UNDERSTANDING
JEWISH LAW

LexisNexis Law School Publishing
Advisory Board

UNDERSTANDING JEWISH LAW

Steven H. Resnicoff
*Professor of Law and Co-Director, DePaul College of Law Center
for Jewish Law & Judaic Studies
DePaul University College of Law*

 LexisNexis®

Library of Congress Cataloging-in-Publication Data

Resnicoff, Steven H.
Understanding Jewish law / Steven H. Resnicoff.
p. cm.
    Includes index.
    ISBN 978-1-4224-9020-4
    1. Jewish law. I. Title.
KBM524.R47 2012
340.5'8—dc23

2012006259

NOTE TO USERS

To ensure that you are using the latest materials available in this area, please be sure to periodically check the LexisNexis Law School web site for downloadable updates and supplements at www.lexisnexis.com/lawschool.

Editorial Offices
121 Chanlon Rd., New Providence, NJ 07974 (908) 464-6800
201 Mission St., San Francisco, CA 94105-1831 (415) 908-3200
www.lexisnexis.com

MATTHEW◆BENDER

(2012–Pub.3327)

PREFACE

Why this Book?

This book can serve either or both of two principal purposes. First, it can serve as the primary text for a survey course in Jewish law, equipping students with the tools necessary for advanced research and analysis. Alternatively, it could constitute a vital supplement in a Jewish law lecture course or in a seminar that is dedicated to specific substantive or philosophical subjects, such as personal autonomy, paternalism, professional responsibility, conflict of laws, and the like.

Consider the challenges confronting those studying, or teaching, Jewish law in American law schools. Jewish law is an extremely broad subject, encompassing all facets of civil law (*e.g.*, contracts, family law, procedure and torts), as well as ritual and spiritual matters, and is hardly amenable to mastery in a single course. Making things worse (or, ironically, more devilish) is the fact that many Jewish law courses compare aspects of Jewish law to their secular law counterparts, thereby requiring students to spend some of their precious time learning, or at least reviewing, relevant secular law.

Another complication is that most students who sign up for Jewish law classes have virtually no background in Jewish law, and there exists no other law school resource designed to provide students an adequate overview of the various institutional, literary and human elements of Jewish law or of how they interact as a legal system.

In addition, most classical Jewish law literature is written in Hebrew and Babylonian Aramaic, languages with which few American law students are familiar. Students are forced to rely on secondary, English language resources. But most of the materials available in English are written for people who are already somewhat knowledgeable about Jewish law. It is difficult for newcomers to the topic to digest these materials. Not only are they confused by the Jewish legal terms they encounter, they are also baffled by the fact that the same term may be transliterated in so many inconsistent ways.

How do law professors respond to these concerns? Frequently, professors try carefully to restrict the substantive scope of their courses. A class may be limited to one or more topics, such as abortion, bioethics, business ethics, capital punishment, dispute resolution, family law, legal ethics and the like. Carefully circumscribing the area covered can certainly help make the course more manageable for all concerned. However, it also makes it more difficult for students to acquire a comprehensive perspective on how Jewish law functions as a legal system. Without such a perspective, a student's appreciation of any particular Jewish law subject is importantly impoverished.

In addition, there is no law school casebook devoted to such narrow Jewish law topics. Consequently, professors often compile their own sets of materials, relying heavily on book chapters and law review articles. While these materials can predicate provocative discussions of diverse topics, they are of little help in understanding Jewish law as a legal system.

This book provides the contextual information necessary to facilitate the study of any Jewish law subject. The main text is divided into Parts (conceptually) and Chapters. Although the various Chapters in each Part interrelate, they are written so that each Chapter stands on its own. A student can profit enormously from this work without reading it from start to finish. In addition, there are nine extremely important Appendices.

Part I of this book, comprising Chapters 1 through 5, provides an overall introduction to Jewish law. Chapter 1 begins by identifying some of the reasons why the study of Jewish law remains vibrantly important. It proceeds to explain what Jewish law is (and is not), identifying its sources and hierarchies of authority. Chapter 2 describes and examines the consequences of a number of fundamental Jewish law assumptions, including the axiom that Jewish law was divinely revealed. Chapter 3 focuses on the interrelationship, under Jewish law, of each member of the community. Chapter 4 discusses disparate categories of Jewish law and underscores important distinctions between biblical and non-biblical Jewish law. Chapter 5 explores the essential institutions of Jewish law. It also describes how the fact that many of these institutions have fallen into desuetude has affected the practical development of Jewish law.

Part II, consisting of Chapters 6, 7, and 8, addresses Jewish law's sources. Chapter 6 identifies the primary literary sources of the law, describes the different types of publications and their functions, and illustrates how they are organized. Chapter 7 examines how personal choice, communal choice, and the law of one's host country serve as additional sources of Jewish law. Finally, Chapter 8 focuses on how Jewish law arises from a rabbinic court's invocation of its extraordinary powers and from the decisions of a Jewish monarch. In doing so, Chapter 8 also addresses the often misunderstood issue of procedural protections in Jewish law. It explains that the nature and scope of these protections depend on whether a rabbinic court acts pursuant to its ordinary authority or whether it exercises its extraordinary authority — and on whether the matter is decided by a Jewish king.

Part III, which includes Chapters 9 through 12, examines the Jewish law process. Chapter 9 discusses competing views as to whether Jewish law "unfolds" or "changes," concluding that, at least as to non-Biblical law, Jewish law changes. Chapter 10 discusses the actual process through which Jewish law develops, and addresses the roles played by individuals, communities and rabbinic authorities within the Jewish law system. Chapter 11 focuses more specifically on the role of personal autonomy within Jewish law. Finally, Chapter 12 describes some of the many significant ways in which Jewish law has developed.

Part IV, which includes Chapters 13 through 16, introduces a number of specific substantive subjects. These chapters do not comprehensively examine their respective topics. Instead, they provide a framework for additional or more sophisticated research. Chapter 13 explores the extremely high value Jewish law places on human life and Jewish law's general opposition to suicide. Chapter 14 compares Jewish and secular debtor-creditor law and discusses how secular bankruptcy law affects Jewish law. Chapter 15 describes Jewish law's approach to professional ethics and, in the case of legal ethics, compares its approach to that of secular law. Chapter 16 explains Jewish law's preference for forms of dispute resolution other than litigation. It also examines how rabbinic arbitration may be conducted so as to lead to a secularly enforceable arbitral award. Chapter 16 discusses the role of alternative dispute resolution within Jewish law.

There are nine appendices. The first provides a glossary of frequently transliterated Jewish law terms. The second is a selected list of post-Talmudic scholars and scholarship. The third prepares students for the multiple systems of transliteration that they will encounter. A fourth provides a general guide to Jewish law legal information available on the Internet. The fifth identifies available non-internet English resources for studying

PREFACE

classical texts such as the Pentateuch, the Mishnah, the Talmuds, and certain Codes of law. A sixth provides a selected bibliography of Jewish law books and journals in English. The seventh offers a brief outline of the development of Jewish legal literature. Appendix eight discusses the Jewish and Catholic systems for counting the years and provides a brief chart of Jewish legal and national history. Finally, Appendix nine identifies the books that are part of the Jewish "canon."

Before sending you off to Chapter 1, I want to express my appreciation — and love — to my wife, Gita, for all of her help and support, which were indispensable to the successful completion of this book. I express the same to my marvelous kids (and grandkids), because this work diverted time and energy that might otherwise have been spent with them. I also especially thank two research assistants, Scott Schreiber, who provided excellent editorial help with early drafts of some of the chapters and Dimitrios Karabetsos, who very carefully and capably helped edit the entire manuscript. I also thank Benzy Fox, Rachelle Ketchum, and my daughter Bela Unell for their kind and effective assistance. Furthermore, I thank my friends, Dean Bell and Larry Rabinovich, for their valuable suggestions. I must also thank Professor Marie Failinger, Linda Berglin and the other faculty, staff and students associated with the *Journal of Law & Religion*, published by Hamline University School of Law. Some of the material incorporated into this book first appeared in articles I published in that terrific journal. Finally, I gratefully acknowledge my indebtedness to the DePaul University College of Law, its past dean, Warren Wolfson, and its current dean, Gregory Mark, for the encouragement and support that made this book possible.

I acknowledge my deepest respect, love and gratitude to my parents, Jack and Blanche Resnicoff, and to my dear friends, Avraham Chaim Nussbaum, Shlomo Bergman, and Shepherd Gerszberg, may they all rest in peace. This book is dedicated to the memory of these five exceptional people. Of course, they are not responsible for any of the mistakes or misjudgments that I have made in connection with the book.

Steven H. Resnicoff, Chicago, Illinois

September 22, 2011

לעילוי נשמות

יצחק יעקב בן הרב מנחם הכהן רעזניקאוו, ע"ה

בתיה פריידא בת אברהם רעזניקאוו, ע"ה

אברהם חיים בן משה נוסבאום, ע"ה

שלמה בן יששכר דוב בערגמאן, ע"ה

שבתאי בן שלמה גערשבערג, ע"ה

TABLE OF CONTENTS

Table of Contents

Table of Contents

Table of Contents

Table of Contents

Table of Contents

Table of Contents

Chapter 1

INTRODUCTION

§ 1.01   THE ROLE OF JEWISH LAW IN AN AMERICAN LAW SCHOOL

There has been a proliferation of Jewish law scholarship[1] at American Law schools.[2] Not only are more and more schools offering Jewish law courses, but an increasing number of schools have centers, institutes, or programs either that focus on Jewish law[3] or that treat Jewish law within a more general law and religion framework.[4] This phenomenon begs the question, "Who studies Jewish law in an

---

[1] There are diverse forms of Jewish law scholarship. For example, some such research focuses purely on Jewish law, while others either compare Jewish and secular law or examine their practical interrelationships.

[2] *See, e.g.,* Samuel J. Levine, *Emerging Applications of Jewish Law in American Legal Scholarship: An Introduction,* 23 J.L. & RELIGION 43 (2007-2008).

[3] These include Berkely School of Law (University of California), Berkely Institute for Jewish Law and Israeli Law, Economy and Society, http://www.law.berkeley.edu/10091.htm; Boston University School of Law, Institute of Jewish Law; Cardozo Law School (Yeshiva University), Yeshiva University Center for Jewish Law and Contemporary Civilization, http://www.cardozo.yu.edu/cjl/; DePaul University College of Law Center for Jewish Law & Judaic Studies (JLJS), http://www.law.depaul.edu/centers_institutes/jljs/; New York University School of Law, Tikvah Center for Law & Jewish Civilization, http://www.nyutikvah.org/; Institute of Jewish Law at Touro College/Jacob D. Fuchsberg Law Center, http://www.tourolaw.edu/academic_ programs/institutes/jewish_law_institute.asp.

[4] These include Emory University School of Law, Center for the Study of Law and Religion,

American law school?"

[A] Personal Importance to Religiously Committed Jewish Lawyers

At least four types of American law students study Jewish law. Some students are personally committed to Jewish law and, therefore, need to know its rules. Not only must they learn what Jewish law requires in a vacuum, but they also need to know how Jewish law interacts with secular law and how this interaction may affect their future practice of law. This concern often arises as to issues concerning legal ethics. For example, does Jewish law permit a practitioner to use certain "offensive," but secularly permissible, forms of cross-examination? Does Jewish law sanction trial tactics designed to trigger an emotional reaction in a witness or party so as to diminish their credibility? Does Jewish law allow an attorney to employ innuendo to influence members of a jury?

The importance of the interaction of Jewish law and secular law is not limited to legal ethics questions, but pervasively affects all areas of practice. For example, a fundamentally important question is whether Jewish law permits an attorney to assist a client in accomplishing a result that is inconsistent with Jewish law, such as collecting money to which, under Jewish law, the client is not entitled. But this issue is only relevant if, in fact, the client is not entitled to the money under Jewish law. Consequently, an attorney must explore the interrelationship between Jewish and secular commercial law. As we will see, Jewish law sometimes accepts secular law as religiously valid and sometimes it does not.

[B] Importance to the Representation of Clients Committed to Jewish Law

Second, some students, although not personally committed to Jewish law, seek to prepare themselves to competently represent Jewish clients for whom Jewish law may be important. Again, Jewish law concerns can arise in a myriad of ways and contexts. For example, a religiously observant client who desires to plan his or her estate wants to do so in a way which will be valid under Jewish law as well as secular law. Indeed, even if the client is not religiously observant, some of the client's intended beneficiaries or legatees may be religiously observant. Unless the secular estate planning is also effective under Jewish law, some of these religiously observant beneficiaries may believe that under Jewish law the estate belongs to others and that their taking property of the estate would contravene Jewish law. As a result, they may refuse to accept such assets, which would frustrate the client's objectives.

---

http://www.law.emory.edu/cms/site/index.php?id=1570; Fordham University School of Law, Institute on Religion, Law and Lawyer's Work, http://law.fordham.edu/lawreligion.htm; Pepperdine University School of Law, Institute on Law, Religion and Ethics, http://law.pepperdine.edu/ilre/; St. John's University Center for Law and Religion, http://www.stjohns.edu/academics/graduate/law/academics/centers/lawreligion; University of Buffalo Law School, Law, Religion and Culture Program, http://law.buffalo.edu/Academic_Programs_And_Research/default.asp?filename=research_centers2#lrp.

[C]   Comparative Law Concerns

Third, even students who do not feel bound by Jewish law may nonetheless respect it or be curious about it. In many ways, neither the human condition nor human nature has changed over the millennia. Many of the competing interests underlying legal questions are also relatively constant. Jewish law is the oldest continuing legal system in the world. It has long wrestled with basic questions such as whether, and if so when, noble ends justify otherwise inappropriate means. Consequently, some students want to see if Jewish law's body of experience can help inform modern debates as to how to approach controversial contemporary legal issues.

Students may also be curious about the institutions and structure of Jewish law, and how it has operated throughout time. Some students are interested in comparative legal systems, and Jewish law provides an unusually rich and aged example.

[D]   Religious Freedom

Fourth, there are those who, even if they are uninterested in Jewish law precepts, are generally concerned lest secular law unnecessarily, and painfully, impinge upon the religious values of others. These students are interested in learning what Jewish law prescribes to help ensure that secular law is carefully circumscribed to avoid any needless conflict.

§ 1.02   WHAT JEWISH LAW IS — AND WHAT IT IS NOT

[A]   Jewish Law Is a Full-Fledged Legal System

The Hebrew word for "Jewish law," is "*halakhah*."[5] Derived from the Hebrew root, "*halokh*," meaning "to go" or "to walk," *halakhah* essentially means, "the way in which one is to walk" or "the path."[6] Halakhah is a full-fledged legal system and comprehensively covers most aspects of an individual's and community's life. It is the oldest practiced legal system in human history, having been in continuous existence for over three thousand years. It has been employed worldwide, in countries with all types of economic and political systems and in all stages of technological development. It has been utilized in times of tranquility[7] and in times of civil unrest. To the extent that Jews from different lands conducted business with each other, Jewish law was perhaps the first version of international law. Moreover, the interaction between Jewish law and the secular law of the countries

---

[5] *Halakhah* is the transliteration most often used for this Hebrew word by Jewish law academics. It is important to note that various systems are used to transliterate Hebrew. Thus, one may find *halakhah* transliterated as *halaka, halacha, halachah*, or even *halacho*. For important information about the transliteration of Hebrew legal terms, see *infra* Appendix 3: Transliterations.

[6] *See* WIKIPEDIA, http://en.wikipedia.org/wiki/Halakha.

[7] Unfortunately, for much of this period of over 3,000 years, periods of tranquility for Jewish communities were relatively rare.

in which Jews have resided, from time to time, has provided interesting conflict of laws questions.

Jewish law has distinct sources and categories of laws. There are biblical laws and non-biblical laws. Some biblical laws are "positive" or "affirmative," while others are "negative" or "passive," and these distinctions have legal consequences. These terms will all be explored in later chapters. Jewish law contains hierarchies of literary, human, and institutional authorities. Before historical developments deprived the Jewish people of their autonomy, specific Jewish law officials and institutions — such as rabbis whose authority could be directly traced back to Moses, a Supreme Council, and a Jewish king — effectively discharged judicial, legislative, and executive functions. These officials and institutions possessed the de facto and de jure powers to enforce the law. As discussed in later chapters, some of these important institutions fell into desuetude. Nonetheless, Jewish law authorities in historical periods earlier than ours continued to enjoy significant tools with which to induce people to observe the law, including local lay governmental bodies as well as official rabbis and rabbinic courts. After the Emancipation of Jews and the breakdown of segregated, self-governing Jewish communities, Jewish authorities largely lost the power to compel compliance.

However, Jewish law is a religiously based system. As such, the religious belief of its adherents, which requires them to obey Jewish law, serves as the engine that continues to drive the Jewish law system today. For the most part, the many Jews who lack such religious commitment are outside of the Jewish law system. There are occasions in which individuals or entities that conduct significant business with religiously observant Jews find it is "good business" to abide by applicable Jewish law.[8]

As a religiously based system, Jewish law is predicated upon a number of significant assumptions, the most important of which will be individually examined in future chapters. In addition to the proposition that the law (or at least part of the law) was divinely ordained, Jewish law assumes that there are legal relationships between and among God, humankind, nations, and individuals. Based

---

[8] For example, Jewish law prohibits the charging (or even the paying) of interest on a loan between Jews. Banks are usually organized as corporations under secular law. Secular law regards commercial corporations as non-religious legal entities separate and apart from the identities of the individuals who own corporate stock or hold executive positions in the corporation. Consequently, under secular law a loan from a bank to a Jew is not a loan from a Jew to a Jew, even if all of the bank's shareholders and executives are Jewish. Many Jewish law authorities, however, would disagree, ruling that the laws against interest apply. *See generally* Steven H. Resnicoff & Michael J. Broyde, *Jewish Law and Modern Business Structures: The Corporate Paradigm*, 43 WAYNE L. REV. 1685 (1997). Nevertheless, if such a bank wants to charge interest, Jewish law provides certain legal "devices" to avoid the prohibition. *See generally* Steven H. Resnicoff, *A Commercial Conundrum: Does Prudence Permit the Jewish "Permissible Venture"?*, 20 SETON HALL L. REV. 77 (1990). One such device, a *hetter iska*, involves some risk that, if the borrower's business fails, the bank may suffer a loss on the loan. When one such case occurred in Israel, the Israeli bank's first response was to argue that the religious device was not intended to have any legal significance and demanded full repayment of the loan. Orthodox community leaders responded by making it clear that without a legally effective *hetter iska* in place, it would be forbidden for Orthodox Jews to borrow from the bank and pay it "interest," or even to lend money to the bank (by making deposits into their accounts) and receive interest. Rather than lose all of this business, the bank chose to treat the *hetter iska* as legally binding.

on these relationships, Jewish law not only proscribes many actions that might harm others but affirmatively prescribes numerous obligations to assist or rescue others.

[B]   What Jewish Law Is Not

Jewish law is *not* Israeli law. Israeli law is simply the secular law of the State of Israel. Although a number of people have lobbied for Israel to adopt various Jewish law rules, their efforts have been largely unsuccessful.[9] Confusion between Israeli law and Jewish law often arises from the fact that the Israeli government appoints two rabbis to serve as its Chief Rabbis. One Chief Rabbi is drawn from and represents Ashkenazi Jews, i.e., those who generally trace their lineage to Franco-German Jewish communities. The other Chief Rabbi is drawn from and represents Sephardi Jews, i.e., those who trace their lineage to Jewish communities that settled in the Iberian Peninsula. These Chief Rabbis do issue Jewish law rulings that enjoy a certain status as a matter of secular law within the Israeli legal system. Nevertheless, these rulings are not necessarily the "last word" as a matter of *halakhah*. Although the individuals holding such positions may well be outstanding scholars, they are not necessarily the foremost Jewish law authorities. The Israeli government's appointment of Chief Rabbis invests the appointees with no greater Jewish law authority than the United Kingdom's designation of a Chief Rabbi for the United Kingdom. In fact, the Israeli Chief Rabbinate seems to lack significant rabbinic authority.[10] The *halakhic* significance of a ruling depends on a variety of factors, including the actual influence within the Jewish law community enjoyed by the particular Chief Rabbi who issued the ruling and the extent to which other leading rabbinic authorities agree.

The Jewish law system is not static. As already mentioned, various historical events have deprived it, at least temporarily, of some of its most vibrant legal institutions.[11] Similarly, many of its rules are importantly influenced by disparate factual variables, and, as economic, political, or sociological circumstances evolve, these circumstances affect the relevant legal conclusions. Chapter 9 will briefly survey the principal perceptions of whether and how Jewish law might be said to "change."

---

[9] The movement to incorporate parts of Jewish law into Israeli law is known as *Mishpat Ivri*. For a discussion of the differences between *halakha* and *Mishpat Ivri*, see Shmuel Shilo, *The Contrast Between Mishpat Ivri and Halakhah*, 20:2 Tradition 91 (1982).

[10] Rabbi Aharon Lichtenstein, head of Yeshivat Har Etzion in Alon Shevut, Israel, writes, "[A]s a quintessentially Rabbinic authority-whether as spiritual leadership in the broader sense or with regard to the specific area of pesak-it [i.e., the Israeli Chief Rabbinate] now carries relatively limited weight. Secularists and Haredim [i.e., those who are more "right-wing" Orthodox] largely ignore it, while the non-Orthodox actively fight it. Its status in the dati-leumi community [i.e., the Religious Zionist community] is more secure, but, even there, many offer it little more than honorific lip-service, having recourse to it only at their convenience." Aharon Lichtenstein, *The Israeli Chief Rabbinate: A Current Halakhic Perspective*, 26:4 Tradition 26, 33 (1992).

[11] It is, of course, possible that some of these "institutions" may someday return. *See, e.g.*, § 5.02, *infra*, as to the possible revival of the institution known as the *Sanhedrin HaGadol* (sometimes translated as the "Supreme Court" and sometimes as the "Great Council" depending on whether its judicial or its legislative function is at issue).

§ 1.03   WHAT THIS BOOK IS — AND WHAT IT IS NOT

[A]   What This Book Is

This book is designed to enable students who know nothing about Jewish law to succeed in an American law school class on Jewish law using a number of different approaches. First, this book explains Jewish law's basic assumptions, institutions, and hierarchies of authorities, as well as the processes by which *halakhah* unfolds or develops. This book supplements these explanations by providing a number of concrete examples. Second, the book attempts to alert students to the typical pitfalls that newcomers to Jewish law usually encounter and to give guidance as to how best to avoid them. Third, this book leads students to a wealth of available resources in English that can facilitate their understanding of Jewish law and their ability to pursue meaningful Jewish law research.

[B]   What This Book Is Not

This book does not explore Jewish ritual law. Nor does it undertake more exotic inquiries concerning Jewish law's perspectives on astrology[12] or how Jewish law might apply in outer space.[13] Of course, these are worthwhile questions, but there is a Talmudic dictum, *tofastah merubah lo tofastah*,[14] i.e., if you try to grab too much, you end up grabbing nothing. Instead, to the extent this book explores substantive issues, it will focus on those for which there are secular law parallels, such as questions of legal ethics, bioethics, and debtor-creditor law. Even then, it cannot possibly consider more than a few examples. After all, even a multi-volume treatise could not cover a large fraction of the interesting topics that are available.

The important point, though, is that after studying this book, the door will be open for students to effectively and efficiently pursue the Jewish law topics that most interest them. This book gives them, gives you, those tools.

---

[12] *See, e.g.*, Yaakov Schwarts, *Jewish Implications of Astrology*, 16 J. HALACHA & CONTEMP. SOC'Y 6 (1988); Fred Rosner, *Unconventional Theories and Remedies*, 19 J. HALACHA & CONTEMP. SOC'Y 81, 92–94 (1990).

[13] *See, e.g.*, J. David Bleich, *Survey of Recent Halakhic Periodical Literature: Mitzvot on the Moon*, 11:3 TRADITION 68 (1970).

[14] This phrase is used frequently in the Talmud and in other rabbinic literature. *See, e.g.*, BABYLONIAN TALMUD, *Yuma* 80a. Similar English expressions abound, such as "Don't bite off more than you can chew."

Chapter 2

FUNDAMENTAL JEWISH LAW ASSUMPTIONS

§ 2.01   INTRODUCTION TO JEWISH LAW'S FUNDAMENTAL ASSUMPTIONS

There are, of course, many core values, principles and assumptions that underlie Judaism. Indeed, various medieval Jewish philosophers offered competing lists of Judaism's "essential principles" (*Ikkarim*).[1] This chapter, however, focuses only on the assumptions that are central to understanding Jewish law, its authority, its hierarchies of authorities, its categories of rules and the punishments it imposes.

Among Jewish law's most fundamental assumptions are: that there is an omnipotent intrinsically good God, who communicated a detailed body of law to the Jewish nation,[2] that everyone is morally obligated to obey the rules applicable to him or her, that in addition to a system of punishment by human authorities, there

---

[1] *See generally* Alexander Altmann, *Articles of Faith, in* 2 ENCYCLOPAEDIA JUDAICA 529, 529–32 (Michael Berenbaum & Fred Skolnik eds., 2d ed. 2007). *See also* MENACHEM KELLNER, DOGMA IN MEDIEVAL JEWISH THOUGHT: FROM MAIMONIDES TO ABRAVANEL (1986).

[2] As explained in Chapter 3, Jewish law also assumes there was an earlier communication of seven

is a divine system of reward and punishment, that there is a life after death, and that much of the system of divine reward and punishment is administered in the afterlife.

§ 2.02 THE ASSUMPTION THAT WRITTEN AND UNWRITTEN BODIES OF LAW WERE DIVINELY TRANSMITTED TO THE JEWISH PEOPLE

The laws that are deemed to have been divinely communicated constitute biblical laws and are core components of the overall corpus of Jewish law.

[A] The Written Law

Jewish law assumes that part of the verbal communication from God to the Jewish nation was, in accordance with God's will, committed to a writing known, alternatively, as the "Written Torah," the "Written Law" (*Torah she-bi-khetav*), the "Pentateuch," or the "Five Books of Moses." Jewish law assumes that the version of the Written Law that the Jewish nation possesses today is identical, or at least virtually identical, to the version that was divinely communicated.

[B] The Oral Law

Jewish law assumes that there was a second portion of the divine communication to Moses that he was specifically commanded not to commit to writing, but, rather, to be transmitted directly from teacher to student. This part of the communication is known as the "Oral Torah" (*Torah she-be-al peh*) or the "Oral Law." Together, the "Written Torah" and the "Oral Torah" constitute the "Torah." As Zevi Hirsch Chajes (1805–55) explains:

> The Torah is divided into two parts, the written and the unwritten law. The former consists of the Pentateuch which was divinely revealed to Moses at Sinai. The latter comprises expositions and interpretations which were communicated to Moses orally as a supplement to the former. Without them the scriptural texts would often be unintelligible since many of them seem to contradict others, and it is only by the aid of oral elucidation that their contradictions can be straightened out.[3]

However, these terms are often used misleadingly. The term "Torah," for instance, is sometimes intended to refer narrowly to the Written Torah alone rather than to the combination of the Written and Oral Torahs. By contrast, the term "Oral Law" is sometimes used broadly to signify not only the Oral Torah communicated by God to Moses but also either to the entire body of non-biblical law (including

---

laws (one to Adam and six more to Noah) and that these seven laws bind all of Noah's descendants. *See generally* AARON LICHTENSTEIN, THE SEVEN LAWS OF NOAH (2d ed. 1986); NAHUM RAKOVER, LAW AND THE NOAHIDES: LAW AS A UNIVERSAL VALUE (1998).

[3] *See* ZEVI HIRSCH CHAJES, THE STUDENTS' GUIDE THROUGH THE TALMUD 1 (Jacob Shachter ed. & trans., 2005). *See also* ARYEH KAPLAN, THE HANDBOOK OF JEWISH THOUGHT 177 (1996) ("We thus speak of two Torahs. There is the written Torah . . . and the Oral Torah. . . . Both are alluded to in God's statement to Moses, 'Come up to Me to the mountain, and I will give you . . . the Torah and the commandments.' ").

rabbinic enactments, communal legislation, customs, etc.) or, sometimes, to all biblical and non-biblical law.

Jewish law is not a "fundamentalist tradition." It does not always interpret the words of the Written Torah literally. In fact, Jewish law authorities openly acknowledge that various Pentateuchal passages, taken by themselves, are incomplete, incomprehensible or even ostensibly inconsistent. It is the Oral Torah that clarifies, resolves and supplements the Written Torah. Indeed, because the Oral Torah is necessary to understand the Written Torah, Jewish legal sources say that the Oral Torah is the more important of the two.[4] Taken together, the Written and Oral Torahs represent divinely ordained *biblical* law.[5]

[C]   Divine Origin of the Torah

Because the assumptions of the divine origin of Jewish law and of the authenticity of the Written Torah text are basic to Jewish law, it is worthwhile to note the extent to which they are well-established. The Written Torah describes the divine revelation at Mount Sinai to the entire Jewish nation.[6] The Mishnah, a compilation of early rabbinic teachings redacted circa 188, repeats this tradition, stating, "Moses received the Torah at Mount Sinai."[7] Similarly, it declares: "All [members of the nation of] Israel have a portion in the world-to-come . . . . But these do not have a portion in the world-to-come: one who says . . . 'The Torah is not from Heaven . . . .' "[8] The Talmud similarly treats this belief as a foundation of Jewish faith.[9]

Moses ben Maimon ("Maimonides"; 1135–1204),[10] the illustrious Jewish philosopher and Jewish law authority, is famous, *inter alia*, for enumerating thirteen fundamental principles of Jewish thought.[11] Maimonides' Eighth Principle declares that God dictated the words of the Written Torah, that Moses wrote them down as would a scribe and that the Torah that we have is identical to that of Moses.[12]

---

[4] *See, e.g.*, MENACHEM ELON, JEWISH LAW: HISTORY, SOURCES, PRINCIPLES vol. 1, 200–03 (Bernard Auerbach & Melvin J. Sykes trans., 1994) (providing a variety of examples in which the Oral Torah clarifies, supplements and resolves apparent contradictions in the Written Torah). *See id.* at 178 (citing various authorities, including the Talmud).

[5] Instead of using the expression "biblical" law, some authorities will refer to "Toraitic" law.

[6] *See, e.g., Exodus* 19:16–25; 20:15.

[7] MISHNAH, *Pirkei Avot* 1:1.

[8] MISHNAH, *Sanhedrin* 10:1.

[9] *See, e.g.*, BABYLONIAN TALMUD, *Berakhot* 5a.

[10] *See infra* Appendix 1: Glossary. For more biographical information, see HERSH GOLDWURM, THE RISHONIM 79 (2d ed. 2001).

[11] Maimonides wrote these Thirteen Principles in his COMMENTARY TO THE MISHNAH, *Sanhedrin* 10:1. *See, e.g.*, MOSES FEINSTEIN (1895–1986), IGGEROT MOSHE, *Yoreh De'ah III*, 104 (Heb.). Indeed, according to Maimonides, anyone who has even a doubt as to the truthfulness of one of these principles would not, after his death, be able to enter "the World to Come." MARC B. SHAPIRO, THE LIMITS OF ORTHODOX THEOLOGY: MAIMONIDES' THIRTEEN PRINCIPLES REAPPRAISED 10 (2004). Many Jewish law authorities disagree with Maimonides as to this last point. *Id.*

[12] *See* FEINSTEIN, *supra* note 11.

Throughout nearly the entire history of the Jewish people, until the nineteenth century rise of the Reform movement in Germany, there was virtually unanimous agreement among religious Jews that the words set forth in the Pentateuch were unquestionably the words of God.[13] For example, Dr. Immanuel Jakobovits (1921–99), former Chief Rabbi of Great Britain, declares:

> To me the belief in *Torah min ha-shamayim* (the divine revelation of the Torah), in its classical formulation by Maimonides, represents a definition of the essence of Judaism as inalienable as the postulate of monotheism. Until the rise of the reform movement in nineteenth-century Germany, this axiom of Judaism was never challenged or varied by any Jewish thinker or movement, whether traditional or sectarian.

> *Torah min ha-shamayim* essentially means that the Pentateuch as we have it today is identical with the Torah revealed to Moses at Mount Sinai and that this expression of God's will is authentic, final, and eternally binding upon the Jewish people. Immaterial to this belief is the mode in which the Torah was communicated to Moses — whether by "dictation," "verbal inspiration," or some other mystic communion peculiar to prophecy.[14]

Similarly, Eliezer Berkovits (1908–92), former Chairman of the department of Jewish philosophy at Hebrew Theological College, affirms:

> I believe that God did indeed speak to Moses, as the Bible says. I am, however, unable to imagine, much less to describe, the actual event. . . . The divine revelation of the Bible is the mysterious contact between God and man by which God communicated His truth and His law to Israel through Moses in a manner that excluded every possibility of doubt in the mind and conscience of the recipient of the revelation. . . . Revelation is a fundamental principle of Judaism.[15]

This view continues to be espoused not only by Orthodox Jewish scholars[16] but even by a number of leading Conservative Jewish thinkers. Thus, Joel Roth, the Louis Finkelstein Professor of Talmud and Jewish Law at the Jewish Theological Seminary, writes, "The document called the Torah embodies the word and will of God, which it behooves man to obey, and is, therefore, authoritative."[17]

---

[13] Of course, there were a few earlier Jewish intellectuals who articulated contrary views. Baruch Spinoza (1632–77), for instance, is said by some to have established the foundation for modern biblical criticism and the reform movement. Even if we were to date the questioning of Torah from Sinai from Spinoza's life, it would still be an extremely recent development. Moreover, the radical nature of Spinoza's beliefs is clear from the fact that they caused him to be put in *Herem*, i.e., to be excommunicated by the Jewish religious authorities of his time.

[14] *See* Immanuel Jakobovits, *Comments, in* THE CONDITION OF JEWISH BELIEF: A SYMPOSIUM, COMPILED BY THE EDITORS OF COMMENTARY MAGAZINE 109, 109–10 (1966) [hereinafter SYMPOSIUM].

[15] *See* Eliezer Berkovits, *Comments, in* SYMPOSIUM, *supra* note 14, at 23–24. *See also id.* at 9 (comments of Norman Lamm, former president of Yeshiva University) and at 236 (comments of Rabbi Moshe Tendler, Professor at Yeshiva University).

[16] *Id.*

[17] *See* JOEL ROTH, THE HALAKHIC PROCESS: A SYSTEMIC ANALYSIS 9 (1986).

Although this book is not the place to examine carefully the different movements within Judaism, a few brief comments may provide helpful context. The most prominent religiously affiliated Jewish groups are the Orthodox, the Conservative and the Reform. None of these groups is monolithic. There are a variety of practices and beliefs within each. Nevertheless, a few generalizations can be fairly made, while emphasizing that these are only generalizations.

The Reform Movement began in Germany in the early nineteenth century. In the United States, at least, the Reform Movement comprised a theologically broad spectrum of adherents. As mentioned more fully below, the Reform Movement's official nineteenth century platform specifically stated that there was no religious obligation to adhere to the rules of Jewish law.

In the United States, more traditional elements of the Reform Movement broke away from it at the end of the nineteenth century. Many point to the 1883 dinner celebrating the graduation of the first class from Hebrew Union College, Reform Judaism's Cincinnati, Ohio, rabbinical seminary, as the catalyst for the establishment of the Conservative Movement. At that dinner, shellfish and other non-kosher foods were served. The Jewish Theological Seminary, the Conservative Movement's first seminary, was established three years later, in 1886.

The Conservative Movement was so named because of its intention to "conserve" or "preserve" Jewish traditions. Although its leadership is more traditional than that of the Reform Movement, it has nevertheless announced many changes to Jewish law and does not consider itself to be as bound to Jewish law "dogma" as Orthodox authorities.[18] The rank and file members of the Conservative Movement are notoriously lax at fulfilling Jewish law (e.g., laws regarding Sabbath observance and kosher foods) even as it is interpreted by Conservative rabbinic leaders. Given this context, Roth's statement is noteworthy.

In short, while some Jewish law scholars are unsure whether God "spoke" the words of the Pentateuch or communicated them in some other effective way,[19] Jewish law, as understood by a majority of its most influential authorities, assumes that the words are God's or God's will.[20]

---

[18] For a discussion of different views within the Conservative Movement regarding Jewish dogma, see generally ELLIOT N. DORFF, CONSERVATIVE JUDAISM: OUR ANCESTORS TO OUR DESCENDANTS (2d ed. 1998).

[19] See, e.g., Berkovits, in SYMPOSIUM, supra note 14. See also the words of Norman Lamm, former president of Yeshiva University, id. at 124:

> The divine will, if it is to be made known, is sufficiently important for it to be revealed in as direct, unequivocal, and unambiguous a manner as possible, so that it will be understood by the largest number of the people to whom this will is addressed. Language, though so faulty an instrument, is still the best means of communication to most human beings. Hence, I accept unapologetically the idea of the verbal revelation of the Torah.

[20] Roth states that the Written Torah "embodies the word and will of God." ROTH, supra note 17. But if the Written Torah words embody God's words, it is not clear what is added by saying that they embody God's will. Of course, but-for Maimonides' principles, it would have been possible for someone to contend that while the words might not all be God's words, they are at least the words that God wants us to have at this point in time.

[D] Scholarly Debate Regarding Minor Exceptions

There is scholarly debate among Orthodox Jewish scholars regarding a few details of the Written Torah. Some scholars question whether all of the Pentateuch's words were written by Moses. The Talmud reports a debate among two of the very early authorities, known as *Tannaim*.[21] One argues that Joshua, rather than Moses, wrote the final handful of narrative verses of Deuteronomy which refer to the period following Moses' demise.[22] Thus, according to this *Tanna*, the Pentateuch we have contains a few concluding verses that were not received by Moses. Nevertheless, even this *Tanna* is assumed to have held that these verses, although recorded by Joshua, were dictated to him by God.[23] Therefore, his position does not affect the assumption that the Pentateuchal text was divinely authored. In fact, it seems unlikely that even Maimonides intended for his Eighth Principle to ban belief in this *Tanna's* position.[24]

Some authorities acknowledge another type of discrepancy, based on the nature of the Hebrew language which may exist between the Pentateuch received by Moses and that which is currently deemed authentic. In Hebrew, some words may be written without a particular vowel without altering the word's meaning or pronunciation. When the word is written without the vowel, the word is "defective," and when it is written with the vowel, it is "plene" or complete. Although most authorities assume that Moses received a tradition as to which words should be written as defective and which as plene, some of these authorities recognize that, in a very small number of instances, the scribes who wrote the Pentateuchal scrolls over the millennia may have introduced discrepancies of this type.[25] None of these possible discrepancies, however, affects the meaning of the words or the normative Jewish laws derived therefrom. Indeed, there is even a view that contends there was no binding tradition as to whether these words should be written in the defective or plene form, but that the scribes were free to choose between the two forms.[26]

Some commentators have argued that, at different points in Jewish history, other variations existed among Pentateuchal manuscripts.[27] Most of these alleged

---

[21] The word *Tanna* (plural, *Tannaim*) is Aramaic. It is used here to refer to a sage who lived in the period from the first century of the Common Era (CE) to about 220 CE. *See* 1 ELON, *supra* note 4, vol. 3, at 1042. *See also* PHILIP BIRNBAUM, A BOOK OF JEWISH CONCEPTS 642–43 (1964).

[22] *See* BABYLONIAN TALMUD, *Sanhedrin* 99.

[23] *See* FEINSTEIN, *supra* note 11.

[24] *See* SHAPIRO, *supra* note 11, at 117. *See generally id.* at 115–21.

[25] If one understands Maimonides literally as saying that not a single letter was changed, one must assume that God not only dictated to Moses the precise words of the Torah but also that He informed Moses whenever a word was to be written deficiently. *See* FEINSTEIN, *supra* note 11.

[26] Abraham Ibn Ezra (1089–1164), for instance, contends that the word itself was important and not the way it was spelled. According to him, each scribe was free to write the word in defective or plene form. *See* SHAPIRO, *supra* note 11, at 100. For biographical information about Ibn Ezra, see GOLDWURM, *supra* note 10, at 73–74.

[27] SHAPIRO, *supra* note 11, at 91–131.

differences are trivial[28] and may have resulted from mere scribal errors.[29] No one seems to have asserted that any such discrepancy affected the legal rules set forth in the Pentateuch. Nor does anyone argue that these changes contradicted any of the Pentateuch's spiritual lessons.[30] Furthermore, the fact that there were discrepancies from time to time does not mean that the version currently deemed to be authentic is not authentic. In short, neither questions about the exact method by which God transmitted His words nor the alleged minor textual discrepancies discussed so far challenge Jewish law's assumption that the acknowledged Pentateuchal text accurately represents God's words.

[E]   Debate Regarding the "Documentary Hypothesis"

Of course, the nineteenth and twentieth centuries witnessed a spate of theories, variations of the "Documentary Hypothesis," which argued that the Pentateuch was not written as a single document or by a single author. According to the Documentary Hypothesis, separate writings were authored by different people in various time periods and were ultimately redacted into a single text. Although many non-Orthodox scholars regard the general idea underlying the Documentary Hypothesis to be established fact, other scholars and traditional Jewish law scholars reject it categorically.

The analyses offered by both sides are complex and extensive and cannot be fully explored in this chapter.[31] Proponents of the theory point to distinct

---

[28] *Id.* at 94 n.25 ("Most of these [textual differences in the medieval period] are very minor differences.").

[29] Interestingly, a thirteenth-century commentator, Moshe ben Nahman (Nahmanides; 1194–1260) suggests that a particular *Tanna* may have intentionally made one such variation in his own Torah scroll based on Jewish mystical considerations. *Id.* at 96 (citing Nahmanides's explanation for a variation in the text possessed by the Tanna Rebbe Meir). For biographical information about Nahmanides, see GOLDWURM, *supra* note 10, at 90–92.

[30] According to Maimonides, anyone who even doubts the veracity of one of his thirteen principles will fail to enter the "World to Come." SHAPIRO, *supra* note 11, at 10. For a description of views concerning the "World to Come," see YECHIEL MICHEL TUCAZINSKY, GESHER HACHAIM (THE BRIDGE OF LIFE) 138–58 (Nissan Aharon Tucazinsky trans., 1983). Although most prominent Jewish authorities disagree with Maimonides about the fate of those who in good faith deny one or more of his Principles, SHAPIRO, *supra* note 11, at 10–12, they continue to assert the truthfulness of the Eighth Principle:

> In popular circles this aspect of the [Maimonides' Eighth Principle] is often repeated dogmatically as if traditional Judaism is unimaginable without it. For example, J. Newman writes: "The version [of the Torah] in our hands today is identical with that which Moses received . . . . [T]he entire text, in every detail, now in our possession is the one given to Moses at Sinai." Louis I. Rabinowitz writes: "The Masoretic text is the sole *textus receptus* of the torah. All other readings represent man-altered variations from that authentic text." Avraham Kushelevsky writes: "The text of the Torah has been preserved as it was given more than 3,000 years ago, without an addition or deletion of a verse, a single word, or even a single letter."

Id. at 90–91(citations omitted). Nevertheless, even if the text had suffered some minor changes, this would not necessarily affect the Torah laws contained within it.

[31] For arguments supporting various versions of the Documentary Hypothesis, see, e.g., ERNEST WILSON NICHOLSON, THE PENTATEUCH IN THE TWENTIETH CENTURY: THE LEGACY OF JULIUS WELLHAUSEN (2003); NORMAN C. HABEL, LITERARY CRITICISM OF THE OLD TESTAMENT (1971); RICHARD E. FRIEDMAN, WHO WROTE THE BIBLE? (1987). For critics of the Documentary Hypothesis, see, e.g., UMBERTO CASSUTO, THE DOCUMENTARY HYPOTHESIS (Israel Abrahams, trans., 2006); Lopes Cardozo, *On Bible Criticism and Its Counterargu-*

Pentateuchal styles and terminology, asserting that these evidence the existence of separate authors, while those who reject the theory often contend that these differences are intentional and convey exquisite homiletical messages.[32]

Traditional Jews also ask fundamental questions regarding the Documentary Hypothesis. For example, the Documentary Hypothesis presumes that various documents were written in different centuries. But there is no record of even a single dramatically new document being disclosed by or to the rabbis or of any new combination of documents being announced. One might have expected the introduction of such a new document to have caused quite a stir. Although one might argue that history is written by the victors of "culture wars," this argument seems less true as to Jewish history which tends to record minority and aberrant opinions. Yet even though the Talmud provides actual examples of deeds by *Sadducees*, members of a well-known early Jewish group who rejected substantial portions of the Oral Law, it provides no examples of anyone who claimed that a dramatically new version of the Written Torah was authored or introduced in his time. Instead, we have evidence of millennia during which the Torah was universally accepted as a single document, the text of which had been transmitted to Moses.

Nevertheless, even if true, the Documentary Hypothesis would not disprove divine authorship of the Pentateuch. The Pentateuch could still represent a verbal communication directly from God. The supposed additional writers may merely have written down an oral tradition originally communicated to, and subsequently transmitted by, Moses. Alternatively, such later writers, if they existed, conceivably could have received prophetic instructions to record God's description of what had transpired in Mosaic and pre-Mosaic times. Of course, these possibilities do not reflect the traditional Jewish law perspective. The point, however, is that the assumption of the Torah's divine origin does not logically depend on whether one accepts the Documentary Hypothesis. After all, at least one leading Conservative rabbi who accepts the Documentary Hypothesis maintains that, at least in theory, Jewish law is binding because it reflects "the [Divine] Will revealed in it."[33]

On the other hand, there are articles by some Conservative rabbis as well as by Reform rabbis, that purport to discuss "Jewish law," but that contend that Jewish law is not "obligatory" and that a person should only follow those Jewish laws which the person considers to be ethically meaningful. They base this conclusion on their adoption of the Documentary Hypothesis. Thus, Conservative Rabbi Edward Feld writes:

> Our changed concept of revelation, induced by our acceptance of modern biblical scholarship, alters the sacred character of the Bible and necessitates a new way of viewing the Halakhah [i.e., Jewish law]. The authority of halakhah stems from its intimate connection with the Bible . . . . Ulti-

---

ments, http://www.simpletoremember.com/articles/a/Bible_Criticism_and_Its_Counterarguments.htm (last visited July 28, 2011). *See also* Steven Shaw, *Orthodox Reactions to the Challenge of Biblical Criticism,* 10:3 TRADITION 61 (1969).

[32] *See, e.g.,* CASSUTO, *supra* note 31; Shaw, *supra* note 31. *See also* David Hoffman, *David Hoffman, Defender of the Faith,* 8:4 TRADITION 91 (Jenny Marmorstein trans., 1966).

[33] *See, e.g.,* ABRAHAM JOSHUA HESCHEL, HEAVENLY TORAH 678 (Gordon Tucker trans., 2005).

mately, in the self-understanding of the tradition, Jewish law is meaningful because God commanded it. Thus the Halakhah is a system of mitzvoth: revealed commandments. Take away the notion of revelation, and halakhah floats like a castle built on air. Yet we have been nurtured on an understanding of revelation that stems from a critical analysis of the Biblical text, different from and more complex than the traditional understanding of revelation. For instance, we do not believe that the contradictions in the text of the Torah were put there to teach us a new halakhah; instead, we know that they are they because the Torah was written over a rather lengthy period of time. Thus, the very basis of Talmudic exegesis is undercut. We may then relate to halakhah as tradition, but not as revelation, not as mitzvah.[34]

This attitude, while only one of many within the Conservative Movement, was at one time the "official" position of the Reform Movement. Consider, for instance, the Pittsburgh Platform adopted in 1885:

We recognize in the Mosaic legislation a system of training the Jewish people for its mission during its national life in Palestine, and today we accept as binding only its moral laws, and maintain only such ceremonies as elevate and sanctify our lives, but reject all such as are not adapted to the views and habits of modern civilization.[35]

In recent years, some individuals in the Reform Movement have become more traditional in their practices, and differences in opinion have arisen regarding the significance of Jewish law. Whereas Solomon B. Freehof clearly stated that he regards responsa literature as "guidance not governance," Walter Jacob contends that "[at] the official level of the [Reform] Conference there is still a good deal of hesitancy about rabbinic authority."[36] Nevertheless, the hallmark of the Reform Movement is that each person may decide for himself how much attention to give Jewish law. This is fundamentally inconsistent with the traditional view that Jewish law is obligatory.

Traditional Jewish law scholars offer a variety of non-technical arguments to demonstrate the divine authorship of the Torah. For example, drawing on the teachings of Rabbi Noah Weinberg, Coopersmith argues that if human beings authored the Pentateuch, they would have been foolish to include some of its laws.[37] For example, the Pentateuch requires that, on the seventh year, farmers in Israel must leave their fields fallow. They are promised that the land will bring forth enough on the sixth year to provide for three years, from the sixth year until after the harvest on the eighth year:

For six years you may plant your fields, prune your vineyards, harvest your crops but the seventh year is the Sabbath of the land in which you may not

---

[34] Edward Feld, *Towards an Aggadic Judaism, in* THE UNFOLDING TRADITION, 207–08 (Elliot N. Dorff, ed., 2005).

[35] *See* Robert Gordis, *Authority in Jewish Law, in* THE UNFOLDING TRADITION: JEWISH LAW AFTER SINAI 99 (Elliot N. Dorff ed., 2006).

[36] *See* WALTER JACOB, CONTEMPORARY AMERICAN REFORM RESPONSA xix (1987).

[37] THE EYE OF A NEEDLE 56–57 (Yitzchak Coopersmith compiler, 1993).

plant your fields nor prune your vineyards. Do not harvest crops that grow on their own. Do not gather the grapes on your unpruned vines since it is a year of rest for the land. And if you ask, what will we eat in the seventh year? We haven't planted nor have we harvested crops. I will direct my blessing to you in the sixth year and the land will produce enough crops for three years.[38]

This is a remarkable claim for a human author to make on his or her own. If the author wanted a religion to last more than six or seven years, why would the author enable people to put the religion to such a difficult test?[39] Similarly, the Torah requires that all males must travel to Jerusalem to celebrate three specific holidays:

Three times each year all your males shall thus present themselves before God the Master, the Lord of Israel [in Jerusalem]. When I expel the nations before you and extend your boundaries, no one will be envious of your land when you go to be seen in God's presence three times each year.[40]

Travel to Jerusalem centuries ago was not as easy as today. There were no cars, trains or planes. Travelling to Jerusalem meant that the men would be leaving their homes, possessions and cities unprotected. Why would human authors, who could not guarantee that other nations would not "be envious of your land," include such a rule in the Pentateuch? Even if there were some perceived practical reason to require all males to visit Jerusalem annually, why not require them to come in staggered shifts? Again, the argument is made, if one assumes human authorship of the Pentateuch, one would also have to assume that the human authors were not too clever.[41]

On the other hand, one might argue that there have been various charismatic cult leaders who have predicted that the world would end on one or more specified dates which came and passed. Yet their followers, or many of them, accepted their lame excuses. If the Torah were written by man, perhaps, one could argue, it was written by the same sort of charismatic leader. Alternatively, one might argue, it may have been written by a person who may have counted on the fact that surely not everyone would leave the land fallow and that not everyone would actually make the three annual pilgrimages to Jerusalem. If so, any non-fulfillment of the divine promises could be blamed on these failures.

§ 2.03   MORAL OBLIGATION TO FULFILL GOD'S COMMANDMENTS

Jewish law fundamentally assumes that God is moral and that, therefore, one is morally obligated to fulfill God's commandments.

---

[38] *Leviticus* 25:3–6.

[39] THE EYE OF A NEEDLE, *supra* note 37, at 64–66.

[40] *Exodus* 34:23–24.

[41] THE EYE OF A NEEDLE, *supra* note 37, at 66–67.

[A] The Assumption That God Is Morally Perfect

If you would ask most people to identify the single way in which Judaism most differed from the religions that preceded it, many would probably answer that it was its belief in one God. Judaism was the first monotheistic religion. But Walter Wurzburger persuasively argues that this answer would not be correct. He states:

> It is no coincidence that ethics play such a pre-eminent role in the Jewish conception of piety. Pagan cults separated ethics and religion and regarded the performance of various cultic rites as the hallmark of religion. They looked upon their deities solely as ultimate powers controlling the forces of nature. In the pre-scientific era human beings could do very little to harness the forces of nature to their purposes. The primitive mind resorted to rites and sacrifices in hope of swaying the gods to respond to human needs.

> Jewish monotheism represents a radically different approach to religion. Its novelty consisted not primarily in the substitution of the belief in one God for the plurality of gods worshipped in polytheism. What was even more revolutionary in the Jewish conception of monotheism was, as against the pagan emphasis upon divine power, the attribution of moral perfection to God.

> His moral attributes rather than His absolute power render Him *worthy* of being worshiped and obeyed. In striking contrast to paganism, worship is no longer dictated primarily by self-serving considerations as a device enabling us to get what we want. To serve Him is not a means to the fulfillment of our needs, but an end in itself.[42]

An examination of the basis for the assumption of God's moral perfection is well beyond the scope of this book. For the purpose of studying Jewish law, however, it is critical to recognize that God's moral perfection is a fundamental assumption. Indeed, God dramatically commands the Jewish people, "You shall be holy, for I, the Lord your God, am holy."[43]

[B] God's Commandments Cannot Be Judged by One's Own Sense of Morality

Accordingly, once the meaning of Torah law is established — and we will soon turn to the process by which it is established — that law, having been authored by a morally perfect God, must be morally correct. Consequently, it would be wrong for a person to refuse to comply with the law simply because it offends the person's subjective sense of morals. As Immanuel Jakobovits, former Chief Rabbi of the United Kingdom, puts it:

> This is fundamental rather than purely fundamentalistic. If ethical laws were good, immutable, and divine because their virtue is manifest to

---

[42] WALTER S. WURZBURGER, ETHICS OF RESPONSIBILITY 4 (1994).

[43] *Leviticus* 19:2. As will be explained in Chapter 8, *infra*, the commandment to be holy is the basis for a number of particular Jewish law rules that are not explicitly expressed in the Written Torah.

reason, intuition, conscience, or any other human faculty, or if the validity of any law in the Torah were subject to human discrimination — accepting those as "divine" which appeal to our present-day notions and rejecting as "man-made" those we do not understand — the whole structure of Judaism as a revealed religion would collapse. We would create a god in man's own image; for man, not God, would determine what is "divine" law, using Him only as a rubber stamp to "authenticate" purely human judgments. Judaism stands or falls by the heteronomy of the law: *"He* hath told thee, O man, what is good" (Mic 6:8), not the reverse.[44]

§ 2.04 BELIEF IN AN AFTERLIFE AND IN THE DOCTRINE OF REWARD AND PUNISHMENT

[A] Belief in an Afterlife

Belief in an afterlife is a central tenet of Jewish law.[45] As Rabbi Maurice Lamm writes:

> The conception of an after-life is fundamental to the Jewish religion. . . . The denial of the after-life constitutes a denial of the cornerstone of the faith. . . . Indeed, the Mishnah (Sanhedrin 10:1) expressly excludes from the reward of the "world beyond" he who holds that the resurrection of the dead is without biblical warrant.
>
> Maimonides considers this belief one of the 13 basic truths which every Jew is commanded to hold.
>
> . . . .
>
> Philosophers, such as Hasdai Crescas in the fourteenth century, changed the formulation of the basic truths, but still kept immortality [of the soul] as a fundamental principle without which Jewish religion is inconceivable. Simon Ben Zemach Duran, in the early fifteenth century, reduced the fundamentals to three, but resurrection was included. Joseph Albo, in the same era, revised the structure of dogmas, and still immortality remained a universally binding belief. No matter how the basic principles were reduced or revised, immortality remained a major tenet of Judaism.[46]

---

[44] *See* SYMPOSIUM, *supra* note 14, at 111. Similarly, Walter Wurzburger states: "In case of conflict with an explicit biblical prohibition, all other considerations must be disregarded, because 'there is no wisdom nor understanding nor counsel against God.'" WURZBURGER, *supra* note 42, at 26 (citing *Proverbs* 21:30, as it is interpreted in BABYLONIAN TALMUD, *Berakhot* 19b).

[45] Traditional Jewish authorities identify separate periods after one's initial physical life, including a spiritual existence separate from one's soul and a period in which the body of the dead is resurrected and rejoined with the soul. Views differ as to the order in which these periods will occur and as to the nature of each period. *See generally* A. COHEN, EVERYMAN'S TALMUD 346–89 (1978); SIMCHA PAULL RAPHAEL, JEWISH VIEWS OF THE AFTERLIFE 117–62 (1994); TUCAZINSKY, *supra* note 30, at 106–58; MOSHE CHAYIM LUZZATTO, THE WAY OF GOD 53–59 (Aryeh Kaplan trans., 1981). Most authorities believe that the resurrection will be the last and ultimate stage, whereas Maimonides thinks that the resurrection will be a temporary stage preceding the soul's separate and eternal existence. *Id.* at 53, 338 n.20.

[46] MAURICE LAMM, THE JEWISH WAY IN DEATH AND DYING 224–25 (1969).

[B] Belief in the Doctrine of Reward and Punishment and Its Connection to the Afterlife

Similarly, the doctrine of reward and punishment is essential to Jewish thought.[47] The Written Torah repeatedly expresses it,[48] Tannaitic writings and the Talmud frequently refer to it,[49] and post-Talmudic Jewish authorities have continuously discussed it.[50]

Moreover, these two doctrines are critically linked. Some people believe that there are evil people who prosper in this world, and this has caused them to question the doctrine of reward and punishment. Many answers to this question have been offered.[51] One response is that this world is ephemeral, and the world to come is eternal. Those who are evil must be recompensed in some way for the good they managed to accomplish, and, therefore, may be allowed some pleasure in this world. It is in the next world where they are punished. Similarly, since any benefit in this transient world pales in comparison to pleasure in the eternal world to come, the righteous must be primarily rewarded there. As a result, most traditional Jewish authorities state that it is precisely the world to come that is the place in which one's principal reward or punishment is administered.[52]

A similar scenario arose in connection with the *Tanna*, Rabbi Elisha ben Abuya. The Mishnah was compiled by Rabbi Yehuda the Prince circa 188 CE. Rabbi Yehuda relied heavily on the teachings of Rabbi Meir. Indeed, the Talmud states that any Mishnah that does not cite a particular person as its author is the teaching of R. Meir. Rabbi Elisha b. Abuya was one of R. Meir's principal teachers. Nevertheless, at some point, Elisha b. Abuya lost his faith in Judaism, and the Talmud refers to him as "*Aher*," "the Other One." The Talmud suggests that it was *Aher's* failure to believe in an afterlife that led him to abandon his faith:

> It was taught: R. Jacob says, There is no precept in the Torah, where reward is stated by its side, from which you cannot infer the doctrine of the resurrection of the dead. Thus, in connection with honouring parents it is written: That thy days may be prolonged, and that it may go well with thee. Again in connection with the law of letting [the dam] go from the nest it is written: "That it may be well with thee, and that thou mayest prolong thy days."
>
> Now, in the case where a man's father said to him, "Go up to the top of the building and bring me down some young birds," and he went up to the

---

[47] *See generally Reward and Punishment*, JEWISH VIRTUAL LIBRARY, http://www.jewishvirtuallibrary.org/jsource/judaica/ejud_0002_0017_0_16693.html (last visited July 28, 2011) (citing the sources in notes 43 and 44, among others).

[48] *See, e.g.*, Exodus 20:12; *Leviticus* 23; *Deuteronomy* 11:13–21; *Deuteronomy* 28.

[49] *See, e.g.*, BABYLONIAN TALMUD, *Sanhedrin* 90a, *Rosh Hashanah* 12a; *Genesis Rabbah* 9:11.

[50] *See, e.g.*, SAADIA GAON, THE BOOK OF BELIEFS AND OPINIONS 323–56 (Samuel Rosenblatt trans., 1955).

[51] *Id.* (citing many reasons). For example, one cannot always trust appearances. Some people who seem to prosper actually commit suicide out of their complete despair and depression. Some people who may seem evil may be quite good and vice versa.

[52] *Id.*; LUZZATTO, *supra* note 45, at 53.

top of the building, let the dam go and took the young ones, and on his return he fell and was killed-where is this man's length of days, and where is this man's happiness? But "that thy days may be prolonged" refers to the world that is wholly long [i.e., the eternal Afterlife], and "that it may go well with thee" refers to the world that is wholly good [i.e., the Afterlife]. . . .

R. Joseph said: Had Aher interpreted this verse as R. Jacob, his daughter's son, did, he would not have sinned. What actually did he [Aher] see? — Some say: He saw such an occurrence [i.e., a boy fatally falling from a tree after fulfilling his father's commandment to send off a mother bird and bring down her young]. Others say, He saw the tongue of R. Huzpith the Interpreter lying on a dung-heap, and he exclaimed, "Shall the mouth that uttered pearls lick the dust!" But he knew not that the verse: "That it may go well with thee," refers to the world that is wholly good, and that the verse: "That thy days may be prolonged" refers to the world that is wholly long.[53]

Because *Aher* disbelieved in an afterlife, he thought that any reward could only be given in this world. As a result, he wrongfully believed that the incidents he observed disproved the central teaching of reward and punishment, therefore disproving Judaism.

Together, the doctrines of an afterlife and of reward and punishment in an afterlife help explain some Jewish punishments. For example, Jewish law maintains that when a person is executed for his sins, his death — at least together with confession and repentance — can achieve atonement for him. Consequently, by putting an offender to death, Jewish authorities provide him with an opportunity for salvation. If he confesses and repents, the offender is rescued from everlasting oblivion to a permanent and rewarding place in the world to come.

---

[53] SONCINO BABYLONIAN TALMUD, *Chullin* 142a (I. Epstein ed.), *available at* http://halakhah.com/pdf/kodoshim/Chullin.pdf.

Chapter 3

RESPONSIBILITY FOR OTHERS

§ 3.01 CONTRASTING JEWISH AND SECULAR VIEWS AS TO ONE'S DUTIES TO OTHERS

[A] The Secular Approach

Common law generally regards each person as an independent being with no responsibilities to or liabilities for others. With few exceptions, the rich have no responsibility to the poor, the powerful have no obligation to the weak, the healthy have no duty to the sick and the protected can callously ignore those in peril.[1] Common law would allow one to watch a person bleed to death without lifting a finger to help or using a cell phone to notify government authorities. More than a century before, the New Hampshire Supreme Court described the common law rule:

> Suppose A., standing close by a railroad, sees a two-year-old babe on the track and a car approaching. He can easily rescue the child with entire safety to himself, and the instincts of humanity require him to do so. If he does not, he may, perhaps, justly be styled a ruthless savage and a moral

---

[1] The few exceptions, other than cases involving parents and children, typically involve scenarios in which two parties have voluntarily entered into a relationship with each other, such as a doctor and patient, and that relationship implicitly includes certain duties.

monster; but he is not liable in damages for the child's injury or indictable under the statute for its death.[2]

This situation remains largely unchanged in the United States. The Restatement (Second) of Torts states: "The fact that the actor realizes or should realize that action on his part is necessary for another's aid or protection does not of itself impose upon him a duty to take such action."[3] Only four states have legislatively imposed limited duties to render direct assistance to those in danger.[4]

Similarly, under common law there was no broad duty to prevent a person from committing a crime or even to help prevent the crime by reporting relevant information to the police. In England, there was a common law offense, "misprision of a felony," which involved (1) knowledge of a felony; (2) a reasonable opportunity to report it without harm to oneself; and (3) failure to do so.[5] Nevertheless, this common law offense was never broadly recognized in the United States. In fact, there may have only been one conviction of the offense in United States history.[6] Although Congress enacted a misprision of felony statute that arguably approximates the English common law offense, courts have consistently construed it as requiring active concealment of the felony rather than a mere failure to report.[7] With a few important exceptions, American law does not require preventing or reporting crimes.[8]

[B] The Jewish Law Approach

Jewish law's perception is quite different. Despite the fact that it treasures the life of each individual,[9] Jewish law also considers each Jewish individual as part of a community, as part of the Jewish people. Jewish law authorities emphasize that the Sinaitic Revelation was given to, and accepted by, the Jewish nation as a whole. As a consequence, Jews are obligated to help each other, materially and spiritually.

Moreover, Jewish law assumes that not only are individuals divinely judged, but the nation as a whole is also judged. As a result, not only are people obligated to

---

[2] Buch v. Amory Mfg. Co., 44 A. 809, 810 (N.H. 1898). This case is frequently cited in legal literature addressing "Good Samaritan" laws.

[3] RESTATEMENT (SECOND) OF TORTS § 314 (1965). *But see* Soldano v. Daniels, 190 Cal. Rptr. 310 (Ct. App. 1983) (plaintiff stated a cause of action in tort against defendant business owner who prevented plaintiff from using public phone in defendant's public place of business to call police for help from an assailant).

[4] *See, e.g.*, MINN. STAT. ANN. § 604A.01 (West 2001); R.I. GEN. LAWS § 11-56-1 (1984); VT. STAT. ANN. tit. 12, § 519(a) (1967); WIS. STAT. ANN. § 940.34(2)(a) (West 2005). For a discussion of these statutes, which seem to have resulted in only one conviction, see Michael N. Rader, *The "Good Samaritan" in Jewish Law*, 22 J. LEGAL MED. 375, 376–91 (2001).

[5] *See, e.g.*, Daniel B. Yeager, *A Radical Community of Aid: A Rejoinder to Opponents of Affirmative Duties to Help Strangers*, 71 WASH. U. L.Q. 1 (1993).

[6] *See* State v. Hann, 40 N.J.L. 228 (1878); Alison M. Arcuri, *Sherrice Iverson Act: Duty to Report Child Abuse and Neglect*, 20 PACE L. REV. 471 (2000).

[7] Arcuri, *supra* note 6, at 475–76.

[8] One major exception pertains to child abuse. Nevertheless, in the vast majority of states, the reporting duty is imposed only on certain "mandated reporters," such as a victim's parents, teachers, or health care providers.

[9] *See infra* Chapter 13.

encourage others to obey Jewish law, they are forbidden to enable another to violate Jewish law. Should others transgress, all Jews may suffer.

§ 3.02 JEWISH LAW DUTIES TO ASSIST OR RESCUE

Jewish law includes many specific duties to assist others, including, for example, the obligation to provide financial assistance to those in need,[10] to visit the sick,[11] to provide hospitality,[12] to return lost property,[13] and to provide physical assistance to someone with his or her burdens.[14] In addition, a number of general Torah commandments are relevant.[15] We will focus, however, on the important duty to save people from physical harm. This obligation is predicated upon three biblical bases.[16]

[A] Duty to Return or Preserve Another's Good Health

One verse states, "If your fellow is missing something, you shall restore it to him."[17] Read in context, this verse primarily refers to returning lost property. Nevertheless, the Talmud understands the verse as requiring one to protect another from a "loss." Returning lost property is only one way to prevent someone from sustaining a monetary loss. More broadly, however, the verse also requires one to protect another from a non-monetary loss, including bodily injuries:

> [To revert to] the above text: "Whence do we know that if a man sees his neighbour drowning, mauled by beasts, or attacked by robbers, he is bound to save him? From the verse, 'Thou shalt not stand by the blood of thy neighbour.'" But is it derived from this verse? Is it not rather from elsewhere? Viz., Whence do we know [that one must save his neighbour from] the loss of himself? From the verse, "And thou shalt restore him [Note: At this point, the Talmud translates the masculine third person singular as "him" instead of as "it"] to himself!" [*Deuteronomy* 22:2] — From that verse I might think that it is only a personal obligation, but that he is not bound to take the trouble of hiring men [if he cannot deliver him himself]: therefore, this verse teaches that he must.[18] [Citations omitted.]

---

[10] *See* SHULHAN ARUKH, *Yoreh De'ah* 247 *et seq.*; *Deuteronomy* 15:7, 8; AVROHOM EHRMAN, JOURNEY TO VIRTUE 463–73 (2002).

[11] EHRMAN, *supra* note 10, at 515–25.

[12] *Id.* at 505–14.

[13] *Id.* at 366–76.

[14] *See, e.g., Exodus* 23:5; ELIEZER BEN SHMUEL OF METZ (d. 1175), SEFER YEREIM (1892) (Heb.), at 229.

[15] These include, for example, the commandment to "love thy neighbor as thyself" (*Leviticus* 19:18).

[16] In addition to the three bases discussed in the ensuing text regarding a "duty" to save someone else, there is a fourth basis that permits, but does not require, a third party to use fatal force against someone who is breaking into an occupied house. *See Exodus* 22:1; *See also* SONCINO BABYLONIAN TALMUD, *Sanhedrin* 72a–72b (I. Epstein ed.), *available at* http://halakhah.com/pdf/nezikin/Sanhedrin.pdf.

[17] *Deuteronomy* 22:2.

[18] SONCINO BABYLONIAN TALMUD, *supra* note 16, at 73a. I altered the punctuation to match American usage. *See also* YOSEF BEN MOSHE BABAD (1801–1874), KOMETZ MINHAH, *Commandment* 232 (Heb.).

[B] Duty Not to Passively Witness Another's Injury or Victimization

The second pertinent verse states, "[Y]ou shall not stand by while your fellow's blood is shed."[19] The Talmudic passage cited above concludes that, taken together, these two verses make it clear that to save someone from loss, one must, if necessary, expend one's own financial resources. When saving someone from financial loss, one need not spend more than the amount being protected. In addition, the person who is saved from loss is liable to reimburse the rescuer for his or her expenses and, in some cases, to compensate the rescuer for the time expended in the rescue.[20]

In Chapter 4, we will explain that Jewish law does not generally impose unlimited obligations. The extent to which someone must go to fulfill a particular biblical obligation usually depends on whether the obligation is characterized as an affirmative duty or a negative duty. There is a debate as to whether this characterization depends on the language in which the Written Torah expresses the obligation (e.g., "Do" versus "Do not") or whether violation of the obligation is passive or active. The obligation not to stand idly by is phrased as a negative commandment,[21] but, because its effect is to require action, it is violated passively, and may be an "affirmative commandment."[22] Nevertheless, because of the importance that Jewish law places on human life, as discussed in Chapter 13, a number of authorities believe that to save another's life one must use all of one's assets. Rabbi Yisroel Meir Kagan (1838–1933), for example, points to a Talmudic passage concerning two people traveling in a desert with only one of them still possessing container of water. If the two share the water, both will die. If the person with the water keeps it for himself or herself, then he or she will survive but the other will die. One view favors sharing the water, while the second view says that the one with the water should (or at least may) refuse to share it.[23] Most later commentators interpret the Talmud as agreeing with the latter opinion, because "one's own life takes precedence over another person's life."[24] R. Kagan argues,

---

[19] *Leviticus* 19:16.

[20] *See* Aaron Kirschenbaum, *The Good Samaritan: Monetary Aspects*, 17 J. HALACHA & CONTEMP. SOC'Y 83, 86–87, 89–92 (1989). Note that this journal incorrectly spells the author's first name as "Aron."

[21] *See, e.g.*, MOSES FEINSTEIN, IGGEROT MOSHE, *Yoreh De'ah* II:174(4) (ruling that this is the source of the duty to rescue and that it is a negative commandment); ZVI HIRSCH SHAPIRO, DARKEI TESHUVAH, *Yoreh De'ah* 157, no. 57 (Heb.) (citing *Shut Zera Emet* II:51).

[22] *See, e.g.*, SHLOMO MORDEKHAI BEN MOSHE SHWADRON, 2 SHUT MAHARSHAM no. 54 (Heb.).

[23] Talmudic commentators disagree as to whether this view requires or merely permits the person with the water to use it all.

[24] Here is a translation of the relevant passage:

> Now how does R. Johanan interpret, "that thy brother may live with thee?" [Lev. 25:36] — He utilises it for that which was taught: If two are traveling on a journey [far from civilisation], and one has a pitcher of water, if both drink, they will [both] die, but if one only drinks, he can reach civilisation, — The Son of Patura taught: It is better that both should drink and die, rather than that one should behold his companion's death. Until R. Akiba came and taught: "that thy brother may live with thee," thy life takes precedence over his life.

SONCINO BABYLONIAN TALMUD, *Bava Metzia* 62a (I. Epstein ed.), *available at* http://halakhah.com/pdf/nezikin/Baba_Metzia.pdf.

one's *life* takes precedence over another's life, but one's *money* does not.[25]

[C] Duty to Protect Someone from an Assailant

The third biblical basis for this rule is far from the plain language of the Written Torah. It arises from a verse regarding the sexual molestation of a partly-married woman. Under Jewish law, there are two distinct stages in becoming completely "married."[26] The first stage, known as *kiddushin* or *eirusin*, typically occurs when the groom recites a stipulated declaration and puts a ring on the bride's finger.[27] Although many may refer to this as a "betrothal" or engagement, under Jewish law it is more than that. After the *kiddushin*, for example, it would be a capital offense for the bride to have consensual coital sex with any man other than the groom.[28] The second stage, known as *nisu'in*, occurs after *kiddushin* and consists of the bride and groom spending a relatively short period of time in seclusion.[29] After *nisu'in*, the marriage is complete.[30]

Modern practice is for these two stages to be completed one right after the other. Before and during the Talmudic era, however, it was customary for the two stages to occur on separate dates.[31] The Written Torah discusses the case of a woman who was raped in a desolate area, such as a field, after *kiddushin* but before *nisu'in*. Although the man who molested her committed a capital offense, the Torah says that the woman is completely innocent because she doubtlessly called out for help, but there was no one to rescue her.[32] From this statement, the Talmud derives that had there been someone there who could have saved her, he would have been obligated to take any steps required to prevent the molestation. If necessary, he would even have been obligated to kill the molester.[33]

Through traditional Jewish law rules of interpretation and argument, the Talmud derives that the same law applies to prevent a Pursuer from committing any similar type of forbidden sexual conduct, such as an act of incest (as defined by Jewish law) or homosexuality.[34] In addition, it applies to prevent a Pursuer from killing another, even if the Pursuer does not intend to kill anyone, and even if the

---

[25] Yisroel Meir Kagan, Ahavat Hessed 20:2 (Heb.). *See also* Ben Zion Meir Chai Uzziel, Piskei Uzziel BiSheelot HaZeman no. 48 (Heb.) (approving view of Yisroel Meir Kagan); Avraham Yitzhak Hakohen Kook, Mishpat Kohen no. 144 (Heb.) (ruling that one must spend all of one's money to save another's life).

[26] *See* Raymond Apple et al., *Marriage, in* 13 Encyclopaedia Judaica 563 (Michael Berenbaum & Fred Skolnik eds., 2d ed. 2007).

[27] *Id.*

[28] *Id.*

[29] *Id.*

[30] *Id.*

[31] *Id.*

[32] *Deuteronomy* 22:21.

[33] *See* Menachem Elon et al., Jewish Law (Mishpat Ivri): Cases and Materials 223–24 (1999); Aaron Kirschenbaum, *The Bystander's Duty to Rescue in Jewish Law*, 8 J. Religious Ethics 204–26 (1980), reprinted in Jewish Law and Legal Theory (Martin P. Golding ed., 1993). *See generally* Steven H. Resnicoff, *Jewish Law Perspectives on Suicide and Physician-Assisted Dying*, 13 J. L. & Religion 289, 308–12 (1998–1999).

[34] *See* Maimonides, Mishneh Torah, *Laws of the Murderer and of the Preservation of Life* 1:10–11.

death would be the indirect cause of the Pursuer's conduct.[35] Of course, if the Pursuer can be stopped by lesser means, one must use such means rather than kill the Pursuer.[36]

§ 3.03 RESPONSIBILITY FOR THE CONDUCT OF OTHERS

The Jewish people accepted the Torah as a unit and they "continue to function as a community rather than as mere individuals."[37] As members of a community, they are responsible, under Jewish law, not only for their own conduct but also for the conduct of their fellows.[38] This mutual responsibility (*arevut*) has a number of significant ramifications.[39] For example, Judaism presupposes that various divine judgments are issued based upon the cumulative merits of the Jewish nation as a whole, and such judgments affect the lot of each individual.[40]

Furthermore, as a matter of Jewish law, this interdependency means that individuals, and not merely official Jewish law authorities, are obligated to try to prevent their fellows from doing evil. The Torah tells each Jew who sees another committing a biblical violation that "You must admonish a member of your nation."[41] Some commentators explain that this obligation comprises two elements. The first is a duty to gently admonish someone who has violated, or seems about to violate, Jewish law — and, according to many authorities, applies even if the person admonished will not alter his conduct. The second, based on the interrelationship established by the biblical oaths the nation took on Mounts *Eval* and *Gerizin*, as described in the twenty-seventh chapter of Deuteronomy, requires more vigorous action to prevent another from breaching Jewish law.[42] Indeed, if a Jew, A, has the ability to prevent another Jew, B, from violating Jewish law and does not do so, A

---

[35] *Id.*

[36] *Id.* at 1:6–16; Elon, *supra* note 33, at 227.

[37] Aryeh Kaplan, 2 Handbook of Jewish Law 136 (1992).

[38] *Id.* (citing authorities).

[39] From a religious perspective, for instance, a spiritual "infection" in any person can adversely affect the entire organic community. *Id.* at n.2.

[40] *Id.* at 336 (entire nations are judged on the Jewish New Year (*Rosh HaShanah*)).

[41] *Leviticus* 19:17. *See also* Shulhan Arukh, *Orah Hayyim* 608; Babad, *supra* note 18, *Commandment* 239 (Heb.) (discusses the commandment of *tokhahah*, *i.e.*, the duty to rebuke one's fellow, based on *Leviticus* 19:17); Joshua H. Smidman, *Rebuke and Reproof, in* Encyclopaedia Judaica, *supra* note 26, vol. 17, at 139. Although many authorities contend that the duty to rebuke does not authorize a person to physically coerce another to comply with Jewish law, other authorities disagree. *See* Yisroel Stefansky, *Tokhahah v'Arvut B'Mitzvot She'Ben Adam L'Makkom u-b'Mitzvot She'Ben Adam L'Havero* (*Rebuke and Interrelationship with Respect to Commandments Between Man and God and Commandments Between Man and Man*), 20 Ohr ha-Mizrach 298 (Heb.) (citing various authorities).

[42] *See* Yitzhak Weiss, 3 Minhat Yitzhak no.79; Moshe Shick, Maharam Shik, *Orah Hayyim* 303 (Heb.). *But see* Eliezer Waldenburg, 17 Tzitz Eliezer, *Kuntras Refuah BeShabbat*, perek 11 (Heb.). One early authority writes:

> All Jews are responsible for each other. If it were not for this responsibility a person would not admonish his fellow about his fellow's sins and he would not pay attention to find out who is a transgressor [and take steps to stop them].

Yehuda Hehasid (1140–1217), Sefer Hasidim 93 (Heb.).

incurs guilt for the offense that B commits.[43]

If the biblical rule being violated is not explicitly stated in the Torah, if B is not purposely violating the law and if A is sure that B will not accept the rebuke, A should not admonish B. In such a case, it is better that B violate Jewish law unknowingly rather than knowingly.[44] On the other hand, if the rule is explicitly stated or B is purposely violating a particular Jewish law provision, A is obligated to rebuke him even if A is certain the rebuke will be ineffective.[45]

Of course, there are exceptions to this obligation. For example, A need not rebuke B if A fears that by doing so he will place himself in danger because B will retaliate against him.[46] In addition, several authorities rule that A is not required to rebuke B if B has completely rejected Jewish law. The Hebrew word for "your nation" (*amkhah*) is spelled with the same Hebrew letters as the word for "with you" (*imkhah*). Consequently, some say that the duty to rebuke only applies as to those Jews who are "with you" in the sense that they generally accept the validity of Jewish law.[47] In light of the large number of contemporary Jews who, unfortunately, do not observe Jewish law, one might think that this latter exception essentially "swallows the rule." Yet there is a very important exception to the exception, because many of today's nonreligious Jews were raised in a nonreligious environment — or even in an environment actively opposed to Orthodox Judaism. According to some authorities:

> [A] person who has been brought up in a nonreligious environment where he never had the opportunity to learn about Judaism, is like a child who was abducted by gentiles, and is not considered to be doing wrong purposely. Even if he is later exposed to authentic Judaism, he is not to be blamed for rejecting it, since it is almost impossible to overcome one's childhood upbringing. Therefore, such a person is not to be counted among the

---

[43] "A person dies because of the iniquity of his brother — to teach you that everyone is responsible for each other. That is where it was possible for them to [effectively] admonish the wrongdoers and they did not do so." BABYLONIAN TALMUD, *Sanhedrin* 27a. *See also* MOSHE ISSERLES, SHULHAN ARUKH, *Yoreh De'ah* 157.

[44] An unknowing violation is a less serious breach of Jewish law. SHULHAN ARUKH, *Orah Hayyim* 608. This sort of situation might arise, for example, when B is so certain that what he is doing is permitted that he will not pay any heed to A (especially if B believes that A is much less learned than he about Jewish law).

[45] In this situation, B is already violating Jewish law knowingly. Consequently, the argument that "it is better for a person to violate unknowingly rather than knowingly" does not apply.

[46] *See, e.g.,* YISROEL MEIR KAGAN, MISHNAH BERURAH, *Orah Hayyim* 608:7 (Heb.). *See also* MOSHE ISSERLES, SHULHAN ARUKH, *Yoreh De'ah* 157, 334. *See also id.* at *Hoshen Mishpat* 12. One might expect that a person would be required to spend up to 20% of his wealth to fulfill the affirmative biblical obligation to admonish another. YAAKOV WEISS, *Minhat Yitzhak* V:8. Nevertheless, Moshe Isserles, *supra* note 43, who cites Rabbi Asher Weil, seems to rule that a person need not spend any money to fulfill the duty to admonish. *See* ASHER WEIL, *Shut Mahariv* 157 (Heb.). *See generally* ZVI HIRSCH EISENSTADT, PISKEI TESHUVAH, *Yoreh De'ah* 157, *sif koton* 5 (Heb.) (citing various views, including one that suggests a possible obligation to spend all of one's money to fulfill this duty) and *Yoreh De'ah* 334, *sif koton* 19.

[47] *See, e.g.,* YISROEL MEIR KAGAN, BIUR HALAKHA, *Orah Hayyim* 608, s.v. *Aval* (Heb.) (citing various authorities); YEHIEL M. EPSTEIN, ARUKH HASHULHAN, *Orah Hayyim* 608:7 (Heb.). If, however, you may convince such a person to do the right thing, some say that you must try to do so. *See, e.g.,* BABAD, *supra* note 18, at *Commandment* 229.

nonbelievers, and he should be approached with love and with every attempt to bring him back to the teachings of our faith. [Citations omitted.][48]

In addition to the duty to verbally dissuade a Jew from violating Jewish law, there is also an affirmative duty, where possible, to take other steps, including the use of physical restraints, to prevent a person from actively violating Jewish law.[49] Nevertheless, just as one is not required to verbally rebuke someone if this will expose one to a significant risk, one need not take non-verbal steps if this will subject one to such a risk. Similarly, one is not required to take non-verbal acts to prevent another from sinning if this would submit one to this type of loss.[50]

[A] Prohibitions Against Enabling or Assisting Others to Sin

There is a biblical prohibition against enabling someone to commit a Jewish law violation that the person could not otherwise commit. This prohibition is referred to as *lifnei iver*. There is a rabbinic prohibition against assisting someone to

---

[48] ARYEH KAPLAN, II HANDBOOK OF JEWISH THOUGHT 151 (1992) (citing authorities, some of which admittedly do not seem to support the precise statements made in his text). A number of poskim indicate that many contemporary Jews, especially those raised by non-observant parents, should be considered to be such "child-abductees." *See, e.g.*, YISROEL REISMAN, THE LAWS OF RIBIS 98, at n.17 (citing Rabbis Shimon Grinfeld (*Maharshag*) and Avraham Isaiah Karelitz (*Hazon Ish*) for the rule that non-observant Jews who were not raised in an orthodox home must be treated just as observant Jews regarding prohibitions concerning interest-bearing loans). *See also* YAAKOV ETTLINGER, BINYON TZIYON HAHADASHOT 23 (Heb.); DAVID ZVI HOFFMANN, MELAMED LEHOYEL, *Orah Hayyim* nos. 5, 29 (Heb.); AVRAHAM ISAIAH KARELITZ, HAZON ISH, *Yoreh De'ah, Hilkhot Shekhitah* 2:16 (Heb.); YEHIEL YAAKOV WEINBERG, 2 SERIDEI EISH no.10 (Heb.); MOSHE STERNBUCH, 1 TESHUVOT VEHANHAGOT, *Orah Hayyim* nos. 132, 319 and 363 (Heb.); CHAIM KOENIG, 4 SHUT HUKEI HAYYIM NISHMAT SARAH, *Hoshen Mishpat* no. 20 (Heb.) (citing authorities); ELIYAHU HENKIN, I KITVEI HAGRAYAH HENKIN 103 (Heb.); FEINSTEIN, *supra* note 21, *Yoreh De'ah* II:52 (Heb.) (they are treated as unintentional violators because they are as children who were kidnapped by Gentiles); SHLOMO ZALMAN AUERBACH, 2 MINHAT SHLOMO no. 97(5) (Heb.) (it is prohibited to help a person who has the status of a "kidnapped child" to commit a transgression). In a letter (on file with the author) dated 29th day of Menachem Av, 5758 (1998), a contemporary Israeli posek, R. Ezra Basri writes that "[T]he non-religious are regarded [literally, 'have a din'] as people who were kidnapped like children just as the Hazon Ish writes." Some authorities argue that there is an obligation to rebuke modern irreligious Jews, because some may well respond positively to such admonition. *See* YITZHAK WEISS, 4 MINHAT YITZHAK no. 79 (Heb.) (citing authority). *But see* BINYOMIN YEHOSHUA SILBER, 9 AZ NIDABRU no. 55 (Heb.); YITZHAK WEISS, 3 MINHAT YITZHAK 79 (Heb.) (using the distinction between observant and non-observant Jews as one of several reasons which, taken together, warranted the leniency of not requiring one to openly object to another's purchase of goods produced by non-observant Jewish workers, even when the purchase might "cause" such non-observant Jews to work on the Sabbath); OVADIA YOSEF, 2 YABIA OMER, *Orah Hayyim* no. 15 (Heb.).

[49] MAIMONIDES, SEFER HAMITZVOT, *Mitzvot Aseh* 205. *See* NAHMANIDES, COMMENTARY TO THE TORAH, *Deuteronomy* 27:26, who says that if one does not prevent others from sinning, the verse, "Cursed is the man who does not uphold all the words of this Torah," applies to him. *See also* KAPLAN, *supra* note 48, at 151–53. Rabbinic authorities disagree as to whether the duty to stop someone from sinning, as opposed to the obligation of admonishing a sinner, is biblical or rabbinic. *See, e.g.*, RABBI AVROHOM SHMUEL BINYOMIN SOFER (1815–1871), KETAV SOFER, *Yoreh De'ah* no. 83 (Heb.) (citing these views); YITZHAK BELZER, 1 PRI YITZHAK no. 53 (Heb.) (printing a responsum of Rabbi Naftali Amsterdam discussing these views and concluding that the duty is biblical).

[50] *See, e.g.*, YEHUDA HEHASID, SEFER HASIDIM no. 405 (Heb.); SHULHAN ARUKH, *Yoreh De'ah* 334:48, *Hoshen Mishpat* 12:1.

commit a violation even if the person could have transgressed without the assistance. This prohibition goes by various names, such as *mesayeah lidei ovrei aveirah, mahzik bidei ovrei aveirah*, or simply *mesayeah*. The *lifnei iver* and *mesayeah* rules have widespread practical implications and will be discussed in order.

[B] Enabling a Transgression: *Lifnei Iver*

The *lifnei iver* doctrine arises from the verse, "in front of the blind (*lifnei iver*), do not place a stumbling block."[51] Interestingly, although there are several aspects to this doctrine, there is a debate among Jewish law authorities as to whether the prohibition applies to the *literal* case in which one places a physical obstacle in front of a person who is visually impaired.[52] All authorities, however, agree that it biblically proscribes enabling people to violate Jewish law. This aspect of *lifnei iver*, not to frustrate the Divine Will, represents an obligation directly owed to God, and applies whether the person assisted is a Jew or a non-Jew.[53]

A classic discussion of this aspect of *lifnei iver* appears in the Talmudic tractate *Avodah Zarah* (Idolatry). The first Mishnah in *Avodah Zarah* states, in part, that it is impermissible to do business with idolaters for three days preceding their religious holidays. The Talmud inquires into the reason for this prohibition. On the one hand, it might be to prevent the idolater from profiting from the transaction. R. Shlomo Yitzhaki, the foremost Talmud commentator, explains that if the idolater profits, then, during his or her holiday, the idolater is likely to give thanks to the idol. In giving thanks to the idol, the idolater will likely invoke the idol's name. Consequently, by conducting such business with the idolater, the Jew would violate a specific Jewish law against causing the name of an idol to be mentioned.[54] Alternatively, the Talmud asks whether the prohibition is lest the idolater use the item purchased to actually serve the idol. By providing merchandise that is so used, the Talmud suggests that the Jew might violate the *lifnei iver* rule.

The Talmud suggests there could be a practical difference between these two reasons in a case in which a Jew wants to sell an animal to an idolater. If the prohibition is based on the possibility that the idolater might profit, the sale should be proscribed. If, however, the prohibition is based on *lifnei iver*, the Talmud suggests that the sale should be permitted, because, presumably, the idolater already owns an animal he could use for a sacrifice. The Talmud, however, queries whether this practical difference is really true:

> If the idolater has his own animal [that he could use as a sacrifice], does this really mean that [if a Jew sells him an animal and the idolater sacrifices that

---

[51] *Leviticus* 19:14.

[52] *See, e.g.*, YITZHAK ADLER, LIFNEI IVER (1988-89), at 15–18 (citing various views); FEINSTEIN, *supra* note 21, *Yoreh De'ah* I:3 (Heb.) (stating that it applies to such a case).

[53] FEINSTEIN, *supra* note 21, *Orah Hayyim* V:13 (9) (causing another to sin is not prohibited because it is a wrong against the sinner but because it is a wrong against the Almighty).

[54] SHLOMO YITZHAKI (*Rashi*; 1040–1105), BABYLONIAN TALMUD, *Avodah Zarah* 6a (citing *Exodus* 23:13). This prohibition, which differs from the rule against idolatry, is cited at SHULHAN ARUKH, *Orah Hayyim* 156:1.

animal instead of the one he already owns] there is no violation of *lifnei iver*? Was the following not taught in a braitha?

> Rabbi Yohanan says: "How do we know that one may not give a cup of wine to a Nazir [a person who has taken a vow which, among other things, makes it forbidden for him to drink wine] or a limb taken from a live animal [which is forbidden food][55] to a Gentile? It is taught 'And before a blind man, do not place a stumbling block.'"

Yet if one does not hand it to him, he [the Nazir or the Gentile] will take it himself![56]

In other words, the Talmud assumes that *lifnei iver* only applies if one enables another to commit a transgression that could not be accomplished without the assistance. If the Nazir could pick up the cup of wine by himself or the Gentile could pick up the limb from a live animal by herself, then, reasons the Talmud, *lifnei iver* should not apply. Consequently, the Talmud questions how Rabbi Yohanan could think that *lifnei iver* could apply.

The Talmud answers this question by saying that Rabbi Yohanan was dealing with cases in which the Nazir and the wine — and the limb from a live animal and the Gentile — were, respectively, "on two [different] sides of the river."[57] In other words, the situations in question were ones in which neither the Nazir nor the Gentile could have gotten the forbidden substances without the assistance of the Jew in question. Consequently, by giving them the substances, the Jew was enabling them to commit a transgression that would not otherwise have been possible.

What if a particular person could not commit a transgression without help from somebody, but there is no need for help from any particular person. There are plenty of people who could provide adequate help and are willing to do so. If one of those people provides the help, has that person violated the *lifnei iver* rule? Although there is a notable minority opinion,[58] most Jewish law authorities ask whether all of the people who are willing to help are Jewish. If they all are Jewish,

---

[55] Jewish law forbids a person from eating a limb taken from a live animal. This prohibition is one of the seven Jewish laws that are known as the "Noahide laws," discussed at § 4.04, *infra*, that apply to Gentiles. In early times, people could not generally afford to eat an entire animal at a time and, given the lack of refrigeration and the scarcity of salt, it was difficult to preserve slaughtered meat. This law forbade the gruesome practice of taking a live animal's limb for one meal, while preserving the rest of the "meat" by keeping the animal alive.

[56] BABYLONIAN TALMUD, *Avodah Zarah* 6a. The Pentateuch discusses a Nazir and a Nazirite vow in the sixth chapter of Numbers.

[57] *Id.*

[58] SOFER, *supra* note 49, *Yoreh De'ah* 183 (Heb.); ELIEZER WALDENBERG, 19 TZITZ ELIEZER 32 (Heb.) (asserting that most *poskim* disagree with R. Rosanes); HAYYIM ELAZAR SHAPIRA, 1 MINHAT ELAZAR no. 53 (Heb.). *See also* OVADIAH YOSEF, 3 YEHAVEH DA'AT no. 67 (Heb.) (citing various views). FEINSTEIN, *supra* note 21, *Orah Hayyim* IV:71 (Heb.), permits a teacher to prepare a child to perform in the synagogue on the Sabbath, despite the strong likelihood that the child will desecrate the Sabbath by traveling to the synagogue in a motor vehicle. Feinstein notes that if the teacher refuses to instruct the child, someone else would do so. For this reason, Feinstein states that only the rabbinic *mesayeah* rule, and not the biblical *lifnei iver* prohibition, is at issue. The responsum does not explicitly state that only Jews could provide the required instruction. If this were the case, however, the responsum would indicate that R. Feinstein disagrees with Rosanes.

then the majority position follows the position of R. Yehuda Rosanes (the *Mishneh LaMelekh*) and rule that *lifnei iver* applies.[59]

The late R. Yaakov Kanievsky (the *Steipler Rav*), for example, a prominent twentieth century Israeli authority (*posek*), followed the *Mishneh LaMelekh* and stated that this was the position taken by the majority of *poskim*. He applied this rule in dealing with a situation in which, because of the great demand for a particular product, the factory making it was open on the Sabbath and its Jewish workers were violating the laws regarding the Sabbath. He believed that if all prospective Jewish customers would refuse to buy the product, even units of the product that were themselves not made on the Sabbath, the factory would produce fewer units and, in fact, would either close on the Sabbath or would reduce the amount of forbidden work done by Jews on the Sabbath. If so, the *Steipler* ruled that a Jew who purchased any units of the product violated the biblical *lifnei iver* rule.[60]

Similarly, another renowned twentieth century Israeli posek, R. Shlomo Zalman Auerbach, applied the *Mishneh LaMelekh* to organ transplants. R. Auerbach held that even if medical tests show that a person had sustained "brain stem death,"[61] the person could not be considered as definitely dead under Jewish law until his heart stopped beating for a certain period of time. R. Auerbach stated that, until such time, any doctor who removed organs from the person — even if the doctor did this to try to save the recipient's life — violated the *halakhic* prohibition against committing a possible murder.[62]

As a result, R. Auerbach announced that, based on the *Mishneh LaMelekh's* view, the *lifnei iver* prohibition forbade any Jew from registering as a potential organ recipient in Israel. Many other Jewish law authorities disagreed with him for

---

[59] *See, e.g.*, YEHUDA ROSANES (d. 1727), MISHNEH LAMELEKH, *Hilkhot Malveh V'Loveh* 4:2 (Heb.); EZRIEL HILDESHEIMER (1820–1899), 1 RESPONSA RABBI EZRIEL, *Yoreh De'ah* no.182 (Heb.) (writing, in the nineteenth century, that this was the majority view); YOSEF BABAD (d. 1874), MINHAT HINUKH, *Mitzvah* 332(3) (Heb.); YOSEF HAYYIM (d. 1909), BEN ISH HAI, cited in AVRAHAM S. AVRAHAM (contemporary), 4 NISHMAT AVRAHAM 86 (Heb.); CHAIM Y. D. AZULEI (d. 1806), BIRKEI YOSEF, *Hoshen Mishpat* no. 9(3) (Heb.) (listing various authorities that so rule and agreeing with them); AVRAHAM DANZIG (d. 1820), HAKHMAT ADAM, *Klal* 130, *siman* 2 (Heb.); SHLOMO KLUGER (d. 1869), 2 RESPONSA TUV TA'AM VADA'AT, TELISA'AH no. 31 (Heb.); HAYYIM MEDINI (d. 1904), SDEI HEMED, *Ma'arakhat Vav, Klal* 26, *s.k.* 9 (Heb.) (stating that this is the majority view); YITZHAK WEISS (twentieth century), 3 MINHAT YITZHAK no.79 (Heb.) (citing R. Hayyim Kaniesvski (twentieth century), *Kehillat Yaakov, Likutim* II:6, as stating, in the twentieth century, that this was the majority view); ADLER, *supra* note 52, at 333 ("Where it is impossible [for the wrongdoer to obtain the object necessary for the sin] except from other Jews, the majority of *poskim* rule strictly.").

[60] *See* YITZHAK WEISS, 3 MINHAT YITZHAK 79 (Heb.) (citing the *Steipler's* work, *Kehillot Yaakov, Likutim* II).

[61] R. Auerbach held that a person who was suspected to have suffered brain stem death was in the category of a *sofek goses* and could not be moved except for his own benefit. Concluding that tests to determine whether a patient was brain stem dead were not intended for the patient's benefit, he ruled that it was forbidden to subject the patient to such tests. *See* letter of R. Auerbach printed in AVRAHAM S. AVRAHAM, 5 NISHMAT AVRAHAM 96.

[62] R. Auerbach held that so long as the patient's hypothalamus was functioning, he could not be conclusively deemed to be dead. He ruled that the hypothalamus of a patient suffering from brain stem death becomes irrevocably nonfunctional approximately five or six minutes after cessation of his heartbeat. *See* letter of R. Auerbach printed in R. AVRAHAM S. AVRAHAM, 5 NISHMAT AVRAHAM 97–98 (Heb.).

reasons unrelated to the view of the *Mishneh LaMalekh*.[63] He recognized that the failure of an individual Jew to register would be unlikely to have any practical impact; Israeli doctors would still routinely remove organs in reliance on the long list of other potential recipients. He reasoned, however, that if all Israeli Jews refused to register, there would be so few people left on the recipient list that doctors would not routinely violate *Halakhah* by removing organs.[64]

What if a client could accomplish his objective without the help of any Jew — so long as a Gentile would help him? For example, assume that a Nazir does not own any wine and can only drink wine if somebody either gives or sells some to him. Assume, further, that there are Gentiles who have wine and are willing to sell it to this Nazir. Some renowned Jewish law authorities, including the Gaon of Vilna[65] and the *Hazon Ish*[66] — and *possibly* Maimonides and R. Aharon HaLevi (the *Hinnukh*) as well[67] — believe that, even in this case, a Jew who sells the Nazir wine violates the biblical *lifnei iver* rule. Nonetheless, most authorities rule that where Gentiles would sell the Nazir wine, the Nazir and the wine are considered to be "on one side of the river" and a Jew who sells the wine does not violate *lifnei iver*, but only the rabbinic rule of *mesayeah*.[68]

[C] Facilitating a Transgression: *Mesayeah*

Suppose a person needs an object in order to violate Jewish law, and that there are Gentiles who are ready, able and willing to sell it to him. As already mentioned, a minority of prestigious authorities believe that a Jew who sells him the object violates the biblical *lifnei iver* rule. The majority view is that in such circumstances

---

[63] *Id.* at 96. *See also* Simha Bunim Lazerson, *Fixing the Moment of Death in Accordance with Halakha*, 14C Assia 55, at 72–73 (describing the views of R. Auerbach, his uncle). R. Auerbach believed that it was permitted to register as a prospective organ recipient outside of Israel, because the organs would be routinely taken in accordance with secular law even if no Jews registered as possible recipients. *See* letter of R. Auerbach printed in Avraham, *supra* note 62, at 95. For various reasons, some *poskim* might disagree with R. Auerbach's conclusions regarding registering in Israel. *See* J. David Bleich, 4 Contemporary Halakhic Problems 343, n.51 (citing these views). This article will not explore the intricacies of the "brain stem death" debate, but merely illustrates R. Auerbach's reliance on the *Mishneh LeMelekh*.

[64] Avraham, *supra* note 62.

[65] Elijah of Vilna, Biur HaGra, *Yoreh De'ah* 151, *s.k.* 8 (Heb.).

[66] Avraham Isaiah Karelitz, Hazon Ish, *Yoreh De'ah*, *siman* 52:13 (Heb.).

[67] For various interpretations as to the positions of Maimonides (1138–1204) and Aharon Halevi (d. circa 1300), see, for example, Babad, *supra* note 18, at *Mitzvah* 68 (Heb.) (saying that, because Maimonides did not differentiate between cases involving "two sides of the river" from those involving "one side of the river," Maimonides presumably held that both cases involved biblical *lifnei iver* violations); Isaac Herzog, Heikhal Yitzhak, *Orah Hayyim* no. 42 (citing views that Maimonides held that providing help in a "one side of the river" constituted a biblical violation); Shalom Yitzhak Tawil, Sha'arei Shalom, *sha'ar* 3, *hakdamah* (Heb.) (surveying the views of numerous commentators, but personally concluding that Maimonides held that the prohibition in a "one side of the river case" was rabbinic); Adler, *supra* note 52, at 21. R. Aaron Samuel Koidonover (1614–1676), and perhaps others, also ruled that the biblical *lifnei iver* rule applied even where the violator could have transgressed without the assister's help. *See generally* Adler, *supra* note 52, at 23–26 (Heb.); Tawil, *supra*, *sha'ar* 3, *halakhah* 1 (Heb.).

[68] *See, e.g.*, Adler, *supra* note 52, at 21.

the person and the object are considered to be "on one side of the river," and *lifnei iver* is inapplicable. Nevertheless, most of these authorities rule that any Jew who provides the object to a Jewish wrongdoer — whether by sale or gift — breaches a rabbinic ban, referred to as *mesayeah lidei ovrei aveirah*, against helping wrongdoers.[69]

The doctrines of *lifnei iver* and *mesayeah*, and some of their specific modern applications, will be explored in later chapters.

---

[69] *See, e.g.*, Shabtai Meir HaKohen (d. 1663), Shakh, *Yoreh De'ah* 151:1, *s.k.* 7 (Heb.); David Halevi, Taz, *Orah Hayyim* 347; Avraham Gombiner (1637–1683), Magan Avraham, *Orah Hayyim* 347 (Heb.); Shmuel Kolin (1720–1806), Mahatzit HaShekel, *Orah Hayyim* 347:1 (Heb.); Shlomo Kluger, 2 Responsa Tov Ta'am VaDa'at, Telisa'ah no. 31 (Heb.); Yitzhak Yehuda Shmelkes (d. 1906), Shut, *Orah Hayyim* no. 25 (Heb.); Shalom M. Shvadron (1835-1911), 2 *Maharsham* no. 93 (Heb.); Shlomo Yehuda ben Pesah Tzvi, Erekh Shai, *Hoshen Mishpat* 26 (Heb.); Yosef Isser, Sha'ar Mishpat, *Hoshen Mishpat* 26:1 (Heb.); Yisroel Meir Kagan, Mishnah Berurah 347:9 (Heb.); Yitzhak Weiss, 2 Minhat Yitzhak no. 106 (Heb.); Hayyim HaKohen (nineteenth century), Lev Shomea, *Ma'arekhet* 30, *oht* 39 (Heb.); Abdallah Someah (1813–1889), Zivhei Tzedek, *Hoshen Mishpat* no. 2 (Heb.) (citing authorities); Ovadiah Yosef (contemporary), 2 Yabia Omer, *Orah Hayyim* no. 15 (Heb.) and 3 *Yehave Da'at* no. 67 (Heb.); Hayyim Ozer Grodzinsky (d. 1940), 3 Ahiezer no. 81 (7) (Heb.); Adler, *supra* note 52, at 332 (Heb.).

Chapter 4

CATEGORIES OF JEWISH LAW RULES

§ 4.01   OVERVIEW REGARDING THE TYPES OF JEWISH LAW RULES

There are various ways in which Jewish law may be categorized. Perhaps the most important distinction is between biblical and non-biblical law. Within biblical law, one might focus on two divisions: (1) between affirmative and negative laws; and (2) laws applicable to non-Jews and laws applicable to Jews.[1]

§ 4.02   BIBLICAL VERSUS NON-BIBLICAL LAWS

There are important differences between biblical and non-biblical laws.

[A]   Biblical laws

Biblical laws are those that were directly communicated by God, but they are not limited to the laws written in the Pentateuch. As explained in Chapters 2 and 6, Jewish law assumes that there were two sections to the Sinaitic revelation. One section, the Written Torah, was written as the Pentateuch. The other section, the

---

[1] There are, of course, other ways of categorizing Jewish law rules. For example, one might differentiate them based on their respective punishments (e.g., capital offenses versus non-capital offenses, offenses punishable in rabbinical courts versus those punishable only by God).

Oral Torah, however, was intended to remain oral and to be transmitted directly by teacher to student. The Oral Torah contains not only specific rules but also instructions as to how to derive additional laws. According to most Jewish law authorities, the laws so derived are also biblical laws.[2]

[B] Rabbinic laws

Rabbinic rules are usually promulgated for one of two reasons. First, rabbinic authorities may believe that a rule is necessary to prevent people from violating a biblical rule. This type of rule is known as a *gezerah* (pl., *gezerot*). For example, suppose one act is biblically permitted and the other is biblically forbidden. It is possible that the rabbis might believe that the differences between these two acts, which make one permitted and the other forbidden, are not apparent to the normal person. As a result, if people see that they are allowed to do the permitted act, they will mistakenly think that the other act is also permitted and may do it. In such a case, the rabbis may prohibit the permitted act to prevent this mistake from being made.

Similarly, the rabbis might believe that if someone were to engage in the biblically permitted activity, they might end up in a situation in which they would be very tempted to do the act that is biblically forbidden. Thus, they prohibit the permitted activity to help prevent people from commiting a biblical violation. An example of this is the rabbinic prohibition against riding a horse on the Sabbath. Biblical law allows one to ride a horse on the Sabbath. However, breaking off a branch from a tree on the Sabbath is biblically forbidden. The rabbis prohibited riding a horse on the Sabbath because someone who rides a horse is inclined to break off a branch to use it to inspire the horse to run faster.[3] In fact, there are many *gezerot* designed to prevent violation of the Sabbath laws. For example, one may not examine his accounts, lest the person end up making notes, thereby violating the biblical law against writing on the Sabbath.[4]

Second, on many occasions the rabbis would issue a different type of rule, known as a *takkanah* (pl., *takkanot*), intended for some specific purpose, such as curing a particular problem or promoting some Torah value. As discussed at more length elsewhere, takkanot were enacted for a variety of reasons, including, for instance, enhancing the rights of women, promoting the operations of economic markets, making it easier for sinners to repent, and preserving the peace.[5]

---

[2] Menachem Elon, Jewish Law: History, Sources, Principles vol. 1, at 209–10 (Bernard Auerbach & Melvin J. Sykes trans., 1994).

[3] There are many examples of other rabbinic *gezerot*. For instance, King David promulgated a rule forbidding a man to be secluded with the wife of another man even if neither did anything untoward. Similarly, the rabbis issued a *gezerah* against the rearing of swine, lest people come to eat pork. *See* H. Chaim Schimmel, The Oral Law 76–77 (2d ed. 1996) (citing these and other instances).

[4] *Id.* at 78.

[5] *See* Chapter 12, *infra*.

[C] The Importance of Distinguishing Biblical from Rabbinic Rules

One cannot always easily determine from a given Talmudic passage whether the rabbis are citing a particular Pentateuchal verse as the *source* of a biblical law, whether they are simply citing it to help "support" a biblical law that was part of the Oral Torah,[6] or whether they are actually citing it to help "support" a law that is actually rabbinic in origin.[7]

[1] A Rule's Type Matters When Its Applicability Is Uncertain

Whether a particular rule is a biblical law rather than a non-biblical law may make a difference to someone spiritually (or motivationally), but is there any *legal* difference?

The answer is yes. One difference arises when a person is legitimately uncertain whether Jewish law proscribes, or prescribes, a particular act.[8] The uncertainty may be based on incomplete knowledge of the relevant circumstances or on the existence of competing and inconsistent legal opinions. [9]

If there is only a de minimus likelihood that a particular act is either forbidden or obligatory, Jewish law assumes that a person possesses discretion to do or to refrain from doing the act.[10]

However, if there is more than a de minimus likelihood that the act is either forbidden or obligatory, how one must act depends on whether the law in question is biblical or rabbinic. If the law is biblical, *i.e.*, if it came from either the Written Law or the Oral Law emanating from God, one must be stringent and assume that it applies. This principle, to act stringently regarding possible violations of biblical law, is known as *safek deoraitha lihumra*.[11] If the possibly applicable biblical law prescribes an act, one must do it. If the law proscribes an act, one must refrain from doing it. Thus, if there is a piece of food and there is more than a de minimus chance that the food is biblically prohibited, one may not eat it.

With respect to the possible violation of a rabbinic prohibition, a different principle applies, *viz.*, we rule leniently (*safek derabbanan likulah*).[12] Thus, suppose there is one piece of food, and we know that it is biblically permitted to eat it. However, the facts as we know them suggest that it is possible that the food is

---

[6] This type of use is referred to as an *asmakhta*, from the Babylonian word for *support*.

[7] SCHIMMEL, *supra* note 3, at 52–57.

[8] If one can easily resolve one's uncertainty, then one cannot rely on the rules regarding cases of legitimate uncertainty. Instead, one should resolve the uncertainty.

[9] 1 ELON, *supra* note 2, at 212.

[10] An event that is so unlikely to be true is referred to as a *mi'ut she'eino matzui*, a minority that does not (normally) occur. Authorities differ as to how much of a risk is deemed de minimus. The Hebrew expression for a doubt that is more than de minimus is *mi'ut hamatzui*.

[11] SCHIMMEL, *supra* note 3, at 59.

[12] *Id.*

rabbinically forbidden. The general rule is that we are allowed to eat the food.[13]

However, there is one more caveat. If there is a very strong possibility that the food is prohibited, then the lenient principle of *safek derabbanan likulah* does not apply, and even if the concern is only about a possible rabbinic prohibition, one may not eat it. Authorities disagree as to precisely where the line between a possibility and a strong possibility is drawn.[14]

[2] Other Issues Depending on a Rule's Biblical or Non-Biblical Status

Various other distinctions between biblical and rabbinic laws include, for instance, the consequences of violating the law (e.g., the penalties that could be imposed[15]) and the likelihood that, in appropriate circumstances, rabbinic authorities might fashion legal exceptions.[16]

Often it is clear whether a particular law is biblical or not. Many provisions are clearly designated as rabbinic enactments (of one sort or another) or as a product of local legislation or custom. Nevertheless, there are exceptions as to which Talmudic and post-Talmudic authorities disagree. For example, when it applies, the doctrine *dina demalkhuta dina* makes secular law binding as a matter of Jewish law. Thus, a violation of such secular law constitutes a violation of Jewish law. However, there is considerable debate as to whether this doctrine is biblical or non-biblical.[17]

---

[13] *See generally* SCHIMMEL, *supra* note 3, at 59.

[14] This work is not the place to examine the various views in detail. However, it is important to note that estimating this likelihood can importantly depend on whether the uncertainty concerns a question of fact or a question of law. Regarding questions of fact, it is sometimes possible to determine the likelihood with precision. The likelihood that one of several inconsistent Jewish law opinions is the "correct" opinion is not amenable to such precision.

[15] For example, if someone were convicted of violating the biblical rule against taking interest on a loan to another Jew, rabbinic authorities would compel the person to return the interest. However, if someone violated a rabbinic rule against the taking of interest, a rabbinic court would not compel him to return the money. Another example involves capital punishment. The biblically prescribed forms of capital punishment would only be imposed for the pertinent biblical offenses. If capital punishment was imposed pursuant to a rabbinical court's extraordinary powers, a different form of capital punishment was used. *See* Chapter 8, *infra*, as to the court's extraordinary powers.

[16] *See* 1 ELON, *supra* note 2, at 212–17.

[17] Indeed, there is considerable debate as to almost all aspects of this doctrine. *See generally* SHMUEL SHILO, DINA DEMALKHUTA DINA (1974) (Heb.); DAYAN I. GRUNFELD, THE JEWISH LAW OF INHERITANCE (1987); Michael J. Broyde & Steven H. Resnicoff, *Jewish Law and Modern Business Structures: The Corporate Paradigm*, 43 WAYNE L. REV. 1685, 1769–73 (1997); 1 ELON, *supra* note 2, at 64–74.

§ 4.03   AFFIRMATIVE (ACTIVE) VERSUS NEGATIVE (PASSIVE) OBLIGATIONS

[A]   General Rules as to the Extent of One's Obligation

Jewish law ordinarily places limits on the sacrifice one must bear to comply with biblical laws. The applicable limit depends on whether the biblical law in question is classified as either affirmative (*aseh*) or negative (*lo ta'aseh*).[18] The general rule is that a person must expend all of his wealth rather than violate a negative commandment.[19] On the other hand, a person need not spend more than 20% of one's wealth to fulfill an affirmative commandment.[20]

[B]   Differentiating Positive from Negative Duties

There is a debate among Jewish law authorities as to what criterion determines whether a commandment is considered negative or affirmative. According to one view, the relevant biblical language is decisive. If the verse that is the literary source of a commandment directs that one should do something, the commandment is an affirmative one. If the verse directs that one should not do something, the commandment is a negative one. Consider, for example, the biblical commandment to protect one's fellow from harm. It arises from the verse, "Do not stand idly by your fellow's blood."[21] Because this commandment is worded as a prohibition ("do not"), it would be a negative commandment, requiring the expenditure of up to all of one's wealth.[22]

The alternative position ignores the form of the biblical language and asks, instead, whether a *violation* of the commandment involves malfeasance or nonfeasance. If a commandment can be violated without doing any act (*i.e.*, if a violation is one of nonfeasance), the commandment in effect affirmatively requires conduct, and there is no need to expend all of one's wealth to avoid a passive

---

[18] Authorities disagree as to whether the same rules that pertain to affirmative and negative biblical commandments apply to affirmative and negative rabbinic laws.

[19] *See* SHULHAN ARUKH, *Orah Hayyim* 656:1 (Heb.). Although this is clearly the accepted rule, for a commentator who questions it, see BARUKH EPSTEIN, TORAH TEMIMAH, *Genesis* 28:22 (Heb.).

[20] *See* MOSES FEINSTEIN, IGGEROT MOSHE, *Yoreh De'ah* II, 174:4 (Heb.). Rabbi Moshe Isserles states that one need not spend a large amount of money (*hon rav*) to fulfill a particular affirmative commandment. He makes reference to a particular rabbinic decree that one should not distribute more than 20% of one's wealth to the poor. SHULHAN ARUKH, *supra* note 19. It is unclear precisely how much a person *must* spend, if an expenditure is necessary, in order to fulfill an affirmative commandment. Rabbi Yehiel Mikhal Epstein seems to believe that one generally need not spend up to the 20% limit. *See* YEHIEL MIKHAL EPSTEIN, ARUKH HASHULHAN, *Orah Hayyim* 656:4 (Heb.). Some say that, if necessary, a person must spend at least 10% of his wealth. *See* YOSEF KARO, BEIT YOSEF, *Orah Hayyim* 656 (Heb.) (citing this view). Rabbi Shlomo Luria, however, disagrees and states that if someone is very poor it is possible that, with two exceptions, he need not spend any money in order to fulfill an affirmative commandment. *See* AVRAHAM ABELI GOMBINER, MAGEN AVRAHAM, *Orah Hayyim* 656:7 (Heb.). *But see* YISROEL MEIR HAKOHEN, BIUR HALAKHA, *Orah Hayyim* 656 (Heb.) (disagreeing with Rabbi Luria).

[21] *Leviticus* 19:16.

[22] *See, e.g.*, FEINSTEIN, *supra* note 20 (ruling that this is the source of the duty to rescue and that it is a negative commandment); ZVI HIRSCH SHAPIRO, DARKEI TESHUVAH, *Yoreh De'ah* 157:57 (Heb.) (citing this view).

violation. However, if a commandment can only be violated actively (i.e., through malfeasance), one must avoid a transgression even at the cost of one's entire fortune. The commandment, "Do not stand idly by," effectively requires action and can only be violated by nonfeasance. According to this view, the duty to rescue another would not require one to use more than one-fifth of one's wealth.[23]

The rule requiring a greater expenditure to avoid a violation involving malfeasance than for one involving nonfeasance is readily understandable according to this alternative position. Intuitively, malfeasance seems to suggest a greater degree of rebellion than nonfeasance.

Before proceeding to the next way in which Jewish laws are differentiated, consider a few interesting issues regarding application of the limits discussed above. For example, consider whether the obligation to use all of one's wealth would require one to draw on his creditworthiness to borrow funds. Rabbi David ben Solomon ibn Abi Zimra (*Radbaz*; c. 1479–1573) was born in Spain but, at age 13 in 1492, was forced to leave when Spain banished all Jews. His family moved to Safed, in Israel, and he later moved to Fes, Turkey, where he became a member of the rabbinical court. When the Turkish government abolished the rabbinical court, he moved to Cairo, Egypt, where he was appointed Egypt's Chief Rabbi, a position in which he served for forty years. Radbaz states that if a Jew is among Gentiles, he must use up all of his money on kosher food rather than eat non-kosher food. Once he has used up his money and cannot afford kosher food, he may, because of duress, eat non-kosher food if it is available. Radbaz rules that the Jew need not borrow money from Gentiles to purchase kosher food, because, should he be unable to repay the loan, the Gentiles from whom he borrowed may place him in physical danger.[24] In the United States, at least, the risk of physical harm from being unable to repay one's debt is negligible, unless one borrows from the Mafia. Therefore, it would seem that in the United States, at least, one would have to borrow before being permitted to violate a negative commandment. One might not, however, be required — or even permitted — to borrow beyond one's expectation to repay, because doing so might violate a different negative commandment, the one against stealing.

Suppose a person has no money and is unable to borrow money. Would he be required to ask for charity rather than eat non-kosher food? Rabbi Moses Feinstein was perhaps the greatest Jewish law authority in the United States from the middle of the twentieth century until his death in 1986. In ruling whether a person is required to make a particular sacrifice in order to avoid violating a negative commandment, Feinstein asks whether the sacrifice is greater than the loss of all of one's wealth. According to Feinstein, only if the answer is "no" must the person sustain the sacrifice and avoid the violation.[25] R. Feinstein's responsum is not clear as to whether, when applying this test, one must: (1) evaluate how much these burdens would mean to a hypothetical "reasonable person" rather than to the

---

[23] *See, e.g.*, SHLOMO MORDEKHAI BEN MOSHE SHWADRON, 2 SHUT MAHARSHAM no. 54 (Heb.). Nevertheless, some authorities believe that the duty to save a life is *sui generis* and, even if otherwise categorized as an affirmative commandment, requires the use of up to all of one's resources. *See* Chapter 3, *supra*.

[24] *See* R. AKIVA EGER, HIDDUSHEI RABBI AKIVA EGER, *Yoreh De'ah* 157 (Heb.) (citing Radbaz).

[25] *See* FEINSTEIN, *supra* note 20.

particular person in question; or (2) evaluate how much the loss of money would mean to the particular person *if he had money*. Of course, neither of these undertakings, but especially the second one, would seem to be easily accomplished.

§ 4.04 LAWS APPLICABLE TO NON-JEWS VERSUS LAWS APPLICABLE TO JEWS

According to Jewish law, God gave seven commandments to the descendants of Noah.[26] Specifically, a *Baraitha*, an early, pre-Talmudic teaching that was not included in the Mishnah, states:

> The Rabbis taught: Seven commandments were given to the descendants of Noah: [to establish] a legal order, [and to refrain from] blasphemy, idolatry, incest, bloodshed, robbery, and eating flesh of a live animal.[27]

These laws are known as the laws of Noah or the Noahide (or Noachide) laws.[28] Jewish law authorities disagree as to whether the commandment to establish a legal order merely required the maintenance of a system of judges or whether it actually included an entire set of civil law similar to those given to the Jewish people.[29] In any event, from the perspective of Jewish law, every non-Jew continues to be bound by these rules. Maimonides states that a non-Jew who accepts these obligations as a resident alien (*ger toshav*) mentioned in Scripture, is among the "righteous" of the non-Jews, and is entitled to "full material support" from the Jewish community.[30]

Jews, as descendants of Noah, were originally subject to the Noahide laws. After the Sinaitic revelation, however, the question arose as to whether Jews were only subject to the new, more detailed laws given to the Jewish people or whether they were obligated both in the new laws and in the Noahide laws. The Talmud seems to reach the latter conclusion, stating broadly that there is nothing that a Jew may do that is prohibited to a non-Jew.[31]

Nevertheless, it does indicate that there are rare instances in which a Jew's new legal responsibilities create "exceptions" not relevant to someone not so charged.[32] In addition, a Jew would not necessarily face the same punishment as a non-Jew for violation of a Noahide law.[33]

---

[26] *See generally* AARON LICHTENSTEIN, THE SEVEN LAWS OF NOAH (2d ed. 1986); NAHUM RAKOVER, LAW AND THE NOAHIDES: LAW AS A UNIVERSAL VALUE (1998).

[27] BABYLONIAN TALMUD, *Sanhedrin* 56a, *translated in* 1 ELON, *supra* note 2, at 194.

[28] *See, e.g.*, Steven S. Schwarzschild, Saul Berman, & Menachem Elon, *Noachide Laws, in* 15 ENCYCLOPAEDIA JUDAICA 284 (Michael Berenbaum & Fred Skolnik eds., 2d ed. 2007).

[29] 1 ELON, *supra* note 2, at 194 (identifying the first view as that of Maimonides and the second as that of Nahmanides).

[30] *Id.*

[31] *See* BABYLONIAN TALMUD, *Sanhedrin* 59a.

[32] *Id.*

[33] *See* Schwarzschild et al., *supra* note 28.

Chapter 5

HUMAN AND INSTITUTIONAL AUTHORITIES

§ 5.01   INTRODUCTION

There are disparate views as to whether, over time, Jewish law has evolved or whether its preexisting essence has merely been increasingly revealed. These views are explored in Chapter 9. Whatever the process through which Jewish law has dealt with changed circumstances — cultural, economic, psychological, sociological and technological — everyone agrees that this process has been largely dependent on the conduct of human and institutional actors, which are the subject of this chapter.

§ 5.02   MOSAIC ORDINATION (*SEMIKHAH*)

Critical to appreciating the process by which the Oral Torah works is the Jewish law "institution" known as Mosaic ordination (*semikhah*). The Pentateuch explains that Moses transferred his authority to his student, Joshua, by placing his hands on him in front of the entire community.[1] By this act, Moses authorized Joshua to exercise leadership over the Jewish nation. Joshua authorized his students by placing his hand on them in the same way, and so on. Anyone who had received this ordination could so ordain others.[2] Thus, those who were ordained in this manner could trace their ordination back to Moses. There are various legal decisions that

---

[1] *Numbers* 27:18–23.

[2] *See, e.g.,* Peretz Segal, *Jewish Law During the Tannaitic Period, in* AN INTRODUCTION TO THE HISTORY

only a sage with this type of ordination is entitled to render.[3]

A sage with this type of ordination also had the right to issue rulings regarding Torah law (based, for instance, on the interpretative rules) even if a majority of other authorities disagreed with him. He would only be bound if there was an assembly of such sages and, at that assembly, the issue was debated, a vote taken and a majority of the sages voted against him.[4]

Individual Jews who were not ordained did not have this luxury. If a consensus developed among rabbinic authorities, then even without an assembly and a vote, Jews who were not themselves qualified to render Jewish law opinions, with rare exceptions, were obligated to abide by the consensus opinion.[5]

Because of Gentile prohibitions against the teaching of Torah law, as well as persecutions of Torah scholars, the chain of Mosaic ordination was broken in 358 C.E.[6] The "ordination" that rabbis now possess is something quite different; it merely means that the holder of the title has his or her teacher's permission to render Jewish law decisions publicly.[7]

§ 5.03 TRIBAL PRINCES

At the time of the Sinaitic revelation, the Jewish nation was a confederation of tribes led by the descendants of the sons of Jacob (the son of Isaac, the son of Abraham). Each tribe was led by a prince or chieftain (a *Nasi*). The princes' responsibilities included participating in the census, the distribution of land, endorsement of pacts or covenants and various communal responsibilities.[8]

§ 5.04 SUPREME COURT (*SANHEDRIN HAGADOL*)

Another important Jewish law institution is the Supreme Court (*Sanhedrin HaGadol*), which consisted of seventy-one judges. The number of Supreme Court judges is based[9] on God's commandment to Moses, "Gather to Me seventy men of the elders of Israel . . . — and bring them to the Tent of Meeting, so that they

---

AND SOURCES OF JEWISH LAW 124–27 (N.S. Hecht et al. eds., 1996). *See generally* PHILIP BIRNBAUM, A BOOK OF JEWISH CONCEPTS 440 (1964).

[3] *See* Segal, *supra* note 2.

[4] *See* MOSES FEINSTEIN, DIBROT MOSHE: SHABBAT 126–27 (Heb.). In the special case in which the highest Jewish rabbinic tribunal, the Sanhedrin HaGadol, issued a judgment, it was a capital offense for a rabbi to rule that someone could affirmatively violate the Sanhedrin HaGadol's judgment. A person who so ruled was called a "rebellious elder" (*zakein mamre*).

[5] *See* WALTER WURZBURGER, ETHICS OF RESPONSIBILITY: PLURALISTIC APPROACHES TO COVENANTAL ETHICS 7 (1994).

[6] *See* ARYEH KAPLAN, THE HANDBOOK OF JEWISH THOUGHT 209 (1979).

[7] *Id.*

[8] *See* Mark Wischnitzer, *Chieftain*, *in* 4 ENCYCLOPAEDIA JUDAICA 614 (Michael Berenbaum & Fred Skolnik eds., 2d ed. 2007).

[9] KAPLAN, *supra* note 6, at 198. With respect to its judicial role, the Sanhedrin HaGadol is referred to as the Supreme Court. With respect to its other powers, the Sanhedrin HaGadol is sometimes referred to as the Great Council.

should stand there with you."[10] Seventy elders plus Moses made seventy-one.[11]

The Sanhedrin HaGadol had the authority to issue Jewish law rulings as to controversies involving Torah law or non-Torah law. These rulings were universally binding, even if more than seventy-one non-members, all possessing Mosaic ordination, disagreed with it.[12] In addition, the Sanhedrin HaGadol was authorized to enact rabbinic legislation which was binding on all Jews as a matter of religious law.[13] Furthermore, the Sanhedrin HaGadol, as well as other official rabbinic courts consisting of judges possessing Mosaic ordination, had the inherent right to implement special emergency measures in cases of general lawlessness.[14]

The Roman government in Byzantium abolished the Sanhedrin HaGadol in the fourth century.[15] Mosaic ordination was one of the prerequisites for membership in the Sanhedrin HaGadol. Therefore, once the chain of Mosaic ordination was broken in the middle of the fourth century, it was impossible to re-establish the Sanhedrin HaGadol.[16] There were efforts, most prominently at the time the Code of Jewish Law was authored, to restore the institution of Mosaic ordination, but the efforts were unsuccessful.[17] Some Jewish law scholars hold the view that if all religious authorities in the Land of Israel were to agree to ordain a qualified person, then that person could ordain others and, ultimately, a new Sanhedrin HaGadol could be formed.[18] Nevertheless, no such agreement among authorities is in sight.

Before it disbanded, the Sanhedrin HaGadol adopted measures to "authorize" subsequent rabbinical courts, which were to act as their "agents" to decide certain types of matters. This authorization continues today. Typically, these matters must involve a common dispute in which one of the litigants suffers an actual loss. Courts consisting of judges lacking Mosaic ordination are not authorized, for example, to rule in cases involving fines or punitive damages.[19] On the other hand, courts consisting of judges lacking Mosaic ordination possess the inherent power to implement emergency measures in times of general lawlessness.[20] Nevertheless, even this power may depend on a court's having the status of an "established" court.

---

[10] *Numbers* 11:16.

[11] There was apparently some larger group of "elders" from whom these seventy were taken. This larger group may also have played some larger role in national government, although its precise role is not clear. The Mishnah states that "Moses received the Torah from Sinai and transmitted it to Joshua, and Joshua handed it to the Elders, and the Elders transmitted it to the Prophets." *Pirkei Avot* 1:1. See GEORGE HOROWITZ, THE SPIRIT OF JEWISH LAW 69–70 (1973).

[12] *See generally* Eli Turkel, *The Nature and Limitations of Rabbinic Authority*, 27:4 TRADITION 80, 80–82 (1993).

[13] KAPLAN, *supra* note 6, at 197.

[14] BABYLONIAN TALMUD, *Yebamot* 90b, *Sanhedrin* 46a.

[15] *See* Turkel, *supra* note 12, at 82.

[16] KAPLAN, *supra* note 6, at 209.

[17] *See, e.g.*, ZECHARIAH FENDEL, LIGHTS OF THE EXILE: EARLY ACHARONIM HASHKAFAH PUBLICATIONS 13–14, 118–20, 145–47 (2001) (discussing efforts to revive Mosaic ordination, which would ultimately permit reestablishment of the Sanhedrin HaGadol).

[18] KAPLAN, *supra* note 6, at 210.

[19] *Id.*

[20] *See Shulhan Arukh, Hoshen Mishpat* 2.

Given the historical dismantling of Jewish communities, the loss of juridical and political autonomy and the highly fragmented nature of most Jewish communities, it seems that no rabbinic court, at least in the Diaspora, enjoys such a status.[21]

§ 5.05 JUDGES (*SHOFTIM*)

After Joshua led the Jewish nation in to Canaan, the settlement period gave rise to a leader known as a "Judge" (*shofet*).[22] These "Judges" (*shoftim*) were not the same as judges in religious courts. Instead, shoftim primarily served as military and as political leaders. The precise procedure through which a person was selected for or elevated to the status of a shofet is uncertain. The institution lasted during the period of enmity between the newly settling Jews and the nations that were already dwelling in Canaan.[23] When the *shofet* Gideon defeated the Midianites, the tribes offered to make him king,[24] but he declined, saying "I shall not rule over you myself, nor shall my son rule over you; the Lord shall rule over you."[25] Nevertheless, the institution of shoftim was the political transition to a monarchical government, discussed below.

§ 5.06 PROPHETS

The Oral Torah also provided information regarding the authority of prophets. Although the Pentateuch states, "In your midst, God will set up for you a prophet like me [Moses] from among your brethren, and it is to him you must listen,"[26] it does not provide much detail.[27] Prophets both receive divine messages and are charged with transmitting them to others.[28] Early prophets were importantly involved in communal and political affairs.[29] For example, the prophet Samuel was involved in the announcement and anointment of Saul[30] and David as king.[31] Similarly, the prophet Nathan criticized King David for his conduct regarding Bath-Sheva and her husband Uriah. Nathan also was instrumental in devising and implementing the method by which he and Bath-Sheva motivated an aged King

---

[21] *See* Turkel, *supra* note 12, at 83–84, 86.

[22] *Topic Overview — History: Beginning Until the Monarchy*, *in* 9 Encyclopaedia Judaica, *supra* note 8, at 169–70.

[23] *Id.*

[24] *Judges* 8:22.

[25] *Id.* at 8:23.

[26] *Deuteronomy* 18:15.

[27] For a general discussion of the role of prophets and prophecy within the Jewish tradition, see, for example, Shalom M. Paul & S. David Sperling, *Prophets and Prophecy*, *in* 16 Encyclopaedia Judaica, *supra* note 8, at 566–80. *See also* Howard Kreisel, *Medieval Jewish Philosophy*, *in* 16 Encyclopaedia Judaica, *supra* note 8, at 581–85. Interestingly, the Written Torah does discuss how to test the genuineness of a person's claim to be a prophet, but the Oral Torah provides important guidance. *See, e.g.*, Maimonides, Maimonides' Introduction to the Talmud 48–63 (Zvi Lampel trans., 1998).

[28] Paul & Sperling, *supra* note 27, at 567.

[29] *Id.* at 570–571.

[30] *I Samuel* 9.

[31] *Id.* at 16.

David to take decisive action to name Bath-Sheva's son, Solomon, his successor.[32] Other prophets played comparable roles in anointing and rejecting kings, castigating political leaders for their misdeeds and providing counsel with respect to specific political decisions.[33]

The Oral Torah provides that prophets have the authority to implement *temporary* emergency measures that might otherwise contradict Torah law.[34] For example, although the Torah forbids the offering of an animal sacrifice outside of the Temple,[35] the prophet Elijah, in a time of religious crisis, offered a sacrifice on Mount Carmel.[36]

However, prophets are not authorized to alter the Oral Torah even by announcing new rules that are purportedly based on the literal language of the Pentateuch,[37] because the Pentateuch says that one may not "add" Torah laws.[38] In addition, a prophet may not even offer an opinion, on the supposed basis of prophecy, about ongoing debates as to existing laws.[39] Although the Torah *came* from Heaven, the Pentateuch says that it is not still "in Heaven."[40] Instead, as dramatically evidenced by the famous Talmudic episode involving "the oven of Akhnai,"[41] one may not use supernatural forces to prove the substance of Torah law.[42] In any event, the Talmud declares that prophecy ended in the fourth century of the Common Era.[43]

---

[32] *I Kings* 1:8–31.

[33] Paul & Sperling, *supra* note 27, at 570–71.

[34] *See* MENACHEM ELON, JEWISH LAW: HISTORY, SOURCES, PRINCIPLES vol. 2, at 519–20 (Bernard Auerbach & Melvin J. Sykes trans., 1994). *See also* KAPLAN, *supra* note 6, at 165–66.

[35] *Deuteronomy* 12:13–14.

[36] *I Kings* 18:3–38.

[37] *See* MAIMONIDES, *supra* note 27, at 50; ELON, *supra* note 34, vol. 1, at 242–43.

[38] Non-Torah rules, however, may be added, for example, by rabbinical or local regulation, by the development of customs, etc.

[39] MAIMONIDES, *supra* note 27, at 50.

[40] *Deuteronomy* 30:12.

[41] *See* discussion *infra* § 10.03[A].

[42] *See* ELON, *supra* note 34, vol. 1, at 17–18, which describes a fascinating event in which one Tanna tried to prove that he was right and his colleagues wrong by calling upon the Heavens for miracles as "proofs." Although the miracles were forthcoming, the colleagues rejected them, insisting that the Torah was given to man and that Jewish law conclusions could only be based on valid Jewish law analysis. See also discussion, *infra* § 10.03.

[43] *See* KAPLAN, *supra* note 6, at 111–12. For the leading theories as to why prophecy lapsed, see Hayyim Angel, *The End of Prophecy: Malachi's Position in the Spiritual Development of Israel*, INSTITUTE FOR JEWISH IDEAS AND IDEALS (Feb. 25, 2011), http://www.jewishideas.org/articles/end-prophecy-malachis-position-spiritual-developmen.

§ 5.07 KINGS

The Pentateuch provides for the institution of a Jewish king: "You shall appoint a king over you, whom God your Lord shall choose."[44] The people petitioned the prophet Samuel for a king to be "like all the nations."[45] Samuel responded disapprovingly to this request, presumably because its apparent motivation was to be like other nations. Samuel warned the people about the broad powers a king could wield.[46] The king's powers, some of which are exceptional and discretionary, include legislative authority.

These powers are elaborated upon in the Oral Torah.[47] The Oral Torah also specifies the method through which a king is appointed. The majority view is that his identity must be declared prophetically and confirmed by the Sanhedrin HaGadol.[48] As a result, until there is a prophet and a Sanhedrin HaGadol, there cannot be another king. In the absence of a king, many Jewish authorities believe that the legislative powers, at least, reside in each local community and the authorities they elect.[49]

It is important to note that a Jewish king did not possess unlimited powers. A king could not initiate an optional war (as opposed to a compulsory war, such as the war to settle the land of Israel or a war of self-defense) without the approval of the Sanhedrin HaGadol.[50] At a time when polygamy was practiced, there was a limit on the number of wives a king could keep, lest he be led astray by them.[51] Similarly, he was not allowed to possess many horses or to amass excessive amounts of gold and silver.[52] The king was obligated to honor Torah scholars[53] and was enjoined to remain humble.[54] In fact, the king was also required to write a Torah scroll for himself and to keep it with him always, even when he went to war, when he sat in judgment and even when he ate.[55] It was to be a constant reminder to him that he, the king, is not the ultimate ruler; the ruler is God.

---

[44] *Deuteronomy* 17:15. As to the institute of a Jewish king, see generally THE JEWISH POLITICAL TRADITION 108–165 (Michael Walzer, Menachem Loerberbaum, & Noam J. Zohar, eds., 2000).

[45] *Deuteronomy* 17:14.

[46] *See generally* Jacob Liver and S. David Sperling, *King, Kingship, in* 12 ENCYCLOPAEDIA JUDAICA, *supra* note 8, at 164 (citing *I Samuel* 8:5–6, 20).

[47] *See also* 4 J. DAVID BLEICH, CONTEMPORARY HALAKHIC PROBLEMS 91 (1995); ELON, *supra* note 34, vol. 1, at 55–57; THE JEWISH POLITICAL QUESTION, *supra* note 44, at 142–143.

[48] MAIMONIDES, MISHNEH TORAH, *Laws of Courts* 5:1; KAPLAN, *supra* note 6, at 166.

[49] ELON, *supra* note 34, vol. 1, at 72, 77–85.

[50] MISHNAH, *Sanhedrin*, 2:4.

[51] *Id.* at 2:5.

[52] *Id.* at 2:5, 6.

[53] MAIMONIDES, MISHNEH TORAH, *Laws of Kings* 2:5.

[54] *Id.* at 2:6.

[55] MISHNAH, *supra* note 50, at 2:6.

§ 5.08 THE EXILARCHATE

The end of Mosaic ordination, the Sanhedrin HaGadol, the age of prophecy and the institution of the Jewish king substantially limited the opportunity for enactment of broad, multi-jurisdictional Jewish legislation. This problem was further exacerbated by the geographical dispersion of the Jewish people, coupled with the quite limited technology for both intranational and international communications. However, Babylonian rulers allowed the large community in Babylon considerable governmental autonomy during the first twelve centuries of the Common Era. The head of this lay Jewish government was the Exilarch. The Exilarch traced his lineage to King David, and his authority was predicated on the notion that the Scepter should never leave the hands of the tribe of Yehudah, David's tribe.[56] Rabbinic authorities declared that the Babylonian Exilarch possessed the same Jewish law authority as a Jewish king.[57]

After the ultimate demise of this institution and the continued dispersion of Jews, a number of host countries allowed Jews some degree of governmental autonomy (at least during those periods when they allowed Jews to live within their countries).[58] In these periods, the local governments were able to promulgate appropriate legislation, often in conjunction with their communities' acknowledged rabbinic leaders. Such legislation had the force of binding religious law, covering a large variety of subjects, including commercial transactions, public education and taxes.[59]

§ 5.09 LATER RABBINIC AUTHORITIES

The same types of factors that hampered lay governmental control over the Jewish community impeded expansive rabbinic action. Despite these challenges, some decrees issued by exceptionally well respected religious authorities, such as Rabbi Gershom ben Yehudah (960–1028), managed to gain quite substantial international acceptance.[60] However, this was certainly the exception rather than the rule. Nevertheless, where Jews were afforded some measure of autonomy,

---

[56] *Genesis* 49:10.

[57] ELON, *supra* note 34, vol. 1, at 58.

[58] Rabbi Abraham Isaac Kook, early twentieth century Chief Rabbi of the Land of Israel, before creation of the State of Israel, justified the authority of local governmental action as arising out of the authority of a king:

> When there is no king, it would seem that because the king's law concerns the general condition of the nation, the king's law-making prerogatives revert to the nation as a whole. . . . In regard to whatever concerns the governance of the public, whoever leads the nation governs according to the king's law, which encompasses the totality of the needs of the people at any time for the general security.

ELON, *supra* note 34, vol. 1, at 59 (providing this translation of Kook's words).

[59] *See* ELON, *supra* note 34, vol. 1, at 71–72, 77–85.

[60] Rabbi Gershom, also known as "the Light of the Diaspora" (*Me'or HaGolah*), issued a number of decrees that were adopted throughout most of the Ashkenazi and some of the Sephardi world. These included prohibitions against polygamy and the unauthorized reading of private mail. *See generally* Shlomo Eidelberg and David Derovan, *Gershom ben Judah Me'or Ha-Golah, in* 7 ENCYCLOPAEDIA JUDAICA, *supra* note 8, at 551–52.

rabbinic officials played a part in Jewish self-governance.

Jewish law has always proceeded on the assumption that at least certain rabbinic authorities possess legislative power. Thus, Moses, other prophets, and the Sanhedrin HaGadol promulgated many decrees.[61] Tannaim, however, disagree as to the precise basis for this authority.

One important Talmudic discussion focuses on the rabbinically established holiday of Hannukah. Before one kindles the Hannukah candles, one recites the following blessing, "Blessed art Thou, O Lord our God, King of the Universe, Who has sanctified us by His commandments and has commanded us to kindle the Hannukah lights." Inasmuch as the holiday of Hannukah and the obligation to kindle Hannukah lights were established by the sages, the Talmud questions why the blessing states that it was a commandment of God:

> Where did He command us? R. Avia said: "In the verse 'You must not deviate [from the verdict that they [the judges] announce to you neither to the right nor to the left]" (Deut 17:11) R. Nehemiah said: "In the verse 'Ask your father, he will inform you, your elders, they will tell you." (Deut 32:7).[62]

The argument is that because God commanded people to obey the judges, doing any commandment ordered by the judges has the status of a Torah commandment ordered by God, thus justifying the language of the blessing.[63] Nevertheless, most authorities disagree, and state that fulfillment of a rabbinic law is not the same as fulfillment of a Torah law.[64] This dispute is important for a number of practical Jewish law reasons, which are discussed in Chapter 3.[65]

Another possible basis for the legislative power of rabbinic authorities is that, in the absence of a Jewish king, rabbinic authorities fulfill the functions of a Jewish king.[66] Indeed, in addition to these legislative powers, rabbinic authorities — at least those who are the recognized leaders of their communities — possess another type of special authority. This authority is to respond to exceptional threats to the community, whether posed by a single, incorrigible wrongdoer or whether presented by a more widespread pattern of lawlessness or licentiousness. In such situations, the Talmud announces that the rabbinic court may punish "not in accordance with the law."[67] In other words, it may convict someone without complying with otherwise applicable procedural rules, and it may impose much more severe punishments than would otherwise have been permitted. The Shulhan Arukh makes it clear that this authority may be used even though the chain of

---

[61] ISAAC HERZOG, 1 THE MAIN INSTITUTIONS OF JEWISH LAW 8–10 (2d ed. 1965).

[62] BABYLONIAN TALMUD, *Berakhot* 19b.

[63] *See* H. CHAIM SCHIMMEL, THE ORAL TORAH 87–88 (2d ed. 1996).

[64] *Id.* (citing view of Nahmanides and others).

[65] *Id.* at 59.

[66] *See, e.g.,* Turkel, *supra* note 12, at 81. *See also* DAVID COHEN, TEMPLATES FOR THE AGES (Sarah Cohen trans., 1999).

[67] *See, e.g.,* ELON, *supra* note 34.

Mosaic ordination was broken.[68] During times in which there was no Jewish king, and perhaps especially in the post-Talmudic period, this authority, discussed in more detail in Chapter 8, has been relied upon heavily.

§ 5.10 CONTEMPORARY INSTITUTIONS

Jews throughout the world no longer live in isolated communities with juridical, legislative or executive autonomy. Even where there is a high concentration of Jews, they generally enjoy no separate, exclusively Jewish governmental infrastructure. Although there are perhaps a few communities, mostly Hassidic groups, which possess some internal governmental structure, they are the exceptions.[69] As will be discussed more in Chapter 8, this has significantly influenced the development of Jewish law.

There is no longer a Jewish king, a Jewish prophet, a Sanhedrin HaGadol, a Shofet, an Exilarch or even a person with Mosaic ordination. In some countries, including Israel, the secular government elects one or more people as the authority on Jewish law, or as a "Chief Rabbi." Nevertheless, because these selections are not made by the religious Jewish communities of those countries, but by secular governments, the religious communities do not generally regard appointment of such rabbis as conferring upon them any special Jewish law "authority."[70]

Instead, recognition of which individual, if any, should be regarded a "great" Jewish law authority (a *Gadol*) is decided informally through a process involving a cluster of complex factors.[71] As one commentator explains:

> Who then is a *Gadol B'Yisroel* [i.e., a great leader in Israel]? Not simply one who has studied much and becomes expert in Torah. Nor is he one who is trained in the intricacies of Talmudic method or procedure. Many know but few are chosen. There are numerous experts in Jewish law, many men who know a great deal of Torah and Talmud and Halakhah. They fill the faculties of yeshvos in America and in Israel. But they are not *Gedolim* [plural of *Gadol*], do not claim to be *Gedolim*, and are not regarded as such by the Torah world. For a *Gadol* is not elected to leadership; no one speaks for his candidacy; no one promotes his image in the eyes of the public. He is selected by a sure and subtle process which knows its leaders and places them in the fore front [sic] of a generation. Call it mystical, call it non-rational: it is both. But somehow the genius of *K'lall Yisroel* [i.e., the Jewish nation] has been able to distinguish between a true *Gadol B'Yisroel* and an ordinary scholar. The *Gadol* not only knows Torah: his life is Torah,

---

[68] SHULHAN ARUKH, *Hoshen Mishpat* 2 (Heb.).

[69] A number of commentators suggest that the heads of certain rabbinical academies serve, for the students and alumni of those academies, some of the same functions as the Hassidic Rebbes fulfill for their Hassidic groups or what local rabbis used to perform for members of their communities. *See generally* Immanuel Jakobovits, *Rabbis and Deans*, 7:4–8:1 (combined issue) TRADITION 95 (1965).

[70] For an interesting article exploring the status of the Israeli Chief Rabbinate, see Aharon Lichtenstein, *The Israeli Chief Rabbinate: A Current Halakhic Perspective*, 26:4 TRADITION 26 (1992).

[71] *See generally* MICHAEL BERGER, RABBINIC AUTHORITY (1998).

his every word, even his ordinary conversation, is Torah, so that he is in a very real sense the repository of Torah on earh.

But even this is not enough to set a *Gadol* apart. For piety, saintliness, integrity and scholarship are qualities not limited to *Gedolim*: *Klal Yisroel* is fortunate in having, if not an abundance, at least numerous such men. What sets a *Gadol* apart is something unique: his perception, his ability to penetrate beyond the surface, his capacity for the intuitive flash of insight which disovers [sic] reality not as it appears to be but as it is: reality in the light of Torah.[72] (Emphasis in original.)

This excerpt is correct in at least two ways. First, it certainly identifies the qualities that are desired in a *Gadol*. Second, it accurately acknowledges that recognition of particular persons as Gedolim is not made by election; the process is far more subtle. However, the excerpt represents an insider's romanticized view[73] when it heralds "the genius of *K'lal Yisroel* [that] has been able to distinguish between a true *Gadol B'Yisroel* and an ordinary scholar." Identifying who is a true *Gadol* has not always been a successful endeavor.

Throughout Jewish history, there have even been times when portions of the Jewish community strayed after false Messiahs. In some instances, such as those involving Sabbatei Zevi (1626–1676) and Jacob Frank (1726–1791), the numbers of Jews who so stumbled were significant.[74] Much more frequently, bitter disagreements raged as to the status of particular individuals or groups. The works of some major rabbinic figures such as Maimonides were censored or publicly burned at the behest of their contemporaries, also prominent rabbinic leaders.[75] Similarly, some major rabbinic leaders, such as Moses Hayyim Luzzatto (1707–1747) and R. Jonathan Eybeschuetz (1690–1767), were accused of participating in the Sabbatei Zevi movement.[76]

The early history of friction between Hasidic leaders and non-Hasidic Lithuanian leaders is replete with well-known clashes.[77] Similarly, within Lithuanian rabbinical

---

[72] Emanuel Feldman, *Trends in the American Yeshivot: A Rejoinder*, 9:4 TRADITION 56, 61 (1968). *See also* Michael Berger, *Rabbinic Authority: A Philosophical Analysis*, 27:4 TRADITION 61 (1993).

[73] Undoubtedly, Feldman would proudly identify himself as an insider. Not all insiders, however, would express as Pollyanish a view.

[74] *See generally* GERSHOM GERHARD SCHOLEM & RAPHAEL JEHUDAH ZWI WERBLOWSKY, SABBATAI SEVI: THE MYSTICAL MESSIAH 1626–1676 (975); MOSHE CARMILLY-WEINBERGER, CENSORSHIP AND FREEDOM OF EXPRESSION IN JEWISH HISTORY (1977); PAWEL MACIEJKO, THE MIXED MULTITUDE: JACOB FRANK AND THE FRANKIST MOVEMENT 1755–1816 (2011).

[75] *See* CARMILLY-WEINBERGER, *supra* note 74.

[76] *Id.* at 76, 84, 86. It should be noted the Turkish government forced Sabbatei Zevi to convert to Islam, and that Sabbatei Zevi died in 1676. Both Luzzatto and Eyebshuetz were born after Sabbatei Zevi. It is true that some of Sabbatei Zevi's followers persisted in their beliefs even after his apostasy and, ultimately, even after his death. However, Luzzatto and Eyebshuetz could not have been influenced by Zevi's personal magnetism, for they never met him. Nor had they committed themselves to his movement prior to Zevi's apostasy. Consequently, the charge, for which some scholars believe there may be some support, *id.*, that either or both were Sabbateans is shocking.

[77] Interestingly, a twentieth century book was banned because it revisited these old wars. *See* Dan Rabinowitz, *The Ban on the Book HaGaon* (Mar. 27, 2006), http://seforim.blogspot.com/2006/03/ban-on-book-hagaon.html.

academies, there have been disagreements leading to the ouster of some who are well recognized as great leaders.[78]

It is true that the Jewish community's perceptions of some of the rabbis whose works were banned, censored or burned, and of some of the rabbis who were forced out from one rabbinical school or another, later changed, and they were later recognized as *Gedolim*. What is not entirely clear is whether there were others whose reputations deserved to be, but were not, so resurrected.

Feldman's assertion that "no one speaks for his [a person's] candidacy [to be recognized as a Gadol]; no one promotes his image in the eyes of the public," is probably a misleading oversimplification. It is disingenuous to assert that politics play no part in the process through which a person acquires a reputation as a Gadol. Some powerful positions in important religious organizations and institutions can be "inherited,"[79] with considerable honor and communal prestige automatically attaching to the new holder of the position.

Interestingly, the position of Rebbe (i.e., leader) of a Hasidic group is typically inherited. Yet even Hasidic groups experience great difficulty in determining who is a Gadol. Ordinarily it is a violation of Jewish law for Jews, especially religious Jews, to sue each other in secular court. Nevertheless, in recent years, the American Jewish community has witnessed sons or other relatives of deceased Hasidic Rebbis actually filing secular lawsuits to fight over which relative should "inherit" the deceased rebbe's leadership position.

Some rabbinical schools are treated as the private "property" of particular rabbis, which perhaps is understandable given that these rabbis established the schools and raised funds to maintain them. Many people associated with these rabbis are in a position to benefit reputationally or materialistically from their enhanced prestige or power, and therefore possess an incentive to further promote the rabbis' public images. This is true whether or not such people are aware of this bias.

These comments are certainly not intended to disparage the status of anyone currently enjoying a reputation as a Gadol. Instead, they are intended to provide a more balanced perspective on the process.

From the perspective of Jewish law, the importance of who is Gadol very heavily depends on the precise role and authority a Gadol possesses. This, in turn, requires discussion of a doctrine known as *da'at torah*, which is taken up in Chapter 9.

It is important to note that, as is also discussed in Chapter 8, each individual has the right, and perhaps the responsibility, to select a Jewish law authority to whom the individual will pose his or her questions about Jewish law.[80] The person so chosen does not have to be a Gadol, but only a competent halakhic decisor (i.e., posek).

---

[78] *See generally* NATHAN KAMANETSKY, THE MAKING OF A GADOL (2002).

[79] JEFFREY I. ROTH, INHERITING THE CROWN IN JEWISH LAW: THE STRUGGLE FOR RABBINIC COMPENSATION, TENURE, AND INHERITANCE RIGHTS (2006).

[80] *See* MISHNAH, *Pirkei Avot* 1:1 (directing each person to make for himself or herself a rabbi).

Chapter 6

JEWISH LAW LITERATURE

§ 6.01 INTRODUCTION

By the time you have finished reading this chapter, you will know Jewish law literature backwards and forwards. This is because the chapter is divided into two parts. Section 6.02 briefly describes the principal, and relatively modern, Jewish law texts to which one would typically refer to resolve a reasonably simple issue that might arise on a daily basis. By contrast, Section 6.03 starts with the earliest Jewish law writings and traces the development of this body of legal literature until the recent texts identified in Section 6.02. The texts in Section 6.03 remain extremely important. When relatively difficult questions arise, scholars meticulously scrutinize the earlier works for guidance.

§ 6.02 RELATIVELY MODERN TEXTS

For an answer to a specific, discrete Jewish law question, particularly one involving daily activities such as prayer or observance of Jewish holidays, many modern religious Jews might simply ask a rabbi. In the alternative, others might turn to a number of contemporary publications dedicated to the specific subject in question. In recent years, a plethora of such publications have appeared, including many written in English. Typically, these works do not represent original Jewish law analysis. Nevertheless, by recording and organizing rulings reached in other, more established Jewish law texts, they can be extremely helpful to those who are relatively well versed in Jewish law and provide references to the underlying rabbinic sources.

More serious students of Jewish law, however, might begin their inquiry by looking at one of the following late nineteenth and early twentieth century texts:

(1) The *Mishnah Berurah* (the "Clear Teaching"), Yisroel Meir Kagan's (1838–1933) commentary on *Orah Hayyim*, one of the four divisions of the sixteenth century *Shulhan Arukh* (the "Set Table"). The Mishnah Berurah was published in parts from 1894 to 1907. Rabbi Kagan provides a gloss tied to individual words or phrases of the Shulhan Arukh, most commonly explaining or elaborating on those words. In addition, he points out cases in which prominent post-Shulhan Arukh authorities disagree with the Shulhan Arukh's rulings. This format enables one to study portions of the Mishnah Berurah in short blocks of time, and it makes quickly looking up answers to specific questions convenient. In modern times, the Mishnah Berurah may be one of the most commonly studied Jewish law texts. From 1981 to 2002, Feldheim Publishers produced a complete multi-volume translation of this work, with each Hebrew page facing its English counterpart.[1]

(2) Yehiel Mikhal Epstein's (1829–1908) publication, the *Arukh HaShulhan*. The literal meaning of this title, "The Table is Set," is a play on Rabbi Karo's title, the "Set Table." Epstein's book is much more comprehensive than Rabbi Kagan's, covering almost all of the Shulhan Arukh. Rabbi Epstein's style is considerably different from that of Rabbi Kagan in the Mishnah Berurah.[2] Although Rabbi Epstein follows the Shulhan Arukh's structure and numbering system, he takes up the subject of each numbered section independently. He explains relevant Talmudic sections and examines the views of various later authorities. Thus, studying the Arukh HaShulhan is typically more challenging than studying the Mishnah Berurah, and translating the Arukh HaShulhan would be a much more complicated task than translating the Mishnah Berurah. Perhaps this explains why an English translation of the Arukh HaShulhan has not yet been published.

(3) Yaakov Haim Sofer's (1870–1939) multi-volume commentary entitled the *Kaf HaHayyim* (the Cup — or Palm — of Life) covers the same division of the Shulhan Arukh as the Mishnah Berurah plus a portion of another division, entitled *Yoreh De'ah*. The Kaf HaHayyim, often citing Rishonim as well as Aharonim, is perhaps

---

[1] MISHNAH BERURAH (Aviel Orenstein ed., 1989).

[2] However, Rabbi Kagan, author of the Mishnah Berurah, also authored another commentary to the Shulhan Arukh, entitled the Be'er Heiteiv, which focuses in considerable detail on a number of individual issues. This commentary is printed with, and as a part of, the Mishnah Berurah.

a more in-depth commentary than that of the Mishnah Berurah, yet offers a less profound analysis than that of the Arukh HaShulhan. Rabbi Sofer was a Sephardi and his work, well appreciated by both Ashkenazi and Sephardi Jews, is especially popular among the Sephardi. The Kaf HaHayyim has not been translated into English.

Rabbi Shlomo Ganzfried's (1804–1886) *Kitzur Shulhan Arukh* (Abbreviated Set Table) should not be confused with the Shulhan Arukh despite the similarity in their titles.[3] It is not, in fact, an abbreviated version of the Shulhan Arukh. It does not even follow the structure of the Shulhan Arukh. It is a popular and fairly comprehensive legal code written clearly and succinctly. It does not provide a detailed examination of the earlier sources upon which it is based. Several English translations are available.[4]

The above sources are built upon tiers of earlier halakhic literature. Often unusual circumstances or sociological, technological, or other developments present novel questions of Jewish law to which the above sources provide no single definitive answer. Serious Jewish law scholars must then plumb the depths of earlier, more fundamental texts. We now turn to those texts, in essentially chronological order.

§ 6.03   EARLY JEWISH LAW LITERATURE

This chapter examines the Sinaitic revelation, other pre-Talmudic writings, the Babylonian and Jerusalem Talmuds and post-Talmudic literature.

[A]   The Sinaitic Revelation — the Written Torah and the Oral Torah

Jewish sources relate that God appeared on Mount Sinai in the year 2448, according to the Jewish calendar's counting of years, which corresponds with the secular year 1313 B.C.[5] According to Jewish law authorities, the Divine law was communicated as two distinct portions. One portion was incorporated into writing as the Five Books of Moses, also known as the Chumash, the Pentateuch, the Written Torah or the Written Law. This portion comprises the books known in English as Genesis (Heb., *Bereishit*), Exodus (Heb., *Shemot*), Leviticus (Heb.,

---

[3] Strangely, there is an even closer relationship between the English title by which the Shulhan Arukh is known, i.e., the "Code of Jewish Law," and the title of a leading translation of the Kitzur Shulhan Arukh, which is also the "Code of Jewish Law." *See* HYMAN E. GOLDIN, CODE OF JEWISH LAW (1963).

[4] *See, e.g., Id.*; THE KLEINMAN EDITION KITZUR SHULCHAN ARUCH (Eliyahu Meir Klugman and Yosaif Asher Weiss trans., 2010), partial translation *available at* http://www.torah.org/learning/halacha/.

[5] Although the Jewish calendar has its own counting of years, it is often impractical, especially when communicating with non-Jews, to refer to the Jewish count. On the other hand, religious Jews prefer not to use the term "B.C.," which stands for "before Christ," because they do not believe that Jesus was Christ. Similarly, they prefer not to use the term "A.D.," which stands for "the year of Our Lord," referring to Jesus. Consequently, when referring to the secular counting of years, Jewish writers often use "C.E.," meaning the "common era," instead of A.D., and use "B.C.E." ("before the common era") instead of B.C.

VaYikra), Numbers (Heb., *Bamidbar*) and Deuteronomy (Heb., *Devarim*).[6] The second portion, known as the Oral Torah or Oral Law,[7] was specifically not to be committed to writing. Instead, it was to be taught orally from teacher to student.

Because of the assumption that the Pentateuch represents the word of God, Jewish law has always assumed that a person's own ethical views "are an inadequate basis for disobeying any clear command of God."[8] But to what extent are God's commands clear?

[1] What the Oral Law Does

Jewish law does not interpret the Pentateuch literally.[9] Jewish law authorities not only admit but actively assert that the words of the Pentateuch are at times incomplete, unclear, or ostensibly self-contradictory. Consider, for instance, just a few examples of rules that are incomplete or unclear. The Pentateuch prohibits "labor" (*melakhah*) on the Sabbath.[10] Not only is violation of this proscription a capital offense,[11] but the observance of this commandment is of central importance in Jewish law.[12] Yet, nowhere does the Pentateuch define what constitutes "labor." Nevertheless, it is universally agreed that the prohibition applies to the simple writing of a word, but not to the lifting of a heavy book or even a heavier table, despite the fact that the latter actions require much more physical exertion.[13] How is this rule known? It is known because the Oral Torah that was taught with the Pentateuch[14] so teaches.[15]

---

[6] It is important to note that the later texts of the Hebrew Bible, identified in Appendix 9, are not generally deemed to be legal texts.

[7] The "Oral Torah" has other meanings as well. *See infra* Appendix 1 — Glossary.

[8] WALTER S. WURZBURGER, ETHICS OF RESPONSIBILITY: PLURALISTIC APPROACHES TO COVENANTAL ETHICS 6 (1994). Similarly, "In case of conflict with an explicit biblical prohibition, all other considerations must be disregarded, because 'there is no wisdom nor understanding nor counsel against God.' " *Id.* at 26 (citing *Proverbs* 21:30, as it is interpreted in BABYLONIAN TALMUD, *Berakhot* 19b).

[9] Eliezer Berkovits (1908–1992), former Chairman of the Department of Jewish Philosophy at Hebrew Theological College, states:

> Only non-Jews have been fundamentalists, never Jews who took their place within Judaism. For them every word of the Torah and, of course, every commandment, has its source in God; but the meaning of the revealed word or commandment is given in the oral tradition, the *Torah she-be'al peh* alone, or is elucidated by its method.

Eliezer Berkovits, *Comments, in* THE CONDITION OF JEWISH BELIEF: A SYMPOSIUM, COMPILED BY THE EDITORS OF COMMENTARY MAGAZINE 23, 23–24 (1966) [hereinafter SYMPOSIUM].

[10] *Exodus* 31:14.

[11] *Exodus* 31:15.

[12] *See, e.g.*, DAYAN DR. I. GRUNFELD, THE SABBATH: A GUIDE TO ITS UNDERSTANDING AND OBSERVANCE 3 (3d ed. 1972) ("Our sages call the Sabbath *Yesod Haemunah*, the very foundation of our faith.").

[13] *See* JUDAH HALEVI, THE KUZARI ¶ 35 in ch. 3 (Hartwig Hirschfeld trans., 1964) (providing many examples).

[14] *See, e.g.*, ZEVI HIRSCH CHAJES, THE STUDENT'S GUIDE THROUGH THE TALMUD 3 (Jacob Schachter trans., 3d ed. 2005) (citing Maimonides as writing: "All the Sinaitic precepts were communicated to Moses with interpretations.").

[15] HALEVI, *supra* note 13.

Similarly, the meat of only certain types of animals is kosher to eat. Knowing which types of animals are acceptable is of enormous practical importance in Jewish law. Furthermore, for the meat to be kosher, it is not enough that the meat be from a certain type of animal; the animal must be slaughtered in a particular way. Nevertheless, the only reference to this rule in the Pentateuch is the divine instruction that states that animals are to be slaughtered "as I [God] commanded you."[16] But no Pentateuchal verse contains such a command or describes the details of the slaughtering process. What type of knife must be used? Where must the cut be made? Are there restrictions as to who may perform the slaughtering? The Oral Torah answers these questions.[17]

With respect to the Jewish holiday of the Feast of Tabernacles (Sukkot), God commanded that each Jew perform a ritual with certain species of vegetation, as it is written in the book of Leviticus, "And you shall take for yourself on the first day the fruit of the beautiful tree, the branches of palms, and the twigs of a plaited tree and brook willows."[18] This verse does not clarify what is meant by the "fruit of the beautiful tree," by "a plaited tree," or by, for that matter, "brook willows." The verse also does not clarify the amount of each of these things any individual is supposed to take. The Oral Torah, however, answers these questions precisely, and Jews around the world fulfill this commandment in accordance with those specifications.

Similarly, the Oral Torah resolves conflicts and apparent inconsistencies in the words of the Torah. The Torah commands that a newborn male be circumcised on the eighth day of his life.[19] However, causing wounds is forbidden on the Sabbath. What if the eighth day of the baby's life falls on the Sabbath? Should the circumcision be performed anyway, despite the prohibition on causing wounds on the Sabbath, or should it be delayed, just as it is delayed if the baby is jaundiced? The Oral Torah resolves this conflict.[20]

Torah law, or biblical law, is thus based on the combination of the Pentateuch and the Oral Torah. In fact, the inadequacy of the Pentateuch to stand alone is often cited as a proof that God communicated an Oral Torah.[21]

---

[16] *Deuteronomy* 12:21.

[17] HALEVI, *supra* note 13.

[18] *Leviticus* 23:40.

[19] *Genesis* 17:12.

[20] *Id.* The Oral Torah also provided clarifications of Pentateuchal statements that do not set forth commandments, although some of them do refer to commandments. For example, in one place (*Deuteronomy* 16:8), the Torah announces that unleavened bread is eaten during Passover for six days, but in another place (*Numbers* 28:17), it says that it is eaten for seven days. The Oral Torah explains that the reference to six days refers to the number of days during which the eating of unleavened bread is purely voluntary. Other than on the first day of the seven-day holiday, there is no commandment to eat unleavened bread. A person can simply choose to eat other foods. On the first day, however, a person is obligated to eat unleavened bread. The reference to seven days, therefore, includes the first day in the count. *See* H. CHAIM SCHIMMEL, THE ORAL TORAH 22 (2d ed. 1996) (citing BABYLONIAN TALMUD, *Pesahim* 120a). For additional examples of ostensible inconsistencies reconciled by the Oral Torah, see CHAJES, *supra* note 14, at 1–2.

[21] SCHIMMEL, *supra* note 20. For this and other proofs, see Gil Student, *The Oral Torah*, at http://www.aishdas.org/student/oral.htm (last visited Sept. 22, 2008); CHAJES, *supra* note 14, at 1–16.

[2] Why the Oral Law was Necessary

But why was the Oral Torah needed? It is needed because, for several reasons, the Pentateuch is not a comprehensive legal text. One reason is practical. Law is "fact-sensitive," and the number of possible factual permutations is unlimited. A truly comprehensive written code would need to be infinitely long and would be impracticable for use by human beings.

Moreover, a comprehensive written code gives rise to two additional problems. First, it would be available to anyone who is literate, irrespective of whether he or she is spiritually qualified to serve as a religious leader. Yet, after mastering a comprehensive code, these persons might be able to pass themselves off as authorities, permitting them to mislead others or to wrongfully promote their personal interests. The existence of the Oral Law, which could only be learned from established rabbinic authorities, enabled these authorities to reject, and thereby screen out, students with flawed characters.

Second, language involves inevitable ambiguities. Consequently, a reader, no matter how intelligent, may be unable to fully discern the intricacies and nuances of a text. By contrast, a teacher who transmits the law orally can explain the text at length and can test students to ensure that they understand the Written Law's messages clearly.[22]

In some instances, the Oral Torah explains that the apparent message is not the correct one. In almost all cases, a close examination of the text, aided by logic, reveals at least strong hints to the nuanced reading provided by the Oral Torah. For example, one of the most commonly misunderstood Pentateuchal laws is derived from the following passage:

> If men shall fight and they collide with a pregnant woman and she miscarries, but there will be no fatality, he shall surely be punished as the husband of the woman shall cause to be assessed against him, and he shall pay it by order of judges. But if there shall be a fatality, then you shall award a life for a life; an eye for an eye, a tooth for a tooth, a hand for a hand, a foot for a foot; a burn for a burn, a wound for a wound, a bruise for a bruise.[23]

Literally, this language clearly *seems* to distinguish between the case in which the pregnant woman does not die and that in which she does. In the former, the tortfeasor makes monetary compensation, but in the latter, a physical, and not a pecuniary, punishment seems to be exacted. Indeed, many people and religions have understood the rule of "an eye for an eye," referred to as *lex talionis*, literally.

Nevertheless, Jewish law never construed this rule literally. This is the position both of the sages of the Talmud and of academic scholars of Jewish law.[24] The

---

[22] MEIR ZVI BERGMAN, GATEWAY TO THE TALMUD 45 (1989).

[23] *Exodus* 21:22–25. This translation is from THE CHUMASH: THE STONE EDITION 423 (Nosson Scherman ed., 1993).

[24] Irene Merker Rosenberg & Yale L. Rosenberg, *Lone Star Liberal Musings on 'Eye for Eye' and the Death Penalty*, 1998 UTAH L. REV. 505, 510 (1998).

Talmudic discussion is extensive and offers various supporting arguments.[25] Here is a sample of the discussion of one such argument:

> It was taught in a Baraisa:[26] R. Dostai ben Yehudah says, [When the Torah states] "an eye for an eye," it refers to [the payment of] money. You say it refers to money, but perhaps it is not so, and the reference is really to an actual eye? To disabuse you of this notion, you should say as follows: Where the eye of this one is large and the eye of that one is small, how can I apply to such a case the penalty of "an eye for an eye"?

> [Author's note: The argument is that the verse cannot be literally referring to an eye for an eye as equivalents, because one person's eye may not be the equivalent of the other person's eye. Although the text refers to the size of the eye, the eyes may differ in other ways. For example, one person's eye may provide greater visual acuity than the other person's eye or one person's eye may be more attractive than the other person's eye.]

> Consequently, the verse must refer to money. And should one say that it is only in a case like this, where the two people's eyes are not the same size, that the assailant pays money, but where the eyes are the same size, the assailant must actually lose his eye, you can respond as follows: The Torah [in the same section as the verse dealing with liability for wounding people], "One law shall be you," (Lev 24:22), which teaches that there shall be the same law for all of you [i.e., there are not different punishments based on whether the assailant and the victim have the same size eyes, etc.].[27]

The consensus of academic scholars agrees with the Talmudic sages.[28] Among other

---

[25] *See, e.g.*, BABYLONIAN TALMUD, *Bava Kamma* 83b.

[26] A "Baraisa" (or "Baraitha" or "Braitha") is a Tannaitic statement that was not included by Rabbi Yehudah ha-Nasi in the Mishnah. *See* PHILIP BIRNBAUM, A BOOK OF JEWISH CONCEPTS 103–04 (1964).

[27] This translation is based very closely on that found in 3 TALMUD BAVLI, *Tractate Bava Kamma*, 83b4–83b5 (Yisroel Simcha Schorr gen. ed., 2001), although I have not followed the complex formatting scheme it employs. Maimonides states that there was never a sage who would say "that one who takes out the eye of his fellow has his eye removed as an observance of the verse, 'Eye replaces eye.' (*Deuteronomy* 19:21)" *See* MAIMONIDES, MAIMONIDES' INTRODUCTION TO THE TALMUD 82 (Zvi Lampel trans., 1998).

[28] *See, e.g.*, Morris J. Fish, *An Eye for an Eye: Proportionality as a Moral Principle of Restraint*, 28 OXFORD J. LEG. STUD. 57, 60 (2008):

> While it seems clear that the lex talionis under Mosaic law advocated the direct punishment of the wrongdoer, scholars who have analysed the text of the Pentateuch have sought more particularly to determine the exact nature of the punishment mandated. Most have concluded that the original meaning of an "eye for an eye" in the Pentateuch related to monetary compensation for the injured eye, rather than the infliction of an identical (or even similar) injury on the wrongdoer. To the Rabbis, "talion was a principle of divine, not human justice."

See also Yung Suk Kim, Lex Talionis *in Exod 21:22–25: Its Origin and Context*, 6 JOURNAL OF HEBREW SCRIPTURES (e-journal), *at* http://www.arts.ualberta.ca/JHS/Articles/article_53.pdf.

> However, it should be noted that Josephus seems to have interpreted the passage literally: He that maimeth anyone let him undergo the like himself and be deprived of the same member whereof he hath deprived the other, unless he that is maimed be willing to accept money instead, for the law makes the sufferer the judge of the value of what he has suffered, and permits him to take compensation unless he would show himself too severe.

GEORGE HOROWITZ, THE SPIRIT OF JEWISH LAW 2 (1973). Horowitz explains that, "[a]s a patrician and

things, these scholars point out:

> This conclusion [that the verse was not intended literally] is supported by a contextual interpretation of the Pentateuch. In Exodus, an "eye for an eye" is preceded, as we have seen, by a "life for a life." The provision does not distinguish between accidental and intentional harm. Mosaic law, however, does not mandate the death penalty for unintentional homicide. It has therefore been argued that neither "life for a life" nor "eye for an eye" can be taken literally, but must instead be understood as mandating proper and full compensation.[29]

Ironically, some of the writers who reject divine authorship of the Pentateuch do so because *they* take the Pentateuch's words, such as the verse regarding "an eye for an eye," *literally* and then criticize the Pentateuch by saying that some of these supposedly literal rules are immoral.[30] Of course, most Pentateuchal rules were interpreted literally. The only major exceptions were when there was an express Oral Law teaching to the contrary or when logic mandated a contrary construction.

[3]   Content of the Oral Torah

The Oral Torah comprises at least two types of material. First, it contains "the basic explanations received directly from Moses."[31] There is no exhaustive list of the rules that fall into this category. Nonetheless, they presumably include all rules that were immediately relevant, including many of the kosher laws and the laws of the Sabbath. Some of these rules provide details or explanations of commandments that were mentioned in the Pentateuch. Other Oral Torah rules provide laws not alluded to in the Pentateuch. Such supplemental laws are known as "Laws Given to Moses at Sinai" (*Halacha LiMoshe MiSinai*),[32] and they are so identified in the Talmud. They include, among other things, standards or measurements in connection with religious requirements as to purity or impurity, rules pertaining to phylacteries (*tefillin*), mezuzot, tithes, torts and crimes.[33] It is said that no disputes ever arose as to these explanations because they were carefully and faithfully guarded, transmitted and preserved.[34]

---

member of a high priestly family, Josephus undoubtedly reported the interpretation of the conservative priestly judges, and not the teachings of the Rabbis, not the 'tradition of the elders.' " *Id.*

[29] Fish, *supra* note 28. *See also* MAIMONIDES, *supra* note 27, at 93 n.6 (citing various classical "proofs" that the phrase, "an eye for an eye" was never intended to be taken literally).

[30] *See* AMMIEL HIRSCH & YOSEF REINMAN, ONE PEOPLE, TWO WORLDS 28 (2002).

[31] MAIMONIDES, *supra* note 27, at 81.

[32] SCHIMMEL, *supra* note 20, at 34; MENACHEM ELON, JEWISH LAW: HISTORY, SOURCES, PRINCIPLES vol. 1, at 204–07 (Bernard Auerbach & Melvin J. Sykes trans., 1994).

[33] *Id.* at 205.

[34] MAIMONIDES, *supra* note 27, at 82–85. The Talmud does contain debates as to whether there are Scriptural "hints" for some of these Torah laws. Maimonides, however, argues that no one actually questioned the validity of the basic rules. Similarly, on occasion there seem to have been disagreements regarding some small facets of these rules. Nevertheless, there is no case concerning a Halacha LeMoshe Misinai in which one Tanna declares an object permissible to eat or permissible to perform while another Tanna declares that the object or act is prohibited. SCHIMMEL, *supra* note 20, at 34 n.8.

Second, the Oral Torah contains instructions as to how the sages could derive Torah laws that were not explicitly communicated.[35] The specific exegetical rules by which the Pentateuch is to be interpreted are the most well-known of these instructions.[36] Many of these rules are technical and not at all intuitive. For example, one rule, known as "Generalization and Specification" (*Klal U'Prat*), states that if a commandment begins with a generalization but is followed by a specification, the commandment only applies to the specified instance. For example, at the beginning of Leviticus, the Pentateuch refers to offering an animal sacrifice "from the beasts."[37] The phrase, "from the beasts," is considered a generalization, because the Hebrew word used for "beasts" refers to both wild animals and domesticated animals. This phrase is followed by the phrase "from the herd and from the flock." The word "herd" refers to cows and bulls, while the word "flocks" refers to sheep and goats. All of these animals are domesticated animals. Consequently, even though the verse begins with a generalization that would include both wild and domesticated animals, the fact that this generalization is followed by a specification of domesticated animals means that only domesticated animals may be offered as animal sacrifices.[38]

Another rule of construction is known as "Generalization, Specification, and Generalization" (*Klal U'Prat U'Klal*). When a rule begins with a generalization, which is followed by a specification, which, in turn, is followed by a second generalization, the law only applies to things that are similar to the specification. For example, in discussing what can be purchased with certain types of funds, the verse states, "You shall give the money for whatever your soul desires," which is a generalization. Then it says, "for any of the herd or for any of the flock or for wine," which is a specification. This is followed by a second generalization, "whatever your soul requests of you." The second generalization means that the rule is not limited only to the items mentioned but also to things that are similar to them. Because the specified items reproduce and derive their sustenance from the earth, one can use such funds to buy any things that reproduce and draw their sustenance from the earth,[39] but may not use the funds for other things.

---

[35] Jewish law assumes that these rules, just as the rest of the Oral Torah, were transmitted by God to Moses. *See, e.g.*, Chajes, *supra* note 14, at 21. Consequently, all of the laws derived therefrom are "the natural development of the text itself." *Id.* at 22. Some significant differences developed between and among Talmudic sages regarding the proper hermeneutic rules. *See* Elon, *supra* note 32, vol. 1, at 316–17. In part, this led to disparate views as to a number of Torah laws. *Cf.* Chajes, *supra* note 14, at 111 (pointing out that many Talmudic disputes involve the proper application of the hermeneutical rules and logic).

[36] *See, e.g.*, Bergman, *supra* note 22, at 120–56; Moses Mielziner, Introduction to the Talmud 117–86 (1968); Bernard Rosensweig, *The Hermeneutic Principles and Their Application*, 12:1 Tradition 49 (1972). The use of several of these rules was subject to significant restrictions. *Id.* at 56 (a sage could not use the rule known as Gezerah Shavah to propose a new Jewish law rule; a sage could only use the rule in a way that he had been expressly taught by his teacher).

[37] *Leviticus* 1:2.

[38] Bergman, *supra* note 22, at 140–41. Inasmuch as the Pentateuch only wanted to include domestic animals, one might wonder why it began with the general term "beasts." The answer is that had the verse been written differently, application of other rules of interpretation would have caused other problems. *Id.*

[39] *Id.* at 141–42.

Interestingly, according to most authorities, laws derived from the hermeneutical principles have the status of Torah law.[40] New circumstances of all sorts — e.g., social, political, and technological — raise innovative scenarios to which these Torah laws must be applied. These resulting decisions themselves reflect Torah law even if Moses did not subjectively imagine all of the practical applications the rules would have in the future.

The sages were also instructed to deduce Torah laws from logic.[41] Thus, at least according to many authorities, the law that one may not kill an innocent person, even when it is necessary to save one's own life, arises from the logical Talmudic proposition stated by Rabbah, "Who said your blood is redder (or sweeter) than the other person's?"[42] While some logical conclusions, such as Rabbah's, are clear, many supposedly "logical" arguments may be subject to considerable debate. The actual number of instances in which the Talmud derives Torah laws by "logic" is small, and these instances usually involve rules for which Pentateuchal proofs arguably exist.[43]

[B] Other Pre-Talmudic Legal Writings

Jewish law literature after the Pentateuch but before the Talmud was written by the Tannaim. It principally consisted of the Mishnah, the Tosefta and Halakhic Midrashim.

[1] The Mishnah

Initially, "no work of the . . . [Oral Torah] was written to be studied publicly."[44] Instead, distinguished individual authorities kept their own private notes regarding the teachings of the Oral Torah. Sometimes these notes might contain the disagreeing views of earlier authorities. Because of draconian measures taken by hostile non-Jewish authorities designed to extirpate the teaching of Torah law, the sages feared that the Oral Torah might be lost if it were not somehow memorialized in writing. As Maimonides explains:

---

[40] *See* SCHIMMEL, *supra* note 20, at 60–63.

[41] *See, e.g.,* BABYLONIAN TALMUD, *Baba Kama* 46b, which asks, "Why bring a proof to your point from a Torah verse; your point is true as a matter of logic!" *See also* BABYLONIAN TALMUD, *Kettuboth* 22a, *Niddah* 25a. *See generally* SCHIMMEL, *supra* note 20, at 50–52; CHAJES, *supra* note 14, at 29–31.

[42] SCHIMMEL, *supra* note 20, at 50–51. Interestingly, a number of important Jewish law commentators question whether the argument that Rabbah articulates is really the basis for his legal conclusion. *See, e.g.,* VIDAL OF TOLUSA (late fourteenth century), MAGGID MISHNEH, *Mishneh Torah, Laws of the Foundations of the Torah* 5:5 (Heb.).

[43] *See, e.g.,* CHAJES, *supra* note 14, at 30 n.9 (identifying a dispute among rabbinic authorities as to whether a particular law is based on logic or on an express Pentateuchal verse). Note, however, that in addition to serving as the source of some Torah laws, "logic" (in the sense of "legal reasoning") plays an important role in applying Torah laws to particular cases. *See, e.g.,* ELON, *supra* note 32, vol. 3, at 987–1014.

[44] *See, e.g.,* MAIMONIDES, *supra* note 27, at 69. Rav Sherira Gaon (906–1006) actually writes that "none of the early sages had written anything [regarding the Oral torah]" until near the end of Rabbi Yehudah HaNasi's life. *See* SHERIRA GAON, THE IGGERES OF RAV SHERIRA GAON 14 (Nosson Dovid Rabinowich trans., 1988). But other commentators disagree, arguing that even before Rabbi Yehudah HaNasi's compilation, there seem to have been some other collections of Tannaitic teachings. *See* NAHUM RAKOVER, A GUIDE TO THE SOURCES OF JEWISH LAW 33 (1994); CHAJES, *supra* note 14, at 254–57.

And why did Rabbaynu Hakadosh [i.e., Rabbi Yehudah HaNasi] do this [i.e., compile and publish the Mishnah], and not leave matters the way they had been up to then? Because he saw that the disciples were diminishing in number and leaving, that the persecutions were intensifying and multiplying, that the Roman Empire was extending its power over the globe and strengthening, and that Israel was continuously being dispersed throughout the extremities of the earth. He therefore compiled this one work to be in the possession of all, so that they could learn quickly and in a way that they would not forget. So he and his Bes Din [i.e., his rabbinic court] sat all their days teaching the Mishna publicly. [Footnote omitted.][45]

Various sages attempted to compile and arrange their teachers' teachings (*Mishnayot*),[46] but the version that was accepted and universally known as the *Mishnah* is the collection of teachings compiled by Rabbi Yehudah HaNasi (also known as "Rebbe") circa 188 C.E.[47] The Mishnah contained not only Torah teachings, but also non-Torah laws that had developed over time, such as rabbinical legislation and local customs. The authorities who preceded the Mishnah and whose views are cited therein are known as Tannaim (singular, Tanna).

Rav Sherira Gaon (906–1006), head of the Yeshiva in Pumbeditha, a city in ancient Babylonia, wrote that "Rebbe arranged and wrote the Mishnah. . . . Rebbe did not produce these words with his own mind; rather, they were the teachings of the early sages who preceded him."[48] Many other commentators agree.[49] However, some disagree, arguing that while Rabbi Yehudah HaNasi may have compiled and arranged these teachings, the teachings were not published during his lifetime.[50] In any event, the Mishnah became the most authoritative collection of Tannaitic teachings and was the focus of the rabbinic debates that were later recorded in the Jerusalem and Babylonian Talmuds.

---

[45] *See* MAIMONIDES, *supra* note 27, at 70. *See also* BERGMAN, *supra* note 22, at 45–46.

[46] BERGMAN, *supra* note 22, at 46–48.

[47] ARYEH KAPLAN, THE HANDBOOK OF JEWISH THOUGHT 187 (1979). Early authorities dispute whether Rabbi Yehuda ha-Nasi merely arranged the Mishnah and taught it orally or whether he actually was the person who published it. BERGMAN, *supra* note 22, at 46.

[48] BERGMAN, *supra* note 22, at 20.

[49] Consider, for instance, the words of Maimonides in his introduction to the Mishnah:

He [Rabbi Yehudah HaNasi] collected all the lectures and the laws, and all the clarifications and explanations heard from Moses, which were taught by the Great Bes Din in each and every generation, on the entire Torah and compiled from it all the book of the Mishna. He reviewed the completed work with the Sages in public and it was revealed to all Israel, and they all copied it. He disseminated it everywhere so that the Oral torah would not become forgotten by Israel.

See, e.g., MAIMONIDES, *supra* note 27, at 69, 74–76, n.15.

[50] CHAJES, *supra* note 14, at 257–61 (citing evidence for this dissenting view, with which he agrees).

[2] The Tosefta

Another volume of Tannaitic statements is entitled the Tosefta. According to tradition, the Tosefta was produced by Rabbi Hiya (and his student, Rabbi Oshaiah).[51] The word "Tosefta" is Aramaic and means "addition." The traditional view is that the Tosefta was written sometime in the third century, after publication of the Mishnah, and serves both to clarify and to supplement the teachings included in the Mishnah.[52] Unsurprisingly, a number of the baraithot that appear in the Tosefta involve teachings that predate publication of the Mishnah itself.

[3] Halakhic Midrashim

The Hebrew word *Midrash* (plural, *Midrashim*) means exposition or interpretation. There are two types of Midrashim: Haggadic Midrashim and Halakhic Midrashim. The former are non-legal teachings that convey ethical or spiritual lessons. By contrast, Halakhic Midrashim explain how Biblical verses provide the basis for specific legal rules. Halakhic Midrashim were primarily taught by Tannaim, the same authorities whose views are cited in the Mishnah. Many of these teachings preceded the Mishnah. Nevertheless, the various sets of Halakhic Midrashim are believed to have been published only after publication of the Mishnah.

Of the various collections of Halakhic Midrashim, a few should be specifically mentioned. Two of these, the *Mekhilta de-Rabbi Yishmael* (attributed by several Rishonim to the Tanna Rabbi Yishmael, but by recent scholars to the school of a different Rabbi Yishmael)[53] and the *Mekhilta de-Rabbi Shimon* (also known by several other names, including *Mekhilta de-Sanya, Mekhilta, Sifrei, Sifri-de-Vei Rav*),[54] focus on the book of Exodus. The *Sifra* (also known as *Torat Kohanim* and *Sifra debe Rab*), attributed to the third century Amora, Rav,[55] addresses the book of Leviticus. *Sifre*, also attributed to Rav,[56] interprets verses in both Numbers and Deuteronomy. Very little of another Halakhic Midrash, *Mekhilta de-Sefer Devarim* (or *Mekhilta* Deuteronomy), is extant.[57]

---

[51] *See, e.g.*, SHLOMO YITZHAKI (Rashi; 1040–1105), BABYLONIAN TALMUD, *Sanhedrin* 33a. *s.v., "ve'afilu ta'ah b'rebbi Hiyya."*

[52] Rav Sherira Gaon writes, "Concerning the Tosefta: Certainly R. Chiyya arranged it, but there is no definite indication whether he arranged it in Rebbe's lifetime or afterwards. However, it undoubtedly was arranged after the halachos of our Mishnah. It is clear that the teachings of the Tosefta are based upon our Mishnah and teach about [its halachos]." *See* GAON, *supra* note 44. Maimonides writes, "Rebbi Yehuda's words, presented in the Mishna, are brief, yet they encompass many concepts. . . . Rabbi Heeya, one of Rebbi's disciples, thereupon decided to compose a text in which he would follow after his master's work, explicating that which might not be easily comprehended from his master's own words. This is the Tosefta [Addition]." *See* MAIMONIDES, *supra* note 27.

[53] *See* Menahem I. Kahana, *Mekhilta of R. Ishmael, in* 13 ENCYCLOPAEDIA JUDAICA 793 (Michael Berenbaum & Fred Skolnick eds., 2d ed. 2007).

[54] *See* Menahem I. Kahana, *Mekhilta of Simeon Ben Yohai, in* ENCYCLOPAEDIA JUDAICA, *supra* note 53, at 795.

[55] Maimonides is among those who so attribute the work. *See* MAIMONIDES, *supra* note 27, at 143.

[56] *See, e.g.*, BERGMAN, *supra* note 22, at 56.

[57] *See* Menahem I. Kahana, *Mekhilta Deuteronomy, in* ENCYCLOPAEDIA JUDAICA, *supra* note 53, at 792.

[C]　Talmudic Writings

None of the Tannaitic halakhic literature was as well received and accepted as the Mishnah. As Maimonides writes, "[T]he Mishna was the basic text to which all the other works were secondary and subordinate, it being the work unanimously esteemed over all the others."[58]

Publication of the Mishnah, however, did not transform the Oral Torah into a super-Written Torah. Not only were the meanings of many of the Mishnaic and other Tannaitic passages ambiguous or unclear, but application of the teachings to concrete cases was frequently uncertain. Moreover, teachings in the names of various Tannaim often disagreed, and it was necessary to determine which teachings were authoritative.

[1]　Debates Leading to the Two Talmuds

From completion of the Mishnah until the end of the fifth century, sages (known as "Amoraim") taught, explained and debated these teachings in rabbinical academies in Jerusalem[59] and Babylonia.[60] Their discussions covered a broad spectrum of topics, including many non-Torah rules. Indeed, often it was unclear whether a particular legal principle was a Torah or non-Torah rule.[61]

[2]　Jerusalem and Babylonian Talmuds, Generally

The debates of the rabbinical academies in the land of Israel were redacted, circa 350, as the Jerusalem Talmud, also known as the Talmud Yerushalmi, the Yerushalmi, the Talmud of the Land of Israel, or the Palestinian Talmud.[62] As will be discussed, below, the Jerusalem Talmud is far less authoritative than the Babylonian Talmud.

The Babylonian academies also produced a Talmud.[63] In fact, deliberations in the Babylonian academies continued well after those in their Jerusalem counterparts

---

[58]　*See* MAIMONIDES, *supra* note 27, at 143–44.

[59]　Rabbi Yohanan was primarily responsible for editing the debates in the Jerusalem academies, and this resulted in publication of the Jerusalem Talmud circa 279. *See, e.g.*, BERGMAN, *supra* note 22. Some say it was redacted later. *See* ELON, *supra* note 32, vol. 3, at 1097.

[60]　BIRNBAUM, *supra* note 26, at 45–50.

[61]　One very important doctrine, for instance, is *dina demalkhuta dina* ("the law of the Kingdom is the [religiously valid] Law"). Nevertheless, authorities disagree as to whether even it is a biblical or a rabbinic rule. *See generally* Michael J. Broyde & Steven H. Resnicoff, *Jewish Law and Modern Business Structures: The Corporate Paradigm*, 43 WAYNE L. REV. 1685, 1769–73 (1997); Steven H. Resnicoff, *Bankruptcy — A Viable Halachic Option?*, 24 J. HALACHA & CONTEMP. SOC'Y 5 (1992); DAYAN I. GRUNFELD, THE JEWISH LAW OF INHERITANCE (1987); SHMUEL SHILO, DINA DEMALKHUTA DINA (1974) (Heb.).

[62]　The appellation "Palestinian Talmud" is essentially equivalent to the "Talmud of the Land of Israel," because the Romans referred to that land as Palestina.

[63]　Horowitz explains that the decision to produce written Talmuds:

Both in Palestine and in Babylon the immediate impulse to commit the Gemara to writing came from without. Persecution of Jewish observances by the Christian masters of Palestine in the one case, and by the Zoroastrian masters of Babylon in the other, aroused fears that the traditional torah might be forgotten and forever lost. . . . In Babylon the mass of comment,

and covered more sections of the Mishnah. Rav Ashi (352–427) and his colleague Ravina (d. 500), who were among the last of the Amoraim, spent many years compiling and redacting these debates into the Babylonian Talmud. The Amoraim attempted to solve Jewish law questions with the teachings of the Tannaim. The last generation of Amoraim, however, confronted a number of problems which they were able to resolve based on their own reasoning but for which they were unable to find Tannaitic support. As a result, they chose not to include their solutions in the Talmud, and left the questions unanswered.[64]

The Savoraim ("Reasoners" or "Ponderers") followed the Amoraim. They added the Amoraim's explanations to the text and sometimes inserted some of their own comments in the form of anonymous narration.[65] The Savoraim were the last to contribute to the actual Talmudic text, which was finally redacted in the sixth century,[66] circa 550.

[3] The Greater Authority of the Babylonian Talmud

The authority of the Babylonian Talmud, however, far eclipsed that of the Jerusalem Talmud. Partly, this is because the Babylonian Jewish community and its rabbinic academies were far larger and more vibrant than their counterparts in Palestine. As Elon explains:

> The character of the redaction, the political conditions, and factors internal to the Jewish community all worked against the widespread study of the Jerusalem Talmud, which was considered less authoritative than the Babylonian Talmud. Pursuant to a principle established in a later period, Talmudic law may be ascertained from both the Babylonian and Jerusalem Talmuds, but in case of a conflict between them, the Babylonian Talmud is determinative.[67]

One indication of the dominance of the Babylonian Talmud over the Jerusalem Talmud is the difference between the numbers and types of editions that have been published of each. Adin Steinsaltz explains:

> The second half of the twentieth century has produced an abundance of photographed editions of the Talmud (based mostly on the Vilna editions) in various sizes and forms, and the number of complete and partial editions must now run into the hundreds. . . . The Jerusalem Talmud has always been regarded as inferior to the work produced in Babylonia. Fewer

---

questions, arguments and counter-arguments was fast becoming unwieldy. Yet it was not until a series of Zoastrian persecutions — meetings of students forbidden, leading men executed, including the exilarch, half the Jews in Ispathan massacred — that "fear for the continuity of the oral law led to a momentous step." Ravina II (474–479) master of the great academy of Sura took the grave responsibility of fixing in writing the fluid mass of the oral tradition of his time.

HOROWITZ, *supra* note 28, at 36–37.

[64] GAON, *supra* note 44 (in the annotation). *See also* BERGMAN, *supra* note 22, at 77.

[65] GAON, *supra* note 44.

[66] *Id.*

[67] *See* ELON, *supra* note 32, vol. 2, at 1097–98. *See also* ADIN STEINSALTZ, THE ESSENTIAL TALMUD, 79–80 (Chaya Galai trans., 1976).

manuscripts of the former were produced, and it was disregarded by the great commentators. . . . Only about thirty editions have been produced to the present day, and they cannot compare in precision and in the quality of the commentary to the Babylonian Talmud. The Jerusalem Talmud still awaits its redeemer.[68]

Interestingly, Mesorah Publications, Ltd., is publishing, one volume at a time, an extensive translation and commentary on the Jerusalem Talmud. These new volumes will make the Jerusalem Talmud considerably more accessible to contemporary scholars and should significantly increase the extent to which it is studied.

Post-Talmudic authorities universally assert that the Babylonian Talmud is the bedrock of Jewish law.[69] They declare that it was accepted "by the entire Jewish people and that, as a result, it is binding on all Jews."[70] As a practical matter, the Talmud became the focal point for Jewish law scholars:

> As the Talmudic literature became complete, the written Torah continued to be the "constitution" of Jewish law, but the Talmudic literature . . . became the exclusive sources for deriving the Halakhah [i.e., Jewish law rulings]. Halakhic authorities taught their disciples, and judges decided

---

[68] STEINSALTZ, *supra* note 67, at 80. Another indication is the fact that when a Jewish law authority refers to the "Talmud" without preceding the reference with either the word "Babylonian" or "Jerusalem," it is assumed that the reference is to the Babylonian Talmud. Note, for example, that in the cited excerpt, when Steinsaltz first refers to the "Talmud," he means the Babylonian Talmud and only later specifically refers to the "Jerusalem Talmud."

[69] Of course, it is much more than that:

> The Talmud is the repository of thousands of years of Jewish wisdom, and the Oral Torah, which is as ancient and significant as the written law (the Torah), finds expression therein. It is a conglomerate of law, legend, and philosophy, a blend of unique logic and shrewd pragmatism, of history and science, anecdotes and humor. It is a collection of paradoxes: its framework is orderly and logical, every word and term subjected to meticulous editing, completed centuries after the actual work of composition came to an end; yet it is still based on free association, on a harnessing together of diverse ideas reminiscent of the modern stream-of-consciousness novel.

Id. at 4.

[70] *See* ELON, *supra* note 32, vol. 1, at 39 (citing Maimonides) and vol. 3, at 1099, quoting Maimonides's Introduction to the Mishneh Torah:

> Everything in the Babylonian Talmud is binding on all Israel. Every town and country must follow the customs, obey the decrees, and carry out the enactments of the Talmudic Sages, because the entire Jewish people accepted everything contained in the Talmud. The Sages who adopted the enactments and decrees, instituted the practices, rendered the decisions, and derived the laws, constituted all or most of the Sages of Israel. It is they who received the tradition of the fundamentals of the entire Torah in unbroken succession going back to Moses, our teacher.

See also KAPLAN, *supra* note 47, at 191 (citing numerous authorities); Berachyahu Lifshitz, *The Age of the Talmud*, *in* AN INTRODUCTION TO THE HISTORY AND SOURCES OF JEWISH LAW 179 (N.S. Hecht et al. eds., 1996). *See also* Jeffrey R. Woolf, *The Parameters of Precedent in Pesak Halakhah*, 27:4 TRADITION 48 n.27 (1993):

> According to Vilna Gaon, the restriction of argument to post-talmudic authorities is based upon the assumption that the authentic chain of the Oral Law ended with the "sealing" of the Talmud in the days of Rav Ashi and Ravina. . . . Subsequent generations are not allowed, therefore, to differ with statements in the Talmud.

cases, exclusively on the basis of the Talmudic literature. They no longer directly consulted the written Torah to solve problems as they arose.[71]

Similarly, Adin Steinsaltz writes:

Even before the Talmud was completed, it was evident that this work was to become the basic text and primary source for Jewish law. It is actually the last book of source material in Jewish literature, since the works that followed were to a large extent based on it, derived their authority from it, and consulted it whenever necessary for elucidation of theoretical and practical problems. In many ways the Talmud is the most important book in Jewish culture, the backbone of creativity and of national life.[72]

[D]   Post-Talmudic Jewish Law Literature

Yet even the Babylonian Talmud failed to constitute a clear written code of Jewish law. Instead, its redaction was followed by eras of ongoing debate by rabbinic scholars who explored the Talmud, composed commentaries to it, replied to countless practical and theoretical legal queries, ruled on actual cases litigated before them and published monographs on specific legal subjects.

The sages who followed the Savoraim who completed that publication were known as "Geonim." In Ashekenazi lands, the Gaonic period lasted from 589 to 1038.[73] The Geonim were followed by another known as "Rishonim" ("First Ones") from the eleventh through the fifteenth centuries.[74] Subsequent authorities became known as "Aharonim" ("Later Ones"). The Aharonim who were closer to the period of the Rishonim are referred to as the Early Aharonim, and the ones who lived more recently are the Later Aharonim.

In the post-Talmudic period, most halakhic literature took one of two forms. One form was "responsa" literature. Individuals — or parties to disputes — would send (either directly or through a local rabbi) legal questions to distinguished Jewish law authorities who often lived out of town. The rabbi receiving such an inquiry would send a response that summarized the facts and rendered a decision, often providing a detailed legal explanation for the decision. The issuance of responsa has continued throughout the entire post-Talmudic period and is alive and well today. There are hundreds of thousands of such responsa literature, which, in a sense, serve as "case law" that informs contemporary authorities confronted with similar questions. Of course, just as is the case in secular case law, different authorities have often reached inconsistent conclusions in ostensibly similar cases. The second form of post-Talmudic halakhic literature is publications of collections of legal rules, organized in various ways.

---

[71] ELON, *supra* note 32, at 40.

[72] STEINSALTZ, *supra* note 67, at 64.

[73] ELON, *supra* note 32, at 83.

[74] *See generally* HERSH GOLDWURM, THE RISHONIM 79 (2d ed. 2001).

[1] The Gaonic Period

The Gaonim were the heads of rabbinical academies from roughly the seventh century through the first half of the eleventh century. Only three comprehensive collections of laws have survived to the present, although more limited treatises on particular topics are also extant. Two of the broader collections, the She'iltot, authored by Rav Ahai Gaon (d. 760), and the Halakhot Gedolot written by R. Shimon Kaira (ninth century), organize the law in accordance with the order of the Written Torah. The other such collection, Rav Yehudai Gaon's (eighth century) Halakhot Pesukot, is arranged according to the order of the Babylonian Talmud. It provides the laws arising out of the Talmudic discussions, but excludes the discussions themselves.

This approach has several benefits. The first is for the reader, who can easily ascertain the Talmudic source for a particular legal conclusion, and can therefore evaluate whether the conclusion is sound. The second benefit is for the writer, is spared the challenging chore of devising a method of organizing the laws more effectively.

The shortcomings of following the order of the Talmud, however, can be best appreciated by those experienced in Talmudic study. The Talmud does not address all of the laws of a particular subject in a single place. Indeed, the Talmud follows a conceptual path. If the applicable legal reasoning is similar, it will move from one subject, such as criminal law, to another, such as a question involving marital relations.[75] As a result, although the various Talmudic tractates are titled, each contains *halakhic* rulings about completely different topics. Consequently, suppose someone wants to learn all of the laws regarding a particular subject. If the legal code follows the order of the Talmud, the only way to be sure one has seen all of the rules about any subject is to read through the entire code. This, of course, is not very practical.

[2] The Period of the Rishonim

The Rishonim were the leading Jewish law authorities immediately after the Gaonic period (from the eleventh through the fifteenth centuries). A number of the Rishonim, including Rav Alfasi (1013–1073), who preceded Maimonides (1135–1204), and Rav Asher ben Yehiel (1250–1328), who followed Maimonides, used Rav Yehudai Gaon's approach of following the order of the Talmud. There were, however, at least three notable innovations during the period of the Rishonim.

The first, and probably the most breathtaking, step was publication of Maimonides' Mishneh Torah. This work was the first truly comprehensive Jewish law code that was clearly, coherently and ingeniously organized according to subject matter. One could find all of the laws pertinent to a particular topic without having to read through the entire work.

However, the Mishneh Torah introduced a new problem, since Maimonides chose not to identify or explain the Talmudic basis for his halakhic rulings. This made it more difficult for a reader to independently evaluate these rulings, and it led to

---

[75] If one misses the conceptual connection, the transition may seem to be a complete tangent.

considerable early criticism of the publication. It has also engendered an enormous body of Jewish scholarly literature regarding those conclusions.[76]

The Talmud states that there are 613 "countable" biblical commandments, 248 affirmative and 365 negative,[77] although there is considerable disagreement as to which commandments are so countable.[78] The second innovation during the period of the Rishonim was the appearance of a number of Jewish law publications organized according to lists of these commandments. One of these books, the *Sefer HaHinnuch*, has been translated and published by Feldheim Publishers in multiple volumes, with each Hebrew page facing a corresponding page of English translation.[79]

The third major innovation was introduced by Rabbi Jacob ben Asher's code, entitled *Sefer HaTurim*, literally, the Book of Rows (Turim).[80] Rabbi Jacob lived more than a thousand years after the Second Temple was destroyed,[81] and he chose not to address laws pertaining to the Holy Temple or the services therein. Instead, he focused on those Jewish laws that continued to have contemporary practical applications. The innovation was in the way he organized his masterpiece. He divided it into four major categories.[82] The first, *Orah Hayyim*, covers issues of daily life, such as blessings, individual and communal prayer, laws regarding the various Jewish holidays and holy days, etc. The second, *Yoreh De'ah*, addresses a variety of topics from kosher food to mourning practices. The third, *Even HaEzer*, primarily encompasses family law, including laws of marriage and divorce. The fourth, *Hoshen Mishpat*, focuses on commercial and criminal law.

[3] The Period of the Aharonim

The term Aharonim refers to the Jewish authorities who followed the period of the Rishonim. The Aharonim have produced a variety of important halakhic publications. The most significant, however, was Joseph Karo's sixteenth century tome known in Hebrew as the Shulhan Arukh (literally, the "Set Table"), but referred to in English as the "Code of Jewish Law." Rabbi Karo, who had previously authored the foremost commentary on Rabbi Jacob ben Asher's Sefer HaTurim, followed that book's structure.

---

[76] Interestingly, over the years, Maimonides' failure to explain his rulings has had an opposite effect by further embellishing his genius and reputation. Why? Because scores of scholars have long labored over apparent nuances and supposed inconsistencies in the Mishneh Torah and have offered brilliant explanations, ascribing them to Maimonides.

[77] BABYLONIAN TALMUD, *Makkot* 23b.

[78] *See generally* Abraham Hirsch Rabinowitz, *The 613 Commandments, in* 5 ENCYCLOPAEDIA JUDAICA, *supra* note 53, vol. 5, at 73, 73–85.

[79] SEFER HAHINNUCH (Charles Wengrov trans., 1992).

[80] The word "Turim" in the title is an allusion to Exodus 28:17 in which the word refers to the four rows of jewels that adorned the High Priest's breastplate. *See, e.g.,* DAVID M. FELDMAN, MARITAL RELATIONS, BIRTH CONTROL AND ABORTION IN JEWISH LAW 12 (1975).

[81] Note, however, that although the Second Temple was destroyed long before the time of Maimonides, this did not cause him to limit the scope of his Mishneh Torah.

[82] This work is therefore sometimes referred to as the *Arba'ah Turim* (literally, the "Four Rows"). It is also known simply as the *Turim*.

The Shulhan Arukh is tightly organized by subject matter and purported to constitute a compendium of Jewish law rules. Yet Jews had been dispersed throughout the Ancient World, and substantial differences had arisen between practices among Sephardic Jews (those who generally lived among Muslims) and Ashkenazi Jews (those who generally lived among Christians). Because Rabbi Karo was a Sephardi and relied heavily on Sephardi customs and authorities, his work was not immediately accepted by Ashkenazic Jews. Shortly after its publication, however, an Ashkenazi authority, Rav Moses Isserles,[83] wrote a commentary, called the *Mappah* (the "tablecloth") to Karo's Code that clarified where the two traditions differed. Soon, Rabbi Karo's and Rabbi Isserles' works were routinely published together, and, as such, became more broadly accepted. As time passed, an increasing number of super-commentaries were written regarding the Code of Jewish Law. Some of these began to be routinely included in newer printings of Karo's Code as well.

Indeed, most of the nineteenth and twentieth century works described in Section 6.02, above, are closely related to the Shulhan Arukh, and all were profoundly influenced by it.

---

[83] Moses Isserles lived from 1530 to 1572. For biographical information, see HERSH GOLDWURM, THE EARLY ACHARONIM 75 (1989).

Chapter 7

SUPPLEMENTAL SOURCES OF JEWISH LAW

§ 7.01 INTRODUCTION

Jewish law arises from a variety of sources. Chapter 5 identified, among other things, the Written and Oral Torah, along with the various literary documents that record how both biblical and non-biblical Jewish law has unfolded. Chapter 5 discussed various Jewish law "institutions" that have played major roles in the history of Jewish law, many of whom contributed to Jewish law's decisional and legislative history.

This chapter identifies a few additional sources that primarily arise as a result of: (1) personal choice; (2) communal choice; and (3) the law of one's host country.

§ 7.02 PERSONAL CHOICE AS A SOURCE OF JEWISH LAW

Many laws, such as biblical laws against desecration of the Sabbath or against the commission of murder, apply before anyone takes any action. Other laws, or at least their specific applications, arguably arise only as the result of independent human action. For example, although there are rules against adultery and against intimacy with relatives of one's spouse, some of these prohibitions, or at least some specific applications of these rules, only attach to two specific people when they marry each other.

Similarly, the Pentateuch states that legal effects will arise from vows (*nedarim*) and oaths (*shavuot*). By taking a vow,[1] a person may biblically obligate himself to perform an act that he was not theretofore duty-bound to perform.[2] He can make it biblically forbidden for him to do something that would otherwise be permitted for him to do.[3] Although Talmudic sages warn against the severity of the punishment for failing to fulfill a vow, the Shulhan Arukh permits making a vow for the purpose of ridding oneself of bad habits.[4]

There are various types of oaths. In some instances, a rabbinic court may require a defendant to take an oath to avoid being found guilty.[5] In other instances, a person may voluntarily take an oath for several reasons, such as to convince an interlocutor that he is telling the truth.[6] In any event, oaths, just as vows, have biblical consequences. Through an oath, for instance, a person may make certain actions biblically forbidden to him or required of him.[7]

§ 7.03 COMMUNAL CHOICE

Elsewhere (such as in §§ 5.09, 5.10 and in Chapter 10) we describe how, through the acts of the lay or rabbinic leaders it chooses, a community may enact religiously binding legislation. There are also additional ways through which a community may formally or informally create law.

[A] Community Custom as Law

Communities may also create law by the customs they adopt for ritual and non-ritual matters. A "custom" is

---

[1] The biblical rules regarding vows are primarily found in *Numbers* 30:1–16.

[2] *Genesis* 28:20.

[3] *See generally* Louis Isaac Rabinowitz, *Vows and Vowing, in* 20 ENCYCLOPAEDIA JUDAICA 585, 585–86 (Michael Berenbaum and Fred Skolnik eds., 2d ed. 2007).

[4] *Id.* at 586 (citing *Shulhan Arukh, Yoreh Deah* 203:7).

[5] For example, a rabbinical court might require a defendant to take an exculpatory oath. *See generally* Moshe Greenberg et al., *Oath, in* 15 ENCYCLOPAEDIA JUDAICA, *supra* note 3, at 358–64.

[6] *Id.*

[7] *Id.*

a practice that is accepted in a given geographic area ("local custom") or among a particular group of people (for example, "merchant custom"). To be defined as "custom," a practice must be widespread, recognized, and performed repeatedly.[8]

[1] Expansive Scope of Custom as Law

Jewish law clearly recognizes that commercial transactions are governed by custom. In tractate Bava Metzia, the Mishnah states:

> One who hires laborers and tells them to come early or stay late: in a place where the custom is not to come early or stay late, the employer is not allowed to force them [to do so]. . . . All [such terms] are governed by local custom."[9]

Moreover, the majority view, at least outside of the State of Israel, seems to be that as to commercial matters, such customs need not have been established by halakhic or communal authorities, or even by Jews.[10] Parties are simply presumed to have implicitly made applicable customs part of their agreement. Rabbi Moses Feinstein explains:

> It is entirely obvious that all of these rules that depend on custom . . . do not have to be customs established by Torah scholars, and not even by Jews specifically. Even if these customs were established by Gentiles, if they are the majority of the inhabitants of the city, the halacha is in accordance with the custom [unless the parties specify otherwise] because [it is deemed that] the parties conditioned their agreement in accordance with the custom of the city [unless they specify otherwise].[11]

There are many examples where custom prevails over what would otherwise be the halakhic rule.[12] For instance, where persons on a caravan hire a guide, halakhah prescribes a formula for determining how much of the guide's fee each person should contribute. That formula takes into consideration both a per capita and a property component so that a person who brings more property pays more. If, however, there is a custom to determine payment based solely on the amount of property each person has with him, then that custom governs.[13] Similarly, although

---

[8] Ron S. Kleinman, *Civil Law as Custom: Jewish Law and Secular Law — Do They Diverge or Converge?*, 14 REV. RABBINIC JUDAISM 11 (2011).

[9] BABYLONIAN TALMUD, *Bava Metzia* 83a.

[10] YOSEF COLON TRABBO (a/k/a *Maharik*; 1420–1480), SHUT MAHARIK 102 (Heb.); SHMUEL DI MEDINA (a/k/a *Maharashdam*; 1506–1589), SHUT MAHARASHDAM no.108 (Heb.) (the questioner makes this argument, and Maharashdam comments approvingly); DAVID HAZAN (nineteenth century), NIDIV LEV no. 12 (Heb.); YISROEL AVRAHAM ALTER LANDAU, BET YISROEL no. 172 (Heb.); MOSES FEINSTEIN (1895–1986), IGGEROT MOSHE, *Hoshen Mishpat* I:72 (Heb.).

[11] *See* JERUSALEM TALMUD, *Bava Metzia* 27b, (statement of Rav Hoshea, "Minhag supersedes halacha"). *See also, e.g.*, PRINCIPLES OF JEWISH LAW columns 97–98 (Menachem Elon ed., 1975).

[12] *See, e.g.*, BABYLONIAN TALMUD, *Bava Metzia* 83a, 94a; MAIMONIDES, MISHNEH TORAH, *Laws of Tenancy* 2:9; SHULHAN ARUKH, *Hoshen Mishpat* 296:5.

[13] PRINCIPLES OF JEWISH LAW, *supra* note 11, at column 103 (citing *Ba'alei Tosafot*, i.e., various twelfth to fifteenth century scholars). *See also* BABYLONIAN TALMUD, *Bava Metzia* 7:13–14, *Bava Kama* 116b and

Jewish law provides that one may become contractually liable only through certain formal procedures (kinyanim), the Talmud states that where people in business use a different method ("s'tumtah"), such as a handshake, this method is valid under Jewish law.[14]

Thus, commercial customs are regarded as "default terms" in any relevant Jewish law contract, similar to the way in which Article 2 of the Uniform Commercial Code treats industry customs as default terms in contracts for the sale of goods. It is as if these customs were written into the commercial contract. It is because Jewish law allows parties to a commercial transaction considerable freedom that these customs can differ from what Jewish law would otherwise prescribe.[15] For the same reason, Jewish law, like secular law, allows parties to avoid the effect of customs, too, by expressly agreeing to different terms.[16]

What about "customs" that arose from, and constitute, compliance with a secularly enacted law?

A custom is frequently based on the fact that secular law requires such action. Many poskim have stated that this fact does not detract from the status of the particular practice as a valid custom under Jewish law. For example, Rabbi Yosef Iggeret argues:

> One cannot cast doubt upon the validity of this custom on the basis that it became established through a decree of the King that required people to so act. Since people always act this way, even though they do so only because of the King's decree, we still properly say that everyone who does business without specifying otherwise does business according to the custom.[17]

Similarly, Rabbi Blau states in the name of Haham Yosef Haim Pe'alim ("Ben Ish Hai," 1832–1909) that if people act in accordance with the secular law, the custom has halakhic validity as custom.[18]

JERUSALEM TALMUD, *Bava Kama* 6:4, 11a; SHULHAN ARUCH, *Hoshen Mishpat* 201:1. For other examples, see, e.g., MOSHE MARGOLIOS (1710–1781), PNEI MOSHE, *Bava Metzia* 27b (Heb.); ASHER BEN YEHIEL (a/k/a *Rosh*; 1250–1327), SHUT HAROSH 64:4 (Heb.).

[14] BABYLONIAN TALMUD, *Bava Metzia* 74a. See also SHULHAN ARUKH, *Hoshen Mishpat* 201:1. For other examples, see, e.g., MARGOLIOS, *supra* note 13; YEHIEL, *supra* note 13. Nevertheless, some Jewish law authorities believe that *s'tumtah* is valid as a matter of biblical law. *See, e.g.,* MOSES SCHREIBER (a/k/a Moses Sofer; 1763–1839), HATAM SOFER, *Yoreh De'ah* 314, *s.v. Nimtza* (Heb.).

[15] BABYLONIAN TALMUD, *Bava Metzia* 94a; MAIMONIDES, MISHNEH TORAH, *Law of Tenancy* 2:9; SHULHAN ARUKH, *Hoshen Mishpat* 296:5.

[16] *See* PRINCIPLES OF JEWISH LAW, *supra* note 11, at columns 251–52.

[17] YOSEF IGGERET, DIVREI YOSEF 21 (Heb.). *See also* DAVID HAZAN, (nineteenth century), NIDIV LEV 12 (Heb.); ELIYAHU HAZAN (nineteenth century), NIDIV LEV 13 (Heb.); YITZCHAK AARON ETTINGER (1827–1891), 2 MAHARIA HALEVI 111 (Heb.); AVRAHAM DUBER KAHANA SHAPIRO (twentieth century), 1 DEVAR AVRAHAM 1 (Heb.). Shmuel Shilo states that Rabbi Iggeret bases his conclusion not only on *minhag* but also on *dina demalkhuta dina. See* SHMUEL SHILO, DINEI DEMALKHUTA DINA 163 (1974) (Heb.). Nevertheless, this does not seem to be a correct construction of Rabbi Iggeret's responsum.

[18] *See* YESHAYA BLAU, PITHEI HOSHEN, *Dinei Halva'ah*, ch. 2, *halakhah* 29, n.82 (Heb.). In PITHEI HOSHEN, *Hilkhot Geneivah*, ch. 1, n. 4, p. 13, Blau explains that, according to the Ben Ish Hai, all disputes between Jews which are adjudged based on secular law are really done so because of custom, not because of *dina demalkhuta dina*.

Rabbi Moses Feinstein has arguably gone further, suggesting that secular law may have the same effect as minhag, even if people do not always act in accordance with the secular law. Thus, in one case, Rabbi Feinstein was told that applicable landlord-tenant law prohibited the landlord from evicting a tenant at the end of the lease, even if the landlord wanted to use the property himself. Although Rabbi Feinstein was asked whether the law was valid under Jewish law because of *dina demalkhuta dina*, a doctrine we discuss next, he chose not to rule on that ground. Instead, he declared that the landlord agreed to the secular law at the time of the lease:

> [C]ertainly the law of the land is no worse than minhag and unless the parties agree otherwise it is deemed as if they agreed according to the secular law, and a fortiori when the minhag is in accordance with the secular law.[19]

[2] Limitations on the Legal Effectiveness of Customs

At least four possible restrictions on the Jewish law effectiveness of some commercial customs need to be mentioned. First, a number of rabbinic authorities from the eleventh to fifteenth centuries (referred to as *Rishonim*) declared that a new commercial custom, as opposed to an ancient custom (a *minhag vatikin*), is only valid under Jewish law if it is also authorized by a communal decree issued with the participation of local rabbinical authorities.[20] Interestingly, this position, which provided rabbinic authorities the ability to supervise and regulate which *customs* would be enforceable, was not mentioned in the Talmud.[21] However, the Talmud had mentioned a requirement that any new communal *legislation* required rabbinic approval.[22] Nevertheless, as mentioned earlier,[23] it seems that the normative rule is that customs validly act as default rules in commercial transactions even without any direct rabbinic involvement in the establishment of those customs.

Second, rabbinic authorities sometimes rule that a particular custom lacks Jewish law validity because the custom is "mistaken," "unreasonable," or "bad."[24] This approach, which has been taken regarding both commercial and non-

---

[19] MOSES FEINSTEIN, IGGEROT MOSHE, *Hoshen Mishpat* I:72 (Heb.). *See also id.* at *Hoshen Mishpat* I:75 (addressing whether an employee may be dismissed without cause).

[20] This approach may have been first taken by Sephardi (North Africa-Spain) authorities in the North African-Spanish Jewish communities. Rabbi Isaac Alfasi (eleventh century) held that a custom was invalid unless approved via a communal decree after consultation with "community elders." Later authorities in this region reiterated this approach, although they sometimes more clearly referred to the need for consultation with or approval by local rabbinic authorities. *See* Kleinman, *supra* note 8, at 17. This same position was adopted by several Ashkenazi (France-Germany) authorities of the same era. *Id.*

[21] *Id.* at 18.

[22] BABYLONIAN TALMUD, *Bava Bathra* 9a. *See also* MAIMONIDES, MISHNEH TORAH, *Laws of Sale* 14:11; SHULHAN ARUKH, *Hoshen Mishpat* 231:28; MENACHEM ELON, JEWISH LAW: HISTORY, SOURCES, PRINCIPLES vol. 2, at 751–59 (Bernard Auerbach and Melvin J. Sykes, trans., 1994). Kleinman contends that these eleventh-to-fifteenth-century authorities "equated enactments and customs." Kleinman, *supra* note 8, at 18.

[23] *See supra* text and accompanying notes 17–19.

[24] *Id.*; ELON, *supra* note 22, vol. 3, at 937–44.

commercial practices,[25] seemingly provides rabbinic authorities with a potentially expansive power with which to challenge commercial customs. Nevertheless, this author's survey of responsa literature, especially recent responsa literature, suggests that this power has been rarely employed.

Third, a custom inconsistent with Jewish law is invalid if Jewish law would not allow parties to expressly agree to the custom. For example, Jewish law forbids one Jewish lender to charge interest to a Jewish borrower for a loan.[26] There happen to be various mechanisms for circumventing this law.[27] Nevertheless, if people did not invoke such devices and simply loaned on interest, this "custom" would not be valid under Jewish law no matter how many people engaged in it.

Fourth, at least some Jewish law authorities state that if a custom is adopted for the purpose of renouncing Jewish law and copying Gentile laws, the custom is invalid. For example, Rabbi Solomon Ben Abraham Adret (Rashba; 1235–1310) addressed a case of a married Jewish woman who died in Perpignan, now part of Southern France, survived by her widower and one daughter.[28] When the daughter later died, the daughter's father sought to recover the dowry he had given the widower at the time of the marriage. The father-in-law advanced two claims, one based on custom. The prevailing Gentile custom was that a father-in-law could recover the dowry under such circumstances. The father-in-law argued that it was common knowledge that the Jews in the land followed Gentile customs and, therefore, when the dowry was given, everyone knew that it was subject to this custom.

Rabbi Adret rejected this reasoning, stating:

> Regardless, I believe that to do so [practice gentile law] by reason of its being gentile law is forbidden because it is imitating the gentiles. This is what the Torah has warned us: "before them and not before the gentiles."[29] And even though both parties agree [to litigation according to gentile law] and it is a monetary matter [it is forbidden to do so] because the Torah does not allow His nation to favor gentile law [over Torah law].[30]

Rabbi Adret's position has been cited favorably by a number of other rabbinic authorities.[31]

---

[25] *Id. See, e.g.*, ASHER BEN YEHIEL, BABYLONIAN TALMUD, *Bava Bathra*, ch. 1, no. 1 (Heb.); MORDECAI BEN HILLEL HAKOHEN (c. 1240–1298), BABYLONIAN TALMUD, *Bava Bathra* 464, *Bava Metzia* 366 (Heb.); YEHOSHUA FALK (*Sema*; 1550–1614), *Hoshen Mishpat* 157:12, 161:7, 163:23 (Heb.); SOLOMON LURIA (*Maharshal*; 1510–1573), YAM SHEL SHLOMO, *Yebamot*, ch. 1, no. 12 (Heb.); SHABTAI HAKOHEN, SHAKH, *Hoshen Mishpat* 72:35 (Heb.). *See generally* 1 ISAAC HERZOG, THE MAIN INSTITUTIONS OF JEWISH LAW 21–22 (1965).

[26] *See, e.g.*, Steven H. Resnicoff, *A Commercial Conundrum: Does Prudence Permit the Jewish "Permissible Venture"?*, 20 SETON HALL L. REV. 77 (1990).

[27] *Id.*

[28] SOLOMON BEN ABRAHAM ADRET (a/k/a *Rashba*; 1235–1310), 6 SHUT RASHBA 254.

[29] *Exodus* 21:1.

[30] ADRET, *supra* note 28 (as translated by Kleinman, *supra* note 8, at 18–19).

[31] *See, e.g.*, YOSEF KARO, BET YOSEF, *Hoshen Mishpat* 26; MORDECAI BEN AVRAHAM YOFFE (1530–1612), LEVUSH, *Hoshen Mishpat* 26:4; HAKOHEN, *supra* note 25, *Hoshen Mishpat*, at 73:39. R. Dov Lior, currently the Rabbi of Kiryat Arbah, Israel, argues that although a "specific" Gentile law in a narrow

At least three factors may limit the effect of Rabbi Adret's ruling. First, although the case involved monetary matters, it arose out of a rather personal, peculiarly intra-faith event, the marriage of two Jews. The notion that Gentile customs would be legally controlling in such a matter might have been especially offensive.

Second, the responsum does not cite any other Jewish case in which this custom had been observed. It is possible that a commercial custom established by the conduct of Gentiles might only be binding as to commercial transactions that could likely occur between a Jew and a Gentile, two Jews or two Gentiles. At the time of Rabbi Adret's ruling, and, in fact, until relatively recent times, the rate of Jewish inter-marriage was quite low. Consequently a custom among Gentiles might not constitute a custom for Jews regarding matters in which Jews almost always dealt only with other Jews.

Finally, several commentators have argued that Rabbi Adret's ruling was not that a secular commercial custom would not be valid under Jewish law. Rather, Adret seemed to focus on the *reason* the Jewish community had for following the custom:

> Rashba evidently attributes great importance to the *intent* behind the adopting of a Gentile norm and the *motivation* that impels its adoption. As long as a practice is adopted for substantive reasons . . . it may be adopted. But it is forbidden to adopt a gentile norm merely because it is a gentile norm, as if therein lies its merit. This was in fact the case in the situation under discussion in which the father argued that they "follow gentile law" and even applied to a gentile court of law . . . . Intent rather than content is the determining factor in his opinion . . . . In monetary matters Jewish society may adopt the norms of the surrounding society, but it may not adopt these norms if the fundamental purpose is to renounce Jewish law. (Emphasis in original)[32]

[B] Communal Abrogation of Law

Not only can community conduct create law, but, in one special way, community conduct can also abrogate certain rabbinic legislation. Suppose, for instance, that a duly authorized rabbinic body issues legislation on the belief that a majority of Jews will abide by it. In fact, however, the majority of the community cannot abide by the regulation. According to some authorities, the legislation automatically becomes void, while according to others, the legislation must be formally repealed.[33]

---

area, such as a labor law or a consumer protection law, may be valid as a "custom" in Jewish law, a general law, such as contract law, may not. *See* Dov Lior, *The Relationship Between Halakha and State Law*, 3 TEHUMIN 247 (1982) (Heb.). Citing Adret, Lior argues that adopting such a general law would be tantamount to uprooting the Torah. *Id.* at 249. *But see* Kleinman, *supra* note 8, at 25–26 (suggesting weaknesses in Lior's argument).

[32] Ya'akov Blidstein, *The Israeli Legal System as Viewed by Contemporary Halakhic Authorities*, DINEI ISRAEL 42 (1986–1988) (Heb.), translated, and agreed to, by Kleinman, *supra* note 8, at 20.

[33] *See* ARYEH KAPLAN, THE HANDBOOK OF JEWISH THOUGHT 228 (1979).

§ 7.04 "THE LAW OF THE KINGDOM IS [RELIGIOUSLY] BINDING" (*DINA DEMALKHUTA DINA*)

The doctrine *dina demalkhuta dina* essentially means that "the law of the kingdom is religiously binding." This is an extremely powerful principle because, where applicable, it supersedes what Jewish law would otherwise provide. Throughout much, if not all, of the last two millennia, most Jews did not live in their own land. Consequently, an expansive version of this doctrine threatened to swallow up all of Jewish civil law. Predictably, the relevant literature is complex and reflects substantial areas of disagreement.[34] The discussion here can only provide an introduction to the topic.

[A]   Sources for the Doctrine

We must first address the Jewish law basis for this doctrine, which the Talmud cites in four places.[35] We will consider seven possibilities.[36] The power and scope of the doctrine may well depend on which, if any, of these explanations is correct. The first five explanations arise from Jewish law authorities of the period from the tenth to fifteenth centuries.[37]

[1]   Implicit Agreement to Secular Law

One approach is suggested by such authorities as Rabbi Shmuel ben Meir (*Rashbam*; 1085–1158),[38] Maimonides (1135–1204),[39] and Israel Isserlein (*Terumat HaDeshin*; 1390–1460).[40] According to their approach, when people live in a country they voluntarily accept the king's authority and subject themselves to the king's laws. Maimonides explains:

> If a king cut down homeowners' trees and made from them a bridge, it is permitted to travel over it. Similarly, if a king demolished houses and made a road or a wall, it is permitted to make use of them, and the same for all like cases, because the law of the king is [religiously valid] law.

---

[34] *See generally* DINA DEMALKHUTA DINA, 7 ENCYCLOPEDIA TALMUDIT 295–308 (S. Zevin ed., 1981) (Heb.); SHILO, *supra* note 17; DAYAN I. GRUNFELD, THE JEWISH LAW OF INHERITANCE 17–46 (1987); Hershel Schacter, *"Dina De'malchusa Dina": Secular Law as a Religious Obligation*, 1 J. HALACHA & CONTEMP. SOC'Y 103 (1981); OVADIAH YOSEF (contemporary), 4 YEHAVE DA'AT no. 65; ELIEZER WALDENBURG (1915–2006), 16 TZITZ ELIEZER no. 49; TRABBO, *supra* note 10, nos. 66, 187; MOSES TEITELBAUM (1769–1841), HESHIV MOSHE no. 90.

[35] *See* BABYLONIAN TALMUD, *Gittin* 10b, *Nedarim* 28a, *Bava Kamma* 113a, *Bava Bathra* 54b.

[36] For arguments offered by some contemporary academics, see, for example, Aaron Kirschenbaum and Jon Trafimow, *The Sovereign Power of the State: A Proposed Theory of Accommodation in Jewish Law*, 12 CARDOZO L. REV. 925 (1991); Chaim Povarsky, *Jewish Law v. the Law of the State: Theories of Accommodation*, 12 CARDOZO L. REV. 941 (1991).

[37] *But see* Asher Weiss, *Lecture Regarding Dina demalkhuta dina*, PARSHAT HUKOT (2010), http://www.scribd.com/doc/33478615/RAW-on-Chukas (last visited July 19, 2011), which examines each of these supposed theories for the doctrine of dina demalkhuta dina and contends that some were not really intended as such.

[38] SHMUEL BAR MEIR (a/k/a *Rashbam*; c. 1085–c. 1158), BABYLONIAN TALMUD, *Bava Bathra* 54b.

[39] MAIMONIDES, *supra* note 12, *Laws of Theft* 5:17–18.

[40] ISRAEL ISSERLEIN (1390–1460), TERUMAT HADESHEN no. 341.

When do these rules apply? [They apply] with respect to a king whose currency is accepted in those lands, because the people of the land accepted him and concluded that he was their master and they were his servants. But if his currency is not accepted, then he is like a thief, an oppressor, and it is similar to a band of armed robbers. Just as their rules are not [religiously valid] laws, so it is with this king and all of his aides, he is [merely] a thief.[41]

[2] Implicit Acceptance Based on the King's Right to Exile

A second approach offered by Rabbi Shlomo Adret (*Rashba*; 1235–1310)[42] and Rabbeinu Nissim ben Reuven (*Ran*; 1320–1376) is also based on implicit consent. But it also provides a specific reason why such consent is implied. They contend that the king is the ultimate owner of the land of his kingdom and has the power to exile the inhabitants. As a result, one who resides in the land does so only upon his agreement to obey the king's laws.[43]

[3] The King's Power to Dispossess a Person of His or Her Property

Rabbeinu Yonah ben Abraham Gerondi (Rabbeinu Yonah; d. 1263) seems to suggest a third basis for the *dina demalkhuta dina* doctrine. He states that the king has the power to dispossess a person of his or her property just as a rabbinic court does. Rabbeinu Yonah appears to argue that the authority to dispossess a person of his property is the basis for the obligation to obey the king's law.

A rabbinic court's power to dispossess a person's property arises from the doctrine known as "what is taken away by a rabbinic court is [validly] taken away" (*hefker bet din hefker*). The obvious question is what is the connection between the power of a rabbinic court and the power of a Gentile king? Rabbi Abraham Duber Kahana Shapiro (1870–1943) contends that the rabbinic court's authority for dispossessing a person of his property does not arise out of the rabbinic court's biblical authority as a religious court but, instead, out of the fact that the court is clothed with the power to govern. Because secular kings possess this same power to govern, he argues that they, too, enjoy the authority to dispossess people of their property.[44]

---

[41] MAIMONIDES, *supra* note 12. *See generally* J. David Bleich, *Jewish Law and the State's Authority to Punish Crime*, 12 CARDOZO L. REV. 829, 834–35 (1991).

[42] SHLOMO BEN ADRET, BABYLONIAN TALMUD, *Nedarim* 28a.

[43] NISSIM BEN REUVEN GERONDI, BABYLONIAN TALMUD, *Nedarim* 28a.

[44] SHAPIRO, *supra* note 17. *But see* Weiss, *supra* note 37, who disagrees with Shapiro's explanation. Weiss argues that Rabbeinu Yonah did not intend to offer an explanation for the basis of the *dina demalkhuta dina* doctrine, but only wanted to explain that the king's power pursuant to that doctrine was no greater than the power of a rabbinical court under the *hefker bet din hefker* doctrine. Specifically, Weiss argues that Rabbeinu Yonah's position was that the power was limited to dispossessing a current owner of ownership. Neither a king nor a rabbinic court could actually transfer ownership to a new person. Instead, the new person needed to do a separate action, a *kinyan*, in order to acquire the original owner's property.

[4] Right of Conquest

A fourth theory is offered by Rabbi Shlomo ben Adret[45] and by Rabbi Yom Tov ben Avraham Asevilli (Ritva; 1250–1330). They contend that the doctrine arises out of the right of conquest.[46] Consequently, they maintain that *dina demalkhuta dina* only religiously validates the laws prescribed by the early kings, the ones that actually conquered the lands.

[5] A Consequence of the Noahide Commandment to Establish Law

Rabbi Shlomo Yitzhaki (Rashi; 1040–1105), the foremost commentator on both the Written Torah and on the Babylonian Talmud, advances a fifth theory. According to Jewish law, seven commandments were given to the descendants of Noah.[47] One of these commandments is to establish a system of laws (*Dinim*). In his commentary on the Babylonian Talmud, Rashi indicates when it requires non-Jewish communities to enact laws, this commandment implicitly validates the laws so passed. Consequently, these laws apply to the Jewish, as well as to the non-Jewish, residents of the land.[48]

[6] Specific Scriptural Source

Moses Schreiber, also known as Moses Sofer (Hatam Sofer; 1762–1839), mentions a sixth theory. In the Babylonian Talmud tractate "Oaths" (Shavuot), Shmuel, the Amora who elsewhere in the Talmud declares the *dina demalkhuta dina* doctrine, provides the following interpretation of a verse in the Scriptural book, "Song of Songs":[49] "My vineyard is before Me. One thousand are for you, Shlomoh [i.e., for the Heavenly Kingdom] and two hundred for those who guard its fruit [i.e., for the earthly kingdom]."[50] Shmuel adduces this verse as a proof that a government that kills up to one-sixth of its population (i.e., that uses up to 1/6th for its personal benefit, including life-endangering military conscription) is not punished, because the verse says that 200 of the total of 1,200, or 1/6th, is for the benefit of the earthly kingdom. This same verse, says Schreiber, which gives the king authority to use 1/6th of his population for his personal benefit, is the source for the *dina demalkhuta dina* doctrine.[51] If the king has the right to demand the lives of up to 1/6th of his citizens, certainly, the argument goes, he has the right to impose lesser demands upon them through the various laws he promulgates.

---

[45] This is the same Rabbi Shlomo ben Adret who, in his commentary to *Nedarim* 28a, offered the second theory described in discussion in the text, *supra*, associated with notes 42 and 43.

[46] *See* Shlomo ben Adret, Babylonian Talmud, *Yebamot* 46a, and Yom Tov Asevilli, Babylonian Talmud, *Yebamot* 46a.

[47] *See, e.g.*, Bleich, *supra* note 41, at 830–31. *See* § 4.04, *supra*.

[48] *See* Shlomo ben Yitzhaki, Babylonian Talmud, *Gittin* 9b; Bleich, *supra* note 41, at 854–56; Weiss, *supra* note 37, who critiqued Rashi's position.

[49] *Song of Songs* 8:12.

[50] Babylonian Talmud, *Shavuot* 35b.

[51] Schreiber, *supra* note 14, *Orah Hayyim* 208 and *Hoshen Mishpat* 44. *See also* Bleich, *supra* note 41, at 844–46 (presenting a slightly different interpretation of Shreiber's proof from the cited text).

[7]   Inherent in the Torah-Recognized Institution of a King

Finally, Asher Weiss, a contemporary rabbi in Jerusalem, contends that the fundamental source of *dina demalkhuta dina* is two-fold.[52] First, Judaism's Scriptural sources axiomatically assume that there is such a legitimate institution as a king. Inherently linked to this assumption is the axiom that the king has authority over his subjects, because without subjects, there can be no king. Second, the doctrine is based on logic, because government is essential, as Tannaitic teachings known as the "Ethics of the Fathers" (*Pirkei Avot*) state: "If there were no government, each person would swallow up his neighbor alive."[53] His argument seems similar to the theory described in § 7.04[A][3], *supra*.

[B]   Practical Application of the Doctrine

Despite some dissenting opinions, the majority view is that *dina demalkhuta dina* is part of biblical law.[54] Similarly, although some important authorities contend that *dina demalkhuta dina* only applies to interactions between two Gentiles or between a Gentile and a Jew, but not between two Jews,[55] the majority view, following Rabbi Moses Isserles, is that it applies even to transactions between two Jews.[56] Again, although some authorities argue that it applies only to laws issued by a king,[57] the majority view appears to be that it also applies to laws promulgated by a democratic form of government.[58]

But are there restrictions as to the types of laws to which the *dina demalkhuta dina* doctrine applies? There are essentially three principal perceptions as to the practical application of *dina demalkhuta dina*, the views of R. Yosef Karo, R. Moses Isserles and R. Shabbatai Hakohen. These authorities broadly agree, based on dicta of the Babylonian Amora Shmuel, that *dina demalkhuta dina* renders religiously effective secular laws concerning taxes, currency regulation and other matters relating directly to the government's financial interests.

R. Karo's view, however, is that these are the only areas to which the doctrine applies. By contrast, R. Isserles envisions the doctrine as enjoying a much more

---

[52] Weiss, *supra* note 37.

[53] MISHNAH, *Pirkei Avot* 3:2.

[54] *See, e.g.*, SCHREIBER, *supra* note 14, *Yoreh De'ah* 114; SHAPIRO, *supra* note 17; Weiss, *supra* note 37. *But see* SHMUEL BEN URI SHRAGA PHOEBUS (second half of seventeenth century), BET SHMUEL, *Even HaEzer* 28:3 (contending that the doctrine is rabbinic).

[55] *See, e.g.*, AVRAHAM YESHAYA KARELITZ (1878–1953), HAZON ISH, *Hoshen Mishpat, Likutim* 16(1) (stating that this was the view of the Rishon, Rabbeinu Yonah).

[56] *See, e.g.*, MOSES ISSERLES, SHULHAN ARUKH, *Hoshen Mishpat* 369:13, who agrees with the view of MORDECAI BEN HILLEL HAKOHEN, *supra* note 25; Weiss, *supra* note 37.

[57] *See, e.g.*, MENASHE KLEIN (contemporary rabbi in Boro Park, New York), 6 MISHNE HALACHOTH no. 277.

[58] This is clearly the opinion of the major Jewish law decisors in the United States during the twentieth century. *See, e.g.*, FEINSTEIN, *supra* note 19, *Hoshen Mishpat* II:62; ELIYAHU HENKIN, TESHUVOT IBRA 2:176. *See also* R. Hershel Schachter, Dina Di'Malchusa Dina: *Secular Law as a Religious Obligation*, 1 J. HALACHA & CONTEMP. SOC'Y 103 (1981); SHILO, *supra* note 17, at 157.

expansive scope. R. Hakohen's concept of *dina demalkhuta dina* is broader than that of Karo, but narrower than that of Isserles.

The controversy reflects a difference of opinion among Rishonim regarding a passage in tractate Gittin.[59] The Mishnah states:

> All documents accepted in non-Jewish courts, even if the witnesses who signed them are non-Jews, are valid under Jewish law, except for writs of divorce and of emancipation. Rav Shimon says that even these are valid; they were only declared invalid when prepared by unauthorized persons.

The Gemara asks why the Mishnah does not differentiate between documents of only evidentiary value and documents which actually effectuate legal changes, such as those purporting to transfer property. The Gemara questions how the latter types of documents could be valid under Jewish law. Two answers are given. First, the Talmud states that the documents are valid because of the doctrine of *dina demalkhuta dina*. Then the Talmud states, "If you like, I could say that the phrase 'except writs of divorce and emancipation' means 'except documents like writs of divorce,' i.e., except documents which themselves change legal status."

Some early Talmudists (*Rishonim*) interpret these two answers as exclusive alternatives. Accordingly, the second answer would constitute an acknowledgment that *dina demalkhuta dina* is limited to matters directly affecting the government's financial interests.[60] Secular documents pertaining to other matters could be considered for evidentiary purposes, but could not themselves effect legal changes. Karo adopts this view.[61]

Other Rishonim construe the two Talmudic answers as supplementary, not exclusive.[62] According to this approach, the first answer, that *dina demalkhuta*

---

[59] BABYLONIAN TALMUD, *Gittin* 10b.

[60] Twelfth through fifteenth century scholars (known as Rishonim) so ruling include, without limitation, Rabbi Yitzchak Alfasi (*Rif*, 1013–1103), reported by Rashba, BABYLONIAN TALMUD, *Gittin* 10b; the majority of the Geonim (various authorities from sixth through early eleventh centuries), reported by VIDAL YOM TOV OF TOLOSA (fourteenth century), MAGGID MISHNEH, *Laws of Lending and Borrowing* 27:1 (reporting views of "Ba'alei Tosafot," leading Talmudic authorities of the eleventh through fifteenth centuries); YEHOSHUA SOAZ BEN SHIMON BARUCH (sixteenth century), SHILTEI GIBORIM, *Bava Basra*, end of ch. 3; SAMUEL HASARDI (1190–1256), BA'AL HATRUMOT, *Sha'ar* 46, part 8, no. 5; MAHARIK, *supra* note 10 (stating this opinion and citing it as the view of Mordecai ben Hillel, a late thirteenth century authority). This is also the view of the Maimonides, according to Maggid Mishneh's interpretation of Maimonides, although others construe Maimonides differently. *See, e.g.*, AVRAHAM BEN MOSHE OF BOTON (sixteenth century), LEHEM MISHNEH, *Laws of Lending and Borrowing* 27:1.

[61] This ruling is implicit in the fact that R. Karo only cites *dina demalkhuta dina* in connection with matters that directly affect the government. SHULHAN ARUKH, *Hoshen Mishpat* 369:6–11. Isserles refers to the view of the other Rishonim in contrast to the rule stated by Karo. *See* SHULHAN ARUKH, *Hoshen Mishpat* 369:8.

[62] For a more complete interpretation of the Gemara based on this second approach, see GRUNFELD, *supra* note 34. Although differing on certain issues, Rishonim interpreting *dina demalkhuta dina* as comprehensively applying to such subjects include, without limitation, Rashi and Mordechai b. Hillel Hakohen, reported in SHAUL YISRAELI (1909–1995), AMUDEI HAYIMINI 8; MEIR, *supra* note 38; MENAHEM MEIRI (1249–1310), BET HABEHIRAH, *Gittin* 10b; Nissim b. Reuven of Gerondi (fourteenth century), COMMENTARY TO RIF, *Talmud Bavli, Gittin* 10b; SHIMON DURAN (thirteenth century), 1 TASHBATZ 158; YITZHAK B. SHESHES (1326–1407), SHUT RIVASH 142, 203; SHLOMO B. LURIA (*Maharshal*; 1510–1573), YAM SHEL

dina broadly applies to all types of civil law, remains valid. Isserles adopts this approach, adding the restriction mentioned by many Rishonim that: "We only apply dina demalkhutah dina where [the secular law] benefits the king [government] *or where it is for the benefit of the people of the land.*" (Emphasis added).[63]

Hakohen, however, argues that even the Rishonim who apply *dina demalkhuta dina* broadly would not apply it to contradict what would otherwise be the rule under Jewish law.[64] But if this were true, asked at least one leading authority of the nineteenth and twentieth centuries, what exactly would the doctrine accomplish? After all, if *dina demalkhuta dina* only applied where it was identical to Jewish law, what purpose would the doctrine serve?[65] It does not seem possible to interpret Hakohen's statement restrictively, as saying that *dina demalkhuta dina* could not contradict a law stated explicitly in the Written Torah, because he makes his statement at a place where the Shulhan Arukh was not discussing such a law.[66]

Isserles agrees, however, that *dina demalkhuta dina* cannot alter any Jewish law that the parties could not alter by agreement, such as the laws of inheritance.[67] But Jewish law allows parties to modify most of the monetary rules that apply to their voluntary transactions. Consequently, *dina demalkhuta dina* could apply to such matters.

Proponents of the Isserles' view cite specific examples in which *dina demalkhuta dina* alters express Jewish law rules regarding financial matters. For instance, Jewish law prescribes that a person who rescues another's property from a lion, a bear, a tidal wave, or a flood may keep the saved property himself. Even if the original owner is standing by and shouting that he does not despair of getting the property back, Jewish law says that his protest is meaningless.[68] Nonetheless, Isserles specifically states that if the king decrees that a person must return such property, then the person must do so because of *dina demalkhuta dina.*[69]

Hakohen's adherents argue that these examples are not inconsistent with Hakohen's view because they require conduct — the return of the lost or stolen

---

SHLOMO, ch. 1, no. 22. Rashba also seems to have shared this view. *See, e.g.*, RASHBA, BABYLONIAN TALMUD, *Gittin* 10b and 3 SHUT RASHBA 63(5), 198. *But see* OVADIAH YOSEF, 4 YIHAVE DA'AT 65 (discussing apparently inconsistent view of Rashba). Moshe B. Nahman believed that *dina demalkhuta dina* applied to all types of secular law, even if they were not enacted for the "public good." Nevertheless, he applied *dina demalkhuta dina* only to laws of ancient origin. *See* HAIM B. ISRAEL BENVENISTE (seventeenth century), KENESSET HAGEDOLAH, *Hoshen Mishpat*, second printing, no. 169:58 (discussing *Rashba's* positions).

[63] MOSES ISSERLES, SHULHAN ARUKH, *Hoshen Mishpat* 369:11. Actually, there are arguably two variations of the Rema's view. At an earlier point in the Shulhan Arukh, the Rema seems to say that *dina demalkhuta dina* applies to all areas of law. He states: "Some believe that dina demalkhuta dina applies only to taxes and charges on real estate . . . . Others disagree and believe that dina demalkhuta dina applies to all areas of law . . . and this is the correct view." *Id.* at *Hoshen Mishpat* 369:8.

[64] *See* SHAKH, *supra* note 25, *Hoshen Mishpat*, at 73:39.

[65] AVRAHAM YESHAYA KARELITZ, HAZON ISH, *Hoshen Mishpat*, Likutim 16(1).

[66] *See* Weiss, *supra* note 37.

[67] *See generally* GRUNFELD, *supra* note 34.

[68] SHULHAN ARUKH, *Hoshen Mishpat* 259:7.

[69] MOSES ISSERLES, SHULHAN ARUKH, *Hoshen Mishpat* 259:7.

object — which is anyway favored, albeit not required, by Jewish law.[70] Other examples are either disputed or distinguished.[71]

Most Jewish law authorities, at least among Ashkenazi Jews and at least in the United States, follow Isserles' view. However, it is necessary to determine whether a particular secular law "is for the benefit of the people of the land." R. Moses Feinstein, perhaps the greatest halakhic authority in the United States during most of the second-half of the twentieth century, applied the Isserles approach. Nevertheless, he articulated a somewhat restrictive perspective regarding the doctrine's scope. Specifically, he stated:

> However, as to things in which this [i.e., either civil unrest among competing creditors or complaints by people about the king's law as inferior to Jewish law] would not result, such as the right of a daughter to inherit along with a son [which might be prescribed by secular law but not by Jewish law], do not so much concern the kingdom, because many people bequeath their possession as they wish [dina demalkhuta dina would not apply]. Similarly as to damages caused by one's animals, for which the Torah imposes liability, even if they [secular laws] exempt [the animals' owners], dina demalkhuta dina does not apply. So, too, regarding the duties of bailees, of neighbors, and of agents, dina demalkhuta does not apply. And also as to the laws that pertain between a man and his wife, such conduct does not concern the kingdom, and each family may conduct itself as it wishes[72] because dina demalkhuta dina does not apply.[73]

The reasons why R. Feinstein excludes some of these categories of law from *dina demalkhuta dina* are unclear, which makes it difficult to predict how he might have ruled regarding other secular laws, such as laws imposing financial obligations on parents for their children or on children for their aged or infirm parents.

---

[70] *See, e.g.*, MAHARIK, *supra* note 10, no. 187; YAAKOV BREISH, 3 HELKAT YAAKOV no. 160.

[71] BREISH, *supra* note 70 (arguing that certain secular methods to transfer ownership of property are valid because, given *dina demalkhuta dina*, a Jew who uses such methods clearly demonstrates his or her intent to transfer ownership and, under Jewish law, the transferor's intent plays the critical role).

[72] Of course, Jews must abide by the Jewish laws that pertain to such relationships and conduct.

[73] MOSES FEINSTEIN, IGGEROT MOSHE, *Hoshen Mishpat* II:62.

Chapter 8

EXTRAORDINARY SOURCES OF LAW: THE EXAMPLE OF CAPITAL PUNISHMENT

§ 8.01   INTRODUCTION

Many Jewish law classes focus on only one of Jewish law's three alternative criminal law enforcement systems, namely the operation of the rabbinic court system pursuant to the rules set forth in the Written Torah and explained by the Talmud. However, focusing solely on this system would cause one to very seriously misunderstand how Jewish law functioned during most of its history. There are two additional law enforcement systems: enforcement by rabbinic courts functioning under their "extraordinary powers" and enforcement by a Jewish king.[1] These systems vary enormously as to the procedural protections they provide and as to their practical consequences. The systems will be compared primarily in the context of capital punishment.

§ 8.01   CAPITAL PUNISHMENT BY RABBINIC COURTS — UNDER ORDINARY RULES

The Written Torah sets forth two non-monetary punishments for criminal offenses: flogging and capital punishment.

---

[1] Although it is not entirely clear why there were two alternative rabbinic "tracts," for a suggestion, see Arnold N. Enker, *Aspects of Interaction Between the Torah Law, the King's Law, and the Noahide Law in Jewish Criminal Law*, 12 Cardozo L. Rev. 1137 (1991).

[A] Prerequisites for Imposing Capital Punishment

For a rabbinic court, operating under ordinary rules, to impose capital punishment, many prerequisites must be satisfied, including the following:

1. Immediately prior to his commission of the offense, the defendant must have been expressly warned that his intended conduct was a crime and that the punishment for the crime was execution.[2]

2. It is not enough for the defendant to have heard or even to have replied, "I hear and understand you." Instead, the defendant must specifically state that he is committing the act despite the fact that it is prohibited and despite the prescribed punishment.[3]

3. Immediately after making this statement, the defendant must commit the act.[4]

4. Two qualified witnesses must have observed the defendant commit the act while observing each other.[5]

5. At the defendant's trial, two qualified witnesses must testify to all of the above. To be qualified, the witnesses must be adult males who are not closely related to the defendant and who have not been disqualified as witnesses because of some prior conduct. In addition, suppose a third person who would not be a qualified witness in this case saw the event together with the other two, intending to serve together with them as a witness. Suppose, also, that this third person does go to court with the other two to serve with them as a witness. In this situation, the other two witnesses are disqualified to testify in the case.[6]

6. Circumstantial evidence or legal presumptions are not enough to predicate a conviction. The testimony of the two qualified witnesses is required.[7]

7. The trial must take place in a court of at least 23 qualified judges.[8]

8. The judges must explain to the witnesses the gravity of testifying in a matter involving capital punishment, and the witnesses must properly respond to the judges' detailed questions.[9]

9. A person's confession was not evidence upon which he could be convicted.[10]

---

[2] MAIMONIDES, MISHNEH TORAH, *Laws of Court* 12:1. In the case of a defendant accused of trying to convince other Jews to commit idolatry, this strict requirement is not required. *See* MISHNAH, *Sanhedrin* 7:10.

[3] MISHNAH, *Sanhedrin* 12:2 (the defendant must say, "on the basis that it is prohibited and that this is the punishment, I am committing the act").

[4] *Id.* (the defendant must commit the act *Tokh Kidei Dibbur*, which means within the time it takes to say three words).

[5] MAIMONIDES, MISHNEH TORAH, *Law Concerning Witnesses*, at 4:1.

[6] *Id.* at 5:3.

[7] MAIMONIDES, MISHNEH TORAH, *Laws of Court*, 20:1.

[8] *Id.* at 11:1.

[9] MAIMONIDES, *supra* note 5; MAIMONIDES, *supra* note 7, at 12:3.

[10] MAIMONIDES, *supra* note 7, at 18:6.

10. The least prestigious judges should speak first, lest the greatest judge speak first against the defendant, and his words deter the other judges from trying to find arguments on the defendant's behalf.[11]

11. The judges must first articulate arguments in favor of the defendant, lest arguments against the defendant predispose the judges towards a conviction.[12]

12. The judges must consider every reasonable argument advanced on behalf of the defendant, even if the argument is advanced by students who are not allowed to argue in favor of conviction.[13]

13. In order for there to be a conviction, at least two more judges must vote for conviction than vote for acquittal.[14]

14. Moreover, a person could only be tried for a capital offense at a time when Jewish law's Supreme Court, the Sanhedrin HaGadol, met at its specific location in the Temple. They ceased meeting at that location even before the Second Temple was destroyed.[15] Thereafter, the Sanhedrin was disbanded, and has not since been reestablished.[16]

There are also a variety of post-conviction, pre-execution procedures to afford a convicted defendant the possibility of offering additional evidence to reverse the sentence.[17]

[B]   Feasibility of Such Prerequisites

Considering all of the above factors, it would seem that a rabbinic court could rarely render a guilty verdict in a case involving capital punishment. Indeed, according to an anonymous view in the Mishnah, a court that executed someone

---

[11] *Id.* at 10:6.

[12] *Id.* at 10:7.

[13] *Id.* at 10:8.

[14] *Id.* at 9:2.

[15] BABYLONIAN TALMUD, *Avodah Zarah* 8b. In explaining the decision to move from this location, the Talmud states that there was a large number of murderers and "when the Sanhedrin saw that murderers were so prevalent that they could not be properly dealt with judicially, they said: 'Rather let us be exiled from place to place than pronounce them guilty [of capital offences]'." *Id.* Citing this passage, some people assert that the Sanhedrin was against capital punishment per se — or at least against its extensive use. I suggest that a closer reading indicates that the court was more concerned that it could not properly judge such a large number of capital cases because of the extensive time and effort required in each instance. As to the move, generally, see AARON M. SCHREIBER, JEWISH LAW AND DECISION-MAKING: A STUDY THROUGH TIME 402 (1979).

[16] The Roman government in Byzantium abolished the Sanhedrin HaGadol in the fourth century. *See generally* Eli Turkel, *The Nature and Limits of Rabbinic Authority*, 27:4 TRADITION 80, 82 (1993).

[17] For example, if the judges feel that they have mistakenly convicted a defendant, they may cancel the judgment and try him again. However, if they feel that they have mistakenly found a defendant not guilty, they may not try him again. MAIMONIDES, *supra* note 7, at 10:9. Similarly, after a guilty verdict is reached, messengers are sent out to announce the verdict and to encourage anyone with exculpatory evidence to go to court so that the court can reconsider its judgment. *Id.* at 13:1. *See also* MISHNAH, *Sanhedrin* 6:1.

once in seven years was called a "hanging court."[18] According to the view of Rabbi Elazar ben Azariah, mentioned in the same Mishnah, this sobriquet was used for a court that executes someone once in seventy years.[19]

Many people cite these rules in arguing that Jewish law opposes the death penalty.[20] Of course, to make this argument, one must respond to the fact that the Written Torah prescribes capital punishment for three dozen types of offenses. Those who are somewhat knowledgeable in Jewish law can argue that the Written Torah and the Oral Torah must be read together. Given that the Talmud elaborates on these various requirements, and these requirements make it relatively infeasible to execute someone, they can contend that Jewish law, as a practical matter, is opposed to capital punishment.[21] Nevertheless, as will be evident from our discussion, below, Jewish law tilts a bit more towards capital punishment, even from a practical perspective, than one might otherwise think.[22]

Many, but not all, of these same requirements were prerequisites for the other principal method of criminal punishment, namely, flogging. Thus, a criminal could not be flogged unless he received a warning that his conduct was illegal and punishable by flogging, he clearly acknowledged that he knew these facts but was still going to commit the act, and, in fact, almost immediately thereafter committed the act.

The question, of course, is how a society could survive if every criminal could escape conviction — even if all of the other multiple prerequisites are satisfied — simply by not responding to a warning with an express statement that he understands his action is criminal, that he knows the punishment is death (or flogging, as the case may be), and that he is nevertheless going to commit the act.

---

[18] MISHNAH, *Makkot* 1:10.

[19] *Id.*

[20] Interestingly, some of those who argue that Jewish law is opposed to capital punishment point to another part of this same Mishnah, which quotes Rabbi Tarfon and Rabbi Akiva as saying that if they had been on the relevant court, the court would never have found a defendant guilty in a capital punishment case. Yet they omit, or underemphasize, Rabban Shimon ben Gamliel's response, namely, that if they had prevented the court from rendering a guilty verdict, they would have increased the number of murderers within the Jewish community. In other words, Rabban Shimon ben Gamliel saw some value in at least the realistic threat of a death penalty.

[21] *See, e.g.*, Chad Baruch, *In the Name of the Father: A Critique of Reliance Upon Jewish Law to Support Capital Punishment in the United States*, 78 U. DET. L. REV. 41 (2000); Daniel A. Rudolph, *Note: The Misguided Reliance in American Jurisprudence on Jewish Law to Support the Moral Legitimacy of Capital Punishment*, 33 AM. CRIM. L. REV. 437 (1996).

[22] Perhaps ironically, some commentators who know enough about Jewish law to cite the Oral Law seem completely ignorant about the various alternative criminal law enforcement procedures and the significant use to which they were put. *See, e.g.*, Baruch, *supra* note 21 (failing to discuss such procedures); Rudolph, *supra* note 21 (substantially understating the significance of these procedures).

In addition, several other Jewish law provisions, in which Jewish law either permits or requires that wrongdoers be killed by extra-judicial action, are also of possible relevance to the debate. For example, the sixth Mishnah in the ninth chapter of Sanhedrin states, in part: "If a Kohen (a member of the priestly tribe) serves [in the Temple] while ritually impure, his brother Kohanim do not bring him to court; rather the young Kohanim remove him from the courtyard and split his skull with clubs." MAIMONIDES, *supra* note 7, at 18:6.

As Arnold Enker writes:

> To properly understand Jewish [biblical] criminal law as it applies to Jews, one must face two problems. First, the system is totally impractical. No one, or at best hardly anyone, could ever be convicted and punished under the system. The strict requirement of direct testimony by two competent witnesses can be satisfied in very few cases. But what criminal would ever "surrender himself" to conviction and punishment by responding to the warning in the required manner. Further, a criminal could literally "get away with murder" by contriving to carry out the killing in slightly less than direct manner. In short, this system is clearly inadequate to the practical needs of law enforcement and the day-to-day protection of society.[23]

The answer is that the society could only survive by virtue of the alternative criminal law enforcement systems, the extraordinary powers of the rabbinic courts and the power of the Jewish king, to which we now turn.[24]

§ 8.02   A RABBINIC COURT'S EXTRAORDINARY POWERS

There are two types of extraordinary rabbinic court powers. One type clothes the court with flexibility in dealing with an individual wrongdoer. The second authorizes the court to take special steps in a time of more general societal lawlessness or licentiousness.

[A]   As to an Individual Wrongdoer

As to the individual wrongdoer, there are two separate cases: a case in which he is deemed an incorrigible recidivist, and a case in which guilt is clear, but some procedural or evidentiary detail precludes a normal conviction. A Mishnah in Tractate Sanhedrin (Court) seems, at first blush, to deal with both of these types of cases:

> He who was twice flogged [for violating the same biblical proscription twice] and then repeats [the same sin], the rabbinical court confines him to a narrow cell, and feeds him barley bread until his stomach bursts [and he dies]. He who commits murder without witnesses is confined in a narrow cell and is fed bread of adversity and water of affliction.[25]

---

[23] Enker, *supra* note 1, at 1139.

[24] Enker states:

> The short answer . . . is that the religious courts had supplementary powers- sometimes called exigency powers — to deviate from the strict substantive, procedural and evidentiary rules and to substitute rational judgment based on the court's assessment of the society's practical law-enforcement needs. Conviction and punishment of a defendant could be inflicted as deemed warranted by the courts. Still another repository of such discretionary powers, also to be used to promote and protect the welfare of the community, was the king, representing the civil authority, who also could, and would, punish criminals free of these formal restraints.

Id. at 1141.

[25] MISHNAH, *Sanhedrin* 9:5. *See also* MAIMONIDES, *supra* note 7, at 18:5.

The Talmud explains that the offender is first fed barley bread, then water, and then barley bread until his stomach bursts.[26]

However, the scope of these two laws is very limited. For example, the first case only applies to persons who committed certain types of crimes punishable by flogging.[27] In addition, the law only applies if the person has committed the same crime three times, despite receiving and expressly responding to the required warnings and despite fulfillment of the other procedural requirements.[28] We have already remarked that it would seem unlikely for these requirements to have been fulfilled in any case; that they should be fulfilled multiple times with respect to the same offender is even more improbable.

With respect to the accused murderer, the Talmud explains that there must be a sound basis for believing him to be guilty. It says that the rule applies, for instance, when there are two witnesses but the witnesses could not see each other at the time they saw the crime.[29] Alternatively, Maimonides states that the procedure was used when some other technicality was not satisfied, such as when the offender received the requisite warning but only acknowledged it with a nod of his head, rather than with the full verbal response that is required.[30]

In addition, it is quite possible that these two laws are not "exceptional powers," but in fact, customary biblical powers prescribed not in the Written Torah but in the Oral Torah. Indeed, this is how the powers are described by most Jewish law authorities who discuss this Mishnah. They say that the powers are Halakhah LiMoshe MiSinai,[31] i.e., laws that were given to Moses at Mount Sinai. Consequently, writes Rabbi Joel Sirkes (1561–1640), when the biblical power to impose capital punishment ended, as a result of the Sanhedrin HaGadol no longer sitting in the designated place in the Temple, the power to impose the penalties specified in this Mishnah ended as well.[32]

---

[26] BABYLONIAN TALMUD, *Sanhedrin* 81b.

[27] *Id.*

[28] SHLOMO YITZHAKI, BABYLONIAN TALMUD, *Sanhedrin* 81b, *s.v. Aveirot Mahzikot* ("His sins establish a presumption.").

[29] BABYLONIAN TALMUD, *Sanhedrin* 81b.

[30] MAIMONIDES, *supra* note 7, at 18:5.

[31] *See generally* MENACHEM ELON, JEWISH LAW: HISTORY, SOURCES, PRINCIPLES vol. 1, at 204–07 (Bernard Auerbach and Melvin J. Sykes trans., 1994) (discussing various meanings of this term).

[32] JOEL SIRKES, BEIT HADASH, *Hoshen Mishpat* 425 (Heb.) (arguing that this authority lapsed when the authority to impose the forms of capital punishment described in the Written Torah lapsed). Although there are various ways in which the term *Halakhah LiMoshe MiSinai* is used, Sirkes' argument clearly links *these* particular exceptional powers with other *biblical* authority by stating that these powers lapsed when the other biblical authority lapsed. As discussed next in the text, the exceptional *rabbinic* authority to impose extraordinary punishment (i.e., punishment "not in accordance with biblical law") continues to exist.

[B] "When the Times Require It"

Rabbinical courts, however, also possess extraordinary authority to impose punishment not in accordance with biblical law when the times require it, and this authority continues to exist.[33] The Babylonian Talmud quotes a Baraitha which states:

> Rabbi Eliezer ben Yaakov says, "I heard [from my teachers] that a rabbinical court may inflict lashes and [capital] punishment not prescribed by the Torah, not [with the intention to] violate the Torah but to build a fence around it [to protect its laws]. During the period of the Greeks, a person rode a horse on the Sabbath, and they took him to court and stoned him. This was not done because [stoning] was prescribed for it [i.e., for such an offense], but because the times demanded it. There was another case in which a man cohabited with his wife under a fig tree [in a public area]. They took him to court and flogged him,[34] not because [flogging] was the prescribed punishment for it [i.e., for such conduct], but because the times demanded it."[35]

The Talmud cites additional cases in which rabbinic authorities either imposed punishments without following the requisite procedural rules or which simply are not otherwise authorized by the Torah.[36] For example, the Talmud describes a case in which Shimon ben Shetach hanged 80 executed Jewish women on one day,[37] even though Jewish law prescribes post-execution hanging only for men,[38] and, even as to men, permits only one person's corpse to be hanged on a single day.[39] In another case, a person who repeatedly hit people was deprived of one of his hands,[40] and, in another case, the Exilarch ruled that if a person was found to have been guilty of

---

[33] See generally Emanuel Quint & Neil Hecht, Jewish Jurisprudence 139–213 (1980).

[34] Some Talmudic commentators actually interpret this passage as stating that this person, too, was executed. See, e.g., Shlomo ben Shimon Duran (1400–1467), Responsa Rashbash no.10 (Heb.).

[35] See Babylonian Talmud, Sanhedrin 46a, Yevamot 90b. A similar version in the Jerusalem Talmud, however, indicates that the relevant violation was biblical rather than rabbinic.

[36] See Schreiber, supra note 15, at 401–402 (describing many cases).

[37] Babylonian Talmud, Sanhedrin 45b (quoting the Mishnah). Although the sages of the Mishnah identify various ways in which Shimon ben Shetach's action contradicted normal biblical law, it did not question the fact that he had the women hanged, even though hanging is not one of the four prescribed forms of capital punishment for Jews. See Haim H. Cohn, Capital Punishment, in The Principles of Jewish Law cols. 526–27 (Menachem Elon ed., 1975). Although hanging is prescribed in the Written Torah with respect to those who are executed, this prescription is only for the post-execution of the corpse. It would therefore seem that Shimon ben Shetach may have first had the women executed in the biblically prescribed manner. But see Jacob Ettlinger (1798–1871), Aruh Laner, Sanhedrin 45b (Heb.) (stating that the Jerusalem Talmud seems to say that Shimon ben Shetach had these women killed by hanging and not by the appropriate biblical form of execution).

[38] Maimonides, supra note 7, at 15:6. See also Babylonian Talmud, Sanhedrin 45b (quoting Mishnah).

[39] Jewish law only permits one person to be convicted of a capital offense on any given day. See Maimonides, supra note 7, at 14:10. Jewish law requires that a person convicted of a capital offense be executed on the same day as the conviction. If the executed person's corpse is to be hung, it is hung on the same day as the execution. Consequently, only one such corpse may be hung on the same day.

[40] Babylonian Talmud, Sanhedrin 58b.

murder, he was to be deprived of one of his eyes.[41] Yet the Torah does not seem to have provided for these types of corporal punishments.[42]

Post-Talmudic authorities provide plentiful evidence of continued reliance on such exceptional rabbinic powers long after the Sanhedrin HaGadol had ceased to exist and the authority to impose biblical forms of capital punishment had lapsed.[43] Rabbi Shlomo ben Adret (Rashba; 1235–1310), for instance, writes:

> It appears to me that if the witnesses are believed by the chosen judges, they (the judges) may impose monetary fines or corporal punishment as seems fit to them. This is in order to preserve the world (society). For should you establish everything according to the laws of the Torah, and act only in accordance with how the Torah punished, in cases of injury and similar cases, the result would be that world society would perish, for we would need witnesses and forewarning.[44]

All of the most authoritative codes of Jewish law assert that this special authority exists. In his work, the Sefer Arba'ah Turim, Yaakov ben Asher (1269–1343), writes:

> If the court sees that the need has arisen, inasmuch as crime is rampant among the people, it may impose the death penalty, monetary fines, or other punishments,° . . . and even if there is no absolute proof, which would have been necessary for a finding of guilt when criminal cases were decided under the strict law, but there is a rational basis for a finding [of guilt] and the facts are common knowledge, then if the judge concludes that the exigencies of the time demand that he so rule, he has such authority ° . . . . But in all matters he should act for the sake of Heaven, and he should not esteem human dignity lightly.[45]

This law is also cited by Rav Yosef Karo in his code, the Shulhan Arukh, perhaps the most authoritative Jewish law code. Known as the Code of Jewish law, the Shulhan Arukh sets forth the following principle:

---

[41] *Id.* at 27a.

[42] The legal doctrine known as *lex talionis*, apparently based on the biblical verses calling for "an eye for an eye." *Exodus* 21:24–25, might suggest that disfigurement is part of Jewish law. Nevertheless, based on the Oral Law, the Talmud explains that those verses are not to be interpreted literally. *See, e.g.*, BABYLONIAN TALMUD, *Sanhedrin* 99a. *See also* RABBI SHLOMO YITZHAKI, BABYLONIAN TALMUD, *Sanhedrin* 99a; Irene Merker Rosenberg & Yale L. Rosenberg, *Lone Star Liberal Musings on "Eye for Eye" and the Death Penalty*, 1998 UTAH L. REV. 505; Steven H. Resnicoff, *Jewish Law: Duties of the Intellect*, 1 U. ST. THOMAS L.J. 386, 387 (2003); Z. H. CHAJES, A STUDENT'S GUIDE THROUGH THE TALMUD 6 (Jacob Schachter trans., 3d ed. 2005). Although *Deuteronomy* 25:12 suggests that the hand of a particular wrongdoer should be amputated, the Talmud explains that a non-corporal punishment is intended. *Id.* at 6, 12. *See also* MAIMONIDES, *supra* note 5, at 18:6 (differentiating court's emergency powers from its ordinary powers).

[43] *See* SIMHA ASSAF, HA-ONSHIM AHAREI HATIMAT HATALMUD (*Punishment After the Redaction of the Talmud*) (1922) (Heb.); SCHREIBER, *supra* note 15, at 402–22.

[44] *See* YOSEF KARO (1488–1575), BEIT YOSEF, *Hoshen Mishpat* 2 (Heb.), *translated in* SCHREIBER, *supra* note 15, at 378.

[45] JACOB BEN ASHER, SEFER ARBA'AH TURIM, *Hoshen Mishpat* 2 (Heb.).

Every rabbinical court, even if they are not [Mosaically] ordained and [convening] in the Land of Israel,[46] if they see that the nation unashamedly transgressing the law, *and that the times so require*, may impose capital punishment, monetary punishment, and all forms of punishment, and even if there is not "complete" evidence.[47]

Citing even earlier authorities, the standard commentators to the Code of Jewish Law, such as Joshua Falk (1555–1614) and Shabbatai HaKohen (1621–62), make it clear that this power applies not only during periods of general lawlessness, but that it also enables the court to deal with individuals who are repeat offenders.[48]

The Code of Jewish Law states that these powers may only be used by the leading rabbinic authority [Gadol Hador] or a City's Lay Leaders, as appointed by the rabbinical court [over the city].[49] The Sefer Arba'ah Turim, however, had referred to the City's Lay Leaders as persons chosen by the community, and J. Falk argues that the Code of Law should be interpreted to mean the same thing, rather than as leaders selected by the rabbinical authorities.[50] Other authorities, even without citing the Sefer Arba'ah Turim, simply state that any lay leader chosen by the community possesses this authority.[51] Of course, in today's world, relatively few communities have selected such lay authorities and, even where such authorities are selected, the secular governments of their host countries do not allow them the autonomy to utilize this power.

§ 8.03 THE POWER OF A JEWISH KING

A Jewish monarch also possessed considerable law enforcement powers. Although there is controversy as to the precise scope of his authority,[52] Jewish law clearly accorded him great latitude as to the types of punishments he could mete out, including those involving physical force and humiliation, as well as to the procedural rules he could follow.[53]

The exceptional powers of court and king, as well as Jewish law's belief in the power of deterrence, are illustrated in Maimonides' description of the treatment of

---

[46] Rabbis who were Mosaically ordained possessed greater Jewish law authority than others. *See* Chapter 5, *supra*. Similarly, there were some rabbinic powers that could only be exercised within the land of Israel.

[47] SHULHAN ARUKH, *Hoshen Mishpat* 2:1.

[48] JOSHUA FALK, ME'EROT EINAYIM, *Hoshen Mishpat* 2:3; SHABBETAI HAKOHEN, SHAKH, *Hoshen Mishpat* 2:2.

[49] SHULHAN ARUKH, *Hoshen Mishpat* 2:1. Given that the city's lay government possesses this authority, one would reasonably assume that the reference to the "Gadol Hador" might be to the leading rabbinic authority in the city. This is especially true according to the view that the city's lay government is appointed by the city's rabbinic authorities. The *literal* translation of "Gadol Hador," however, is "the greatest [rabbi] of the generation."

[50] FALK, *supra* note 48, at 2:9.

[51] *See, e.g.*, HAKOHEN, *supra* note 48, at 2:10.

[52] *See, e.g.*, THE PRINCIPLES OF JEWISH LAW cols. 30-1(Menachem Elon ed., 1975); 1 THE JEWISH POLITICAL TRADITION 142–47 (Michael Walzer, Menachem Lorberbaum & Noam J. Zohar eds., 2000).

[53] *See, e.g.*, SCHREIBER, *supra* note 15, at 236–37. *See also* Enker, *supra* note 1, at n.23 (citing sources).

those who caused human deaths but, for technical reasons, were not subject to the Torah's death penalty:

> Regarding any of these or similar murderers who are not subject to being condemned to die by verdict of the court [because of some lack of evidence or because the murderer killed only indirectly], if a king of Israel wishes to put them to death by royal decree for the benefit of society, he has a right to do so. Similarly, if the court deems it proper to put them to death as an emergency measure, it has the authority to do so as it deems fit, provided that circumstances warrant such action.[54] If the king does not kill them, and the needs of the time do not demand their death as a preventive measure, it is nevertheless the duty of the court to flog them almost to the point of death, to imprison them in a fortress or a prison for many years, and to inflict severe punishment on them in order to frighten and terrify other wicked persons, lest such a case become a pitfall and a snare, enticing one to say, "I will arrange to kill my enemy in a roundabout way, as did So-and-So; then I will be acquitted."[55]

In any event, there is now no Jewish king. As a result, according to most authorities, this criminal law enforcement mechanism is also unavailable.[56] Some authorities, such as Rabbi Abraham Yitzhak HaKohen Kook, however, held that in the absence of a Jewish king, the powers of a king reside in the people and in any government that the people elect.[57]

---

[54] MAIMONIDES, MISHNEH TORAH, *Laws Concerning a Murderer and the Preservation of Life* 2:4 (Heb.).

[55] *Id.* at 2:5.

[56] Interestingly, some authorities contend that the king's power to maintain law and order is fundamental and extends to non-Jewish kings as well. See generally discussion, *supra* Ch. 6, on the doctrine of *dina demalkhuta dina.*

[57] *See* ELON, *supra* note 31, at 59 (citing and translating the view of Rabbi Kook).

Chapter 9

PERSPECTIVES ON THE UNFOLDING OF JEWISH LAW

§ 9.01   INTRODUCTION

It would be surprising if a course on Jewish law did not at some time and in some way include a discussion of the unfolding or evolution of Jewish law. This topic typically arises when discussing whether Jewish law could "accommodate" changed cultural, economic, or sociological circumstances or whether Jewish law could change to be more consistent with the desires of members of the Jewish community.

There are a variety of relevant views. Indeed, although the terms "unfolding" and "evolution" may sound similar to some, to others the two words may appear to be antonyms. This chapter will not survey the field; it will simply describe a few of the most prominent perspectives.

§ 9.02   THE "LITERALIST VIEW"

One position might be described as the "Literalist View." Relying on certain literal Talmudic and Midrashic statements, this approach regards the Sinaitic revelation as having exhaustively transmitted all Torah Law. The Sifra, a legal Midrash on Leviticus, states:

> *And the Lord spoke unto Moses at Mount Sinai* — What do the words *at Mount Sinai* come to teach us? Was not the entire Torah given at Sinai? Scripture wishes to teach us that just as all the rules of Sabbatical — its principles, details and minutia — were revealed at Sinai, so the rules of all

the Commandments — their principles, details and minutiae — were all given at Sinai. [Sifra on Leviticus 25:1][1]

Similarly, the Palestinian Talmud states: "Even that which a conscientious student will one day teach in the presence of his master was already revealed to Moses at Sinai."[2] Many traditional Jewish law scholars seem to have adopted this Literalist View.[3]

At least one Talmudic passage seems to contradict the Literal View:

> Rab Judah said in the name of Rab, When Moses ascended on high he found the Holy One, blessed be He, engaged in affixing coronets to the letters.[4] Said Moses, "Lord of the Universe, Who stays Thy hand?" [i.e., Does the Written Torah lack anything that would require You to add to it by affixing these coronets?] He answered, "There will arise a man, at the end of many generations, Akiba b. Joseph by name, who will expound upon each tittle heaps and heaps of laws." "Lord of the Universe," said Moses; "permit me to see him," He replied, "Turn thee round." Moses went and sat down behind eight rows [and listened to the discourses upon the law]. Not being able to follow their arguments he was ill at ease, but when they came to a certain subject and the disciples said to the master "Whence do you know it?" and the latter replied "It is a law given unto Moses at Sinai" he was comforted.[5] [Citations omitted.]

According to this passage, it would seem that there were teachings that Moses had not received.

Some supporters of the Literalist View have offered explanations why this passage does not disprove it. For instance, one argues that although God transmitted every Torah law to Moses, God did not show Moses how these laws could be derived from the Written Torah. Thus, although Moses knew the law that he heard Rabbi Akiba teach, he did not know the "proof" that Rabbi Akiva provided.[6]

Another clever solution points out that, in context, the Talmudic passage in which Moses observes Rabbi Akiba seems to be referring to the time just *before* God

---

[1] Aaron Kirschenbaum, *Subjectivity in Rabbinic Decision-Making, in* RABBINIC AUTHORITY AND PERSONAL AUTONOMY 64 (Moshe Sokol ed., 1992) (citing the *Sifra*).

[2] TALMUD YERUSHALMI, *Pe'ah* 2:4.

[3] *See, e.g.*, MAIMONIDES, MAIMONIDES' INTRODUCTION TO THE TALMUD 35 (Zvi Lampel trans., 1998) ("It should be understood that every mitzva [commandment] that the Holy-One-blessed-be-He gave to Moshe Rabbaynu [Moses Our Teacher], peace unto him, was given to him together with its Explanation."). Kirschenbaum, *supra* note 1, at 64, states that Maimonides, whom he describes as "a classic exponent of the conservative approach," took the Sifra "literally." *See generally* ABRAHAM HIRSCH RABINOWITZ, THE JEWISH MIND IN ITS HALACHIC TALMUDIC EXPRESSION 101 (1978) (citing Meir Leibush Malbim, author of HaTorah VeHamitzvah, as an adherent of this view).

[4] These are three additional strokes that are added at the top of certain letters as they appear in the Written Torah.

[5] SONCINO BABYLONIAN TALMUD, *Menachoth* 29b (I. Epstein, ed.), *available at* http://halakhah.com/pdf/kodoshim/Menachoth.pdf.

[6] *See* HAYYIM BEN MOSES IBN ATTAR (1696–1733), OHR HAHAYYIM, *Leviticus* 13:37. *See also* MEIR ZVI BERGMAN, GATEWAY TO THE TALMUD 19–20 (1989) (citing *Ohr HaHayyim*).

actually gave the Torah to Moses. This clearly explains not only Moses' unfamiliarity with the proof Rabbi Akiba articulated but even with the rule.[7]

§ 9.03 THE "A PRIORI VIEW"

A second approach rejects the notion that Moses was literally taught how each and every Torah law would apply in all future fact patterns.[8] Instead, this approach, which might be called the "A Priori View," posits that Moses learned the substantive and interpretative rules that, a priori, provided the answers to all questions of biblical law that would arise in the future.[9] Accordingly, the sages' rulings throughout history "reveal" what always has been Jewish law from the start. As Rabbi J. D. Bleich bluntly states, "Let it be stated unequivocally: *Jewish law does not change.*" (Emphasis in original.)[10] Rather, changed circumstances are simply a stimulus to look deeper into the Torah's teachings to ascertain what the relevant a priori law is:

> Even that which a conscientious student will one day teach in the presence of his master was already revealed to Moses at Sinai (Palestinian Talmud, Pe'ah 2:4). All of Halakhah is inherent in the original revelation at Mt. Sinai. Some portions of the Halakha were fully formulated; others remain latent, awaiting investigation and analysis. . . . It is a priori in the sense that it was always present in Torah; it is synthetic only in the sense that it requires a stimulus to prompt the investigation which serves to reveal that which had already been available to the human mind at any time in any age.[11]

§ 9.04 THE "AGENCY VIEW"

A third approach might be described as the "Agency View."[12] It denies that Moses was taught all of the minutiae of the law and that the sages' decisions throughout history accurately reflect God's "original intent." Instead, the Agency View is that God entrusted the Jewish sages with a Written Text and interpretative rules, and authorized them to issue binding rulings even if these rulings did not represent God's original intent. Kirschenbaum states that Nahmanides described this view when he wrote: "One must say, 'The Lord who enjoined the command-

---

[7] Unfortunately, I do not recall who offers this explanation.

[8] *See, e.g.*, NATHAN T. LOPES CARDOZO, THE INFINITE CHAIN: TORAH, MASORAH AND MAN (1989):

> One should not infer that Moshe was consciously aware of all the Torah insights that were to originate with future generations. Rather, he was a complete master of the fundamentals of the Torah, upon which all later deductions were based. . . . Nevertheless, later sages were confronted with new situations that had no clear halachic precedents. A steady stream of important halakhic questions begged for elucidation. The Torah therefore had to contain provisions for deriving *halachot* in any eventuality. These are the laws that Rambam writes were extracted by *sevarah* and *drash*.

[9] This view seems to be the first of the two perspectives that Kirschenbaum describes as the "Explicative Approach." *See* Kirschenbaum, *supra* note 1, at 64.

[10] J. David Bleich, *Halakhah as an Absolute*, 29:1 JUDAISM 30, 31 (1980).

[11] *Id.*

[12] This view is one of the two views that Kirschenbaum, *supra* note 1, at 64–65, labels as the "Explicative Approach."

ments commanded that I perform all His commandments in accordance with all that [the Sages] . . . teach me to do. He gave me the Torah as taught by them, *even if they were to err.'* "[13] (Emphasis added by Kirschenbaum.)

The Agency View is arguably consistent with the Talmudic passage involving Moses and Rabbi Akiba which was mentioned above as a possible problem to the Literal View. According to the Agency View, there is no reason why Moses would be expected to know the specific ruling issued by Rabbi Akiba in a particular case. The critical point is that Rabbi Akiba reached his conclusion by following the Oral Torah's rules. Similarly, the Agency View would fit well with other additional Talmudic passages that at least appear problematic for both the Literal View and the A Priori View. In one of these passages, Rabbi Abba, the son of Shmuel states:

> For three years there was a dispute between Bet Shammai and Bet Hillel, the former asserting, "The halakha is in agreement with our views," and the latter contending, "The halakha is in agreement with our views." Then a bat kol [i.e., a Heavenly Voice] issued announcing, "The utterances of both are the words of the living God [*Elu Va-Elu Divre Elokim Hayyim*], but the halakha is in agreement with the ruling of Bet Hillel."[14]

As already stated, the Agency View acknowledges that the conclusions of qualified rabbinic authorities, reached through the processes prescribed by the Oral Law, enjoy Jewish law "validity," even if the conclusions do not correspond with God's original intent. This arguably implies that scholars laboring in good faith could reach more than one conclusion. Each would enjoy true Jewish law "value." In fact, it is even consistent with the Agency View that the sages, in employing the interpretive rules provided by the Oral Torah, may perceive and characterize the operative facts in accordance with their respective — and unique — experiences and frames of reference, which could understandably result in different conclusions.

Of course, when contradictory views are reached by the various rabbinic leaders of a particular time and place, there needs to be some mechanism to reach a definitive ruling that could consistently govern people's conduct and transactions. The Torah rule is that the law must be determined according to the majority of the qualified Jewish law authorities.[15]

---

[13] *Id.* at 65, *citing* Nahmanides' Commentary to the Torah.

[14] BABYLONIAN TALMUD, *supra* note 5, *Eruvin* 13b. The bracketed words are inserted by me.

[15] The Talmudic passage states that Bet Hillel merited having the law determined according to it because they were kindly, modest and humble. *Id.* However, this may have explained why they were more numerous, because these traits may have attracted more students and produced more scholars. This Talmudic passage, in which a dispute among sages is ostensibly resolved by a Heavenly Voice, is often posed as an apparent contradiction to the principle that "the Torah is not in the Heavens," discussed in Chapter 8. A typical answer is that the doctrine of majority rule was well-established, and Bet Hillel constituted the majority. The sages of Bet Shammai, however, may have possessed more wisdom than those of Bet Hillel. Consequently, there was a fundamental issue as to whether it is the majority in number or the "majority" in intellect that prevails. The Heavenly Voice was therefore needed only to clarify this general principle. Nonetheless, this response must not be shared by all commentators, because a number of post-Talmudic authorities (ironically, apparently a minority of such authorities) actually held that the view of a minority of sages prevails over the view of the majority if the minority possess greater wisdom. *See* Shmuel Shilo, *Majority Rule, in* 13 ENCYCLOPEDIA JUDAICA 414 (Michael Berenbaum & Fred Skolnik eds., 2d ed. 1997).

However, how would the Literal View and the A Priori View explain this passage? These two approaches seem to maintain that only Bet Hillel or Bet Shammai, but not both, could be correct. If so, why does the Talmud say that the words of both are the words of the "Living God"?

One possible explanation interprets this Talmudic statement as referring not to the two rulings issued by Bet Hillel and Bet Shammai, but to the *process* of studying Jewish law in order to reach a legal conclusion. According to this explanation, the Talmud is not saying that the conclusions reached by each were "correct," but that the participants on both sides of the debate were meritorious because their respective "words," the arguments that they raised, were all instrumental in reaching fully reasoned Jewish law conclusions. In making this point, Rabbi Michael Rosensweig cites Rabbi Yaakov Lorberbaum (1760–1832), who states:

> [O]ne cannot successfully establish halakhic truth without some measure of initial failure. The early stages of halakhic analysis bear a similarity to a diver who is not yet capable of distinguishing worthless stones from the treasure he wishes to retrieve. More often than not, he surfaces with the former rather than the latter. However, once he has analyzed his error he emerges with an enhanced capacity to discern. The very process of failure increases his sensitivity to the nuances that distinguish precious jewels from stones, enhancing his future prospects for success. . . . As the Rabbis indicate — if he had not drawn worthless objects, we would not have discovered the valuable item which they camouflaged. For this entire process there is heavenly reward.[16]

§ 9.05 A HYBRID OF THE "A PRIORI" AND "AGENCY" VIEWS

A fourth view might be described as a hybrid of the A Priori View and the Agency View. As articulated by Rabbi Yom Tov ben Abraham of Seville, this view assumes that God communicated to Moses an exhaustive set of laws, but that these laws did not contain a single definitive answer for each fact pattern that could arise. Rather, the Torah provided ranges of "permissible outcomes" for every particular case, leaving it to the sages of each generation to determine, in light of the attendant circumstances, which option ought to be followed.[17]

§ 9.06 THE "ACCUMULATIVE APPROACH"

While discussing these views, Kirschenbaum introduces a fifth, which he labels the "Accumulative Approach." This approach, as he explains it, perceives the sages' role as much more creative.[18] Specifically, he argues that the Torah authorized the

---

[16] Michael Rosensweig, *Elu Va-Elu Divre Elokim Hayyim: Halakhic Pluralism and Theories of Controversy*, 26:3 TRADITION 4, 9 (1992) (citing and translating from the introduction to Lorberbaum's *Netivot HaMishpat*).

[17] *See* Jeffrey I. Roth, *Responding to Dissent in Jewish Law: Suppression Versus Self-Restraint*, RUTGERS L. REV. 40, 33 and n.6 (1987), cited by Kirschenbaum, *supra* note 1, at 66.

[18] *Id.* at 66.

sages in each generation to employ concepts of equity to "correct" miscarriages of justice that application of strict law would produce.[19] In this way, he argues, the sages accomplish "the 'true' intent of the law" by accommodating formal Scriptural rules to the circumstances of particular cases.[20]

To the extent that Kirschenbaum's examples can be explained as rabbinic invocations of their authority under *hefker beit din hefker* or under any other doctrine allowing rabbinical authorities to create non-biblical law, the proponents of the alternative views might agree that the equities of individual cases are relevant. If, however, Kirschenbaum intends to make the broader statement that the rabbis possess some other inherent power to "correct" supposed inequities that the application of biblical law would produce, Kirschenbaum's approach appears quite unconventional.[21]

§ 9.07 THE DEVELOPMENT OF NON-BIBLICAL LAW

None of these first five approaches is quite as absolute as it sounds. Each appears to recognize that the details of future non-biblical Jewish law, such as rabbinic decrees and communal customs, were not transmitted to Moses.[22] For example, this appears implicit in the words of Bleich, a staunch proponent of the A Priori View, when he dismisses the charge that institution of the rabbinic institution known as Prosbul represented a change in the law.

To understand Bleich's comments, one must first learn a little about the Jewish law of the Sabbatical Year. Biblical law provides that certain unsecured debts become uncollectible on the seventh year (the Sabbatical year) of a seven-year cycle. As the Sabbatical year approached, lenders became decreasingly willing to extend loans for fear that they would become uncollectible. Consequently, the Tanna, Hillel, instituted a device, known as Prosbul, to circumvent the scope of Sabbatical and, thus, to encourage lending. It is unnecessary to examine the details of this device.

In rejecting the charge that this represented a change in biblical law, Bleich points to, and comments upon, the two justifications the Talmud provides for rabbinic establishment of Prosbul. First, the Talmud suggests that Hillel could have instituted Prosbul pursuant to the Jewish law doctrine of *hefker beit din hefker*, which authorizes rabbinic authorities to dispossess people of their property when necessary for the public good.[23] Bleich states that the exercise of this doctrinal authority is "fully consistent with Halakhah."[24] Bleich in no way suggests that it was

---

[19] *Id.* at 73–74.

[20] *Id.* at 78.

[21] For a critical assessment of the Accumulative Approach, as described by Kirschenbaum, see Alan J. Yuter, *Review Essay: Rabbinic Authority and Personal Autonomy, ed. Moshe Z. Sokol*, 27:4 TRADITION 140, 141–44 (1993) and associated endnotes.

[22] *See* BABYLONIAN TALMUD, *Sabbath* 30a.

[23] *See* Chapter 10, *infra* (describing this doctrine). Bleich compares the doctrine to the secular law power of "eminent domain." *Id.*

[24] *Id.*

preordained that Hillel would choose to institute Prosbul when he did, if ever.[25] Second, the Talmud suggests that Prosbul was only instituted after, for technical reasons, the biblical law of Sabbatical was no longer applicable. Instead, the rules of Sabbatical only applied because of a rabbinic decree, and, Bleich argues, Jewish law authorizes the rabbis to create exceptions to their own rules.[26]

Indeed, it seems incontrovertible that, as to certain non-biblical law issues, rabbinic authorities have responded to sociological circumstances.[27] The next three chapters will focus on such developments.

---

[25] *Id.*

[26] *Id.*

[27] *See, e.g.*, Marc B. Shapiro, *Review Essay: Sociology and Halakha*, 27:1 TRADITION 75 (1992).

Chapter 10

THE DEVELOPMENT OF JEWISH LAW

§ 10.01   INTRODUCTION

Previous chapters have examined Jewish law's basic assumptions, its sources, its institutions and its categories of law. All of these, of course, play roles in the unfolding of Jewish law. This chapter focuses primarily on the role of human beings in the Jewish law process. Before doing so, however, it is important to discuss two biblical commandments which might be perceived as obstacles to this process, and it is to them that we now turn.

§ 10.02   PROHIBITIONS ON ADDING OR SUBTRACTING FROM THE TORAH

The Torah prohibits adding to, or subtracting from, any of the laws of the Torah: "Everything that I command you, that shall you be careful to do; you shall not add to it and you shall not detract from it."[1] At first blush, these prohibitions might appear to represent formidable obstacles for any corpus of law intended to regulate the actions of human beings in all countries, at all times, and under diverse economic, political and social systems and circumstances. Nevertheless, as we shall see in this chapter and the next, there have been many legal developments and

---

[1] *Deuteronomy* 13:1. This verses strictures are counted as separate commandments. *See* R. HALEVI, SEFER HAHINNUCH nos. 454–55.

changes in Jewish law. How is this possible in light of these two biblical prohibitions?

There are two principal explanations. One is offered, for example, by both Maimonides and Nahmanides. It is that the law permits certain changes provided that the changes are not characterized as *biblical*.[2] Another approach interprets the prohibitions as only applying to changes made with respect to the manner of performing affirmative biblical commandments.[3]

§ 10.03   ROLE OF HUMAN BEINGS IN THE JEWISH LAW PROCESS

The participation of people is a necessary and vital part of the Jewish law process. Consider just a few of the critical roles people play. Even if the Written Torah were a complete repository of biblical law, human Jewish law authorities would need to read and interpret the Written Torah in order to reconcile its apparent contradictions. However, the Written Torah is not complete. It is explained and supplemented by the Oral Torah, the transmission of which from generation to generation was entrusted to human agents. Moreover, even if a complete list of biblical legal principles were unambiguously provided in an immutable writing, human authorities would be required to apply the principles to a myriad of fact patterns involving a countless number of complex economic, social, psychological and technological variables.

As Joseph Albo, a medieval Jewish philosopher, explains:

> [T]he law of God can not be perfect so as to be adequate for all times, because the ever new details of human relations, their customs and their acts, are too numerous to be embraced in a book. Therefore Moses was given orally certain general principles, only briefly alluded to in the Torah, by means of which the wise men in every generation may work out the details as they appear.[4]

The Written Torah itself announces that although the Jewish law originated from God, "it is not in the heavens,"[5] i.e., it is to be interpreted and applied by human beings, not by heavenly signs. Even a "prophet" cannot advance legal rulings by basing them on prophecy. Instead, he must rely on halakhic analysis. Rabbi J. D. Bleich states, "[A] prophet who claims the ability to resolve disputed legal points by virtue of his prophetic power stands convicted by his own mouth of being a false prophet."[6] Indeed, as Maimonides wrote approximately 900 years earlier, "Altering the Oral Law in any way is equally as well a manifestation of false prophecy, even

---

[2] MOSHE BEN MAIMON (MAIMONIDES), MISHNEH TORAH, *Laws of Mamrim* 2:9; MOSHE BEN NAHMAN (NAHMANIDES), COMMENTARY TO TORAH, *Deuteronomy* 4:2.

[3] *See, e.g.*, RAAVAD, MISHNEH TORAH, *Laws of Mamrim* 2:9 (Heb.); AHARON HALEVI, SEFER HAHINNUKH, *Commandment* 554 (Heb.). *See* Appendix 1: Glossary, *infra*, entry 104, as to the controversy over authorship of *Sefer Hahinnukh*.

[4] JOSEPH ALBO, 3 SEFER HA-IKKARIM, BOOK OF PRINCIPLES 203 (Isaac Husik trans., 1946).

[5] *Deuteronomy* 30:12.

[6] *See* J. DAVID BLEICH, 1 CONTEMPORARY HALAKHIC PROBLEMS xiv (1977). *See also* MAIMONIDES, MAIMONIDES'

if the prophet is ostensibly supported by a literal interpretation of a verse, as opposed to its actual meaning."[7]

[A]   The Torah is "Not in Heaven"

Several famous Talmudic passages underscore the message that the Torah is no longer "in Heaven."[8] Of these, perhaps the episode most frequently cited is the debate between Rebbe Eliezer and the other sages as to whether a particular oven, referred to as the oven of Akhnai, was ritually clean:

> It has been taught: On that day R. Eliezer brought forward every imaginable argument, but they [i.e., the other sages] did not accept them. Said he to them: "If the halachah agrees with me, let this carob-tree prove it!" Thereupon the carob-tree was torn a hundred cubits out of its place — others affirm, four hundred cubits. "No proof can be brought from a carob-tree," they retorted.

> Again he said to them: "If the halachah agrees with me, let the stream of water prove it!" Whereupon the stream of water flowed backwards — "No proof can be brought from a stream of water," they rejoined.

> Again he urged: "If the halachah agrees with me, let the walls of the schoolhouse prove it," whereupon the walls inclined to fall. But R. Joshua rebuked them, saying: "When scholars are engaged in a halachic dispute, what have ye to interfere?" Hence they did not fall, in honour of R. Joshua, nor did they resume the upright, in honour of R. Eliezer; and they are still standing thus inclined.

> Again he said to them: "If the halachah agrees with me, let it be proved from Heaven!" Whereupon a Heavenly Voice cried out: "Why do ye dispute with R. Eliezer, seeing that in all matters the halachah agrees with him!" But R. Joshua arose and exclaimed: "It is not in heaven."[9] What did he mean by this? — Said R. Jeremiah: That the Torah had already been given at Mount Sinai; we pay no attention to a Heavenly Voice, because Thou hast long since written in the Torah at Mount Sinai, "After the majority must one incline."[10]

> R. Nathan met Elijah [the prophet] and asked him: What did the Holy One, Blessed be He, do in that hour? — He laughed [with joy], he replied, saying, "My sons have defeated Me, My sons have defeated Me."[11]

INTRODUCTION TO THE TALMUD 50 (Zvi Lampel trans., 1998); BABYLONIAN TALMUD, *Yebamot* 102a, *Avodah Zarah* 36a.

[7] MAIMONIDES, *supra* note 6, at 50.

[8] *Deuteronomy* 30:12.

[9] *Id.*

[10] *Exodus* 23:2.

[11] SONCINO BABYLONIAN TALMUD, *Bava Metzia* 59b (I. Epstein general ed.), *available at* http://halakhah.com/pdf/nezikin/Baba_Metzia.pdf. According to Jewish tradition, the prophet Elijah never died. Instead, he ascended to Heaven alive, but, from time to time, he would return to earth and have a brief encounter with one of the sages.

In the passage R. Jeremiah cites, a verse instructs us to follow the majority. The Oral Torah explains that this is the rule when either the Sanhedrin HaGadol convened or when all of the recognized sages convened to debate and vote upon the law.[12] Consequently, none of the miracles, not even the heavenly voice, offered by R. Eliezer were in any way probative.[13] Similarly, the Talmud reports that even if the Prophet Elijah were to come down from Heaven and declare that Jewish law as to a particular practice was really different from the way the people observed it, Elijah's words would not be followed.[14]

Elsewhere, the Talmud actually describes a supposed dispute between God and His Heavenly Court[15] about a particular Jewish law issue. The Talmud states that the ultimate ruling would be left to the Jewish sage, Rabba bar Nahmani, because he was the expert in this field.[16] Obviously, God did not need Rabba bar Nahmani's help in interpreting His Torah.[17] The message is that once the Torah was given to humankind, it was for human Torah authorities to interpret.

[B] "Safeguarding" the Oral Law by Putting Much of it in Writing

Having established that the Torah was placed in the hands of humankind and that human agents play an integral role in its development, it is appropriate to describe how, in fact, Torah law has unfolded. As discussed in Chapter 4 and Chapter 6, the Oral Torah, which was originally intended to be transmitted by word of mouth from teacher to pupil, has been substantially committed to writing, lest fierce Roman persecution of Jewish law scholars and teaching cause the Oral Torah to be lost. Maimonides explains:

> And why did Rabbaynu Hakadosh [i.e., Rebbe] do this [i.e., compile and publish the Mishnah], and not leave matters the way they had been up to then? Because he saw that the disciples were diminishing in number and leaving, that the persecutions were intensifying and multiplying, that the Roman Empire was extending its power over the globe and strengthening, and that Israel was continuously being dispersed throughout the extremities of the earth. He therefore compiled this one work to be in the possession of all, so that they could learn quickly and in a way that they

---

[12] *See* MOSES FEINSTEIN, DIBROT MOSHE, *Shabbat* 126–7 (Heb.).

[13] For a variety of non-literal and allegorical interpretations of this episode by Torah authorities over many centuries, see Itzhak Englard, *Majority Decision vs. Individual Truth: The Interpretations of the "Oven of Achnai" Aggadah*, 15:1 TRADITION 137 (1975).

[14] SONCINO BABYLONIAN TALMUD, *supra* note 11, at *Avodah Zarah* 36a, *Yebamot* 102a. *See also* MAIMONIDES, COMMENTARY TO THE MISHNAH, *Sanhedrin* 1:3 (stating that the Messiah may not alter Jewish law).

[15] The concept of a "Heavenly Court" (or "Celestial Retinue") is, of course, provocative, given that monotheism is an absolutely core Jewish belief. Surveying the various possible explanations would surpass the scope of this book. Probably the simplest way to understand this Aggadic passage is as an allegory. For a detailed discussion of this concept, see, for example, EPHRAIM E. UHRBACH, I THE SAGES: THEIR CONCEPTS AND BELIEFS 135–83 (Israel Abrahams trans., 1975).

[16] SONCINO BABYLONIAN TALMUD, *supra* note 11, at *Bava Metzia* 6a.

[17] *See* BLEICH, *supra* note 6.

would not forget. So he and his Bes Din [i.e., his rabbinic court] sat all their days teaching the Mishna publicly. (Footnote omitted.)[18]

The transformation to writing began with Tannaitic teachings, such as the Mishnah, Tosefta and legal Midrashim, and then continued to the Jerusalem and Babylonian Talmuds, as described in Chapter 6.

Early authorities agree that the Babylonian Talmud was deemed to have been "accepted" by all Jews. As Maimonides writes:

> Everything in the Babylonian Talmud is binding on all Israel. Every town and country must follow the customs, obey the decrees, and carry out the enactments of the Talmudic Sages, because the entire Jewish people accepted everything contained in the Talmud. The Sages who adopted the enactments and decrees, instituted the practices, rendered the decisions, and derived the laws, constituted all or most of the Sages of Israel. It is they who received the tradition of the fundamentals of the entire Torah in unbroken succession going back to Moses, our teacher.[19]

Indeed, based on this acceptance of the Babylonian Talmud, it is often said that later authorities may not issue rulings that contradict that Talmud. As Woolf writes:

> Similarly, according to Vilna Gaon, the restriction of argument to post-talmudic authorities is based upon the assumption that the authentic chain of the Oral Law ended with the "sealing" of the Talmud in the days of Rav Ashi and Ravina. . . . Subsequent generations are not allowed, therefore, to differ with statements in the Talmud.[20]

Nevertheless, teachings in the Babylonian Talmud were not always clear. Statements by Tannaim conflicted with each other, Amoraim often failed to agree, and the various Talmudic discussions of a single issue were sometimes ostensibly, or actually, incompatible. The Jerusalem Talmud sometimes provided solutions, but not often. For these reasons, and other reasons that will soon be discussed, Jewish law continued to rely on the efforts of human agents.

[C]   Human Autonomy As to the Interpretation and Creation of Jewish Law

Jewish law provided for important areas of intellectual creativity and innovation for rabbis possessing Mosaic ordination, for the Sanhedrin HaGadol and for Jewish kings. The fact that none of these legal "institutions" currently exist curtails the scope of Jewish law flexibility, but certainly does not quash it. Substantial flexibility continues to be afforded to laity, to communities and to rabbinic and lay leadership in interpreting, applying and creating the law.

---

[18] *See* MAIMONIDES, *supra* note 6, at 70. *See also* MEIR ZVI BERGMAN, GATEWAY TO THE TALMUD 45 (1989).

[19] *See* MENACHEM ELON, JEWISH LAW: HISTORY, SOURCES, PRINCIPLES, vol. 1, at 39 and vol. 3, at 1099 (Bernard Auerbach & Melvin J. Sykes trans., 1994). *See also* ARYEH KAPLAN (1934–83), THE HANDBOOK OF JEWISH THOUGHT 191 (1996); Berachyahu Lifshitz, *The Age of the Talmud, in* AN INTRODUCTION TO THE HISTORY AND SOURCES OF JEWISH LAW 179 (N.S. Hecht et al. eds., 1996).

[20] Jeffrey R. Woolf, *The Parameters of Precedent in Pesak Halakhah,* 27:4 TRADITION 41, 48, n.27 (1993).

We will first broadly survey the scope of autonomy historically and then focus more on contemporary times.

[1] Historical Autonomy in *Interpreting* the Law

Most lay people did not have a direct role in reaching decisions regarding existing Jewish law. People are required to follow the law correctly. If they are unable to discern the law themselves, they must go to those who can.[21] Communities, however, could indirectly influence the interpretation of Jewish law by their selection of rabbinic leaders. Rabbinic leaders have always possessed substantial flexibility, despite the generally accepted proposition that whenever the Babylonian Talmud reached a consensus as to a particular Torah or non-Torah law, that conclusion became normative law, not to be changed by later authorities.[22]

One reason such flexibility survived is that determining whether Talmudic authorities reached a consensus and, if so, what consensus was reached is no simple task.[23] The Talmud is a terse, reticulate, multi-volume work. Its debates are pitched at a sophisticated, conceptual level. Moreover, as much, or perhaps more, of the Talmud's meaning is inferred from what is *not* said as from what *is* said. The Amoraim are assumed to be both brilliant thinkers and masters of all Pentateuchal and Tannaitic materials. As a result, if it seems that three pieces of evidence could have been adduced to prove a particular proposition, but only two were actually proffered, commentators assume that there was a reason why the third was ignored.[24] Similarly, if four objections appear to have been possible but only one was raised, commentators assume that the other three ostensible arguments must be irrelevant. By identifying the unstated analytical or factual bases for each omission, commentators refine their understanding of the jurisprudential rule at issue.[25]

It is critical to identify the underlying purpose or function of a particular rule. This analytical process is referred to as "Lomdut." In most cases, the details would be too complex — involving numerous variables and requiring knowledge of multiple Jewish law doctrines — to provide an example in this type of book. But here is a simple illustration:[26] Jewish law prescribes three main prayer services per

---

[21] MISHNAH, *Pirkei Avot* 1:6 ("Joshua ben P'rahyah said: Provide yourself with a teacher."). *See* IRVING M. BUNIM, I ETHICS FROM SINAI 62 (1964), explaining that this means: "Commit yourself to his authority [i.e., the authority of the rabbi you have chosen for yourself] and abide by his decisions."

[22] *See, e.g.,* MAIMONIDES, 4A MISHNEH TORAH (Moses Hyamson ed. & trans., 1974); YEHUDAH LEVI, TORAH STUDY: A SURVEY OF CLASSICAL SOURCES ON TIMELY ISSUES 105, 319 n.14 (1990) (citing the views of additional authorities).

[23] There are, however, some general rules for determining whether the Talmud reached a consensus on a particular issue. *See generally* ZEVI HIRSCH CHAJES, 1 KOL KITVEI MAHARITZ, *Darkei Hora'ah* (1958) (Heb.); BERGMAN, *supra* note 18, at 92–98.

[24] *See generally* ABRAHAM HIRSCH RABINOWITZ, THE JEWISH MIND: A STUDY IN ITS HALACHIC EXPRESSION (1978).

[25] This particular aspect of Talmudic analysis is one of many reasons why neophytes are limited as to what they can accomplish. Those who lack experience and knowledge of the background literature are unaware of the various possible proofs or disproofs that are omitted.

[26] *See* J. David Bleich, *Lomdut and Pesak: Theoretical Analysis and Halakhic Decision-Making, in* THE CONCEPTUAL APPROACH TO JEWISH LEARNING (Yosef Blau ed., 2006) (explaining this example, providing other examples and providing a fuller description of Jewish law's analytical process). For discussions of

day, one in the evening, afternoon and morning.[27] The principal part of each service is a Silent Prayer.[28] If someone forgets to recite this prayer on one occasion, he has a chance to make up the missed prayer at the next prayer session. Thus, if one unintentionally fails to pray in the evening, then he can say the Silent Prayer twice in the morning. The first time counts as his morning prayer, and the second counts as the make-up.

The evening prayer recited every Saturday night after the conclusion of the Sabbath contains an extra paragraph acknowledging the end of the Sabbath and the beginning of the new week. Suppose someone unintentionally fails to recite this evening service and wants to make up for it on Sunday morning by reciting the Silent Prayer twice. Suppose also that the person not only failed to recite the Silent Prayer on Saturday night, but also failed to recite a special prayer (known as Havdallah) to mark the end of the Sabbath, and, therefore, still needs to include the extra paragraph acknowledging the end of the Sabbath in his Silent Prayer.[29] On Sunday morning, should this person recite the extra paragraph in his first recitation of the Silent Prayer (which is the recitation for Sunday morning) or should he include it in his second recitation (which is the make-up for Saturday night)?

The text of the Silent Prayer was established by ancient rabbinic authorities. The answer to our question seems to depend on the reason these rabbinic authorities prescribed the extra paragraph in the prayer for Saturday night. Some authorities rule that the extra paragraph has nothing essentially to do with an evening prayer, per se. Rather, the paragraph, which announces the end of the Sabbath, was to be included in the first prayer after the end of the Sabbath, which is supposed to be the Saturday night prayer. However, for a person who fails to pray on Saturday night, his first prayer on Sunday morning is his first prayer after the Sabbath. Consequently, these authorities conclude, the extra paragraph should be included in this person's first prayer on Sunday morning.[30] Although a very simple example, it provides at least a sense of what is involved.

Second, even if the Talmud contained a clear set of rules, it would not be easy to extrapolate correctly from those rules to novel contexts. As is obvious to secular

---

this analytical approach, see also, for example, David C. Flatto, *Tradition and Modernity in the House of Study: Reconsidering the Relationship Between the Conceptual and Critical Methods of Studying Talmud*, 43:4 TRADITION 1 (2010); Marc B. Shapiro, *Review Essay: The Brisker Method Reconsidered*, 31:3 TRADITION 78 (1997).

[27] In the Jewish week, a day is measured from evening to evening, rather than from morning to morning.

[28] This prayer is said while standing, and is referred to as the "Amidah," which, in Hebrew, means "standing." It is also referred to as the *Shemoneh Esrei* (Eighteen), because it originally comprised eighteen separate blessings. Although a nineteenth was later added, the name remained the same. (Remember: The "Big Ten" football conference was still commonly called the "Big Ten" even when there were more than ten teams.)

[29] If the person had recited this separate prayer acknowledging the end of the Sabbath, he would not recite the special paragraphs in either of the two Silent Prayers on Sunday. *See* YISROEL MEIR KAGAN, MISHNAH BERURAH, *Orah Hayyim* 294:2 (Heb.).

[30] Bleich, *supra* note 26, states that R. Moses Schreiber (a/k/a Moses Sofer or *Hatam Sofer*; 1762–1839) and R. Akiva Eger (1761–1837) so ruled, even though R. Kagan (a/k/a *Hafetz Hayyim*; 1838–1933) disagreed.

lawyers, laws are often intensely fact-sensitive. In order to identify which facts are germane, one must have a fairly comprehensive grasp of Jewish law.[31]

Even after the relevant facts are identified, the task remains daunting. Typically, there are at least ostensibly significant factual differences between the Talmudic paradigms and the cases which the Jewish law decisor confronts. The continuous stream of significant economic, geographical, political, sociological and technological changes and scientific discoveries almost ensures such differences. In such circumstances, the applicability of Talmudic rulings becomes increasingly ambiguous and uncertain.

Third, Jewish law accounts for the absence of the Sanhedrin HaGadol by providing flexibility. Once the Sanhedrin HaGadol had debated a matter and ruled upon it, no sage could issue a contrary ruling. In the absence of such a binding vote, an expert Jewish law authority who is certain of his opinion is not bound by the majority view of his contemporaries.[32] Given the absence of the Sanhedrin HaGadol, some argue that a consensus of the rabbinic leaders of the generation has the same effect as the vote of the Sanhedrin.[33] Yet, even if this were true, given the diverse factions and perspectives among the religious Jewish population, such a consensus is rarely, if ever, reached.[34] It follows that if an authority, through his own analytical Jewish law skills, cannot reach a position of certainty on an issue, he must regard more closely the views of other qualified authorities. If a Torah prohibition is at stake, the authority would have to rule strictly even if other authorities were evenly split.[35] On a matter involving a rabbinic prohibition, the authority would have to rule strictly only if a majority of the other authorities so ruled.[36]

In any event, throughout much of Jewish history, the absence of telecommunication systems — and of efficient, safe transportation — made timely conferral with out-of-town scholars a practical impossibility. Moreover, because questions often presented an unusual set of variables and circumstances, it was difficult to determine whether there were true "majority views" as to the questions which arose. In addition, the fact that a particular rabbi was the recognized authority in a particular locality historically clothed him with some additional stature and

---

[31] To emphasize the importance of "issue-spotting" in reaching Jewish law conclusions, David Bleich recounts an episode involving R. Soloveitchik, renowned for his use of Lomdut, and another rabbi who criticized Lomdut. To prove his point, R. Soloveitchik presented the other rabbi with a hypothetical question. He showed the rabbi that imprecision as to the facts led to one mistake after another. Although the example is too complex for those who are beginners in Jewish law, those who have some Jewish law background may find this episode both illuminating and humorous. *See id.* at 92–94.

[32] *See* FEINSTEIN, *supra* note 12, at 127; Woolf, *supra* note 20, at 44–5.

[33] *See* Woolf, *supra* note 20, at 46 n.3: "According to the Vilna Gaon, the authority of consensus approximates that of an enactment of the Sanhedrin which was adopted by all of Israel (*Bi'ur ha-Gra, Hoshen Mishpat* 25:7 citing *Babylonian Talmud, Avodah Zarah* 36a)."

[34] "[A]s noted by Rambam (Introduction to the Mishneh Torah *s.v.* u-devarim halalu and cf. Hil. Mamrim 2:5–7), in our time such absolute consensus is exceedingly rare and is, at most, only regionally valid." Woolf, *supra* note 20, at 46 n.3.

[35] *Id.*

[36] *Id.*

discretion.[37] Consequently, in many cases, local authorities possessed both the responsibility to render decisions and considerable flexibility with which to do so.

[2] Historical Flexibility in *Applying* the Law

As already mentioned, the application of many Jewish law rules depends on a variety of factual findings. Some of these "facts" are not easy to evaluate. For example, in some cases, Jewish law permits a person to perform an otherwise proscribed act if refraining from that act would cause the person "great loss."[38] The amount that constitutes a "great loss" is relative. In reaching a decision in a particular case, a rabbi needs to know quite a lot about the people who will be affected by the ruling, including their economic and emotional well-being, in order to gauge the practical consequences of a stringent ruling.

Similarly, a particular act, such as the involuntary administration of life-preserving medical care, may in some circumstances appear to be required by Jewish law.[39] Yet if a patient adamantly refuses the treatment, administering it could be counter-productive; it could actually impair the patient's health. If so, such treatment would be proscribed rather than prescribed.[40] To rule, a rabbi must, among other things, evaluate the psychological factors at play. Likewise, other medical procedures may be permissible only if necessary to save someone from particular levels of physical or emotional harm. In evaluating these cases, a rabbi needs to consider the opinions of medical experts as to their professional prognoses regarding likely medical or psychological consequences, not as to those experts' ethical opinions. Other decisions, such as whether it is permissible to trade land in Israel for certain concessions from neighboring countries or other groups, involve predictions as to the likely ramifications. Reaching conclusions in such cases often involves cultural, political, sociological or technological factors.

Some commentators believe that, in making these evaluations, individual rabbis may well be influenced, in subtle ways and to a limited extent, by some of the rabbi's own approaches, assessments and priorities.[41] As will be discussed later in this chapter, other commentators deny that such subjective factors play any role in the Jewish law process.

[3] Historical Flexibility in *Making* the Law

After the end of Mosaic ordination, the Sanhedrin HaGadol, the age of prophecy, and the institution of the Jewish king, there remained virtually no vehicle for the enactment of legislation for the Jewish people as a whole. Nevertheless, Jews lived

---

[37] *See, e.g.*, Aaron Kirschenbaum, *Mara De-Atra: A Brief Sketch*, 27:4 TRADITION 35 (1993).

[38] R. Isserles' gloss to the *Shulhan Arukh* contains countless examples of cases in which lenient approaches are adopted to avoid a "great loss." *See, e.g.*, SHULHAN ARUKH, *Yoreh Deah* 23, 31, 35, and 36 (Heb.).

[39] *See, e.g.*, Steven H. Resnicoff, *Jewish Perspectives on Assisted Suicide and Euthanasia*, 13 J.L. & RELIGION 289, 347–48 (1998–99).

[40] *Id.*

[41] Marc D. Angel, *A Study of the Halakhic Approaches of Two Modern Posekim*, 23:3 TRADITION 41 (1988).

in structured communities. In many lands, these communities were afforded official political and juridical autonomy. These communities had both lay and rabbinic leaderships; each was able to promulgate appropriate legislation, which had the force of binding religious law, covering a large variety of subjects, including commercial transactions, public education and taxes.[42] Even if the Talmudic rulings were unambiguous and even if their application to new fact patterns were obvious, there was autonomy in the enactment of such legislation. Individuals shared in this process indirectly by helping to select lay and rabbinic leaders and directly, on occasions when specific questions were put to a vote.

In addition, rabbinic leaders enjoyed autonomy to "create" law because a number of Jewish law doctrines specifically delegate to them considerable discretion. For example, as discussed in Chapter 8, Jewish law provides rabbis with exceptional criminal law enforcement authority when the times require it — either to prevent some pernicious impact on the community, to restrain an already lawless community, or to deal with a recidivist offender.[43] Rabbis exercise their own judgment as to whether the times require special action,[44] whether to take such action (because they are not required to do so),[45] and what specific action to take.[46]

The authority to adopt extraordinary measures was not limited to criminal affairs. Just as Jewish law prizes the value of human life, it prizes the value of preserving the Jewish nation and its link to God. Thus, if these are threatened, the leading Jewish law authorities of the generation are permitted, or even required, to order people to violate biblical law *temporarily*. Maimonides describes this authority:

> If they [the court] should deem it necessary temporarily to set aside a positive commandment or to nullify a negative commandment in order to restore the people to the faith or to save many Jews from becoming lax in other matters, they may act as the needs of the time dictate. Just as a physician amputates a hand or foot to save a life, so a court in appropriate circumstances may decree a temporary violation of some of the commandments to preserve all of them, in line with the approach of the early Sages who said: "One should violate . . . one sabbath in order to enable the observance of many sabbaths."[47]

The Talmud derives this authority from the Scriptural event in which the prophet Elijah challenged the priests of Baal to see whether their sacrificial offering or his would be accepted.[48] Elijah did this in order to "rescue" the many Jews who were

---

[42] *See* ELON, *supra* note 19, vol. 1, at 71–72, 77–85.

[43] *See, e.g.,* JOSHUA FALK, ME'EROT EINAYIM, *Hoshen Mishpat* 2:3; SHABBATAI HAKOHEN, SHAKH, *Hoshen Mishpat* 2:2.

[44] Jewish law provides no specific standard for the rabbis to apply.

[45] As set forth in the *Shulhan Arukh* by Rabbi Yosef Karo, the rabbis possess exceptional authority but need not choose to exercise it.

[46] For example, they must decide whether the deficient evidence that is available warrants action, and they must decide what particular punishment to impose.

[47] *See* MAIMONIDES, MISHNEH TORAH, *Laws of "Mamrim"* 2:4, *translated in* ELON, *supra* note 19, at 519.

[48] *See* BABYLONIAN TALMUD, *Yebamot* 90b.

being lured to the idolatry of serving Baal. Because, for a number of reasons, this "competition" could not be held in the Temple, Elijah offered the sacrifice on Mount Carmel. At that time period, Jewish law required that any such sacrifice be offered only in the Holy Temple. By offering the sacrifice on Mount Carmel instead, Elijah violated two biblical transgressions.[49] Most Jewish law authorities explain that Elijah's authority to temporarily suspend the two biblical prohibitions came not from his standing as a prophet, but from the fact that he was the leading rabbinic authority.[50] This is understood to be one of the situations in which the Scriptural statement, "It is a time to act for the Lord, for they have violated Your Torah," applies.[51] The Hebrew words permit the interpretation, "It is a time to act for the Lord, [therefore, to bring the people back to Him] violate your Torah." This type of temporary, emergency measure is referred to as a *hora'at sha'ah* (a ruling for the "hour").

In less extreme circumstances, rabbinic authorities could also instruct people to passively ignore a biblical commandment if doing so was necessary to prevent violation of a biblical proscription. This type of legislation is described as *lemigdar milta* (to safeguard the matter). For example, there is a biblical commandment to blow a shofar, a wind instrument made from a horn of certain animals, on Rosh Hashanah, the Jewish New Year. Nevertheless, there is also a biblical proscription against carrying any object, for even a very short distance, in a public area on the Sabbath. Because of concerns that people might come to carry a shofar in a public area on the Sabbath, the rabbis in the time of the Talmud instituted a decree forbidding the blowing of a shofar on any Rosh Hashanah which fell on a Sabbath.

Rabbinic authorities also possessed power to legislate and authority as to individual disputes regarding monetary matters. Pursuant to the doctrine, *hefker bet din hefker* (that which a rabbinic court declares to be ownerless becomes ownerless), rabbinic courts had the power, for the public good, to dispossess people of their property.[52]

---

[49] *See* SHLOMO YITZHAKI (a/k/a *Rashi*; 1040–1105), BABYLONIAN TALMUD, *Yebamot* 90b, s.v. *Kegon Eliyahu beHar HaCarmel.*

[50] *See* ELON, *supra* note 19, vol. 2, at 520 n.117.

[51] *Psalms* 119:1:26. Uhrbach explains:

Sometimes the breaking of the law is in effect its observance, as R. Johanan and Resh Laqish taught when they expounded the verse "It is time to work for the Lord, they have made void thy law" (Psalms cxiv 126), saying: "Rather let a letter of the Torah be uprooted than the Torah be forgotten in Israel."

UHRBACH, *supra* note 15, at 294. *See also* SONCINO BABYLONIAN TALMUD, *supra* note 11, at *Temurah* 14b (translating the statements by R Johanan and Resh Laquish).

[52] *See generally* Hermann Cohn, *Confiscation, Expropriation, Forfeiture, in* 5 ENCYCLOPEDIA JUDAICA 150, 150–51 (Michael Berenbaum and Fred Skolnik eds., 2d ed. 1997). *See also* BABYLONIAN TALMUD, *Gittin* 36b, *Yebamot* 89b. Sometimes the doctrine of *Hefker Bet Din Hefker* actually dramatically affected non-monetary law. For example, in one case, a man betrothed a girl who was a minor. When she became an adult, he was about to wed her when another man ran off with her and married her. Apparently the bride changed her mind and wanted to dissolve this marriage and went to R. Beruna and R. Hananel. *See* HANINA BEN-MENAHEM, JUDICIAL DEVIATION IN TALMUDIC LAW: GOVERNED BY MEN, NOT BY RULES 42 (1991). They declared the marriage to be invalid and ruled that she could remarry without even receiving an official writ of divorce. This ruling seemed to contradict the normative law that would require such a writ. In explaining the rabbis' action, Rav Ashi declared, "He [the man who ran off with her] had acted

The Talmud cites two alternative sources for this doctrine. Interestingly, although the Talmud does not usually derive legal principles from Scripture other than the Pentateuch, Rabbi Isaac points to an event discussed in the Book of Ezra. Ezra announced a proclamation commanding all of Jews of the exile to gather in Jerusalem, declaring that, "Whoever fails to appear within three days, in accordance with the counsel of the officials and the elders, all his property would be destroyed[53] and he will be separated from the congregation of the exile."[54]

Rabbi Eliezer, however, points to yet a different non-Pentateuchal verse: "These are the inheritances, which Eleazar the priest, and Joshua the son of Nun, and the heads of the fathers' houses of the tribes of the children of Israel, distributed for inheritance."[55] R. Eliezer focuses on the fact that the word "fathers'" seems unnecessary, and asks as to the connection between "heads" and "fathers." He says the message is that just as fathers may distribute their property to their children in whatever manner they wish, the heads of the community may also distribute the community's property as they wish.[56]

The hefker bet din hefker doctrine was not to be used lightly. Nevertheless, it served as an underlying explanation for a variety of forms of rabbinic discretion,[57] as well as for legislation prescribed by lay leadership or approved by direct vote of the people in a community.[58]

A variety of other legal and equitable doctrines afforded rabbinic authorities discretion in financial disputes. In one case, a person from out of town came to Rav Hisda, claimed to be a brother of Mari bar Isaac, and asked for a share of the estate of Mari bar Isaac's deceased father.[59] Mari denied that the person was his brother. Rav Hisda told the claimant to bring witnesses. The claimant replied that he had witnesses but they were afraid to testify against Mari, who was a powerful and violent person. Rav Hisda then turned to Mari and told him to bring witnesses that the claimant was not his brother. Mari asked, "Is this the law?" After all, the customary rule is that the burden of proof is on the claimant. Rav Hisda replied, "This is how I judge your case and all cases involving powerful people like you."[60]

Another case involved porters:

---

improperly, therefore they [Beth Din] treated him improperly and deprived him of the right to a valid betrothal." *See* BABYLONIAN TALMUD, *Yebamot* 110a. The question remains as to how, *technically*, these rabbis justified their ruling. One Talmudic explanation is that the marriage was effected by the groom's giving the bride a sum of money. The rabbis retroactively dispossessed the groom of ownership of the money, so that, retroactively, no marital bond was created.

[53] It is possible that, in this context, the word "destroyed" might have been used to mean "forfeited."

[54] *Ezra* 10:8. For an explanation of how this declaration by Ezra demonstrates the *hefker bet din hefker* doctrine, one should look to Talmudic commentaries.

[55] *Joshua* 19:5, *translated in* AARON SCHREIBER, JEWISH LAW AND DECISION-MAKING: A STUDY THROUGH TIME 216 (1979).

[56] BABYLONIAN TALMUD, *Yebamot* 89b.

[57] *See* Cohn, *supra* note 52, at 150.

[58] *Id.*

[59] BABYLONIAN TALMUD, *Bava Metzia* 39b.

[60] *Id.*

Some porters [negligently] broke a barrel of wine belonging to Rabbah son of R. Huna. Thereupon he seized their garments; so they went and complained to Rab. "Return them their garments,' he [Rab] ordered. "Is that the law?" he [Rabbah son of R. Huna] enquired. "Even so," he rejoined: "That thou mayest walk in the way of good men." Their garments having been returned, they observed, "We are poor men, have worked all day, and are in need: are we to get nothing?" "Go and pay them," he ordered. "Is that the law?" he asked. "Even so," was his reply: "and keep the path of the righteous."[61]

There are many more specific doctrines, but reviewing them in detail exceeds the scope of this book. One commentator who examines many of them provocatively suggests that Jewish law is more the rule of men than the rule of law.[62] In cases in which disputants authorize rabbinic courts to render decisions based on the principle of "pesharah" (i.e., compromise) rather than strict law, judges have still more leeway.[63]

Communities could also create law by the customs they adopt for ritual and non-ritual matters. Commercial customs, for instance, are regarded as part of any pertinent Jewish law contract, unless the parties expressly contract to the contrary.[64] In one special way, communities can also cause the abrogation of certain rabbinic legislation. Before a duly authorized rabbinic body issues a decree, it is supposed to evaluate whether a majority of the citizenry will be able to accept it. Only if it concludes that it will be so accepted, should the rabbinic body issue the decree.[65] Suppose that such a rabbinic body issues a decree on the erroneous belief that a majority of Jews will abide by it. According to some authorities, the legislation automatically becomes void, while according to others, the legislation must be formally repealed.[66]

Individuals may in many ways "create" the law pertaining to their commercial interactions because Jewish law allows them the flexibility to alter, by contract, many of the rules that would otherwise apply to them.[67] Individuals also possess the ability to create certain other types of "law" by virtue of voluntarily made oaths or vows. For example, it may be perfectly permissible for a person to refrain from a particular act. But if the person makes an oath to do it, the failure to perform the act becomes a violation of Torah law.[68] Similarly, it may be totally permissible for someone to eat a particular food. However, if the person takes a vow that the food

---

[61] Soncino Babylonian Talmud, *supra* note 11, at *Bava Metzia* 83a. The word that Epstein translates as "Even so," seems to be translated by others as "yes." *See, e.g.,* Ben-Menahem, *supra* note 52, at 75.

[62] Ben-Menahem includes this statement in the book's subtitle. *See* Ben-Menahem, *supra* note 52.

[63] *See generally* Tzvi Spitz, 3 Mishpatei HaTorah 113–15 (Heb.).

[64] *See* Steven H. Resnicoff, *Bankruptcy — A Viable Halachic Option?*, 24 J. Halacha & Contemp. Soc'y 5, 10–21 (1992); Elon, *supra* note 19, vol. 1, at 87–96.

[65] Maimonides, Mishneh Torah, *Laws of Mamrim* 2:5.

[66] *See* Kaplan, *supra* note 19, at 228. Maimonides, *supra* note 6, at 2:6 is one of the authorities that believes the decree is automatically invalid.

[67] *See* The Principles of Jewish Law cols. 251–52 (Menachem Elon ed., 1975).

[68] *See* Moshe Greenberg, Haim Cohn & Menachem Elon, *Oath, in* 15 Encyclopedia Judaica, *supra* note 52, at 358–64.

is forbidden to him, then his eating it would violate Torah law.

[4] How Modernity Affects Autonomy

One historical change in western countries during the modern period was the enfranchisement of Jews as voting citizens. As discussed in Chapter 7, the Jewish law doctrine of *dina demalkhuta dina* validates certain secular legislation as religiously binding law. To the extent that, as voters, individual Jews can influence the enactment of such legislation, they posses greater autonomy to create Jewish law indirectly.

More dramatic and pervasive changes, however, arise from transformations in the internal structure and demographics of the Jewish community. In the United States, at least, neither the federal government nor the various state governments imbue any Jewish organizations with official authority, whether legislative or juridical, over their Jewish citizens and residents. Nor have many American Jewish communities established quasi-legislative community institutions. Although some communities have rabbinic courts, secular law does not authorize such rabbinic courts to employ coercive powers to enforce Jewish law. Even if secular law permitted the use of such power, there is typically no official, fixed rabbinic court that enjoys authority under Jewish law to do so. In a large Jewish community, such as New York City, there may be many competing rabbinic courts, none of which was established by the community as a whole.

Within any metropolitan area, there may be numerous Jewish factions representing groups from diverse geographic origins, possessing discrete and dissimilar customs. For example, greater New York is home to many disparate groups of Sephardi and Ashkenazi Jews, Hasidic and Non-Hasidic Jews, Yeshivah-oriented and non-Yeshivah-oriented Jews, as well as Orthodox and non-Orthodox Jews. Indeed, each such faction may comprise various sub-groups, and the members of each sub-group may look to its own rabbinic authority or authorities for rulings. If a person affiliated with one Jewish sub-group falls out of favor with the other members of that sub-group, he can often switch to another sub-group or faction in the same city with relatively minimal adverse social consequences. Indeed, in many cities, it is quite possible for a religiously observant Jew to live a socially rewarding life without being an official member of any particular Jewish faction and without being linked to any particular Jewish law authorities.

Technology has also increased individual autonomy. A person may now live in one location but pose his or her religious questions to authorities who live on the other side of the world. Furthermore, mobility between cities, states and even nations is greater than ever before. Such freedom of movement increasingly insulates individual Jews from the informal sanction of social ostracism, and makes it easier for them to follow the rulings of far away authorities or to flout rabbinic rulings altogether.

As modernity has expanded the practical ability of Jewish individuals to choose which rabbinic authority to follow and which community to join, it has restricted the practical flexibility of rabbinic authorities.[69] First and foremost, in the United States, most cities have neither an official rabbinic authority nor an official Jewish lay governing council. Consequently, today's rabbis largely lack the Jewish law authority to enact binding legislation. As Eli Turkel explains:

> In modern times, no single organization is accepted as authoritative by all Torah observant Jews and, as a result, no group has the right to impose its views on individuals who do not voluntarily accept them. The late chief rabbi of Israel, Rabbi Yizhak Halevi Herzog, claimed that the court of the Chief Rabbinate of Israel was, in fact, such a central organization and that all Jews in Israel are required to follow its rulings. He stressed that this was based on the authority of the institution itself and was independent of the specific person who occupied the position of the chief rabbi. However, his ruling was not accepted by those groups who did not recognize the Halakhic validity of the Israeli government or any of its agencies. Similarly, Rabbi David Friedman of Karlin disputed the right of Rabbi Joshua Leib Diskin of Jerusalem to issue general bans on secular studies that affected other communities outside of his own. Hence, we conclude that a modern rabbi's authority is limited to his immediate community or to those people who ask his opinion. No rabbi has the right to impose his views on anyone else. [Citations omitted.][70]

In addition, historically, difficulties associated with travel and communication generally prevented rabbis in small towns from being second-guessed.[71] Modern technology, however, permits a rabbi's decision to be instantly broadcast to the entire world and subject to intense and immediate scrutiny and criticism. Indeed, it is almost guaranteed that a decision on any important matter will be criticized by somebody. The sting from such criticism can be painful, even if it comes from only a relatively small number of people and even if those people are not as qualified as the author of the ruling. All the more daunting is the danger of a sharp rebuke from a well-known authority from elsewhere in the United States or Israel. Consequently, by deterring authorities from making bold decisions, modern technology may have had a stifling effect on Jewish law's ongoing development.[72]

It is possible that this effect may be especially pronounced with respect to Jewish customs. Although the Talmud may have had the last word with respect to many

---

[69] Daniel Sperber, *Paralysis in Contemporary Halakha?*, 22:3 TRADITION 10 (2002).

[70] *See, e.g.*, Eli Turkel, *The Nature and Limits of Rabbinic Authority*, 27:4 TRADITION 83–84 (1993). *See also id.* at 86–87 (citing responsum of R. Moses Feinstein). Similar statements were issued in much earlier times as well. R. Issac ben Sheshet Perfet (*Rivash*; 1326–1408) wrote: "A rabbi is [entitled to make pronouncements binding] only for his students or his congregation; and certainly, [it is not possible] for one rabbi to make decrees or ordinances for a country other than his own.") *See* Alfred Cohen, *Da'at Torah*, 45 J. HALACHA & CONTEMP. SOC'Y 61, 74 (citing and translating Rivash). R. Joseph Colon Trobatto (*Maharik*; c. 1420–1480) expressed the same view. *Id.* at 73. Kirschenbaum suggests that technological innovations may *expand* the concept of a particular sage's "jurisdiction," although he makes no firm prediction. *See* Aaron Kirschenbaum, *Mara De-Atra: A Brief Sketch*, 27:4 TRADITION 35, 38–39 (1993). To my mind, the lack of a transparent or even remotely democratic process for the selection of a rabbinical authority makes this highly unlikely as well as unattractive.

[71] *See, e.g.*, Chaim I. Waxman, *Toward a Sociology of Psak*, 25:3 TRADITION 12, 22 (1991).

[72] Sperber, *supra* note 69.

Jewish law rulings, it is far from clear that it should prevent changes in some types of customs. Indeed, some customs mentioned in the Talmud have changed, including, for instance, many pertaining to the prayer service, including the communal recitation of Hallel.[73] A variety of Jewish law innovations will be briefly surveyed in Chapter 12.

Furthermore, it seems that many customs developed in response to "cultural circumstances" rather than abstract religious values. If so, where there has been substantial cultural change within a community, pressure may build up to alter those customs. Rabbinic authorities in an entirely different social milieu, where cultural circumstances have not so substantially changed or have changed in different ways, may not be sufficiently sensitive to the need for, or benefits of, change elsewhere.

In some respects, this may be characteristic of the differences between the Orthodox communities in the United States and in Israel. In the United States, increasing numbers of Orthodox men, including Yeshivah-trained men, enjoy extensive secular educations. Similarly, increasing numbers of Orthodox women, including those married to Yeshivah-trained men, are educated both secularly and religiously. Neither of these facts is characteristic of the Haredi Yeshivah communities in Israel. The socio-economic status of Americans who are actually part of, or who view themselves as part of, Yeshivah communities also differs importantly from that of members of the Israeli Haredi community. Furthermore, a large percentage of Orthodox Americans, including those who are Yeshivah-trained, are culturally "sophisticated" by extensive experience with non-Jews and non-Jewish institutions. By contrast, many members of the Israeli Haredi community are culturally sheltered. Yet, large segments of the Orthodox community in the United States, including modern Orthodox Jews, continue to look to prominent Israeli Haredi rabbis for Jewish law decisions — as well as for "social guidance."

Some segments of the United States Orthodox community do look to American rabbis for guidance. Hasidim defer to their Rebbe, the head of their respective Hasidic group. In addition, many Hareidi Orthodox Jews who have attended American rabbinic academies modeled after pre-World War II Lithuanian yeshivot, defer to their Roshei Yeshivot, the rabbis who head these academies for guidance as to Jewish law, or the official Jewish law decisors (*poskim*) at their Yeshivah. (For simplicity I will simply use the term Roshei Yeshivot to refer to all three of these groups, Rebbes, Roshei Yeshivot and poskim.) Even many who would follow the opinions of Israeli Gedolim on some matters will often ask many everyday questions to their Roshei Yeshivah. Even those who might pose some questions to certain Israeli authorities will ask many everyday questions to their American rabbis.

Some commentators contend that the increased role of Roshei Yeshivah in the process of rendering Jewish law decisions has lessened the role of local congregational or community rabbis. They argue that various factors bias the former toward stricter rulings.[74] For example, Roshei Yeshivot are surrounded by some of the most

---

[73] For a description regarding *Hallel*, see 8 Encyclopedia Judaica, *supra* note 52, at 279–80.

[74] *See, e.g.*, Lord Rabbi Immanuel Jakobovits, *Rabbis and Deans*, 7:4–8:1 (combined volume) Tradition 95 (Winter 1965–Spring 1966); Waxman, *supra* note 71, at 16–20.

religiously motivated young people who aspire to do more than that which is minimally required. Indeed, Roshei Yeshivot may believe that part of their function is to inspire such students to greater heights, and their rulings may be pitched to that purpose. By contrast, this argument continues, congregational or community rabbis need to respond to all segments of their communities, from the least religiously motivated members to the most motivated. Similarly, local rabbis may more often need to provide answers to Jews who face all types of challenges and hardships. Sometimes, especially when those facing hardships are the less religiously motivated, community rabbis may more extensively search for, and perhaps may sometimes find, grounds for more flexible rulings. Failing to find a legitimate leniency may result in "marginally" religious members leaving the fold completely, certainly a result to be avoided if possible. Lord Rabbi Immanuel Jakobovits, former Chief Rabbi of the United Kingdom, makes this argument somewhat provocatively:

> Moreover, judgments rendered in the isolation of *Yeshivot* can afford to be rigid if not dogmatic, in their reasoning. Rabbis, on the other hand, must endeavor to vindicate their decisions before public opinion. They must also take into account the ramifications and consequence of their rulings on relations and attitudes within the larger community. They must have their feet planted firmly on earth even if their heads reach to heaven in arriving at a verdict on problems posed to them.[75]

Some other commentators disagree with Jakobovits' sentiments.[76] One aspect of Jakobovits' argument, that the Roshei Yeshivot respond to questions of a narrow, student community, is partly blunted by the fact that vibrant local Orthodox communities have developed around some rabbinic academies. Such communities include not only current students but also working and professional Orthodox Jews who were never otherwise connected to these academies, and the Roshei Yeshivot are asked an entire gamut of questions.

In addition, some commentators have expressed concern over a "climate" that has allegedly developed among Roshei Yeshivot in the United States during and after World War II. This climate is markedly skewed towards strictures rather than leniencies, and any rabbis who might issue lenient decisions would face considerable criticism. It has even been alleged that, as to some areas of Jewish law, "a major Talmudic premise, *koach d'heter adif*, to uncover possibilities of permissiveness within the law demonstrates a higher power," has been eliminated.[77]

---

[75] Waxman, *supra* note 71, at 98. A few years later, Rabbi Oscar Fasman expressed similar sentiments, along with other criticisms of Roshei Yeshivah, in even more strident terms. *See* Oscar Z. Fasman, *Trends in the American Yeshiva Today*, 9:3 TRADITION 48, 53 (1967). Rabbi Emanuel Feldman strongly protested Fasman's article, arguing, among other things, that it was especially inappropriate for Fasman to criticize rabbinic leadership because the leadership had been unusually successful in bringing Jews back to Judaism. *See* Emanuel Feldman, *Trends in the American Yeshivot: A Rejoinder*, 9:4 TRADITION 56 (1968).

[76] Many of the Roshei Yeshivah would not, or at least, have not typically published in *Tradition*, a more modern/centrist Orthodox journal. Nevertheless, at least one objector responded to Jakobovits. *See* Marvin Schick, *Communications*, 8:4 TRADITION 121 (1966). Jakobovits briefly replied, *id.* at 125–26.

[77] *See, e.g.*, Fasman, *supra* note 75, at 51. *See also* Sperber, *supra* note 69; Waxman, *supra* note 71; Jakobovits, *supra* note 74, at 98; Mark B. Shapiro, *Review Essay: Sociology and Halakha*, 27:1 TRADITION

Interestingly, some commentators argue that Sephardi rabbinic leaders have responded proactively, and effectively, to sociological changes introduced by the Enlightenment. In a review of Rabbi Marc Angel's *Voices in Exile*, Henry Toledano writes:

> Another interesting aspect of the Sephardic response to modernity was the bold and forthright manner in which Sephardic poskim responded to modern problems. Angel discusses representative responsa of such Sephardic halakhic authorities as R. Eliyahu Hazan, R. Hayyim Yosef David Azulai (the Hida), R. Yaacov Moshe Toledano, and R. Benzion Uziel, and shows how they were able to apply traditional principles of halakha in a spirit of creativity and innovation, and provided halakhic insight with which to deal with many modern problems, including the vexing problem of the aguna.[78]

Similarly, Marc Shapiro, in a review of *The Uses of Tradition*, edited by Jack Wertheimer, writes:

> One point left unmentioned by [Harvey] Goldberg [in his essay on modernization and traditional responses in North Africa] is that, not having to face the threat of Reform, North African halakha was able to develop in different ways from what is found in Europe. This is particularly true with regard to Morocco. Here one finds many seemingly radical decisions by eminent figures (in particular R. Joseph Messas), such as are generally not found in Europe, at least not in the writings of mainstream *halakhists*. For example, not only did Moroccan rabbis generally have a lenient attitude towards conversion, but rulings were given that the *hazzan* [i.e., the person who leads the prayer service] need not repeat the shemoneh esreh, married women need not cover their hair, the law of *eruvei hatzerot* [a particular rabbinic requirement] is no longer applicable, non-Jewish milk is permissible, wine handled by a Muslim can be consumed, Jews can be buried in the same cemetery as Gentiles (with a separation of four cubits), and flowers may be placed on the coffin.

> Morocco is also the only modern Diaspora country in which the Bet Din was still a moving force behind *halakhic* development. *Takkanot* were issued on a wide range of issues, and unlike what occurred when the Chief Rabbinate of Israel issued *takkanot*, there was no right wing opposition. In general, the Ashkenazic trends of separatism and extremism found no echo in North Africa, or among Sephardim in general, and incidentally, this is one of the reasons why the Sephardic Chief Rabbis in Israel have not had to confront

---

75 (1992); Marc D. Angel, *Authority and Dissent: A Discussion of Boundaries*, 25:2 TRADITION 18 (1990); Francis Nataf, *Religious Censorship in the Information Age: Libertarian Implications of Contemporary Realia*, http://www.francisnataf.com/ideas-35.html (last visited Aug. 7, 2011). Marc Stern describes Roshei Yeshivot as "rabbis who themselves are hostile to, and have (nevertheless) little direct experience with, modern life." Marc D. Stern, *On Constructively Harnessing the Tensions Between Laity and Clergy, in* RABBINIC AND LAY COMMUNAL AUTHORITY 131, 131–32 (Suzanne Last Stone ed., 2006).

[78] *See, e.g.*, Henry Toledano, *Book Review*, 28:2 TRADITION 74, 77 (1994). *See also* Marc Angel, *A Study of the Halakhic Approach of Two Modern Posekim*, 23:3 TRADITION 41 (1988).

a significant right wing challenge to their legitimacy from within their own communities.[79]

There is one other, major issue regarding the role of individual autonomy and Jewish law. This involves the rabbinic doctrine know as *da'at Torah* (the "Torah View"). Chapter 11 is dedicated to this topic.

---

[79] Marc B. Shapiro, Book Review, 28:2 TRADITION 74, 80 (1994) (brackets added).

Chapter 11

PERSONAL AUTONOMY & *DA'AT TORAH*

SYNOPSIS

§ 11.01 PERSONAL AUTONOMY & THE BROAD COMMANDMENT TO "BE HOLY"

This chapter explores the very important, timely and controversial topic of the interaction between personal autonomy and the doctrine known as *"da'at Torah."* One way in which Jewish law provides for autonomous choice is by refraining from ruling on various matters. The number of relevant, detailed Torah law commands is quite limited. Yet God commands, "You shall be holy, for I, the Lord your God, am holy."[1] Rabbi Moses ben Nahman (a/k/a *Nahmanides*)[2] argues that a person could technically fulfill all of the Torah's particularized rules while still leading a morally repulsive life. He construes this commandment to be "holy" as requiring each person to exercise *responsible* discretion as to acts which are technically permitted. By doing so, the person will be "holy." It is not enough to observe only the specific Torah law provisions.[3] Indeed, we are told that one of the reasons why Jerusalem was destroyed was because people only acted in accordance with the letter of the law.[4] God wants us to "walk in his ways"[5] and those ways are the "doing of

---

[1] *Leviticus* 19:2.

[2] Moshe ben Nahman (1194 to 1256).

[3] As Rabbi Joseph B. Soloveitchik is reported to have said, "Halakha [i.e., Jewish law] is not a ceiling but a floor." *See* WALTER WURZBURGER, ETHICS OF RESPONSIBILITY: PLURALISTIC APPROACHES TO COVENANTAL ETHICS 32 (1994).

[4] BABYLONIAN TALMUD, *Bava Metzia* 30b.

[5] *Deuteronomy* 28:9.

righteousness and justice."[6] Similarly, God wants us "to do that which is right and good in the eyes of God."[7] Commenting on this verse, Nahmanides explains:

> First it [the Pentateuch] says that you shall keep the statutes and observances which He has commanded you. Then it states that even with respect to what has not been commanded, be mindful to the good and the right. This is an important matter, because it is impossible to mention in the Torah all forms of conduct of man with his neighbors, all his business affairs and the institutions of all civilizations. . . . After mentioning a good many of them, such as "thou shalt not slander," "thou shalt not take revenge nor bear a grudge," "thou shalt not curse the deaf," "thou shalt rise before the elderly," etc., then there is the general statement that "one should do the good and the right" in every matter.[8]

Of course, a question arises as to how someone is to discern the proper ways to act when they are not specified.[9] Although a full discussion of alternatives exceeds the scope of this book, one method is described by Walter Wurzburger (1920–2000), a rabbi and professor of philosophy at Yeshiva University.[10] He contends that Nahmanides' comments suggest an inductive approach.[11] By following the Torah's explicit laws and by studying the moral lessons it imparts,[12] a person develops moral sensitivities and intuitions that enable him to make proper ethical judgments as to cases to which no clear rule applies.[13]

Such individual autonomy applies to a broad range of activities, including many serious matters, including, in no particular order, one's choice of jobs, homes, communities, schools, synagogues, religious advisors, spouses, political parties, public interest projects, charitable contributions, social activities and the like.

§ 11.02 THE "TORAH WAY" (*DA'AT TORAH*)

A number of modern commentators argue that many members of the Orthodox rabbinate not only fail to provide helpful halakhic leniencies, but invoke an expansive version of the *da'at Torah* doctrine to curtail significantly the scope of an individual's personal autonomy. There are a variety of views and considerable

---

[6] *Genesis* 18:19.

[7] *Deuteronomy* 6:18.

[8] NAHMANIDES, COMMENTARY TO TORAH, *Deuteronomy* 6:18, translated in WURZBURGER, *supra* note 3, at 26–27.

[9] Sometimes various Tannaitic writings, including the Mishnah, Tosefta and Midrashim, provide guidance. Applying this guidance to the myriad of factual settings in which questions arise, however, is not always easy.

[10] Interestingly, Wurzburger writes, "Far from being disappointed that the formal Halakhah is silent on so many questions, I am glad that Halakhah makes space for the input of individuality and subjectivity on religiously significant issues." WURZBURGER, *supra* note 3, at 31.

[11] *Id.* at 37.

[12] Rabbi Tzvi Yehudah Berlin argues that one of the reasons why the Torah contains narratives about the Patriarchs is to provide models for our ethical choices. *Id.*

[13] *Id.* For a respectful, but critical review of parts of Wurzburger's analysis, see David Shatz, *Beyond Obedience: Walter Wurzburger's Ethics of Responsibility*, 30:2 TRADITION 74 (1996).

controversy concerning *da'at Torah*.[14] Sociologist M. Herbert Danzger, who is himself an Orthodox Jew, argues that one's perspective about the nature of rabbinic authority best differentiates between the more traditional Orthodox Jew and the more modern Orthodox Jew:

> [Earlier] . . . we noted that dress styles identify different subcommunities of Orthodox Jews, which hold different attitudes toward Israel, secular education, and relations between men and women. . . . Some observers . . . have argued that these differences derive from the fact that traditionalists are world-rejecting sectarians whereas modernists are world-accepting denominationalists. . . . We suggest, instead, that the critical feature distinguishing the modernist from the traditionalist is *the nature and scope of the authority to which each is committed.* Traditionalists allow their leaders authority in political and personal matters, and the leadership attempts to exercise authority beyond the specifics of halakhah. . . . Modernists, in contrast, seek maximum scope for personal decision making, and their leadership limits its authority to halakhah.[15] [Emphasis in original.]

[A]   The Expansive View of *Da'at Torah*

Rabbi Lawrence Kaplan, who criticizes the present form of the *da'at Torah* doctrine, points to statements by Rabbis Abraham Karelitz (*Hazon Ish*; 1878–1953), Eliyahu Dessler (1892–1953) and Bernard Weinberger, a contemporary rabbi, as representing the view of *da'at Torah* held by more traditional Orthodox Jews. It is a view that equates *da'at Torah* with the doctrine of *Emunat Hakhamim* (Faith in the Sages) and that calls on Jews to follow the guidance of the rabbinic authorities (Gedolim) in all areas of life, even those in which Jewish law seems to allow individuals discretion.

---

[14] For a variety of views, see generally, Binyomin Brown, *Doctrine of "Da'at Torah": Three Levels, in* JERUSALEM STUDIES: IN JEWISH THOUGHT vol. xix, at 537 (Yohayada Amir ed., 2005) (Heb.); Shalom Carmy, *"The Heart Pained by the Pain of the People": Rabbinic Leadership in Two Discussions by R. Joseph B. Soloveitchik,* 13 TORAH U-MADDA JOURNAL 1 (2005), *available at* http://www.yutorah.org/lectures/lecture.cfm/715601/Rabbi_Shalom_Carmy/01_'The_Heart_Pained_by_the_Pain_of_the_People':_Rabbi nic_Leadership_in_Two_Discussions_by_R_Joseph_B_Soloveitchik; Rabbi Alfred Cohen, *Daat Torah,* 45 J. HALACHA & CONTEMP. SOC'Y 67 (Spring 2003); Aaron Cohen, *The Parameters of Rabbinic Authority: A Study of Three Sources,* 27 TRADITION 4 (1993); Lawrence Kaplan, *Daas Torah: A Modern Conception of Rabbinic Authority, in* RABBINIC AUTHORITY AND PERSONAL AUTONOMY 1 (Moshe Sokol ed., Jason Aronson 1992); Jacob Katz, *Da'at Torah — The Unqualified Authority Claimed for Halachists,* 11 JEWISH HISTORY 41 (1992), *available at* http://www.law.harvard.edu/programs/Gruss/katz.html; Rabbi Berel Wein, *Daas Torah: An Ancient Definition of Authority and Responsibility in Jewish Life,* JEWISH OBSERVER 4 (Oct. 1994); Marc B. Shapiro, *The Uses of Tradition: Jewish Continuity in the Modern Era,* 28:2 TRADITION 78, 80–84 (1994). For an excellent review of Kaplan's article and of other articles on rabbinic authority and personal autonomy, see Alan J. Yuter, *Review Essay: Rabbinic Authority and Personal Autonomy,* 27:4 TRADITION 140 (Moshe Z. Sokol ed., 1993).

[15] M. HERBERT DANZGER, RETURNING TO TRADITION: THE CONTEMPORARY REVIVAL OF ORTHODOX JUDAISM 164 (1989). Steven Bayme makes the same point: "[D]a'at Torah has come to mean ex cathedra pronouncements of the rabbis, and the acceptance of rabbinic authority signals the critical divide between Ultra-Orthodox and Modern Orthodox Jews." *See* Steven Bayme, *New Conditions and Models of Authority: Changing Patterns Within Contemporary Orthodoxy, in* RABBINIC AND LAY COMMUNAL AUTHORITY (Suzanne Last Stone ed., 2006).

R. Karelitz writes:

> The viewpoint that divides the Torah in two: questions of *issur ve-hetter* [e.g., matters regarding what is prohibited and permitted, such as kosher laws, laws regarding what is permitted on the Sabbath, *etc.*] on the one hand and guidance in everyday life on the other; and that holds that for *issur ve-heter* one should subjugate oneself to the sages of one's time, while leaving other matters to one's own free choice — this is the viewpoint held by the heretics of old in Germany who drove their brethren to assimilate with the other nations. . . . [F]or one to distinguish between instruction regarding *issur ve-heter* and matters of legislation constitutes denigration of *talmidei hakhamim* and places one in the category of those who have no portion in the world to come.[16]

Similarly, Rabbi Dessler states:

> Our rabbis have told us to listen to the words of the Sages, even if they tell us that right is left, and not to say, heaven forbid, that they certainly erred because (one as inadequate as) little me can see their error with my own eyes. Rather, my seeing is null and void compared with the clarity of intellect and the divine aid they receive. . . . This is the Torah view [da'at Torah] concerning faith in the Sages [emunat hakhamim]. The absence of self-negation toward our Rabbis is the root of all sin and the beginning of all destruction, while all merits are as night compared to the root of all — faith in the Sages.[17]

R. Weinberger refers to this divine aid as a form of divine inspiration:

> Gedolei Yisroel [i.e., great rabbinic leaders of Israel] possess a special endowment or capacity to penetrate objective reality, recognize the facts as they really are and apply the pertinent halakhic principles. This endowment is a form of ruah ha-kodesh [divine inspiration], as it were, bordering, if only remotely, on the periphery of prophecy.[18]

One might distinguish the statements by Rabbis Karelitz and Dessler, two extremely distinguished rabbinical authorities from an earlier generation, from those of Rabbi Weinberger or other contemporary rabbis who express views similar to his. The former focus primarily on the superior insight[19] and intellect of Torah leaders and the need, whether practical and/or divinely commanded, for the Jewish people to abide by rabbinic legislation. At least as quoted, these views are not logically inconsistent with the possibility that in any particular case, a particular piece of rabbinic legislation might in fact be misguided. Nevertheless, it is still possible that those who espouse these views may deny that we can evaluate whether

---

[16] Kaplan, *supra* note 14, at 15–16 (1996).

[17] *Id.* at 16–17.

[18] *Id.* at 17.

[19] Indeed, just as Wurzburger argues that each individual Jew develops an intuition for the Divine Will by virtue of the person's immersion in the Torah and its teachings, one might argue that great Torah scholars, whose immersion is all the more complete, acquire a commensurately keener Torah intuition.

a particular rabbinic decision was correct even after witnessing the ensuing consequences.

The latter approach, asserting that the rabbinic leaders enjoy "a form of ruah ha-kodesh [i.e., "Divine spirit"], as it were, bordering, if only remotely, on the periphery of prophecy," claims, or appears to claim, that all such legislation is necessarily appropriate. Accordingly, in the early days of Hitler, the advice given to many Eastern European Jews to remain in Europe when they might otherwise have safely fled must be deemed necessarily correct. Of course, it is possible that the advice was "correct." We do not know what horrors might have ensued from different advice. In addition, the advice may have been "correct" in the sense that it was the advice that God, through this "form of ruah ha-kodesh," wanted to be given. This book is not the place to debate such philosophical issues. The point, however, is that this absolutist approach to da'at Torah seemingly contends that the advice *must* have been right.

[B]   Problems with the Absolutist View of *Da'at Torah*

However, the absolutist approach is problematic, first, because Jewish history is replete with major controversies between and among the most renowned rabbinic authorities.[20] These disagreements focused not only on strictly halakhic questions, but also on broader matters regarding the proper approach to Jewish studies and worship. Some of the major controversies in the last few centuries have included conflicts involving the rise of the Hasidic and Mussar movements.[21]

A second problem with the absolutist approach is that the Torah itself acknowledges that even the most erudite and revered sages are not infallible. Indeed, the Torah provides precise laws as to the types of animal sacrifices that must be brought when various leaders of the Jewish nation, including the Great Council (the Sanhedrin Hagadol), an institution composed of the foremost Jewish law scholars, err. The Talmud elaborates on these laws, especially in the tractate entitled "Rulings" (*Horayot*). Similarly, the Talmud discusses cases in which rabbinic authorities or courts err, explaining when the rabbis might bear financial liability to the litigants who suffered injury from such decisions. In fact, in analyzing the scope of such liability, a number of authorities emphasize that an individual cannot blindly rely on a rabbi's decisions. Consider, for example, the words of Zerahiah ben Yitzhak Halevi Gerondi (*Ba'al HaMaor*; 1125–1186):

> If you were to ask: We hold [the prevailing view] that cases of *garmi* (damages resulting from direct and predictable cause) are liable for court adjudication. Why then do we say that when a judge errs in something stated explicitly in a Mishnah, he simply reverses his ruling but is not responsible for any losses, even if the damage incurred by the litigant due to his error is irrevocable? [For example,] the case of the cow of Bet

---

[20] MOSHE CARMILLY-WEINBERGER, CENSORSHIP AND FREEDOM OF EXPRESSION IN JEWISH HISTORY (1977).

[21] For a description of early opposition to the Mussar Movement, see IMMANUEL ETKES, RABBI ISRAEL SALANTER AND THE MUSSAR MOVEMENT 194–99 (1993). For an even more explosive, far-ranging and extended controversy over the Hasidic movement, see, e.g., H.H. BEN-SASSON, A HISTORY OF THE JEWISH PEOPLE 768–76 (1976).

Menahem whose meat can not be returned because R. Tarfon [the judge] had already [caused it to be] fed to the dogs [by those who followed his ruling].

The answer is: The litigant was negligent. Since the error is in that which is stated explicitly in a Mishnah, the error is obvious, and the litigant should not have relied upon him and should not have acted upon what he was told. He should have questioned [the judge] and demonstrated the error, for this was as obvious as an explicit Mishnah. Therefore it is the litigant who was negligent; the judge's ruling is superfluous. This is what is meant by: It is as if the judge never issued the ruling; he did nothing at all [to the litigant.][22]

One or both of these approaches might accept some limitations on the breadth of their application. For example, these statements refer to the "Gedolim" of each generation, and this group may not be synonymous with the membership of any particular rabbinic organization or council. Second, to the extent that the comments refer to rabbinic "legislation," they may be subject to the restrictions that have historically applied to rabbinic legislation. These include, for instance, the rule that even well-respected rabbinic authorities could typically legislate only within their respective geographic jurisdictions. Similarly, legislation that a majority of the community could not abide was invalid. Furthermore, there may be some limits as to how deeply or extensively rabbinic "legislation" traditionally applied to everyday matters.

[C] Competing Views of *Da'at Torah*

In any event, there are a variety of other views that regard *da'at Torah* differently. Some contend that the expansive version of *da'at Torah* is not a *legal or halakhic* doctrine at all.[23] Instead, they interpret *emunat hakhamim* (and *da'at Torah*, to the extent it is said to be a synonym) as a deep respect for the sages' intellect, insights and spiritual motives, a respect that impels a person to assiduously study the sages' words and be enlightened by them.[24]

[1] Suggested Limitations on *Da'at Torah*

Some of those holding this view argue that it is unprecedented for rabbinic authorities to attempt to restrict everyday actions as comprehensively as is attempted today. They question whether, or assert that, this supposed new version of *da'at Torah* is employed as a political strategy to preserve the cultural practices of pre-World War II East European Jews rather than to promote or protect the practice of Jewish law.[25]

---

[22] Nachum Eliezer Rabinovitch, *What Is "Emunat Hakhamim"?*, 5 HAKIRAH 35, 38–39 (2007) (citing and providing translation).

[23] *See, e.g.*, Katz, *supra* note 14.

[24] Rabinovitch, *supra* note 22, at 45.

[25] *See, e.g., id.*; Katz, *supra* note 14.

[2]   Who Has the Authority to Declare *Da'at Torah*

Some question the authority of a rabbi who issues rulings over communities other than that in which he lives or other than that which has selected him as a rabbinic authority.[26] The significance of this objection is most compelling when the community in which the Gadol lives differs economically, educationally and experientially from that of the person raising the objection. The decree, even if appropriate for the rabbi's community, may be deleterious to the objector's community, with which the rabbi is relatively unacquainted.

In some specific cases, a question may arise as to whether a particular person really was, or was as of a particular point in time, qualified to be regarded as a "great rabbinic authority."[27] In the past, some widely acclaimed rabbinical leaders have suffered physical or other challenges that may have put their subsequent status in question. For example, Rabbi Menachem Mendel Schneerson (1902–1994), the Seventh Rebbe of the Chabad-Lubavitch movement, suffered a serious stroke in 1992 which left him unable to speak and paralyzed on the right side of his body. It is reported that he continued to answer queries by nodding his head or by making hand movements. Nevertheless, those outside his immediate circle had no meaningful opportunity to ascertain whether Rabbi Schneerson was still able to process complex questions or, assuming he could, whether his physical motions were being properly construed by those sending out "answers" to those queries.

[3]   The *Process* by Which *Da'at Torah* is Determined

A number of commentators question the process by which a person recognized as a Gadol reaches a decision as to *da'at Torah*. Many contend that the information presented to the Gadol is filtered, slanted, or even misrepresented and that decisions reached in such a manner need not be followed.[28] A number of factors adversely affect the communication process. For example, the Gadol may only speak Yiddish, and the person with the question may not. Even if the person with the question does speak Yiddish, he or she may not be allowed direct access to the Gadol, whose schedule is more than busy and whose strength may be limited. In addition, because of the lack of direct access, the questioner cannot be sure that the person who ultimately did convey the question did so accurately. Because Jewish law questions, as all legal questions, are often complex and fact-sensitive, even an *apparently* minor miscommunication can be critically important. Furthermore, even if upon receiving an answer the questioner suspects that the question may not

---

[26] *See, e.g.*, Eli Turkel, *The Nature and Limits of Rabbinic Authority*, 27:4 TRADITION 83–84 (1993).

[27] *See* Chapter 4 for a discussion of the process by which rabbis are identified as "Gedolim."

[28] *See, e.g.*, Oscar Z. Fasman, *Trends in the American Yeshiva Today*, 9:3 TRADITION 48, 56 (1967). There have been occasional specific reports that some assistants have misleadingly relayed questions directed to the sages. *See* http://www.zootorah.com/controversy/gedolim.html (posting a letter to R. Slifkin) (last visited Aug. 4, 2011); Emes Ve-Emunah, *Manipulating a Godol*, http://haemtza.blogspot.com/search?q=Manipulating+a+Gadol (last visited Aug. 4, 2011); Shaya Goldmeier, Emes Ve-Emunah, *Comment on "Manipulating a Godol,"* http://www.haloscan.com/comments/hmaryles/6233571016777353622/ (last visited Aug. 4, 2011) (reporting a story heard from Chicago Rabbi Zev Cohen in which a sage's executive assistant allegedly attempted to manipulate the sage by altering the question that was put to him).

have been understood, it is rare that the questioner will be given a chance to have the answer clarified.

Sometimes misinformation may even cause a rabbinic authority to issue an opinion that is completely unfounded. In one well-publicized case involving the banning of a planned music concert, one prominent American rabbi acknowledged that he had signed the ban because he had been misled as to the position of other major rabbis and not because he had made an independent decision that a ban was appropriate.[29]

[D] Possible "New Wrinkles" Regarding *Da'at Torah*

Others argue that the broadened use of *da'at Torah* is not a twentieth century phenomenon, but one that began much earlier.[30] For example, book-banning *within* the Jewish community, an activity justified in recent years by references to da'at Torah, certainly has a long and troubling history. However, there are arguably new wrinkles on this issue.

In the United States, at least, there is a large religious Jewish laity that is not only intellectually sophisticated but *relatively* well-educated about Jewish law.[31] For better or worse, it is a laity that is familiar with democratic practices[32] and the right to participate in decision making. Some members of this laity allege personal knowledge of instances in which rabbinic authorities impaired communal interests by relying on their own judgment without adequate consultation with those with more specialized knowledge or experience.[33] Indeed, some of the laity seem to regard unrestrained invocation of da'at Torah as a matter of personal affront. This sense of indignation appears evident in the words of Marc Stern:

> The depth and breadth of religious studies had surely improved over time. My sons and their friends know far more than my peers and I did at a comparable age. The overwhelming majority of today's students spend at

---

[29] An article in the Jewish Star reported:

Rabbi Kamenetsky . . . said that he had understood that he request for the ban originally came "from rabbis in Erez Yisroel [i.e., Israel]. We didn't want to differ with them. It was expressed that certain performers . . . upset some people." The Rosh Yeshiva [i.e., Kamenetsky] was asked whether anybody had confirmed the origin of the request. "It seems that it was a request from mouth to ear and everyone went along with them," he responded. "What they said was that it was a request from Rav Elyashiv and Rav Steinman. I didn't confirm that." Asked if it is unusual for distinguished rabbonim to sign a kol korei [i.e., a public statement against a particular action, such as attending the Big Event], Rabbi Kamenetzky was candid: "Usually we meet together. This time, with time pressing, we did not get together. And maybe it was not the right thing." The concert was supposed to have been a benefit for Simchat Tzion, a group that makes weddings for orphaned brides and grooms in Israel.

The article can be found at Blog in DM, http://blogindm.blogspot.com/2008_02_01_archive.html (last visited Nov. 1, 2008).

[30] Katz, *supra* note 14; Marc B. Shapiro, *Review Essay: Sociology and Halakha*, 27:1 Tradition 75 (1992).

[31] *See* Marc D. Stern, *On Constructively Harnessing the Tensions Between Laity and Clergy, in* Rabbinic and Lay Communal Authority 142 (Suzanne Last Stone ed., 2006).

[32] Whether it is better or worse is an interesting subject for another time.

[33] *See* Stern, *supra* note 31, at 153–54.

least a year in Israel devoted exclusively to Torah studies — a phenomenon
that is now two generations old. (Of course, for many, formal Torah
education does not stop even there.) The broad dispersion of knowledge
means that no longer is the rabbi the only person in town with a serious and
sustained exposure to Talmudic text and codes. Some of the lay people will
themselves have rabbinic ordination. People so educated cannot be dictated
to and will not be swayed by a bare assertion of authority. It is inevitable
— and a good thing — that lay people so educated will from time to time
challenge their rabbi's judgment or his interpretation of a text or application of a code or decision. Often, lay people will be wrong. But not always.
And it is always a mistake to infantalize educated people.[34]

Some may well argue that Stern overstates the extent of the laity's Jewish
education. The quality of Jewish law education that one derives from a year or two
of post-high school study in Israel varies substantially from person to person. Even
those for whom the experience is most successful do not acquire a command of
Jewish law that can be compared to that of those who devoted themselves to Jewish
law for many years. However, a substantial percentage of the laity is qualified to
appreciate, and certainly wants the chance to evaluate, clear halakhic analyses
rather than unexplained edicts. Even more people are qualified to appreciate, and
evaluate, proposed courses of action regarding pragmatic communal decisions.

The clash between differing perspectives as to *da'at Torah* is undoubtedly an
issue of major concern both within the Jewish community at large and within
competing perspectives on the role of autonomy in Jewish law.

---

[34] *Id.* at 143.

Chapter 12

ILLUSTRATIVE EXAMPLES OF JEWISH LAW INNOVATIONS

§ 12.01 INTRODUCTION: MOST JEWISH LAWS ARE NON-BIBLICAL

Most Jewish laws that affect a Jew's everyday life are not biblical. For example, although there *may* be a biblical obligation to engage in some prayer every day, the obligation to pray three times — morning, afternoon and evening — is rabbinic.[1] In addition, the basic structure of prayer services and the texts of the prayers are not biblically prescribed, but were rabbinically formulated.[2] Even after these early formulations, diverse customs continued to develop, so that liturgical differences exist not only based on the particular country in which one is located, or in which one's ancestors were raised, but also between the prayers of Ashkenazic and Sephardic Jews, Hasidic and non-Hasidic Jews, Orthodox and Centrist Jews and so on.

Similarly, most of the blessings or rituals with respect to eating are rabbinic. For example, the obligation to recite a blessing before eating or drinking any food is rabbinic, as is the obligation to wash one's hands prior to partaking of any meal at which bread is eaten.

---

[1] *Compare* MAIMONIDES, BOOK OF COMMANDMENTS, *Affirmative Commandment* 5 (stating that there is a basic biblical commandment to pray) *to* NAHMANIDES, COMMENTARY TO BOOK OF COMMANDMENTS, *Affirmative Commandment* 5 (arguing that there is no biblical commandment to pray daily but that there is a biblical obligation to pray in response to a crisis).

[2] *See, e.g., Ezra* 2:65; I *Chronicles* 16.

Many of the most common dietary laws are also non-biblical. Although it is biblically forbidden to eat meat and dairy products that have been cooked together, "meat," for purposes of this biblical rule, does not include fowl. Nevertheless, rabbinical authorities decreed that fowl must be treated as if it were "meat," lest people err as to real meat. Similarly, it is biblically permitted to eat meat and cheese together so long they were not cooked together. However, this is non-biblically forbidden. Indeed, a custom developed not to eat cold dairy products and meat products at the same meal. A further custom developed that, after eating meat, a person would not eat a dairy product until the normal amount of time between meals had elapsed. In many Jewish communities, this was a six-hour period. Another custom developed so that two people could not eat at the same table if one ate meat products and the other dairy products and the relationship between the people was such that they might come to share their food with each other. Within Jewish jurisprudence, customs attain the status of *law*. Consequently, these rabbinic rules and these customs are set forth in Jewish law codes, such as the Rabbi Yosef Karo's Shulhan Arukh, as *legal obligations*.

Jewish law regulates intimate relations between man and wife. For example, biblical law precludes conjugal relations with a woman who is menstruating — and even thereafter until certain ritual requirements are fulfilled. Non-biblical rules and customs, however, have importantly increased the number of days during which such relations are forbidden. In addition, during the period in which conjugal relations are proscribed, many other types of interactions between husband and wife, including many activities involving no physical contact, are rabbinically forbidden, lest they lead to physical interaction.[3]

As mentioned in Chapter 10, countless Jewish law innovations have developed in response to evolving economic, political and social circumstances including, of course, anti-Jewish persecution. Although it is impossible to review all of these changes, examining a relatively small number should be illustrative.[4] We will first examine some of the innovations that occurred prior to the closing of the Babylonian Talmud, which took place circa 500 C.E. Then we will move on to post-Talmudic developments.

§ 12.02   INNOVATIONS PRIOR TO THE CLOSING OF THE BABYLONIAN TALMUD

Even prior to the closing of the Babylonian Talmud, there had been substantial development in various areas of Jewish law.

---

[3] *See generally* BINYOMIN FORST, THE LAWS OF NIDDAH: A COMPREHENSIVE EXPOSITION OF THEIR UNDERLYING CONCEPTS AND APPLICATIONS (2002).

[4] *See, e.g.*, MENACHEM ELON, 2 JEWISH LAW: HISTORY, SOURCES, PRINCIPLES 545–879 (Bernard Auerbach & Melvin J. Sykes, trans., 1994) (extensively examining rabbinic rules and decrees).

[A] Marketplace Regulation

As a matter of biblical law, a purchaser of personal property obtains ownership of the property as soon as he pays the purchase price.[5] Nevertheless, the rabbis thought that this could lead to problems. For example, assume Buyer pays for a large quantity of goods that fill Seller's warehouse. Under biblical law, the goods immediately become Buyer's. If a fire breaks out in the warehouse, Seller, who would no longer be responsible for the goods, would have relatively little incentive to exhaust its energies and resources in attempting to extinguish the fire, and Buyer would suffer a loss.[6] Consequently, the rabbis decreed that Buyer does not obtain ownership of such property until Buyer does a physical act with them, called a *kinyan*.[7] Typically, this would occur at the time Buyer takes possession of the property.

One of the most important rabbinic innovations regarding commerce is known as *takkanat hashuk* (a decree regarding the marketplace) and pertains to the sale of stolen personal property. Secular law principally takes two alternative approaches to the rights of a purchaser of such property. In the United States, a person who purchases stolen property does not receive good title.[8] Therefore, if there is no statute of limitations or latches problem, the true owner may recover the property from the purchaser without paying any compensation. The only way for the purchaser to recover the purchase price it paid would be to sue the person from whom it bought the property.

By contrast, in common law countries, including most European nations, a good faith purchaser without knowledge or notice that property was stolen acquires good title to the property.[9] Therefore, the original owner is unable to recover the property. Purchasers who do not buy in good faith or who buy with knowledge or notice that the property was stolen do not acquire title and, as to them, the result is the same as in the United States.

Under biblical law, whether a purchaser acquires good title importantly depends on whether the original owner despaired of ever recovering the property. If a

---

[5] *See* Babylonian Talmud, *Bava Metzia* 47a. *See generally* Shalom Albeck, *Acquisition, in* 1 Encyclopaedia Judaica 361 (Michael Berenbaum & Fred Skolnik eds., 2d ed. 1997).

[6] This is the explanation provided by the Talmud. It is also true that, under the biblical rule, a deceitful Seller could possibly "stage" a fire, making it appear as if the property, which Seller has hidden elsewhere, burned in the fire. The rabbinic rule would make such conduct unprofitable for a wrongdoing seller.

[7] *See* Albeck, *supra* note 5.

[8] *See, e.g.,* Autocephalous Greek-Orthodox Church of Cyprus v. Goldberg and Feldman Fine Arts, Inc., 917 F.2d 278 (7th Cir. 1990) (applying Indiana law); Northern Insurance Company of New York v. 1996 Searay Model 370DA Yacht, 453 F. Supp. 2d 905 (D.S.C. 2006) (applying Florida law); Schrier v. Home Indem. Co., 273 A.2d 248, 250 (D.C. 1971) ("[A] possessor of stolen goods, no matter how innocently acquired, can never convey good title."); O'Keeffe v. Snyder, 416 A.2d 862, 867 (N.J. 1980); Basset v. Spofford, 45 N.Y. 387, 391 (1871).

[9] "Though the possessory rights of bona fide purchasers are never recognized under the property law of the United States, the laws of continental Europe, in contrast, strongly protect innocent purchasers and allow them to acquire legitimate title to the stolen goods." Monique Lee, *A Choice of Law Dilemma: The Conflict and Reconciliation of Laws Governing Cross-Border Transfers of Stolen Art,* 7 Cardozo Pub. L. Pol'y & Ethics J. 719, 721 (2009).

person buys the property after such despair (*yeush*), the person acquires good title.[10] Whether an owner has despaired is determined in a particular case either by evidence regarding the owner's actions or statements or by operation of law. With respect to some types of property, there may be legal presumptions against a finding of despair.[11] Consequently, in cases in which there was no despair, the owner could recover the property from the purchaser without providing any compensation. This result might have been satisfactory in a small, closely-knit community or even in larger communities with relatively few purveyors of personal property. In such settings, purchasers knew and trusted the few merchants with whom they dealt. But as conditions changed, profitable opportunities for purchasing goods from non-local merchants increased, particularly at large regional fairs. The Talmud explains that the rabbis recognized the economic benefits of a robust economy. They feared that the biblical law, and the attendant possibility that a consumer would lose both the purchase price and the property purchased, would deter people from buying goods. They therefore promulgated a decree, takkanat hashuk, providing that owners of stolen personal property could only recover the property from a good faith buyer after yeush by reimbursing the buyer the purchase price the buyer had paid.[12]

The rabbis also affected monetary rights by action intended to increase the availability of credit to the poor. When the Jewish people dwelt in Israel, biblical law provided for the years to be counted, and every seventh year was a Sabbatical year. At the end of the Sabbatical year, many forms of unsecured debt were canceled. The Torah was concerned that, as a Sabbatical year approached, creditors might be reluctant to lend money for fear they would not be repaid. The Torah specifically enjoined creditors from such conduct.[13] Nevertheless, the rabbis saw that credit in fact dried up as the Sabbatical year neared, creating a cruel hardship for the poor. Hillel instituted a mechanism, known as *Prosbul*, which was designed to circumvent the effect of the Sabbatical year in order to encourage lending.[14] It is not important for our purposes to examine the details of this procedure. What is important is to note that, according to one Talmudic view at least, *Prosbul* circumvented a significant, biblically based rule.[15]

Other rabbinical laws were designed to protect the public against price gouging. Thus, the rabbis prohibited the hoarding of essential goods to prevent excessive

---

[10] According to some authorities, yeush must occur before the purchase. According to others, the purchaser acquires title even if yeush occurs after the purchase was made. *See* Shulhan Arukh, *Hoshen Mishpat* 356:2. *See also* Steven H. Resnicoff, *Theft of Art During World War II: Its Legal and Ethical Consequences*, X 10 DePaul-LCA J. Art & Ent. L. 67 (Fall 1999); J. David Bleich, 3 Contemporary Halakhic Problems 352, n.9 (1989).

[11] *See generally* Bleich, *supra* note 10, at 352–56; Simcha Krauss, *The Sotheby's Case — A Halachic Perspective*, 9 J. Halacha & Contemp. Soc'y 5, 10–13 (1985).

[12] Shulhan Arukh, *Hoshen Mishpat* 356:7; Yehiel Michel Epstein, Arukh ha-Shulhan, *Hoshen Mishpat* 368:4.

[13] *Deuteronomy* 15:9. *See also* Mishnah, *Shavuot* 9:3; Aaron Rothkoff, *Prosbul*, *in* 12 Encyclopaedia Judaica 586–87, *supra* note 5.

[14] *See* Mishnah, *Gittin* 4:3.

[15] *See* Babylonian Talmud, *Gittin* 36a (explaining how the rabbis possessed the power to circumvent the biblical law).

prices.[16] Similarly, the rabbis tried to limit the prices of essential goods by controlling the number of middlemen between the producer and the ultimate consumer. In some cases, rabbinic law required that sales be made directly to the consumer. In other cases, the rabbis limited the number of times such products could be resold.[17]

[B] Developments Designed to Promote Societal Peace

Some property rights were rabbinically altered in order to promote societal peace. For example, under biblical law, a minor lacked the legal capacity to acquire ownership of personal property that he or she might find. Thus, if a minor found such property, an adult could acquire ownership simply by taking the property from the minor. The rabbis felt that such conduct, however, would lead to strife between such an adult and the minor's family. The rabbis therefore decreed that taking such property from a minor would constitute stealing.[18]

Similarly, under biblical law, if a person puts out an animal trap in the public domain and an animal becomes trapped in it, the animal does not automatically become the property of the trapper. Instead, anyone who sees the animal in the trap can legally take it. Believing that such conduct could lead to conflict between the person taking the trapped animals and the trapper, the rabbis decreed that taking such trapped animals constitutes stealing.[19]

In addition, to minimize the possibility of quarrels between people, the rabbis decreed that in a public area a person can acquire any ownerless property within a four cubit radius of him or her without performing any of the biblical forms of acquisition. Without this rule, the rabbis were concerned that, as one person reached out to the property, another person might see and snatch the item up first, leading the two people to quarrel.[20]

The rabbis also enacted a decree affecting property rights for the purpose of making it easier for a thief to repent. Under biblical law, a person who stole personal property was obligated to return the stolen property itself. It was not sufficient to pay the value of the property. Thus, if a person stole a wooden beam and then used the beam to construct a building, the biblical law would require the person to return the beam, even if doing so meant that he or she would have to deconstruct part or all of the building. The rabbis were concerned that the harshness of this rule might discourage a person from repenting of his crime. Therefore, they promulgated *takkanot hashavim* (a decree for the repenting), which provided that, in such situations, a thief was only obligated to reimburse the

---

[16] Nahum Rakover, Ethics in the Market Place: A Jewish Perspective 39 (2000). This restriction, however, did not apply to goods produced by the person himself or herself, but only as to goods purchased from elsewhere. *Id.* at 40. *See also* Maimonides, Mishneh Torah, *Laws of Sales* 14:5; Shulhan Arukh, *supra* note 12, at 231:24.

[17] Rakover, *supra* note 16, at 71–74.

[18] Babylonian Talmud, *Gittin* 59a–59b.

[19] Eliezer Berkovits, Not in Heaven 38–39 (2010).

[20] *Id.* at 37. Babylonian Talmud, *Bava Metzia* 10a.

owner for the value of the property that was stolen. This enactment was to promote peace between the thief and God.

[C] Family Law Innovations

Some of the most important changes occurred in the context of family law. Consider, first, the relations between husband and wife. Under biblical law, a husband completely controlled family dissolution issues. He could divorce his wife for any reason, or without any reason, and without her consent. By contrast, a wife had no right to force her husband to grant a divorce. In fact, a writ of divorce from her husband was only effective if it was given "voluntarily." Meanwhile, the husband had very few financial obligations during the marriage and perhaps none thereafter. Furthermore, there were various ways, some of which we will describe, whereby a husband could cause his wife serious problems. By the time the Babylonian Talmud was closed, many of these issues were substantially ameliorated.

For example, under biblical law, a man could divorce his wife even if she were mentally incompetent. The rabbis feared what might become of such a woman, especially if she had no other relative to take care of her. Consequently, they ruled that a man could not divorce a mentally incompetent wife.[21]

In addition, the rabbis decreed that in certain scenarios, a wife had the legal right to have her husband grant a divorce. One such situation was where a husband refused to perform his conjugal duties.[22] Furthermore, where a wife was legally entitled to a divorce but her husband refused to cooperate, the rabbinic court would coerce him to do so, even resorting, if necessary, to physical force. If, as a result of such coercion, the husband would orally declare that he authorizes or "wants" the court to prepare and deliver the writ of divorce, the rabbinical court would do so. At first blush, at least, this procedure seems problematic given the biblical requirement that the husband grant the divorce "voluntarily." The rabbinic response, however, was to treat the husband's oral statement as adequate evidence of voluntariness, at least if the husband was still a member of the Jewish community.[23] Maimonides explains that we assume that such a person, in his heart of hearts, really desires to fulfill his Jewish law obligations. It is only that the "evil inclination," whether spite or some other evil sentiment, is overcoming that desire. The physical afflictions, in turn, neutralize the evil inclination and allow the person's sincere sentiments to be expressed. If, however, the husband rejected Judaism and had become attached to a non-Jewish community, this rationale could not be employed.[24]

---

[21] Babylonian Talmud, *Yebamot* 112b; Berkovits, *supra* note 19, at 51.

[22] Berkovits, *supra* note 19, at 59–60; R. Shimon ben Tzadok (1361–1444), 2 Shut Tashbat no. 8.

[23] On the other hand, if the husband had embraced some other faith, the issue became more complicated.

[24] This is similar to one of the classical explanations attempting to reconcile God's "hardening" of Pharaoh's heart, with the notion of Pharaoh's "free will." The explanation is that the royal court, fearful of the harm from additional plagues, had already begun to plead with Pharaoh to let the Jews go. This political pressure might have forced Pharaoh to release the Jews, even though Pharaoh had not recognized the intrinsic correctness of the decision. Accordingly, God only hardened Pharaoh's heart to

Under biblical law, a man could authorize an agent to deliver a writ of divorce to the man's wife. When the writ of divorce was delivered, the woman would be divorced. But biblical law also empowered the husband to annul the agency outside of the presence of the agent and without the agent's knowledge. If a man did that, and the agent delivered the divorce, the woman would think she were free to remarry. If, however, she had relations with a second man, she would be guilty of unknowingly committing adultery and any child resulting from those relations would have the status of a "*Mamzer.*" This rule drastically reduces the child's chances of ever finding a spouse.

The rabbis reversed this result in two steps. First, they prohibited a man from annulling his agent's authority other than by announcing this annulment in the presence of the agent. Of course, it was still possible that a man might wrongfully violate this rabbinic rule and annul the agency outside of the presence of the agent. Consequently, the rabbis ruled that if a man did that, the marriage itself was retroactively annulled ab initio.[25] The Talmud provides various explanations as to the source of this rabbinic power. For example, suppose the first step of marriage ("*kiddushin*") was accomplished through the man's giving the woman something of value that he owned. The rabbis could annul that marriage by using their power to dispossess someone of property, *hefker beit din hefker*, to dispossess the man of ownership of that very piece of property so that the kiddushin never happened.[26] Alternatively, it is possible that all marriages are effectuated on the condition that they be subject to possible rabbinic annulment.[27]

Another way a man could cause terrible problems for his wife would be by abandoning her and leaving town. In this situation, not only could the wife not obtain a divorce, but she might never be free even if her husband were to die because she might be unable to prove to a rabbinic court that he had died. Eliezer Berkovits explains how the rabbis modified the normal evidentiary rules in this case:

> According to biblical law, one may testify only from direct personal knowledge, but not on the basis of knowledge learned from another person's testimony. Neither is the testimony of a woman or a slave admitted. But in this case, it was ruled not only that the testimony of one witness was sufficient, but that the witness may testify on the basis of hearsay, and that the witness may be a woman or even a slave.[28]

The Talmud explains, "Because of the danger of her becoming an agunah [i.e., without a husband but nonetheless unable to remarry], it was made easier for her."[29]

---

the extent necessary to neutralize such political pressure, enabling Pharaoh to exercise his "free will."

[25] BABYLONIAN TALMUD, *Gittin* 33a.

[26] *Id.*

[27] *Id.*

[28] BERKOVITS, *supra* note 19, at 65.

[29] BABYLONIAN TALMUD, *Yebamot* 87b–88a.

A woman could also be an agunah, trapped and unable to remarry, while her husband was still alive. This might arise, for example, if her husband simply abandoned her without any intention to return. For various reasons, including the need to earn a living, a husband may have already been living in another land, sending money home to his wife and family. If the husband decided to divorce his wife, he might be marginally willing to send a divorce decree with an agent. Nevertheless, if some legal glitch made this process difficult or expensive, he might forego it. As a result, the rabbis made the process a bit easier. Not everyone in Talmudic times knew how to sign their names. The rabbis allowed the signatures of the witnesses on a writ of divorce to be outlined by someone else (such as a scribe). The witnesses only had to fill in the outlines with ink. This was not permitted on other documents. The reason for the exception, explained Rabbi Elazar, "[S]o that the daughters of Israel not become agunot."[30]

As a matter of biblical law, a husband's financial duties to his wife were limited to providing food and clothing. The rabbis, however, enacted a requirement of a prenuptial agreement ("ketubah") which detailed the husband's obligations in the event that he divorced his wife. A variety of additional obligations were ordinarily included in the ketubah, such as the husband's duty to pay for his wife's medical treatment if she became ill, to ransom her if she were kidnapped, to pay her burial expenses should she predecease him, and to provide certain financial benefits to the children that she may bear from him.[31] The rabbis prescribed the minimum obligations for a normal marriage, and these requirements, which were referred to as "tenai ketubah," were presumed applicable to each marriage even if one or more of these obligations were not expressly included in a particular ketubah.[32]

Under biblical law, a man could not marry his wife's sister, during his wife's lifetime, even while polygamy was practiced. Nevertheless, as a matter of biblical law, it was possible for the man and this wife's sister to enter into a binding marriage contract on the condition that it would only be effective upon the wife's death. Similarly, a man could betroth a married woman on the condition that the betrothal only become effective on her current husband's death. Nevertheless, the rabbis felt that these types of betrothals "would lead to enmity between husband and wife, between sister and sister, between one man and another. This consideration invalidated a marriage contract that was legally binding according to biblical law."[33]

Additional innovations affected other parts of family law. For example, a father's biblical duty to provide financial support for a child ends when the child is six years old.[34] The rabbis extended this duty until the child legally becomes an adult, i.e., to

---

[30] Babylonian Talmud, *Gittin* 19b.

[31] Maimonides, Mishneh Torah, *Laws of Personal Status* 12:2. *See also* Berkovits, *supra* note 19, at 50. In exchange, the husband was entitled to any money the wife earned and any property that she found, that he inherits her if she predeceases him, and that, during her married life to him, he is entitled to any profits realized from her property. Maimonides, *supra* at 12:3.

[32] Maimonides, *supra* note 31, at 12:5. *See* Babylonian Talmud, *Ketubot* 111a, 56b.

[33] Berkovits, *supra* note 19, at 38. *See also* Babylonian Talmud, *Kiddushin* 63a.

[34] Maimonides, *supra* note 31, at 12:14. Babylonian Talmud, *Ketubot* 49a–b.

age twelve for a daughter and age thirteen for a son.[35]

Laws and customs also responded either to evolving circumstances or increased sensitivity to the circumstances. For example, under Jewish law, if a man dies childless, leaving a widow, it is an obligation mitzvah for the deceased's brother, referred to in this situation as the "levir," to marry the widow, so that the widow can bear a child and, in some sense, continue the deceased's legacy.[36] The value the Torah attributes to this deed is underscored by two facts. First, in other circumstances, such as where the widow already has a child, it is actually biblically forbidden for the deceased's brother to marry her. The marriage is only permitted in order to continue the deceased's legacy. Second, although the levir is permitted to refuse to marry the widow, if he does so, the Torah requires him to participate in a humiliating procedure in front of the elders:

> If the man like not to take his brother's wife, then his brother's wife shall go up to the gate unto the elders, and say: "My husband's brother refuseth to raise up unto his brother a name in Israel; he will not perform the duty of a husband's brother unto me." Then the elders of his city shall call him, and speak unto him; and if he stand, and say: "I like not to take her"; then shall his brother's wife draw nigh unto him in the presence of the elders, and loose his shoe from off his foot, and spit in his face;[37] and she shall answer and say: "So shall it be done unto the man that doth not build up his brother's house." And his name shall be called in Israel "The house of him that had his shoe loosed."[38]

Nevertheless, the Mishnah states, "Originally, when they [levirs] acted [i.e., married their brothers' widows] for the sake of fulfilling the commandment of yebum [i.e., to produce a child that would continue their deceased brothers' legacy], it was preferable that they marry their brothers' widows than undergo halizah. Now that they [levirs] do not act for the sake of fulfilling the commandment of yebum [i.e., but, rather, for some personal objective] it is preferable that they undergo halizah."[39] Interestingly, Rabbi Samuel Belkin (1911-1976), former president of Yeshiva University, points out that the rabbinic attitudes regarding yebum and halizah changed over time. After citing various Tannaitic views that seem to prefer *halizah*, he states:

> The tannaitic emphasis that the fulfillment of the law is not through the levirate act but by *halizah* did not, however, remain the established doctrine. At the end of the second century CE and in the following centuries, the Rabbis again encouraged levirate marriage. The Jerusalem Talmud relates an unusual story of a levir who was confronted with the

---

[35] Maimonides, *supra* note 31, at 12:14–15.

[36] *Deuteronomy* 25:6 (stating that by having a child with his brother's widow, the levir prevents his brother's name from being "blotted out in Israel").

[37] The Oral Law explains that she does not literally spit in his face, but, rather, on the ground in front of him. *See, e.g.,* Menachem Elon, *Levirate Marriage and Halizah, in* 12 Encyclopaedia Judaica 727, *supra* note 5. *See also* Louis Isaac Rabinowitz, *The Ceremony of Halizah, in id.* at 729.

[38] *Deuteronomy* 25:7-10, as translated in Elon, *supra* note 37, at 725.

[39] Mishnah, *Bekhorot* 1:7.

burdensome duty of performing levirate with twelve childless widows of his dead brothers. He obviously refused to perform the duty because he could not support them. R. Judah the Prince, however, urged him to marry the women, and R. Judah himself promised to contribute towards their support. The Babylonian Rabbis of the fourth century likewise favored levirate marriage.[40]

[D] Miscellaneous Developments

Various other areas of Jewish law also reflect important responses to changed circumstances. According to biblical law, a person is obligated to annually offer the person's "first fruits" at the Holy Temple in Jerusalem. At that time, the person is supposed to make a specific declaration in Hebrew as set forth in the Written Torah. Originally, those who could read would read the declaration. Those who could not read would repeat it after someone else read it for them. This shamed those who could not read, and many of them simply did not go to offer their first fruits. Consequently, the rabbis decreed that a particular Temple official would read the text on behalf of everyone.[41]

Similarly, changes were effected in customs regarding mourning rituals and the burying of the dead:

Originally, the food [traditionally brought to the house of the mourner after the funeral] was brought to the rich in silver and gold baskets, and to the poor in baskets made of stripped willow twigs. The poor were ashamed. Because of the honor of the poor, it was ordered that one would have to come to all homes with twig baskets. Originally, in the houses of the rich the drinks would be offered to the mourners in costly white glass; for the poor, they would use cheap, colored glass. The poor were ashamed. Because of the honor of the poor, it was ordered that in all homes only colored glass was to be used.

Originally, the faces of the dead of the rich would be uncovered [for the funeral]. The faces of the poor would be covered, however, because they often showed the signs of starvation. The poor were ashamed. Because of the honor of the poor, it was ordered that at all funerals the face of the dead was to be covered. Originally, the dead of the rich would be carried to their burial on couches; but of the poor in cheap, wooden boxes. The poor were ashamed. Because of the honor of the poor, it was ordered that all dead were to be carried in boxes.

Originally, the apparel in which the dead were clothed for the funeral was so expensive that the poor could not afford it, so that [it was said] it was harder for them to raise the money than even to bear their sorrow for the dead. They would leave the body and run away. Until R. Gamliel, the head of the Sanhedrin, ordered "irreverent" treatment of himself, that he be

---

[40] Samuel Belkin, *Levirate and Agnate Marriage in Rabbinic and Cognate Literature*, 60 Jewish Q. Rev., *New Series* 329 (1970).

[41] Mishnah, *Bikkurim* 3:7.

carried out in a cheap, cotton shroud. After that, the people followed his example, and they too used cheap shrouds made from cotton.[42]

§ 12.03   INNOVATIONS AFTER THE CLOSING OF THE BABYLONIAN TALMUD

Jewish law continued, and continues, to change after the closing of the Talmud. Many non-biblical laws were adopted by individual communities, particularly to regulate commercial practices.

[A]   Family Law Issues

Some changes, however, were widespread and dramatic. For example, Rabbenu Gershom ben Yehuda (960–1028), one of the foremost rabbis in the world at that time, convoked a rabbinical synod circa 1000 C.E. At this gathering, several important takkanot were adopted. One of these decrees prohibited men from practicing polygamy, which was biblically permitted to men.[43] Another decree forbade a husband from divorcing his wife against her consent even though doing so was biblically permitted.[44]

Similarly, there were important, and controversial, rabbinic responses to the family law problems produced by the increase in the numbers and percentages of Jews who, especially since the "Enlightenment," relied on secular divorces, which, according to most authorities, are invalid under Jewish law. The rising rates of divorce exacerbated this problem. Women denied a religious divorce could not remarry, and if they bore a child to a second man while still religiously married to the first, their offspring would be mamzerim, unable to marry any other Jew who was not also a mamzer.

Over the years, various partial solutions have been proposed, including, for example, pre-nuptial agreements requiring rabbinic court involvement in the event of an action for a civil divorce and promoting secular law legislation placing halakhically permissible financial pressure on parties to a secular divorce to cooperate in the granting of a religious divorce. Some of the proposals have been quite controversial.[45] None has been universally implemented.

---

[42] Berkovits, *supra* note 19, at 35–36 (translating excerpts from Babylonian Talmud, *Moed Katan* 29b).

[43] Ben-Zion (Benno) Schereschewsky, *Bigamy and Polygamy, in* 3 Encyclopaedia Judaica 691–94, *supra* note 5; Shlomo Eidelberg and David Derovan, *Gershom Ben Judah Me'or Ha-Golah* (960–1028), *id.* vol. 7, at 551–52.

[44] Eidelberg & Derovan, *supra* note 43, at 552.

[45] For a taste of the controversies surrounding some of these proposals, see, for example, *The Plight of the Agunah and a Summary of Possible Solutions*, http://ohr.edu/ask_db/ask_main.php/253/Q1/; Chaim Z. Malinowtiz & Michael J. Broyde, *The 1992 N.Y. Get Law: An Exchange*, 31:3 Tradition 23 (1977); Dr. Israel Drazin, *Thoughts on the Agunah Problem*, http://www.jewishideas.org/articles/thoughts-agunah-problem; David Hartman, *The God Who Hates Lies: Confronting and Rethinking Jewish Tradition* (Woodstock, Vt: Jewish Lights Publishing, 2011); Statement by Michael Broyde, http://www.jlaw.com/Recent/Agunah.html; Naomi Ragen, *The Great Agunah Debacle — Part I, available at* http://www.naomiragen.com/israel/the-great-agunah-debacle-part-i/; Aviad Hacohen and Blue

Rabbi Moses Feinstein, probably the greatest Jewish law authority in the United States during the mid and latter parts of the twentieth century, took a rather controversial approach. Various criteria must be satisfied for a Jewish marriage to be valid. For example, all of the witnesses must be qualified as such under Jewish law, which, among other things, means that they must be men, that they must be religiously observant and that they may not be related to each other. Only two witnesses are required. Nevertheless, if there are 100 witnesses, and two of them are related, all of the witnesses are disqualified. Similarly, even if one of the 100 witnesses is ineligible to serve as a witness for some other reason, all of the 100 witnesses are disqualified.[46] Where the witnesses are not qualified, the marriage is not effective. Another requirement is that if a groom effectuates the *kiddushin* (i.e., the first step in the two-step marriage process), by giving the bride a ring, the ring must definitively belong to the groom at the time he gives it to the bride. If, however, the ring belongs to the groom's mother, and the mother had not effectively given it to the groom to be "his," the marriage is religiously ineffective. Of course, these are serious questions and each case might require specific evaluation of the facts. Nevertheless, Feinstein ruled that if the marriage service was conducted by a Reform rabbi, the marriage was presumptively invalid. Not having been religiously married, the woman involved would not require a religious divorce and any subsequent offspring from a different man would not be mamzerim. Although this ruling incensed many Reform Jews, it saved many women whose husbands refused to divorce them. Some rabbinic authorities who were students of Feinstein have definitely relied on this ruling, but it is unclear just how widely it has been accepted.[47]

[B] A Long History of Innovation Regarding Interest Bearing Loans

Another example of major halakhic innovation involves the biblical prohibitions against giving and receiving interest on loans. In Exodus, the Torah says, "When you lend money to My people, to the poor person who is with you, do not act toward

---

GREENBERG, TEARS OF THE OPPRESSED: AN EXAMINATION OF THE AGUNAH PROBLEM: BACKGROUND AND HALAKHIC SOURCES (2004); SHLOMO RISKIN, WOMEN AND JEWISH DIVORCE : THE REBELLIOUS WIFE, THE AGUNAH, AND THE RIGHT OF WOMEN TO INITIATE DIVORCE IN JEWISH LAW, A HALAKHIC SOLUTION (1989); Jeremy Wieder, *Hafka'at Kiddushin: A Rebuttal*, 36:4 TRADITION 91 (2002); Gedalia Dav Schwartz, *Book Review: The Rebellious Wife, the Agunah, and the Right of Women to Initiate Divorce in Jewish Law, a Halachic Solution by Shlomo Riskin* (Ktav, 1989), 25:2 TRADITION 94 (1990). References to some of the organizations offering support to Agunot may be found at a web site maintained by JOFA, the Jewish Orthodox Feminine Alliance, *available at* http://www.jofa.org/about.php/advocacy/otheragunaho.

[46] There are ways to avoid this problem, such as by designating two specific, qualified and unrelated men to serve as the witnesses, to the exclusion of all of the other people present.

[47] One commentator writes:

The decision of R. Moshe Feinstein not to recognize the halakhic validity of Conservative and Reform marriage ceremonies has, more than any other single piece of halakhic legislation, freed countless Jewish children from the stigma of mamzerut, a problem with which Berkovits has grappled both here and in his earlier works.

See Allan L. Nadler, *Review Essay: Eliezer Berkovits' Not in Heaven*, 21:3 TRADITION 91, 96 (Fall 1984).

him as a creditor; do not lay interest upon him."[48] In Leviticus, the Torah says, "If your brother becomes impoverished and his means falter in your proximity, you shall strengthen him — proselyte or resident — so that he can live with you. Do not take from him interest and increase."[49] Finally, in Deuteronomy, the Torah states:

> You shall not cause your brother to take interest, interest of money or interest of food, interest of anything that he may take as interest. You may cause a gentile to take interest, but you may not cause your brother to take interest, so that Hashem, your God, will bless you in every undertaking on the Land to which you are coming, to possess it."[50]

The Talmud clearly interprets these verses as making it biblically forbidden for a Jewish lender and a Jewish borrower to stipulate or pay interest for any loan between them. The prohibition not only applies to the lender, but also to the borrower. In fact, it applies to the scribe who prepares a loan document specifying such interest and to the witnesses to the transaction.[51]

Jewish law authorities underscore the seriousness of the prohibition against interest. They state that if a person violates this law, it is as if he or she denied the existence of God and the exodus from Egypt.[52] The Talmud compares a lender who collects interest to a murderer[53] and states that someone who either pays or collects interest is ineligible to serve as a witness in any legal case.[54] Furthermore, the Talmud states that the divine punishment for charging interest is permanent impoverishment.[55]

The Talmud also explains that the sages rabbinically banned many other types of transactions involving interest. For example, suppose the borrower and lender do not stipulate that any interest will be paid. When the borrower repays the loan, it is rabbinically forbidden for the borrower to give anything extra to the lender.[56] The borrower may not even perform a minor favor for the lender, such as providing the

---

[48] *Exodus* 22:24. The translation is found in THE CHUMASH: THE STONE EDITION 431–432 (Nosson Sherman, ed., 1993).

[49] *Leviticus* 25:35–36. *See* Sherman, *supra* note 48, at 703.

[50] *Deuteronomy* 23:20–21. *See* THE CHUMASH, *supra* note 48, at 1057.

[51] MAIMONIDES, MISHNEH TORAH, *Laws of Lenders and Borrowers* 4:2 (explaining that the prohibition also applies to the scribe who writes the relevant legal document and the witnesses who sign it).

[52] *Id.*, at 4:7.

[53] BABYLONIAN TALMUD, *Bava Metzia* 61b, 62a, *Temurah* 6b.

[54] BABYLONIAN TALMUD, *Sanhedrin* 25a.

[55] The Talmud states:

> It has been taught: R. Simeon b. Eleazar said: He who has money and lends it without interest, of him Scripture writes. He that putteth not out his money to usury, nor taketh reward against the innocent. He that doeth these things shall never be moved; thus you learn that he who does lend on interest, his wealth dissolves. But do we not see [people] who do not lend on interest, yet their wealth dissolves? — R. Eleazar said: The latter sink [into poverty] but re-ascend, whereas the former sink but do not re-ascend. [Footnotes omitted]

EPSTEIN, SONCINO BABYLONIAN TALMUD, *Bava Metzia* 71a, *available at* http://halakhah.com/pdf/nezikin/Baba_Metzia.pdf.

[56] BABYLONIAN TALMUD, *Bava Metzia* 75b.

lender with useful information, if the borrower's motive is to reward the lender for making the loan.[57] The Mishnah reports that the sages even prohibited a number of transactions simply because they could "seem" as if they involved interest. For instance, the Mishnah declares that it is forbidden for someone to sell a field and say, "If you pay me now, it is yours for a thousand zuz; if [you pay me] in the harvest time, [you must pay] twelve maneh [1200 zuz]."[58] Similarly, the rabbis ruled that a person may not say to another, "Weed [my field] with me, and I will hoe [your field] with you" or "Hoe [my field] with me, and I will weed [your field] with you."[59] The reason is that one type of work may be more difficult than the other.

A variety of important innovations which permitted commercial practices to effectively skirt these prohibitions occurred even during Talmudic times. Rabbi Hillel Gamoran skillfully traces how a device, known as an *iska* or a *hetter iska*, began as a commercially meaningful transaction and developed into little more than a legal fiction.[60] As initially conceived, an *iska* requires the person providing the funds (the "Financier") and the person receiving the funds (the "Recipient") to form a venture, probably best described as a partnership, to use the money for a profit-making purpose. The Financier would lend, at no interest, half of the money and would "invest" the other half. The half of the money that the Financier invested was "at risk" based on the profitability of the enterprise.

The agreement would also contain a provision providing some financial benefit to the Recipient in exchange for the Recipient's personal services on behalf of the venture. Without such a provision, the Recipient's personal services, provided for free, might be deemed to constitute forbidden interest.

In the post-Talmudic era, however, the hetter iska mechanism has undergone dramatic changes. The amount paid for the Recipient's services has become trivial. Unless the Recipient becomes personally bankrupt, the likelihood that the Financier will bear any portion of the business losses has become de minimus. Indeed, the likelihood that the Financier will fail to realize a specifically agreed upon percentage return on his investment is close to nil. Thus, through a series of rabbinic innovations, the various biblical prohibitions involved in interest bearing loans have become largely irrelevant.[61]

The Mishnah states that, for his services to the enterprise, the Recipient should be paid but does not specify how much.[62] The Talmud cites a braitha reporting a dispute between three early authorities (Tannaim). Rabbi Shimon states that the worker must be fully compensated. Rabbi Yehudah declares that the Recipient need only be paid a symbolic amount. Rabbi Meir rules that the Recipient should be paid "much or little." Another version of the braitha quotes Rabbi Meir as saying that the

---

[57] *Id.* (citing the *Mishnah*).

[58] MISHNAH, *Bava Metzia* 5:2.

[59] BABYLONIAN TALMUD, *Bava Metzia* 75a–b (citing the *Mishnah*).

[60] *See generally* HILLEL GAMORAN, JEWISH LAW IN TRANSITION: HOW ECONOMIC FORCES OVERCAME THE PROHIBITION AGAINST LENDING ON INTEREST (2008).

[61] Ironically, many of the rabbinic prohibitions which involve sale transactions rather than actual loans, are now more practically relevant than the biblical prohibitions.

[62] MISHNAH, *Bava Metzia* 5:4.

Recipient should be paid as a "worker" or as an "idle worker." The Talmud explains that the pay of an "idle worker" depends on the job that the worker gave up to work on the iska enterprise.[63]

In the Geonic period (approximately 650–1050), it seems that rabbinic authorities "exercised care to enforce the working partner's [right to meaningful] compensation."[64] Similarly, R. Yitzhak Alfasi (Rif; 1013–1103) ruled in accordance with Rabbi Meir, saying that "much or little, as they have contracted and agreed with each other, according to the job from which he was idle."[65] If the Recipient's former job was at a high salary, then the Financier had to pay him a relatively high amount. If the Recipient's job was not at a high salary, the Financier could pay him relatively little.[66]

Rabbi Yehudah of Barcelona, an early twelfth century authority, is said to have been "[t]he first authority to relax the requirement for the working partner's pay."[67] R. Abraham B. David of Posquieres (Rabad), also a twelfth century authority, similarly wrote that the Financier could stipulate that the Recipient would be paid a specific amount, even a token amount, although the Recipient's services were worth much more.[68] In the centuries after Rabad, rabbinic authorities adopted his approach that required the Financier to make only a relatively trivial payment to the Recipient for his services to the partnership.[69] The early Aharonim continued this approach. Rav Abraham Halevi (1650–1712) states:

> It is good for the . . . [Financier] to pay the . . . [Recipient] at the start, for whatever he gives him then is sufficient. And we have learned from the words of the poskim that we do not have to be concerned about the amount of this payment; whatever he gives him is enough.[70]

Similar developments importantly reduced the risk that the Financier would suffer a loss of his or her investment. The iska was designed as half loan and half investment. The Recipient was surely personally responsible as to the amount of the loan, but a number of Geonim ruled that, absent negligence, the Recipient was not personally responsible for the Financier's investment.[71] This position was adopted by a number of the most significant early Rishonim, including R. Hananel (Rah), R. Yitzhak Alfasi and Maimonides.[72]

Nevertheless, Rabad suggested a way in which all of the business losses could be placed on the Recipient. In Jewish law, if a bailee or agent fails to follow instructions, then his use of property deposited with him is unauthorized and he or

---

[63] GAMORAN, *supra* note 60, at 134.

[64] *Id.* at 132–35.

[65] *Id.* at 136–37 (citing from the Rif's *Halakhot, Bava Metzia* 39b).

[66] *Id.* at 137.

[67] *Id.*

[68] *Id.* (citing *Rabad's Teshuvot U-fesakim* (Joseph Kafih, ed., 1964) no. 132).

[69] *Id.* at 149.

[70] *Id.* at 156 (citing Halevi's *Ginat Veradim*).

[71] *Id.* at 150.

[72] *Id.*

she is fully liable for return of the property. Rabad suggested that the Financier could, at the outset, specify commercially unreasonable instructions that the Recipient would not follow, resulting in the Recipient's full liability to the Financier for any loss. For example, the Financier could specify that the Recipient will only lend out the money if he receives gold or silver collateral and that the Recipient must bury such collateral in the ground. The Rabad's novel ruling was adopted by subsequent Rishonim.[73]

In the fifteenth century, Rabbi Yisroel Isserlein went a step further by stating that it was permissible for the Financier to make such stipulations:

> even though everyone knows that it is not at all the intention of the investor or of the recipient that the stipulation be fulfilled, that is, that he will lend only on silver and gold and will bury it in the ground, but rather, he will lend on debts without any pledges at all, or on pledges which are not silver or gold, or if they are silver or gold, he will surely not bury them in the ground. Nevertheless it is allowed.[74]

Isserlein suggested an additional way for the Financier to avoid any losses. The agreement between the Financier and the Recipient would provide both that the Recipient is liable for gross negligence and that the Recipient would not be believed that he was not grossly negligent even if he takes a solemn biblical oath and even if he has numerous witnesses. The only way he would be believed is if the Rabbi and cantor and similar people in the city would testify that he was not grossly negligent. According to Isserlein:

> And in this way will [the Financier's] principal be secure as he always wishes. For if it is lost . . . [the Financier] may claim that it was lost [by the Recipient] intentionally, and . . . [the Recipient] will be able to uphold his claim . . . with the testimony of the Rabbi and the cantor. And it is almost entirely certain that they will not know all [of the relevant facts and, therefore, will be unable to testify].[75]

After various other versions of the hetter iska device, Rabbi Abraham Halevi suggested an agreement that included a sum as the amount of expected profit and provided that if the profit exceeded that sum, all of the extra would belong to the Recipient. On the other hand, if the Recipient were to claim that the profits were less than the stated sum, the Recipient would not be believed unless he took a stern oath. If he failed to take the oath, the Recipient would have to pay the Financier half of the amount fixed as the expected profit. Based on the aversion religious Jews had to the taking of an oath, it was almost certain that the Financier would receive half of the expected profit.[76] Even if the Recipient knew that he did not profit, so long as he had an alternative right to avoid payment by taking an oath, making the payment did not violate the laws against paying interest.[77]

---

[73] *Id.* at 151–52.

[74] *Id.* at 152–53 (translating from Isserlein's *Terumat Hadeshen* no. 302).

[75] *Id.* at 153. The bracketed words are mine.

[76] *Id.* at 165.

[77] *Id.* at 165–66.

The period of the later Aharonim ushered in at least equally dramatic innovations. The hetter iska device was approved for use in the making of a personal loan, i.e., a loan in which the Financier knows that the Recipient is not using the money for a business.[78] Similarly, the notion of a "general hetter iska agreement" was adopted in which a bank resolves that all of its transactions are done according to the terms of a particular hetter iska agreement. As far as borrowers are concerned, they may think that they are entering into ordinary interest bearing loans. Under Jewish law, however, the transaction is governed by the terms of the hetter iska agreement adopted by the bank. This agreement may be framed and hung on the bank's wall, but the bank need not draw the customer's attention to it.

There are countless ways in which Jewish law has responded over time to changed circumstances and needs. This chapter simply provides a few illustrative examples.

---

[78] *Id.* at 170–71.

Chapter 13

IMPORTANCE OF LIFE

§ 13.01   INTRODUCTION

Judaism's perspectives on the importance of life lead to a variety of legal ramifications. Consequently, this chapter begins by briefly discussing Judaism's view of the purpose and value of life and then turns to a view of the related legal implications.

§ 13.02   A PERSON AS THE CREATOR'S "BAILEE"

In creating life, God joins a spiritual soul and a physical body. Is it good for the soul to be so joined? A Talmudic passage records an ancient debate on this question. The conclusion is that it would be better for a person never to have been born.[1] Although the Talmud does not state the reasons for this determination, it can be partially explained by the dangerous spiritual trials a soul experiences in this world and the risks attendant to failure. In any event, it is clear that life is not merely a divine gift; it is a responsibility.[2] Man is the Creator's "bailee," entrusted with life, His "property," and charged with living. Rabbi David Ibn Avi Zimra, who served for forty years as the Chief Rabbi of Egypt, explains: "a person's soul is not his property; it is the property of the Holy One, Blessed be He, as it is written, 'And the souls are Mine.' "[3]

---

[1] *See* BABYLONIAN TALMUD, *Eruvin* 13b.

[2] *See* MISHNAH, *Pirkei Avot* 4:29: "Against your will, you live, and against your will, you will die."

[3] *See* DAVID BEN SOLOMON IBN ABI ZIMRI (*Radbaz*; 1479–1573), COMMENTARY ON MISHNEH TORAH, *in Law*

§ 13.02 THE IMMEASURABLY GREAT VALUE OF EACH LIFE

Each life is considered supremely valuable. In discussing the creation of Adam, the Talmud explains:

Adam [the first human being] was created alone to teach you that if any person causes a single soul to perish, Scripture regards him as if he has caused an entire world to perish — and if any human being saves a single soul, Scripture regards him as if he has saved an entire world."[4]

Perhaps life is so important because of the holiness that can be achieved through it. Man is supposed to subordinate his desires and logic to God's will, as manifested in specific Jewish law tenets. As Rabbi Eliezer ben Azariah states:

How do you know that a person should not say, "Pork disgusts me. I do not want to wear clothes made from a combination of wool and linen," but should instead say, "I would like [to eat pork or wear such clothes] but what can I do? My father in heaven has decreed upon me [that I cannot]"? It is learned from the fact the verse says, "I have separated you from the nations to be mine." [The message is that] "your separation should be for me. Separate yourselves from sin and accept the yoke of the kingship of heaven."[5]

Judaism believes that by fulfilling this mission, despite life's diverse challenges, such as poverty or illness, a person realizes inner potentialities, perfects one's character, becomes holy and draws closer to God.[6] Ephemeral life is the training ground for the eternal afterlife. As Rabbi Yaakov states, "This World is like a

---

of Courts 18:6 (explaining that this is the reason why a rabbinical court exercising its ordinary powers does not impose corporal punishment based on a defendant's admission of guilt). *See also* ELIEZER WALDENBURG (1915–2006), 5 TZITZ ELIEZER, *Ramat Rachel* 29(1); Abraham S. Abraham, *Euthanasia*, MEDICINE AND JEWISH LAW 123, (Fred Rosner ed., 1990); J. David Bleich, *Life as an Intrinsic Rather Than Instrumental Good: The "Spiritual" Case Against Euthanasia*, 9 ISSUES LAW & MEDICINE 139, 144 (1993) ("[m]an's interest in his life and in his body are subservient to those of the Creator . . . . [I]t is the Creator who is the ultimate proprietor of human life.").

[4] JERUSALEM TALMUD, *Sanhedrin* 22a. *Compare* BABYLONIAN TALMUD, *Sanhedrin* 37a, that refers to a "single Jewish soul" rather than simply to a "single soul."

[5] *See* SHLOMO YITZHAKI (*Rashi*; 1040–1105), COMMENTARY TO THE TORAH, *Leviticus* 20:26 (Heb.) (quoting source). Similarly, as Rabbi Haim Shmuelevitz states, a Jew's job is to be God's servant, who fulfills the Master's commands without independently evaluating the appropriateness of the command. This is reflected in the Jewish tradition that emphasizes that, when God offered the Torah to the Jewish people, they immediately agreed to accept it — before looking to see what it required. *See* HAIM SHMUELEVITZ, SIHOT MUSAR 36 (Heb.).

[6] As Rabbi Aryeh Kaplan explains:

It is extremely difficult to understand why innocent children are born blind or crippled, and are thereby condemned to suffer throughout their lives. It is also difficult to understand why unborn children are taken, or why orphans or the children of the righteous die when there is no parental sin. Likewise, the tortures and brutal deaths of absolute saints are not sufficiently explained. . . . However, all of these cases must be considered in terms of the overall plan for creation. According to this master plan, every soul that has ever been born in this world must reach a minimum degree of perfection before God. In order to achieve this, many souls must be born or reincarnated more than once. [Citations omitted.]

See, e.g., ARYEH KAPLAN, 2 HANDBOOK OF JEWISH THOUGHT 332–33 (1992).

corridor leading to the World to Come. Prepare yourself in the corridor so that you can enter the banquet hall."[7]

Every person's life is also precious to the community. Each person plays a role in the development of other people's spirituality not only by providing them the opportunity to exercise mercy, to extend charity, or to acknowledge gratitude for their own more favorable plights, but also by serving as an example as to how to act under like circumstances. Jewish law explicitly requires that a Jew play a direct role in the religious lives of others. Every Jew has a duty to discourage others from sin and to encourage them to be religiously observant.[8] This obligation arises, in part, from the fact that each Jew is considered a member of a national and of a global community that God annually judges based on the accumulated religious accomplishments and shortcomings of all community members.[9] An adverse judgment deleteriously affects even those individuals who are themselves righteous.[10] Merely by being alive at the time of the judgment, a person is counted as a part of the community, and his deeds during the year are considered when the community is evaluated.

§ 13.03 LEGAL IMPLICATIONS

The significance of human life explains a number of legal rules, including:

A. The Obligation to Protect Oneself from Harm and to Preserve One's Life;

B. The Prohibition Against Suicide;

C. The Proscription Against Murder.[11]

[A] Obligation to Protect Oneself from Harm and to Preserve One's Life

Life is not merely a privilege but a duty with which a human being is charged. A person must strive to fulfill this duty faithfully. Good health is a critical asset in this endeavor and, as a result, one must try to safeguard that health. Certainly, a person may not abandon this duty altogether by committing suicide. Thus, Jewish law generally rejects the modern mantra that a person has the "right" to do that which the person wants with his or her own body. Similarly, as will be discussed in more detail, Jewish law, at least on the theoretical basis, rejects the unlimited claim for patient autonomy.

---

[7] *See* MISHNAH, *Pirkei Avot* 4:21.

[8] *See supra* Chapter 11.

[9] MAIMONIDES, MISHNEH TORAH, *Laws of Repentence* 3:4.

[10] *Id.*

[11] *See* AHARON HALEVI, SEFER HAHINNUCH, *Commandment* 34 (Heb.). *See also* THE PRINCIPLES OF JEWISH LAW, 526–29 (Menachem Elon ed., 1975) (in carefully circumscribed circumstances, however, Jewish law recognizes that those who are guilty of particular offenses may be killed). *See* discussion *supra* Chapter 7.

Authorities cite at least four possible Scriptural sources for the duty to protect one's health. Some point to the verse, "Be careful, very careful for your lives."[12] At least one authority identifies, "and your brother shall live with you," as the source of this obligation.[13] The argument is that by using this verse to establish that one must give preference to preserving one's own life over saving another, the Talmud implies that there is a duty to save oneself.[14] Rabbi Yehudah HeHasid derives this duty from the verse, "The blood of your own souls will I require":

> The blood of your own souls I will seek: . . . [I]f a person goes to a place fraught with danger [for example, if] during the winter [he treads] on ice which is likely to break [causing his] drowning, or if a person enters a ruin which collapses on him, or if a person quarrels with a violent man who becomes exceedingly angry [and kills him], these people will be punished, for they caused their own deaths.[15]

Others suggest that the obligation emanates from the verse, "Do not stand idly by your fellow's blood,"[16] reasoning that Jewish law regards a person as his own relative and may consider him his own "fellow" as well.[17]

[1] Spending Money to Save Life

As a matter of Jewish law, it might theoretically be important which verse is actually the source for the rule mandating self-protection. As discussed in Chapter 4, biblical commandments are categorized as either negative or positive. Jewish law requires much more of a person to avoid violating a negative commandment than for merely failing to fulfill an affirmative one. As discussed in Chapter 4, there is some debate as to how to characterize a particular obligation, whether one follows the form in which the commandment is phrased (i.e., if it directs one to do something it is affirmative, if it prohibits something, it is negative) or whether it depends on whether the commandment can be violated passively (if it can be violated passively, it is an affirmative commandment, and if it can only be violated actively, it is a negative commandment). The practical difference is that one generally must use up to only twenty percent of one's wealth to perform an affirmative commandment, but must use up to all of one's wealth to avoid violating a negative commandment.[18] Nevertheless, some authorities believe that with respect to saving life, especially one's own life, one must use up to all of one's assets irrespective of the particular verse that gives rise to the obligation.[19]

---

[12] *Deuteronomy* 4:9. *See, e.g.,* MAIMONIDES, MISHNEH TORAH, *Hilkhot Rozeah U'Shemirat Nefesh* 11:4; MOSHE SCHREIBER (a/k/a Moses Sofer; 1763–1839); HATAM SOFER, *Yoreh De'ah* 326 (Heb.) (also citing the verse, *Leviticus* 18:5, "and you shall live by [the commandments]").

[13] *Leviticus* 25:38.

[14] *See* J. David Bleich, *Treatment of the Terminally Ill*, 30 TRADITION 51, 79 at note 12 (1996) (referring to BABYLONIAN TALMUD, *Bava Metzia* 52a).

[15] *See* YEHUDA HEHASID (1660–1700), SEFER HASIDIM no. 675 (Heb.).

[16] *Leviticus* 19:16.

[17] *See* Bleich, *supra* note 14, at 79, note 12 (citing authorities discussing this argument).

[18] *See* discussion *supra* Chapter 11.

[19] Even Rabbi Yitzhak Zilberstein, who appears to conclude that one need not use all of one's money

[2] Transgressing Jewish Law to Save Life

Sometimes, however, saving one's life involves something other than expending resources. Instead, it may be that the only way to save one's life would be by violating some other Jewish law precept. Suppose, for example, on the Sabbath a person is suffering from an illness that threatens his or her life, and the only way for the person to stay alive is by an act that would otherwise violate the Sabbath laws. For example, it might be necessary to make medicine, to cook food, to boil water, or to build a fire, all of which are forbidden on the Sabbath. In such a situation, virtually all Jewish law authorities rule that, despite the religious centrality of the Sabbath, one *must* violate the applicable Sabbath laws to preserve one's life.[20] Rabbenu Nissim, a fourteenth century authority, states that a person who, out of a misguided sense of righteousness, fails to desecrate the Sabbath to save his own life, "is a murderer and is culpable for [losing] his life."[21] Similarly, Rabbi David ben Shlomo ibn Avi Zimra (the Radbaz), a sixteenth century authority, comments: "There is no righteousness in his refusal, for it constitutes suicide . . . and Hashem [God] will hold him accountable for his [loss of] life."[22] These rules apply even if a person's life can be only momentarily extended, for Jewish law regards each instant of life as of transcendent value.

Sometimes, however, the only "need" to violate Jewish law is because of some other person's threat. In other words, someone says "Do this, or I will kill you," and the "this" is an act that violates Jewish law. The rules in this situation depend on additional facts. For example, suppose it is the Sabbath, and the person wants you to cook him food or to build him a fire because he is hungry or cold. In other words, the person wants the act done for his own personal benefit. In this case, Jewish law says you must perform the act and save your life.

Suppose, however, that the person does not really want the food cooked or the fire built. Rather, the person issues the threat for the purpose of forcing you to

---

to save someone else's life, agrees. His logic is that: (1) one must spend all of one's money to avoid violating a Sabbath prohibition, and (2) one must violate a Sabbath prohibition to preserve his life, even briefly. Consequently, he argues, one must spend all of one's money to preserve his life. *See* Yitzhak Zilberstein, *Monetary Considerations Regarding the Saving of Human Life*, 12:3 Assia 50 (1958) (Heb.). Rabbi Zilberstein's logic, however, is questionable. For example, Jewish law requires the circumcision of a child on the eighth day of his life, even if the eighth day is Sabbath and even if such circumcision involves what would otherwise be a Sabbath violation. Nevertheless, one is not obligated to spend all of one's money in order to perform such circumcision on that Sabbath. In any event, assuming, arguendo, that Zilberstein's logic were valid, it seems that the same logic would require a person to spend all of his money to save the life of another person because: (1) one must spend all of one's money to avoid violating a Sabbath prohibition, and (2) one must violate a Sabbath prohibition to preserve someone else's life, even briefly. Indeed, the classical Talmudic passage that requires violating the Sabbath even to temporarily extend life does not deal with someone's saving his own life but, rather, with someone's violating the Sabbath in order to save another person's life. *See* Babylonian Talmud, *Yoma* 85a.

[20] *See* Abraham S. Abraham, The Comprehensive Guide to Medical Halachah 23–24 (1996) (citing rules and authorities).

[21] Nissim ben Reuven Girondi (*Ran*; 1320–1376), Commentary to Sefer HaHalakhot, *Yuma*.

[22] *See* Yaakov Weiner, Ye Shall Surely Heal at 4 (1995) (citing this view of the Radbaz). *See also* Maimonides, Mishneh Torah, *Yesodei HaTorah* 5:1. *But see* Alfred Cohen, *Whose Body? Living with Pain*, 32 J. Halacha & Contemp. Soc'y 32, 45 (1996) (citing an early dissenting rabbinic view, which Cohen states is not reflective of normative Jewish law).

violate Jewish law. But the person only demands that you commit the violation privately, not in front of others. In this case, all Jewish law authorities agree that you are permitted to violate the law, but there is disagreement as to whether you are obligated to do so. Some rule that in this case you are allowed to act stringently and allow yourself to be killed, because this fervent display of religious commitment, while not required, sanctifies God's name.[23] Others disagree, arguing that the duty to live by the commandments takes precedence and that if one allows oneself to be killed, it is considered as if one had committed suicide.[24]

There are three scenarios in which it is forbidden to accede to the threat. First, if the required act involves idolatry, murder or certain forms of sexual impropriety, one must allow oneself to be murdered rather than comply. Second, even if the threat does not involve idolatry, murder or sexual impropriety, if the threatener demands that the violation be performed in public, i.e., before ten or more Jews, one may not comply. Third, even if the threat does not involve idolatry, murder or sexual impropriety, if it is a time of religious persecution, and the person's purpose is to coerce a violation of Jewish law, one may not give in.

[B]   The Prohibition Against Suicide

The prohibition against suicide may arise from the same verses that require one to safeguard one's life; because a suicidal act would be inconsistent with the duty to safeguard one's life.[25] Most authorities learn the prohibition against suicide from the verse, "The blood of your lives will I require."[26] At least one authority derives this ban from the verse "Thou shalt not murder."[27] Given that all life belongs to God, the argument can easily be made that there should be no difference between killing someone else or killing oneself.[28]

Someone who violates this prohibition by committing suicide is considered a murderer and is punishable at the hands of heaven. Jewish theology recognizes that there is a World to Come after this physical life, and, as a general rule, all Jews — even sinners — are promised a place in the World to Come.[29] Suicides,

---

[23] *See, e.g.*, YAAKOV BEN ASHER (1269–1343), TUR, *Yoreh De'ah* 157; ISRAEL ISSERLEIN (1390–1460), TERUMAT HADESHEN no. 199. *Compare* YOSEF KARO, KESEF MISHNEH, *Hilkhot Yesodei HaTorah* 5:4.

[24] *See, e.g.*, MAIMONIDES, *supra* note 22, at 5:1, 4.

[25] *See, e.g.*, GIRONDI, *supra* note 21, at *Shevuot* 28a (citing *Deuteronomy* 4:9 as one of two verses establishing the prohibition against suicide).

[26] *Genesis* 9:5. *See* MAIMONIDES, *supra* note 12, at 2:3 (Heb.). *See also* GIRONDI, *supra* note 21 (citing this verse as one of two that establish the prohibition against suicide); THE PRINCIPLES OF JEWISH LAW, *supra* note 11, at columns 477–78 (identifying this verse as the source of the prohibition). Rabbi Yosef ben Moshe Babad identifies this verse as the source for the proscription against suicide and then, saying that this verse does not apply to non-Jews, contends that non-Jews are not forbidden from committing suicide. *See* YOSEF BEN MOSHE BABAD (1801–1874), MINHAT HINNUKH, *Commandment* 34.

[27] *Exodus* 20:13. *See* Bleich, *supra* note 14 (citing this view).

[28] *See* YEHIEL MICHOEL TUKAZINSKY, GESHER HAHAYYIM I at 269.

[29] MISHNAH, *Sanhedrin* 10:1: "All Israelites have a share in the World to Come, as it is said [Isaiah 60:21]: 'And all your people will be righteous. They will inherit the land forever. They are the plants of my hands, wherein I am glorified.' "

however, have no place in the World to Come.[30] Moreover, as a practical matter, suicides are denied certain mourning rites and are buried in a separate, distant place in the cemetery.[31]

Jewish law views suicide as especially opprobrious for many reasons. First, suicide constitutes a denial that God is the origin and master of one's life[32] and a rejection of one's religious responsibility to cope with the challenges of this world. Second, it frustrates both God's wish that the world be populated and that each individual live and strive to "be holy." Third, because man is made in God's image, suicide degrades that image and, indirectly, God.[33] Fourth, one who commits suicide out of despair demonstrates a lack of trust in God's ability to remedy one's predicaments or to punish one for his transgressions.[34] Fifth, suicide deprives one of a chance to repent for past sins, because one may only repent while one is alive. In fact, the very act of suicide, complete only upon the suicide's death, counts as another sin.[35] Sixth, suicide denies a person the invaluable atonement that death typically effectuates.[36]

There is considerable controversy as to whether there are any exceptions to the rule against suicide and, if so, what those exceptions are. Jewish law scholars analyze these issues by examining how ancient authorities dealt with biblical or Talmudic examples of suicide. Although this is not the place to examine all of these details, there are considerable English language materials available for those who are interested to pursue.[37] In any event, there certainly are circumstances which render prohibitions on certain burial rights inapplicable. For example, although the sixteenth century code of law, the Shulhan Arukh, which continues to be a major

---

[30] *See* BABYLONIAN TALMUD, *Sanhedrin* 90a. *See also* EPHRAIM OSHRY, 1 SHUT MIMA'AMAKIM no. 6, at 46–47 (Heb.) (citing various authorities); SHLOMO KLUGER, HAELEF LEKHAH SHLOMO, *Yoreh De'ah* 321; ELIEZER WALDENBURG, 7 TZITZ ELIEZER no. 49, *Kuntras Even Yaakov*, Chapter 1 (Heb.).

[31] SHULHAN ARUKH, *Yoreh De'ah* 345; MAIMONIDES, MISHNEH TORAH, *Hilkhot Avel* 1:11. *See also* BABYLONIAN TALMUD, *Semahot* 2:1.

[32] Fred Rosner, *Suicide in Jewish Law*, JEWISH BIOETHICS 317, 326–27 (1979). *See also* TUKAZINSKY, *supra* note 28.

[33] Similarly, a person is compared to a Torah scroll and just as it is a sin to destroy a Torah scroll it is a sin to kill a person. *See* TUKAZINSKY, *supra* note 28. An analogous concern is reflected in the rule that, although every person executed by the rabbinical court had to be hanged, the person had to be taken down and buried before nightfall. *Deuteronomy* 21:22, 23. To leave a human body hanging longer than that was considered to be an offense to God in whose image man was made. *See* SHLOMO YITZHAKI, COMMENTARY TO THE TORAH, *Deuteronomy* 21:23. *See also* NAHMANIDES, COMMENTARY TO THE TORAH, *Deuteronomy* 21:22.

[34] *See* TUKAZINSKY, *supra* note 28, at 269–70.

[35] *See* Rosner, *supra* note 32, at 327. The Mishnah explains that Rabbi Yaakov used to say: "Better is one hour of repentance and good deeds in this world than all of the life in the world to come." MISHNAH, *Pirkei Avot* 4:22.

[36] *See* Rosner, *supra* note 32, at 326 ("stating [that] [d]eath in most circumstances is the greatest atonement for one's sins (Yoma 86); however, in a suicide's death there has been committed a cardinal transgression rather than expiation"). *See also* MAIMONIDES, *supra* note 9, at 1:4, 2:1.

[37] *See, e.g.*, Steven H. Resnicoff, *Jewish Law Perspectives on Suicide and Physician-Assisted Dying*, 13 J. LAW & RELIGION 289 (1998–1999); WEINER, *supra* note 22, at 7; BASIL F. HERRING, JEWISH ETHICS AND HALAKHAH FOR OUR TIME 47–65 (1984); Rosner, *supra* note 32, at 326–27; NOAM J. ZOHAR, ALTERNATIVES IN JEWISH BIOETHICS 54–58 (1977); EPHRAIM OSHRY, RESPONSA FROM THE HOLOCAUST 34 (1989).

Jewish law authority, explains that a person who commits suicide is generally not to be eulogized, it provides an explicit exception for a person who, "as [King] Saul," committed suicide while under duress.[38]

Chapter 3 discusses a person's responsibility to others. Among other things, it explains that it is not only biblically forbidden to enable a person to transgress Jewish law if the person could not otherwise do so, but it is rabbinically forbidden to assist another Jew to commit a transgression even if the person could have done so without the help. These rules would apply to collaborating in someone else's suicide.

[C] The Proscription Against Murder

The biblical rule, "[t]hou shalt not murder," is clear.[39] However, there are various procedural rules that apply before a rabbinic court exercising its customary authority may convict and execute a murderer. Theoretically, at least, it is also possible for a Jewish king and a rabbinic court utilizing its "special powers" to execute or cause the death of murderers with far fewer procedural requirements. Chapter 8 discusses this subject in some detail.

Jewish law authorities use the following biblical language to conclude that a murderer who escapes humanly imposed punishment is divinely punished:

> The blood of your lives will I require; from the hand of every beast will I require it, and from the hand of man, from the hand of a person's brother, will I require the life of man. If one spills the blood of a man, one's [own] blood will be spilled by man. [40]

Such persons will be punished not only for direct acts of murder but also for acts that indirectly cause the loss of life.[41] For example, the phrase, "From the hand of every beast will I require it," promises punishment to those who incapacitate someone, such as by tying him up, thereby leaving him defenseless to the fatal attack of a wild animal.[42] "From the hand of man" assures punishment to those who hire someone to commit murder for them.[43]

The rule against murder cannot be contravened even to save one's own life.[44] Assume, for example, that Reuven holds a gun to Shimon's head and tells Shimon: "Here's a knife. Either you use it to kill Levi, who is tied to this chair, or I will use

---

[38] SHULHAN ARUKH, *Yoreh De'ah* 345:2.

[39] *Exodus* 20:12; *Deuteronomy* 5:16.

[40] *Genesis* 9:6.

[41] *See, e.g.*, MAIMONIDES, *supra* note 12, at 3:10:

> But one who ties up another and leaves him to die of hunger, or ties him in a place in which cold or heat will result in his death . . . in any of these [cases] he is not liable for capital punishment [imposed by a rabbinic court], but is still considered a murderer. The One that seeks blood will seek from him the blood which he spilled.

[42] *Id.*

[43] *Id.* at 2:2.

[44] MAIMONIDES, *supra* note 12, at 5:1. *See also* ABRAHAM, *supra* note 20, at 23–24 (citing rules and authorities).

this gun to kill you." Even if Shimon fully believes Reuven's threat, Shimon is not allowed to kill Levi.[45] It would not matter even if it were certain that Levi had only an instant left to live.[46] Nor would it make any difference if Levi were comatose, mentally deranged, physically handicapped,[47] terminally ill,[48] and apparently unable to perform any commandments.[49] All innocent life is sacrosanct and cannot be sacrificed.[50]

What if Levi were in great pain and begged Shimon to kill him so that Levi could find "relief"? This, too, would generally be forbidden, because, as noted before, a person does not possess a proprietary interest in his life.[51] In addition, Rabbi Jacob Zevi Mecklenburg, a nineteenth century scholar, derives the prohibition from a close examination of the passage cited above. He asks what lesson is learned from the phrase, "from the hand of a person's brother, will I require the life of man."[52] A proscription against fratricide would seem to follow logically from the prohibition against ordinary homicide. Indeed, fratricide may even appear more abhorrent than simple murder of a stranger. According to Jewish law's oral tradition, if a rule can be logically derived, there is no need for it to be explicitly stated in the Torah. Consequently, this biblical passage must communicate some additional message. Rabbi Mecklenburg argues that the apparent surplusage is necessary to outlaw an act of killing even when the act is motivated by "brotherly love," for example, by a misguided desire to mercifully end the life of a person suffering from excruciating pain.[53]

---

[45] MAIMONIDES, *supra* note 12, at 5:2, 7.

[46] BABAD, *supra* note 26 (the prohibition against murder applies equally to someone with only a moment to live as to someone with many years to live).

[47] *See, e.g.*, ELIEZER FLECKELES, 1 TESHUVAH MEAHAVAH 53 (there was an affirmative obligation to preserve the life of a child born with animal-like organs and features); 13 ELIEZER WALDENBURG, TZITZ ELIEZER 88 (the lives of children born with severe birth defects must be preserved just as the lives of any other children); YEHUDA HEHASID, SEFER HASIDIM no. 186.

[48] MAIMONIDES, *supra* note 12, at 2:7: "There is no difference between a person who kills either a healthy person or one who is ill and dying or even a *goses* [e.g., someone manifesting certain symptoms of imminent death]. In all of these cases, the murderer is put to death."

[49] *See, e.g.*, SHLOMO ZALMAN AUERBACH, MINHAT SHLOMO no. 91 (Heb.).

[50] HALEVI, *supra* note 11.

[51] *See, e.g.*, ELIEZER WALDENBURG, 9 TZITZ ELIEZER, *Ramat Rachel* no. 29; YEHIEL M. EPSTEIN, ARUKH HASHULHAN, *Yoreh De'ah* 331.

[52] *Genesis* 9:5, as translated by Bleich, *supra* note 3, at 139.

[53] JACOB ZEVI MECKLENBURG, HAKETAV VEHAKABBALAH no 20 (5th ed. 1946), cited by Bleich, *supra* note 3, at 139–40. *See also* ABRAHAM, GUIDE TO MEDICAL HALACHAH at 193 (citing sources). A number of authorities explain that Jewish law believes that life, even a life with suffering, is in a person's own best interests. To support this proposition, they cite a Talmudic passage regarding a Soteh, a woman accused of adultery under certain specific circumstances. In the times of the Temple, a Soteh might be required to drink a certain potion. *Numbers* 5:11–31. If guilty, she would die — but not always immediately. The Talmud explains that if, unrelated to the adultery, the woman had other merits, the potion would cause a degenerative, lingering death. Although this condition would presumably involve physical and emotional pain, it was nonetheless considered a reward in contrast to immediate death. *See, e.g.*, Bleich, *supra* note 3, at 141 (citing *Psalms* 118:18, which states that this "sentiment . . . is reflected in the words of the Psalmist: 'The Lord has indeed punished me, but He has not left me to die.' "). *See also* AUERBACH, *supra* note 49; ABRAHAM S. ABRAHAM, NISHMAT AVRAHAM, *Yoreh De'ah* 339(4). Of course, it may be that a particular person's suffering could exceed the pain involved in a Soteh's lingering death. If so, the case

According to some Jewish law authorities, the prohibition against murder is also relevant to the discussion of abortion. Jewish law definitely permits the abortion of a Jewish fetus if both of the following are true: (1) neither the fetus' head nor the majority of the fetus' body has emerged from the mother, and (2) the fetus represents a threat to the mother's life. Whether there are other exceptions depends, in part, on the nature of the offense involved in an impermissible abortion. Some authorities believe that an illegal abortion falls within the Jewish legal category of "murder," although it is not a full-fledged murder. If it were a full-fledged murder, there would be no exception. But the fact that the transgression even falls within the category of murder is enough to prevent there from being many exceptions. Other authorities, however, believe that an illegal abortion does not constitute "murder." Consequently, they identify a number of other exceptions.[54] Note, however, that irrespective of the nature of the transgression, the biblical doctrine of *lifnei iver*, as described in Chapter 3, would prohibit someone from enabling an illegal abortion that could not have been performed without such assistance. Similarly, the rabbinic doctrine of *mesayeah*, also discussed in Chapter 3, would proscribe helping a Jew commit a forbidden abortion even if the abortion could have been done without the help.

---

of the Soteh would not prove that continued life coupled with excessive pain would be a boon. As to the general issue whether a life with pain and suffering is considered preferable to death, see WEINER, *supra* note 22, at 33–46.

[54] *See generally* BASIL F. HERRING, JEWISH ETHICS AND HALAKHAH FOR OUR TIME 24 (1984).

Chapter 14

JEWISH AND SECULAR DEBTOR-CREDITOR AND BANKRUPTCY LAW

§ 14.01   INTRODUCTION

This chapter:

1. compares and contrasts the American and Jewish law perspectives on the moral obligation to pay one's debts; and

2. examines some of the interrelationships between American bankruptcy law and Jewish law.

§ 14.02   AMERICAN AND JEWISH PERSPECTIVES ON THE DUTY TO PAY DEBTS

There are consensual debts and non-consensual debts. Consensual debts usually result from some voluntary contractual interaction between two parties. For example, Able may enter into a contract with Baker, whereby Able promises to pay Baker in exchange for receipt of Baker's services, the use or transfer of ownership of Baker's property, or the loan of Baker's money. Able's non-payment constitutes a breach by Able of his promise. Able's non-consensual debts to Baker do not arise from Baker's voluntary acts. Rather, they are the product of Able's having stolen property from Baker or Able's having tortiously damaged Baker or Baker's property. For example, if Able runs his car into Baker's, damaging it, Baker becomes a non-consensual creditor of Able.

[A]   American View of Contract Versus Non-Contract Debts

[1]   No Moral Wrong in Breaching Contract

Interestingly, the prevailing perspective in American legal theory seems to be that a breach of contract is morally blameless. Even if the language of a contract provides that a party *promises* to provide a specific performance, rather than just *agreeing* to do so, the party is perceived as having only agreed *either* to perform or to be legally responsible for the contract law consequences.[1] As a result, under American law, there is no *moral* imperative to fulfill one's contractual commitment. Thus, the amount of recoverable contract damages is limited. A contract defendant need only pay damages that were foreseeable at the time the contract was formed, even if at the time the defendant intentionally decides to breach the contract it is clear that the breach will cause considerably greater harm.[2] Indeed, this limitation is intended to encourage breaches that are perceived to be "economically efficient,"[3] thereby increasing overall societal wealth.[4]

An example of a supposed efficient breach is a case in which Able is under contract to sell product ("Gizmo") to Baker for $1,000. This sale is going to allow Baker to increase the value of his property by $1,100 (for a net profit to Baker of $100, i.e., $1,100 minus the $1,000 price for Gizmo) in a process that will completely consume the Gizmo. However, before performing the contract by delivering Gizmo, Able finds another use for Gizmo — whether for Able himself or some third person — which has a value of $1,200. According to the theory of efficient breach, society's

---

[1] *See, e.g.*, Oliver Wendall Holmes, *The Path of the Law*, 10 Harv. L. Rev. 457, 462 (1896-1897); Avery Katz, *The Option Element in Contracting*, 90 Va. L. Rev. 2187, 2192 (2004).

[2] Restatement (Second) of Law of Contracts § 351. *See also* Steven J. Burton, Principles of Contract Law 349 (2d ed. 2001).

[3] Of course, on the individual transaction level, rather than on the overall rule level, calculating foreseeable damages at the time of the decision to breach would appear to be more efficient. *Id.*

[4] *See, e.g.*, XCO International, Inc. v. Pacific Scientific Co., 369 F.3d 998, 1001 (7th Cir. 2004) ("breaches that confer a greater benefit on the contract breaker than [damage] on the victim of the breach, in which event breach plus compensation for the victim produces a net gain with no losers and should be encouraged"); Richard Posner, Economic Analysis of the Law § 4.1 (4th ed. 1992); Howard O. Hunter, Modern Law of Contracts § 1.3 (2006).

overall wealth would be $100 greater if Able would breach the contract with Baker and realize Gizmo's $1,200 value rather than deliver it to Baker who will only realize Gizmo's $1,100 value. Furthermore, according to the theory, Able can pay Baker the $100 loss in expected profit that Baker suffered (again, the difference between the $1,100 benefit Baker would have realized and the $1,000 price Baker would have paid).

There is, of course, serious questions both as to whether the theory of efficient breach really results in greater societal wealth and, even if it does, whether this would justify the breach's effect on the allocation of wealth.[5] In practice, a party that breaches a contract often denies the breach and only pays compensation if it is legally compelled to do so. Prosecuting a civil lawsuit in the United States, however, is quite an expensive undertaking, including court costs, deposition fees, expert witness' fees (where applicable), the plaintiff's time being available for the trial,[6] and, often most importantly, attorney's fees. Yet a successful plaintiff is typically not permitted to recover these costs. Consequently, under American contract law, Able would have an incentive to violate the contract even if the gain to it were less than Baker's loss.[7] Why? Because Able realizes that Baker will likely not file suit. In our example, for instance, Baker's loss was only $100, and the likely costs to it of filing a lawsuit would be thousands of dollars.

Suppose we change the numbers in the example so that purchase price is $1,000,000, the benefit to Baker, $1,100,000, and the value of the new use that Able discovered, $1,200,000. It may remain unlikely that Baker would sue. First, the costs of litigation could still exceed the $100,000 difference between the $1,000,000 contract price and the $1,100,000 profit Baker was going to realize. Second, Baker must consider the possibility that he may not prevail at trial even though his claim is meritorious. Baker may simply be unable to prove the breach, that it incurred recoverable damages because of the breach, or the amount of such damages.[8] Such uncertainty as to its possible success may persuade Baker that it is not worthwhile to invest in a lawsuit.

Also consistent with the notion that a party who breaches a contract commits no moral wrong is the fact that, under American law, no punitive damages are imposed for breach of contract. In addition, non-breaching parties are not allowed to recover any damages that they could have reasonably avoided — even in cases in which a

---

[5] *See, e.g.,* Daniel Friedmann, *The Efficient Breach Fallacy,* 18 J. LEGAL STUD. 1 (1989).

[6] Often the plaintiff, or one or more agents of the plaintiff, has to spend time consulting with the plaintiff's attorney, participating in depositions, and being available to testify in court. Sometimes a lawsuit can only be filed in a court which is not in a location that is convenient for the plaintiff or the plaintiff's agents. In addition, sometimes, court proceedings are postponed, even at the last minute, creating additional burdens for the parties.

[7] For example, suppose Able found an alternative use with a value of $1,050, which is less than the $1,100 value of Baker's use. If it is clear that Baker will not sue, Able still may have an incentive to breach and get the $1,050 value rather than the $1,000 contract price. Of course, breaching the contract may cause Able to incur other costs, such as reputational injury, more difficulties in finding future contract partners, etc. Consideration of these factors is beyond the scope of this book.

[8] Under American contract law, the plaintiff must prove its damages "with reasonable certainty."

defendant's breach was willful.[9] If, however, breaching a contract were deemed a moral wrong, it would seem appropriate to place the loss on the willfully breaching party than on the innocent, albeit negligent, victim. Furthermore, in most American jurisdictions, payments that the aggrieved party receives from collateral sources, such as insurance, can reduce the amount that the defendant is obligated to pay. In other words, "the collateral source rule," which prevents such payments from resuding a plaintiff's recovery generally does not apply to contract cases.[10]

[2] A Tortfeasor is a Wrongdoer

By contrast, tort law obligations are not voluntarily undertaken. They are externally imposed. These duties, at least when based on "fault," reflect society's moral norms, and a violator is a "wrongdoer."[11] Accordingly, American tort law is designed not only to compensate victims, but also to punish tortfeasors[12] and to deter future wrongdoing.[13] All proximately caused damages are collectible, the collateral rule does not reduce the defendant's liability, and, in egregious cases, punitive damages are imposed.

[3] Possible Connection to American Bankruptcy Law

Of course, it is possible to distinguish between the American moral perspective on the breaching of a contract and its moral perspective on the failure to pay a debt for having breached a contract. Nevertheless, there is no evidence of such a distinction. Just as American contract law limits a party's liability for breach of contract in order to promote the perceived public policy favoring "efficient" breaches, American bankruptcy law, for a variety of other perceived public policies, broadly allows a person to obtain a discharge of consensually incurred debt.[14] Admittedly, it allows a discharge of some tortiously incurred debt as well. Nevertheless, American bankruptcy law makes it difficult or impossible for an individual debtor to obtain a discharge from a number of debts incurred by morally culpable conduct, such as fraud, defalcation, and willful damage to person or

---

[9] *See* E. ALLAN FARNSWORTH, CONTRACTS § 12.12, at 778 *et seq.* (4th ed. 2004).

[10] For a discussion of the differences between the American and Jewish law approaches to the collateral source rule, see Steven H. Resnicoff, *May Plaintiffs Enjoy a Double Recovery? The "Collateral Source Rule" and Jewish Law*, 18 JEWISH LAW ASS'N STUD. 187 (Joseph Fleishman ed., 2008).

[11] *See* Richard C. Witzel, Jr., Note, *The Collateral Source Rule and State-Provided Special Education and Therapy*, 75 WASH. U. L.Q. 697, 702 (1997), who argues that "[i]n the latter part of the nineteenth century [i.e., when the collateral source rule was first recognized in the United States], a tortfeasor would only be liable under the 'rather strict concepts of negligence'" which were then prevalent. Certainly, the "wrongdoer" appellation would seem an inappropriate appellation for many persons liable under modern "no-fault" approaches. This is one of the policy arguments in favor of restricting the scope of America's collateral source rule.

[12] Shipler v. General Motors Corp., 710 N.W.2d 807 (Neb. 2006) (purpose of collateral source rule is to prevent wrongdoer from escaping duty to pay for the damage it caused).

[13] RESTATEMENT (SECOND) OF LAW OF TORT § 901(c).

[14] One such policy is to encourage capitalistic entrepreneurism. Similarly, generous early state laws that prevented creditors from executing on certain types of property held by creditors were initially enacted by Western States to encourage pioneers to take the risks inherent in blazing the frontiers.

property.[15] Similarly, if the debtor is guilty of trying to subvert the bankruptcy process itself, the debtor may be denied a discharge of any of the debtor's debts.[16]

[B] Jewish Law View of Contract Obligations

By contrast to American law, Jewish law regards the repayment of debt to Jewish creditors as a moral and religious imperative. Most authorities characterize the payment of one's debts as an affirmative biblical commandment no less than others, such as hearing the Shofar blown on the Jewish New Year (Rosh Hashanah).[17] Rabbi Yisroel Meir Kagan (1838–1933) states that if a debtor possessing the resources to repay a debt refuses to do so, he also violates the negative biblical commandment not to oppress (*lo ta'ashok*) one's neighbor.[18] This verse applies to the case of a person who became indebted consensually, such as a person who borrowed money from a lender and promised to repay.[19] In fact, the Psalms call such as person "wicked": "The wicked one borrows but does not repay."[20] In the Tannaitic Teachings of the Fathers (Pirkei Avot), Rabban Yohanan ben Zakhai asks his five prize students to identify the evil path that would alienate a person from others. Rabbi Shimon bar Yohai answers, "An evil person borrows and does not repay."[21]

R. Kagan explains that it is to such persons that the sages apply the verse, "Those who acquire wealth in violation of halakhah, in mid-life *it(they) will leave them(it)*" (emphasis added). The italicized words represent alternative translations of two ambiguous Hebrew words. Thus, the phrase "it (they) will leave them (it)" has two meanings. Sometimes the wealth ("it") leaves the people ("them") — i.e., the people become impoverished while still young. Sometimes the people ("they") leave the wealth ("it") — i.e., the people die before they can enjoy the weath.

The Jewish sources cited so far deal with loans, but Jewish law takes a similarly moralistic view of other contractual duties. It places a high value on fulfilling the commitments that one makes. Indeed, it believes that doing so is important not only to protect the interests of others but also to perfect one's own character. Ideally, one should abide by a commitment even if it was only made mentally, in one's own heart. Thus, the Babylonian Talmud makes the following comment regarding Psalm 15:

"Who may sojourn in Your Tent? Who may dwell on Your Holy Mountain? One who walks in perfect innocence, does what is right and speaks

---

[15] *See, e.g.,* 11 U.S.C. §§ 523, 1141(d), 1328(a), 1328(b).

[16] *See, e.g.,* 11 U.S.C. § 727.

[17] *See* SHLOMO YITZHAKI (a/k/a *Rashi*; 1040–1105), BABYLONIAN TALMUD, *Ketuboth* 86a (citing *Leviticus* 19:36); YAAKOV YESHAYA BLAU, PITHEI HOSHEN, *Dinei Halva'ah*, ch. 2, *halakhah* 1, n.1 (Heb.) (citing various authorities).

[18] YISROEL MEIR KAGAN, 2 AHAVAT HESSED, ch. 24 (Heb.).

[19] SHULHAN ARUKH, *Hoshen Mishpat* 359:8.

[20] *Psalms* 37:21.

[21] MISHNAH, *Pirkei Avot* 2:14.

truthfully from his heart." . . . [Psalm 15] . . . "[S]peaks truthfully from his heart" — [this refers to a person] such as Rav Safra.[22]

Rabbi Solomon Yitzhaki (*Rashi*; 1040–1105) explains this reference to Rav Safra:

Rav Safra — [found] in the She'iltot of Rav Aha (She'iltot 36). Here is how the episode goes: Rav Safra had an item to sell and a person came up to him while he [Rav Safra] was reciting Kriyat Shema. The person said, "Give me the object for such-and-such amount of money," and Rav Safra did not answer him because he was reciting Kriyat Shema. The person thought that he [Rav Safra] was unwilling to give him the object for that price, and he increased the amount, saying, "Give it to me for such-and-such higher price." After he finished reciting Kriyat Shema, he [Rav Safra] told the man, "Take it for the [lower] price you mentioned first, because I had [mentally] decided to give it to you for that amount."[23]

Had Rav Safra failed to fulfill his mental commitment,[24] the purchaser would have suffered no adverse emotional or psychological harm, because he was unaware of that commitment. Nor could the purchaser be said to have suffered a financial "loss," even if he or she would have paid the higher price, because the purchaser had no legally enforceable right to purchase at the lower price. Consequently, the reason for the Psalm's emphasis on fulfilling such a mental commitment is the perfection of one's own character. Because this standard appears to be relatively lofty,[25] most authorities agree that a person who fails to reach it not only faces no sanction in this world but is also guiltless in the world to come. Yet such conduct is certainly encouraged.

Under Jewish law, certain formalities must be fulfilled before a person becomes contractually bound. Suppose a buyer of personal property pays the purchase price but does not fulfill the necessary formality (which, in this case, is to take possession of the personalty). Suppose further that the seller changes his mind and sends the money back, whereupon the buyer sues. The court will not force the seller to transfer ownership of the property or pay damages. Nevertheless, the court will proclaim a "curse" on the party who backed out. The curse, in part, states that "He who exacted payment from the generation of the Flood and from the generation of the Tower of Bavel will in the future exact payment from anyone who does not abide by his word."[26] The phrase, "anyone who does not abide by his word," seems to refer to the person who backed out in the third person. According to some authorities, the curse actually names the person explicitly.[27] According to the majority view, this rule applies even if the person backs out because the market price of the object

---

[22] BABYLONIAN TALMUD, *Makkot* 24a.

[23] SHLOMO YITZHAKI, BABYLONIAN TALMUD, *Makkot* 24a.

[24] *See* WITH PERFECT FAITH: THE FOUNDATIONS OF JEWISH BELIEF 1–2, n.2 (J. David Bleich ed., 1983) (discussing that, in "medieval usage," the "heart" is often used to represent the intellect).

[25] *See* YEHUDAH HEHASID (d. 1217), SEFER HASIDIM, § 1059 (Heb.) (suggesting that it would be good for a person to specifically intend that his thoughts not count as "decisions" until and unless he articulates them aloud).

[26] SHULHAN ARUKH, *Hoshen Mishpat* 204:4.

[27] MOSHE ISSERLES (a/k/a *Rema*; 1525 or 1530–1572), SHULHAN ARUKH, *Hoshen Mishpat* 204:4.

changed.[28] In fact, even if no money has changed hands, if one of the parties backs out after having made an oral commitment, the person is labeled "untrustworthy" (*mehusar amanah*).[29]

§ 14.03 JEWISH LAW PROTECTIONS

Jewish law traditionally provided various protections for a debtor that were unavailable in other legal systems. Nevertheless, it did not offer a true discharge of indebtedness.

[A] Protections, Generally

Creditors were enjoined from oppressive collection tactics. Secured creditors, for example, were precluded from entering a debtor's home to seize collateral. In addition, certain properties — such as particular tools of one's trade, money for food for thirty days, clothing for twelve months, and rent for a particular period of time — were altogether exempt from collection.[30] Moreover, except for thieves who were unable to return or repay the value of what they stole, Jewish debtors could be neither imprisoned nor subjected to involuntary servitude.[31] Nonetheless, it must be acknowledged that, despite objections by many Jewish law authorities, various Jewish communities throughout history issued local legislation that imposed imprisonment on debtors who failed to pay despite possessing the ability to do so.[32]

[B] No Equivalent to a Bankruptcy Discharge Law

Notwithstanding these generally pro-debtor rules, Jewish law does not provide a debtor with the equivalent of a general discharge of indebtedness. Instead, if property collected from a debtor is insufficiently valuable to pay off the debtor's debts, the debtor remains personally liable for any unpaid amounts. If and when the debtor acquires additional assets, the debtor is obligated to pay, and this obligation is enforceable by rabbinic court (*bet din*).

People frequently confuse the effect of the biblical law pertaining to the Sabbatical year (*Shemittah* year), which was every seventh year,[33] with the effect

---

[28] *See generally* Steven H. Resnicoff, *Keeping One's Word in Commercial & Non-Commercial Contexts, in* JEWISH LAW ASSOCIATION STUDIES XVI (Elliot Dorff ed., 2007).

[29] *Id.*

[30] *See* SHULHAN ARUKH, *Hoshen Mishpat* 97:23–29.

[31] *Id.* at 97:15. Thieves could be forced to work off restitutive obligations. *See* THE PRINCIPLES OF JEWISH LAW 622–24 (Menachem Elon ed., 1975).

[32] *See, e.g.*, Jonathan M. Lewis, *Insolvency in Jewish Law, in* JEWISH LAW ASSOCIATION STUDIES IX: THE LONDON CONFERENCE 103, 124–25 (Bernard S. Jackson ed., 1997) (citing sources). Note that some Jewish law writers avoid addressing the Jewish law status of this legislation. *See, e.g.*, Meir Tamari, *Ethical Issues in Bankruptcy: A Jewish Perspective*, 9 J. BUS. ETHICS 785, 786 (1990) ("There is no trace in Judaism of bodily punishment, exile or jail for debts.").

[33] *See Deuteronomy* 15:1–2. The biblical *Sabbatical* year law only applied when the law of the Jubilee year (the fiftieth year) applied, and the latter only applied under certain conditions, one of which was that

of an American bankruptcy discharge.[34] On the Sabbatical year, certain debts were automatically discharged. Nevertheless, the Sabbatical year's rules — as well as its apparent function — importantly differed from bankruptcy law in several ways. In many ways, the debt relief granted by the Sabbatical year was far narrower than that afforded by bankruptcy law. The Sabbatical year only discharged a debt that was in the nature of a "loan." It did not, for example, discharge an employer's obligations to pay an employee's wages,[35] a shopper's obligation to repay credit extended by merchants,[36] a thief's responsibility to make restitution,[37] a tortfeasor's obligation to pay certain biblical fines,[38] or a lender's obligation to return interest received from Jewish borrowers in violation of Jewish law.[39] Nor did it apply to a debt that did not mature prior to the end of the Sabbatical year,[40] to a judgment debt (even if the judgment did no more than order a debtor to repay a loan), or to a debt that a creditor had turned over to a rabbinical court for collection.[41] Even as to debts in the nature of a "loan," the Sabbatical year only canceled debts that were unsecured. If there was collateral for a debt, the debt was not canceled.[42] According to some authorities, even the amount, if any, by which the debt exceeded the value of the collateral was not canceled.[43]

In another way, however, the Sabbatical year provided far broader relief than American bankruptcy law. With respect to the kinds of debts to which it applied, the Sabbatical year canceled the obligations of the rich and poor alike. This rule makes it clear that Sabbatical was not only intended to protect the poor, but also to teach other lessons. Indeed, it seems to be part of a larger plan of periodic renewal designed to remind humankind of its impermanent place in this material world.[44] This theme also resonates with respect to the laws of the Jubilee year, which occurred at the end of seven Sabbatical years. In the Jubilee year, real estate was returned to its original owners and slaves were emancipated.[45]

Jewish legal history, however, provides strong evidence of rabbinic efforts to delimit the protections provided by Sabbatical.[46] The Talmud makes it clear that even if the debt were canceled, the debtor was strongly urged to pay it. Indeed, the

---

the majority of the Jewish people live in the land of Israel. *See Leviticus* 25:10. Rabbinically, however, the *Sabbatical* law applies even now. *See* SHULHAN ARUKH, *Hoshen Mishpat* 67:1.

[34] Of course, it is certainly possible that the *Sabbatical* paradigm did, at some level, politically inspire early bankruptcy law.

[35] SHULHAN ARUKH, *Hoshen Mishpat* 67:15.

[36] *Id.* at 67:14.

[37] *See generally* YISROEL REISMAN, THE LAWS OF RIBIS 357–71 (1995).

[38] SHULHAN ARUKH, *Hoshen Mishpat* 67:16.

[39] *See* THE PRINCIPLES OF JEWISH LAW, *supra* note 31, cols. 76, 267; REISMAN, *supra* note 37, at 365–71.

[40] SHULHAN ARUKH, *Hoshen Mishpat* 67:10.

[41] *Id.* at 67:11. *See, e.g.*, BABYLONIAN TALMUD, *Gittin* 37b.

[42] SHULHAN ARUKH, *Hoshen Mishpat* 67:12.

[43] *Id.*

[44] AHARON HALEVI (1235–1290), SEFER HAHINNUKH 330 (Heb.). *See* Appendix 1: Glossary, *infra*, as to the controversy over authorship of this work.

[45] *Id.*

[46] One major exception, of course, is that, although for technical reasons the biblical law of the

creditor may even be allowed to take certain physical steps to motivate the debtor to pay.[47] Furthermore, the Talmud states that the sages established a procedure, known as *Prosbul*, that made it extremely easy to turn a debt over to a rabbinic court for collection and, thus, prevent the debt from being canceled.[48] The Talmud explains that the sages created *Prosbul* for the benefit of borrowers rather than to protect the rights of creditors. The sages saw that as the Sabbatical year would approach, lenders were increasingly unwilling to provide loans, and this led the poor to suffer. *Prosbul* encouraged creditors by protecting the enforceability of their claims and, in doing so, benefitted the poor by enabling them to find willing lenders.

In earlier chapters, we discussed the fact that, as a practical matter, much of the legislative power in the Jewish law system has been lost because some legal institutions are in desuetude and because the traditionally close-knit, structured nature of Jewish communities has changed. Even if such legislative power prevailed today, it is far from certain that Jewish law authorities would agree with the secular policy analysis that regards bankruptcy discharge law as desirable.

Nonetheless, we have also learned that there are two major Jewish law doctrines that sometimes operate to import into halakhah the secular laws or practices of the communities within which Jews live. These doctrines are *dina demalkhuta dina* (the Law of the Kingdom is religiously valid law) and *minhag hasoharim* (business custom). We now examine how American law and Jewish law interrelate, primarily in light of these two principles.

§ 14.04   INTERRELATIONSHIPS BETWEEN AMERICAN BANKRUPTCY LAW AND JEWISH LAW

American Bankruptcy law provides certain benefits to debtors. In addition, it provides rules regarding the rights of creditors with respect to each other and with respect to the bankruptcy "estate," a term that will soon be described. We will investigate the extent to which Jewish law allows such benefits and rights to be enjoyed.

[A]   American Bankruptcy Law Benefits to Debtors

First, we will focus on the benefits provided to debtors. The American Bankruptcy Code is codified in Title 11 of the United States Code. Title 11 consists of a number of individual chapters, some setting forth generally applicable rules and others devoted to various types of bankruptcies. These various proceedings can be characterized as falling into one of two categories: liquidations and reorganizations. There are two principal benefits that liquidations and reorganizations both offer: an immediate respite from debt collection efforts and an

---

Sabbatical year became inapplicable a millennium ago, rabbinical authorities decided to impose it rabbinically.

[47] *See, e.g.*, Babylonian Talmud, *Gittin* 37b.

[48] *See* The Principles of Jewish Law, *supra* note 31, cols. 76, 267; Reisman, *supra* note 37, at 365–71.

ultimate discharge of personal liability for many or all of one's debts.[49]

Both liquidations and reorganizations allow a debtor a discharge from personal liability for many of his or her debts without obtaining the consent of even a majority of the debtor's creditors. A liquidation bankruptcy is conducted pursuant to chapter 7 of the Bankruptcy Code. The debtor may deliver to the court all of the debtor's property (except for certain "exempt" property which the debtor is allowed to keep) for distribution to creditors. In "exchange" for the surrender of such property, the debtor can generally be relieved of personal liability for any unpaid debt. Certain types of debts, usually tax debts to the government or debts arising out of the debtor's wrongful conduct, are not discharged.[50] Similarly, if the debtor engaged in certain specific types of conduct deemed to be an abuse of the bankruptcy laws, the debtor might be denied a discharge of any debts.[51] This discharge can be obtained without the consent of any of the creditors.

In a reorganization bankruptcy, the debtor must make payments to creditors over a number of years pursuant to a "plan" that must be approved ("confirmed") by the court. There are two types of reorganization bankruptcies available to individuals.[52] One type, designed for individuals with *relatively* little debt, is governed by Bankruptcy Code chapter 13. A more complex procedure, available not only to individuals but also to entities such as corporations and partnerships, is set forth in Bankruptcy Code chapter 11. In each case, statutory rules determine the minimum amount the debtor must pay to the various creditors.[53] In chapter 13 liquidations, the debtor ordinarily receives a discharge of its remaining debt only upon successful completion of the partial payments specified in its plan.[54] The same is true for individuals in chapter 11, unless the court, after notice and a hearing, enters an order effectuating the discharge at some earlier point in time.[55] In both chapter 13 and chapter 11 cases, an individual debtor may be denied a discharge of liability for certain types of debts or for any debts. As in chapter 7, these exceptions to discharge typically arise from the debtor's misconduct either when incurring particular debts or with respect to the bankruptcy proceeding itself.[56]

The second principal benefit available to debtors is protection from creditors' collection efforts. There are various Bankruptcy Code provisions that provide such

---

[49] Reorganizations provide debtors a third, extremely important benefit. They allow the debtor the opportunity to become financially rehabilitated while retaining even non-exempt property by permitting the debtors to restructure their debt, enabling them to stay afloat until their income flow increases.

[50] 11 U.S.C. § 523(a).

[51] 11 U.S.C. § 727.

[52] A third type of reorganization, similar to that of chapter 13, is available to individuals who fit the statutory definition of a "family farmer." This third type of reorganization is set forth in Bankruptcy Code chapter 12. There are comparatively few chapter 12 bankruptcies. In any event, for our purposes, there is nothing particularly remarkable about them.

[53] 11 U.S.C. §§ 1129, 1325.

[54] 11 U.S.C. § 1328(a). In certain exceptional cases, a more narrow discharge may be granted even if not all payments prescribed by the plan were made. 11 U.S.C. § 1328(b).

[55] 11 U.S.C. § 1141(d)(5)(A).

[56] 11 U.S.C. §§ 1141(d), 1328.

protection. The principal ones are the "automatic stay" (or simply, the "stay")[57] and the "discharge injunction."[58] A debtor's voluntary filing of a bankruptcy petition automatically triggers the automatic stay.[59] Compensatory and even punitive damages may be imposed on a creditor who willfully violates the stay.[60] The stay prevents virtually all types of collection activities, including courteously worded dunning letters, the filing or continuation of lawsuits and repossessions of collateral. After a discharge of indebtedness is granted in a bankruptcy proceeding, the automatic stay lapses (unless it has already lapsed). But the discharge itself gives rise to a discharge injunction that prohibits any actions to collect or enforce the discharged debt.

[B] Bankruptcy Law and Jewish Law's Doctrine of Commercial Custom (*Minhag Hasoharim*)

Jewish law might recognize the validity of American bankruptcy law rules based on either its doctrine of commercial custom (*minhag hasoharim*) or its doctrine that the law of the kingdom is religiously valid law (*dina demalkhuta dina*).

Chapter 7 explained that:

(1)   the *minhag hasoharim* doctrine treats commercial customs as if they were default terms in every contract unless the parties expressly agree to the contrary;

(2)   according to an apparent majority rule, especially of rabbinic authorities in the United States, it does not matter whether the people whose conduct established a custom were Jewish or non-Jewish; and

(3)   according to the majority rule, it also does not matter if the custom arose out of compliance with a secular statute.

A number of poskim have discussed whether a creditor's rights against an impoverished debtor may be limited or annulled through applicable commercial custom, minhag hasoharim. Most of these poskim refer to responsa of Rabbi Moses Hakohen (a/k/a *Maharshakh*), an authority in sixteenth century Salonika.[61] Hakohen was asked about a case in which a majority of creditors agreed to give a

---

[57]   11 U.S.C. § 362.

[58]   11 U.S.C. § 524(a)(2).

[59]   If one or more creditors file an involuntary bankruptcy petition against a debtor, then the automatic stay goes into effect upon the court's issuance of "an order for relief." Involuntary bankruptcies are relatively rare.

[60]   11 U.S.C. § 362(k).

[61]   MOSES HAKOHEN (1530–1602), 2 SHUT MAHARSHAKH nos. 8, 113(Heb.). Rabbi Chaim Yosef Azulei (*Hida*; nineteenth century) quotes Rabbi Yaakov Alfandari as saying: "To us, *Mahari ibn Lev* [Rabbi Yosef ibn Lev], *Maharashdam* [Rabbi Shmuel de Medina] and Hakohen are to be considered like Rif, Rambam and Rosh." HAYYIM YOSEF AZULEI, SHEM HAGEDOLIM, *s.v. Hakohen.* Jewish law authorities typically honor earlier authorities, and Rif, Rambam and Rosh were leading rabbinical authorities hundreds of years before R. Alfandari's time. Consequently, this comment speaks volumes as to the awe in which Hakohen was held.

debtor an extension of time to pay his debts.[62] One creditor objected and sought to enforce his halakhic rights in rabbinic court. Local custom entitled a majority of creditors to force minority creditors to a compromise with the debtor. Hakohen cited a Talmudic passage discussing a particular procedure, s'tumtah, used by business people for transferring property. Even though the procedure was not otherwise biblically or rabbinically prescribed, the Talmud concluded that the procedure was effective as a matter of Jewish law. The reason for this ruling was that Jewish law recognizes commercial customs as valid even if the customs contradict what halakhah would otherwise provide. Consequently, Hakohen ruled that the local commercial custom allowing a majority of creditors to bind a minority as to a compromise with a debtor was also effective under Jewish law, and Hakohen ruled against the minority creditor.

This view of Hakohen has been cited favorably by a number of early halachic authorities.[63] Similarly, a letter sent to the Rabbi Shmuel de Medina (a/k/a Maharashdam) stated Hakohen's argument, and Maharashdam commented on it approvingly.[64] Some of the authorities citing Hakohen considered compromises that, as in Hakohen's case, extended the debtor's time to pay. Others considered compromises that affected the creditors' respective rights regarding the distribution of the debtor's assets.[65] None of these authorities indicated that Hakohen's logic was limited to such cases.[66]

Most poskim either explicitly or implicitly addressing this issue appear to apply Hakohen's approach broadly, ruling that a local custom[67] enabling a majority of creditors to force a minority of creditors to agree to a compromise is effective under Jewish law.[68] In discharging part of the debtor's debt, these compromises operated substantially as secular bankruptcy discharges. Indeed, for a number of years, in order for a debtor to obtain a discharge of debt in a "liquidation bankruptcy," a debtor needed to obtain the consent, or to at least avoid the dissent, of a majority of its creditors.[69] In "reorganization bankruptcies," the consent of

---

[62] HAKOHEN, supra note 61, no. 113.

[63] See generally Steven H. Resnicoff, Bankruptcy — A Viable Halachic Option?, 24 J. HALACHA & CONTEMP. SOC'Y 5 (Fall 1992) (citing numerous authorities). Countless authorities before and after Hakohen more generally attest to the halakhic force of commercial custom. See, e.g., SHLOMO ADRET (a/k/a Rashba; 1235–1310), 2 SHUT HARASHBA 268 (Heb.).

[64] SHMUEL DE MEDINA, SHUT MAHARASHDAM, Hoshen Mishpat 108 (Heb.).

[65] See, e.g., YEHUDA LIRME (seventeenth century), PELEITAT BEIT YEHUDA nos. 21, 22 (Heb.); HASDEI HAKOHEN PRACHYA (seventeenth century), TORAT HESSED no. 225 (Heb.); HAYYIM ESHEL (eighteenth century), SOM HAYYEI no. 33 (Heb.).

[66] See Resnicoff, supra note 63, at 16 n.37.

[67] See also HAIM ARYEH KAHANE (nineteenth century), DIVREI GEONIM, klal 14, no. 18 (Heb.) (failing to mention a requirement that there be a preexisting custom).

[68] See, e.g., MOSHE YISROEL, MASES MOSHE no. 62 (Heb.) (compromise involving discharge of debt); YITZHAK HAKOHEN, OHEL YITZHAK no. 33 (Heb.) (same); HAIM AZULAI (nineteenth century), BIRKEI YOSEF no. 12, n.14 (Heb.) (broad statement); KAHANE, supra note 67; ELIYAHU HAZAN, NIDIV LEV no. 13 (Heb.) (compromise involving discharge of debt); AVRAHAM YISROEL ALTER LANDAU, BEIT YISROEL no. 172 (Heb.) (same). See also SHMUEL SHILO, DINA DEMALKHUTA DINA 163–64 (1974) (Heb.); EZRA BASRI, 1 DINEI MAMANOT 71 (Heb.).

[69] See, e.g., American Bankruptcy Act of 1800, ch. 19, 36, 2 Stat. 19, 31, 36 (1800) (repealed 1803)

some creditors is still required.[70] Nevertheless, current bankruptcy discharge law allows a debtor to obtain a discharge in a liquidation without the consent of any creditors and in a reorganization with the consent of very few creditors.

Rabbi Yeshaya Blau and Professor Shmuel Shilo are among the relatively few contemporary commentators who explicitly discuss one or more of the R. Moses Hakohen responsa in connection with bankruptcy discharge law. Shilo correctly describes the Hakohen responsa as based on *minhag hasoharim* and states that they support secular bankruptcy law.[71] Blau does not mention Hakohen but refers to him indirectly. Blau points out that Rabbi Akiva Eger refers to a ruling by Rabbi Moses Yisroel. Rabbi Yisroel's ruling, however, cites Hakohen. Yisroel concludes that a discharge of debt obtained through an agreement with a majority of creditors binds even those creditors who objected.

Blau rules that bankruptcy law should be effective as to corporate debt[72] because corporations are creatures of secular law and it is therefore reasonable that secular law govern their affairs.[73] Blau denies that bankruptcy law is effective as to individual debtors, arguing that rare "customs" are not effective under Jewish law, implicitly suggesting that bankruptcy filings by individuals are "rare." Blau is a rabbi in Israel. In the United States, at least, such filings are quite common. Blau parenthetically refers to R. Shabbetai Hakohen (a/k/a *Shakh*; 1621–1662) and R. Rafael Hazan who, Blau believes, limit the halachic validity of the customs of non-Jews. But, as we have already seen in Chapter 7, many authorities, including R. Moses Feinstein, the leading halakhic decisor in the United States during most of the second half of the twentieth century, argue that such customs are halakhically valid. Moreover, R. David Hazan explains the view of R. Raphael Hazan, his father, as allowing a halakhically binding custom to be derived from non-Jews where the custom would be enforceable against Jews under secular law.[74]

Interestingly, a number of rabbinic authorities have ruled that a compromise reached "under coercion" is not valid without a *kinyan*, i.e., without the performance of one of the traditional Jewish law mechanisms that make a legal commitment enforceable.[75] Consequently, they characterize a compromise made

---

(discharge only with consent of two-thirds of creditors in number and in amount of debt; only creditors owed at least $50 counted); Bankruptcy Act of 1841, ch. 9, 4, 5 Stat. 443–44 (repealed 1843) (need majority of creditors in number and in amount of debt to be non-dissenting); Bankruptcy Act of 1867, ch. 176, 33, 14 Stat. 51, 533 (one who voluntarily files for bankruptcy more than one year from effective date of Act must pay creditors at least 50% and need consent of creditors holding 50% of debt in order to obtain a discharge) (amended in 1874). Either some minimum payment or consent of some minimum percentage of creditors was required in liquidation bankruptcies until the Bankruptcy Act of 1898, ch. 541, 30 Stat. 548.

[70] The confirmation requirements concerning creditor consent are too detailed to discuss here.

[71] SHILO, *supra* note 68, at 163–64.

[72] For a general discussion of the way Jewish law perceives and treats a corporation, see Steven H. Resnicoff & Michael J. Broyde, *Jewish Law and Modern Business Structures: The Corporate Paradigm*, 43 WAYNE L. REV. 1685 (1997).

[73] BLAU, *supra* note 17, *Dinei Halva'ah*, ch. 2, n.63, at 27.

[74] DAVID HAZAN, NIDIV LEV no. 12.

[75] *See* BETSALEL STERN, 3 BETSEIL HAHOKHMAH 215, resp. no. 124 (1975) (Heb.) (citing several such authorities and appearing to agree with them).

because a creditor fears he or she will otherwise receive nothing as a coerced compromise.[76] These rulings make no reference to the Moses Hakohen responsa or their progeny. It is uncertain whether these poskim would reject Moses Hakohen's approach or distinguish it in some way. How that approach might be distinguished raises tantalizing questions, exploration of which would exceed the scope of this book.

One of the authorities that initially did not cite the Moshe Hakohen responsa published a second opinion in 1986, eleven years after his first. In this second responsum, he cites the Moshe Hakohen responsa, acknowledges that his first opinion did not mention those responsa, and concludes that there is a disagreement among rabbinic authorities as to whether the conclusions of the Moshe Hakohen responsa are valid.[77]

[C] Bankruptcy Law and the "Law of the Kingdom is [Religiously] Valid Law" (*Dina Demalkhuta Dina*)

As described in Chapter 7, there are three principal approaches regarding the scope of the Jewish law doctrine that the law of the kingdom is [religiously] valid law (*dina demalkhuta dina*). The first approach, articulated by Rav Joseph Karo in his Shulhan Arukh and followed by many Sephardi rabbinic authorities, limits *dina demalkhuta dina* to laws enacted for the direct benefit of the sovereign, such as tax laws.[78] The second, espoused by Rabbi Moses Isserles, provides that, with some exceptions, *dina demalkhuta dina* also covers all laws enacted for the public good.[79] The third view, set forth by Rabbi Shabbetai Hakohen, is that although *dina demalkhuta dina* applies both to legislation directly benefiting the king and to legislation to benefit the public, it does not apply to laws that specifically purport to overrule Jewish law.[80]

[1] American Bankruptcy Law and R. Isserles' View of *Dina Demalkhuta Dina*

Most Jewish law authorities, especially in the United States, follow either Karo's or Isserles' views, with the latter being the most widely accepted view.[81] According to both of these views, the purpose underlying the American bankruptcy law is very important. Nevertheless, neither the United States Constitution, which authorizes Congress to enact a bankruptcy law, nor the federal Bankruptcy Code explicitly declares the purpose of the bankruptcy discharge. The numerous, complex Bankruptcy Code provisions limiting the availability of a discharge reflect a variety of

---

[76] *Id.*

[77] STERN, *supra* note 75, vol. 5, no. 114, at 166 (Heb.).

[78] SHULHAN ARUKH, *Hoshen Mishpat* 369:6–11.

[79] *Id.* 369:8.

[80] SHAKH, SHULHAN ARUKH, *Hoshen Mishpat* 73:39.

[81] In the United States, for example, the foremost halakhic authority of the latter twentieth century, R. Moses Feinstein, as well as his predecessor, R. Eliyahu Henkin, followed R. Isserles' approach. *See, e.g.*, MOSES FEINSTEIN, IGGEROT MOSHE, *Hoshen Mishpat* II:62; ELIYAHU HENKIN, 2 TESHUVOT IVRA 62.

often conflicting and changing purposes.[82] Congressional hearings, academic literature, and case law mention the following objectives:

(1)   Minimizing the likelihood that a penniless debtor would commit antisocial or criminal acts and, thereby, protecting the rest of the public from such conduct;[83]

(2)   Motivating the debtor to become economically productive to advance the national economy[84] and to avoid having to support the debtor through programs that drain the government's coffers;[85]

(3)   Encouraging people to engage in entrepreneurial activity by eliminating the discouraging specter of unlimited, nondischargeable debt;[86]

(4)   Providing a discharge to debtors who honestly cooperate in the bankruptcy proceeding encourages such cooperation which, in turn, furthers the goal of distributing the debtor's assets fairly;[87]

(5)   Freeing the debtor from the heavy yoke of "oppressive indebtedness"[88] serves a social welfare function,[89] affording the debtor "a new opportunity in life";[90]

(6)   Minimizing the probability that a financially burdened debtor would be forced to engage in immoral conduct in order to make ends meet;[91] and

(7)   Promoting the economically efficient extension of credit by alerting creditors to the fact that, should the debtor fail and the debt discharged, the creditors will bear the loss.[92]

---

[82] *See* Charles G. Hallinan, *The "Fresh Start" Policy in Consumer Bankruptcy: A Historical Inventory and an Interpretation*, 21 U. Rich. L. Rev. 49, 96 (1986) ("the idea of the 'fresh start' has long incorporated and been shaped by a complex multiplicity of policy concerns, which have been founded in turn upon equally complex and often shifting combinations of assumptions about creditors, debtors, credit markets and the social function of bankruptcy").

[83] Margaret Howard, *A Theory of Discharge in Consumer Bankruptcy*, 48 Ohio L.J. 999, 1061 n.99 (1987) (citing this view).

[84] *See, e.g.*, Luthor Zeigler, Note, *The Fraud Exception to Discharge in Bankruptcy: A Reappraisal*, 38 Stan. L. Rev. 891, 910 (hereafter "Zeigler") n.81, citing Weistart, *The Costs of Bankruptcy*, 41 Law & Contemp. Probs. 107, 111 (1977).

[85] Zeigler, *supra* note 84, at 910, n.82 (1986) (citing this view).

[86] In a phone interview on March 13, 1992, Rabbi Moshe Heinemann mentioned this possible argument as one which might establish that the discharge law was intended for the general benefit of citizens, allowing *dina demalkhuta dina* to apply. Rabbi Heinemann concluded by telling me that he was uncertain (*mesupak*) as to whether to accept this policy reason. I have not seen this point precisely expressed in print by secular bankruptcy scholars.

[87] United States v. Kras, 409 U.S. 434, 447 (1973) (citing this view).

[88] Williams v. Fidelity, 236 U.S. 549, 554–55 (1914).

[89] *See, e.g.*, Anthony T. Kronman, *Paternalism and the Law of Contracts*, 92 Yale L.J. 763, 785–86 (1983).

[90] Local Loan Co. v. Hunt, 292 U.S. 235, 244 (1934).

[91] Frank R. Kennedy, *Reflections on the Bankruptcy Laws of the United States: The Debtor's Fresh Start*, 76 W. Va. L. Rev. 427, 441 (1974).

[92] For a thorough discussion of this argument, see, for example, Howard, *supra* note 83, at 1063–68.

The fact that the Bankruptcy Code allows many debts owed to the government to be *discharged* ironically suggests that the discharge law operates *against* the government's financial interests. According to R. Karo's view, it would therefore seem that *dina demalkhuta dina* would not apply to bankruptcy's discharge law.

On the other hand, some of the objectives enumerated above could save the government money. For instance, if discharging a person's debts prevented the person from being driven into a life of crime (objective #(1)), the government might save money on police personnel, on criminal prosecutors, and on the costs of incarceration. Similarly, the federal government would save money if motivating a debtor to be economically productive (objective #(2)) keeps the person off of federal government welfare programs. Furthermore, if the availability of a bankruptcy discharge spurs profitable entrepreneurial activity, the government may realize greater tax revenues. Nevertheless, it is unclear whether these types of possible benefits would be enough to characterize the discharge law as having been enacted for the direct benefit of the government.

The various purposes, however, appear more than adequate according to R. Isserles' criterion; the law certainly was intended to benefit the public. The goal of preventing criminal activity, for instance, certainly promotes the public welfare, even if, for some reason, the federal government fails to realize any financial savings as a result. Similarly, the objective of preventing other legal but immoral conduct may also satisfy R. Isserles' requirement, because Jewish law would recognize this goal as beneficial to the public.

The fact that the government believes that the policy of providing a discharge benefits the public is clear from the very fact that it allows debts owed to the government to be discharged. It is also evidenced by the many rules restricting a debtor's right to renounce the right to a discharge. For example, bankruptcy law makes it impossible for someone to waive his right to discharge at the time a debt is incurred.[93] Although a debtor may waive the discharge of particular debts while the bankruptcy case is proceeding, the ability to do so is extremely restricted.[94] Even where the proper procedures are followed, the court may veto the waiver if it finds that the agreement conflicts with the best interests of the debtor or the debtor's dependents.[95] Once a discharge is obtained, there can be no waiver.[96]

A relatively small number of rabbinic authorities have specifically stated that *dina demalkhuta dina* does not apply to a bankruptcy discharge. Surprisingly, although some of these authorities make reference to the relevance of the law's purposes, none of them delves deeply into those purposes.

Rabbis Yaakov Breish and Yeshaya Blau are among those who have ruled that *dina demalkhuta dina* does not give Jewish law effect to a secular bankruptcy

---

[93] 11 U.S.C. § 524(a).

[94] 11 U.S.C. § 524(c). The bankruptcy code refers to this as a "reaffirmation" of a debt.

[95] 11 U.S.C. § 524.

[96] Prior to adoption of § 524(c) of the Bankruptcy Code, if a debtor renewed, in writing, its promise to repay discharged debt, state law often made such promise enforceable. Although the obligee provided no new consideration in exchange for the debtor's promise, these states found that the debtor was morally obligated to pay and that this moral obligation constituted "consideration."

discharge of an individual's debt. Without any explanation, Rabbi Breish enigmatically declares that there is no basis on which the bankruptcy law could be considered "for the benefit of the people of the land."[97]

Rabbi Blau states:

> It seems that if the secular law is for the benefit of the people of the land [*l'to'ellet bnei hamedinah*], such as price controls or commercial matters between one person and another, the opinion of most poskim is that *dina demalkhuta dina* applies, apparently even between one Jew and another. Thus we find in many, many laws [*halakhot*], such as in employment law [*hilkhot sekhirot*], etc., that poskim judge according to *dina demalkhuta dina* or *minhag hamedinah* [i.e., the custom of the land].[98]

Thus, Blau seems to acknowledge that the Isserles' view is the majority opinion.

Yet, when specifically addressing bankruptcy law, Blau comments:

> [T]here is some doubt in our times whether secular bankruptcy law is enforceable because of *dina demalkhuta dina*. It appears from the words of poskim that in such a case where there is no connection to the government [*inyan limalkhut*], *dina demalkhuta dina* is inapplicable.[99]

The expression *inyan limalkhut* is ambiguous. Based on the fact that Blau acknowledged that Isserles' approach is the majority opinion,[100] it seems that his point here is that bankruptcy law is not for the benefit of the people of the land. If so, his conclusion is unsupported by any explicit evaluation of the various alleged purposes of bankruptcy law.

Only one of the poskim Blau names, Rabbi Weiss,[101] dealt with a bankruptcy scenario. In a very brief responsa, Weiss considered a case in which a debtor filed bankruptcy, and the court ordered that each creditor be paid thirty percent of its claim with the rest discharged. In stating the question, the responsum specifically indicates that the court order could be entered only if no creditor objected. The creditor in the case had not objected. The creditor contended that its failure to object was irrelevant because: (1) it did not know that its particular loan would be affected by the bankruptcy order; and (2) the reason it did not object was that it did not wish to interfere with the debtor's ability to obtain bankruptcy relief, if halakhically permissible, from its other creditors.

Rabbi Weiss did not rule whether a bankruptcy discharge is per se invalid.[102] Rather, he announced that the court's ruling was halakhically invalid because of a

---

[97] YAAKOV BREISH, 3 HELKAT YAAKOV no. 160 (Heb.).

[98] BLAU, *supra* note 17, *Hilkhot Geneivah*, ch. 1, n.4, p. 13.

[99] BLAU, *supra* note 17, *Dinei Halva'ah*, ch. 2, n.63, p. 27.

[100] By contrast, according to Karo's minority opinion, "inyan l'malkhut" could mean "direct benefit to the king."

[101] YITZHAK WEISS (1902–1989), 3 MINHAT YITZHAK no. 134.

[102] Had the creditor's silence been construed as consent to the court order, there would have been an issue as to whether or not such consent was the product of economic duress. Consideration of this issue might have led to discussion of *dina demalkhuta dina*. Nevertheless, Rabbi Weiss did not discuss the

procedural ground — that a court may not rule against someone simply because he does not appear to assert his claims. This interpretation of Weiss' responsum is supported by the fact that, in another responsum, Weiss suggests that Isserles' approach to *dina demalkhuta dina* is valid.[103] Consequently, it would have been odd for Weiss, in the responsum cited by Blau, to have held a bankruptcy discharge halakhically ineffective without mentioning Isserles or Hakohen and without declaring that the bankruptcy discharge law was not for the benefit of the people of the land.

Rabbis Blau and Weiss made their statements while residing in Israel. As mentioned in Chapter 7, one view understands dina demalkhuta dina as based on the king's (or the government's) authority to exile people from the land. For the privilege of remaining in the land, people are deemed to have implicitly agreed to abide by the laws of the land. Under Jewish law, however, each Jew is entitled to live in Israel. Consequently, even though the Israeli government may have the power to prevent a Jew from residing in Israel, under Jewish law, it lacks the authority to do so. Consequently, it has been suggested that opinions issued by Israeli poskim regarding *dina demalkhuta dina* may not be persuasive authority outside of Israel.[104] Nor is it even clear that Blau or Weiss intended their rulings to apply outside of Israel.

If Jewish law does not recognize a secular bankruptcy discharge, then it would also not recognize secular bankruptcy's permanent discharge injunction that bans efforts to collect discharged debts. Nevertheless, Jewish law might still recognize the temporary relief afforded by the automatic stay, and it is to this issue that we now turn.

[2] Does Jewish Law Recognize the Automatic Stay?

The purpose of the temporary relief afforded by the automatic stay is to enable the bankruptcy to proceed effectively and efficiently and, in a liquidation bankruptcy, to permit the debtor's assets to be distributed as set forth in the Bankruptcy Code.

R. Moses Feinstein ruled that *dina demalkhuta dina* applied to require compliance with Switzerland's bankruptcy distribution laws.[105] In the specific case presented to Feinstein, the debtor was a corporation. Although the facts are not entirely clear, it seems that just after the debtor filed bankruptcy, its directors paid $36,000 to a Jewish creditor who was legitimately owed $72,000. Under Swiss law,

---

merits of the economic duress argument, because the creditor had not satisfied the formal preconditions necessary to have raised the issue.

[103] Rabbi Weiss at least ruled that a litigant was entitled to assert the Isserles' view was correct and to rely thereon successfully against an adversary invoking Shabbetai Hakohen's view. WEISS, *supra* note 101, vol. 2, no. 86:3.

[104] SHILO, *supra* note 68, at 157; HENKIN, *supra* note 81, at 176 (limiting Shabbetai Hakohen's view to context in which there are organized Jewish communities with their own communal leaders, a situation which may exist in parts of Israel).

[105] By applying dina demalkhuta dina to the secular distribution laws even though they differed from Jewish law's distribution laws, R. Feinstein implicitly rejects Shabbetai Hakohen's approach to *dina demalkhuta dina*.

as Feinstein describes it, once a bankruptcy petition is filed, a debtor's directors are forbidden to take or use any of the debtor's assets, even to pay the debtor's authentic debts. Instead, a three-person panel is appointed to distribute the debtor's assets on a pro rata basis in accordance with the amount of the creditors' respective claims.

Feinstein emphasized that the details of the dina demalkhuta dina doctrine are quite complex and controversial. Nevertheless, applying Isserles' approach, he ruled that *dina demalkhuta dina* applied to the Swiss bankruptcy distribution of assets laws. Feinstein had no difficulty finding that the law was enacted for the public good, stating that it could help prevent conflicts among competing creditors. Indeed, he noted that Jewish law has similar, but not identical rules, for the disposition of a debtor's resources. Undoubtedly aware of a minority view that *dina demalkhuta dina* is inapplicable to transactions between or among Jews, Feinstein emphasized that *dina demalkhuta dina* should *a fortiori* apply in the case of a corporate debtor with many shareholders, because the distribution of the debtors assets might affect the rights of non-Jews as well as of Jews. It would seem that this *a fortiori* argument would apply to any debtor whose affairs affect both Jews and non-Jews inasmuch as the argument was not analytically linked to the debtor's corporate identity.

Feinstein specifically ruled that if the Jewish creditor had in fact been given the $36,000 *after* the bankruptcy filing, in violation of Swiss bankruptcy law, the creditor was obligated under Jewish law to deliver the $36,000 to the three-person panel. This decision is especially noteworthy because Jewish law often differentiates between a person's obligation ex ante, where the rules are usually stricter, and a person's obligation post facto, where there is frequently greater room for leniency. Yet Feinstein found no leniency available in this case.

The reasoning underlying Feinstein's responsum would also apply to bankruptcy law's automatic stay. If a creditor must return property received in violation of Swiss bankruptcy law, it seems clear that a creditor must comply with a law banning him or her from trying to obtain the property in the first place. This is an important point because a debtor's creditors, perhaps especially its employees, often feel that they have been wronged by the debtor's filing of a bankruptcy, and, therefore, justified in resorting to self-help, by seizing from the debtor whatever property they can. According to Feinstein's analysis, such conduct would not only violate secular law but would violate Jewish law.

[D]   An Unintended Interaction: Bankruptcy Law and the Jewish Doctrine of *Yeush*

Suppose a person loses a piece of property. If the person despairs of ever recovering the object, there is *yeush* (i.e., despair). If the object is found after *yeush*, it belongs to the finder. Arguably, if a creditor is convinced that he will never be paid, there is *yeush*, and the "debt," which, in a sense, is in "the possession" of the one who owes it, i.e., the debtor, becomes the debtor's and is automatically extinguished. If this argument is valid, then the extent that issuance of a bankruptcy discharge order affects a creditor's expectation of being repaid, the discharge has Jewish law significance quite apart from *minhag hasoharim* and *dina demalkhuta dina.*

There are several approaches as to whether a creditor's *yeush* cancels a borrower's debt. At one extreme, R. Yosef Karo[106] broadly declares that *yeush* does not eliminate a debt. R. Blau states that most poskim agree that the mere fact that a debtor appears to have become impoverished does not discharge his debts.[107]

On the other hand, many poskim conclude that where circumstances would lead any reasonable creditor to despair, such as where the debtor's fields are ruined by floods, there is *yeush* and the debt is discharged.[108] According to Rabbi Aryeh Leib Hakohen Heller, this is the view of Rabbi Yosef Colon (a/k/a *Maharik*; 1420–1480) and R. Moses Isserles.[109]

A final view is offered by Rabbi Meir Auerbach. He states that a debt is generally discharged whenever the creditor despairs of repayment, even if this is because the debtor becomes impoverished. The only exception is that a debtor cannot extinguish his debt if his own purposeful, wrongful act caused the owner's *yeush*, such as where a debtor simply refuses to pay.[110]

According to the Rabbis Heller and Auerbach, under Jewish law, a debtor's financial woes may cause his or her debts to be discharged without resort to secular bankruptcy law. Ironically, however, the very existence of secular bankruptcy discharge law may *prevent* such a discharge. Suppose, for example, that there were no secular bankruptcy law, and that a particular debtor had an overwhelming amount of debt. According to Rabbis Heller and Auerbach, if a reasonable creditor would despair of repayment, because of the debtor's overwhelming financial burden, the debt would be discharged.

Suppose, however, that there were a secular bankruptcy law. Suppose also most of the debtor's debts were owed to "secular" creditors (i.e., non-Jewish creditors and, possibly, even non-religious Jewish creditors) and that Jewish law recognized that secular bankruptcy law was valid to discharge the claims of secular creditors but not to discharge the claims of religious Jewish creditors. But if the debt to secular creditors were discharged, it would be much more likely that the debtor could pay the remaining debts owed to religious Jewish creditors. As a result, because a reasonable religious Jewish creditor might not despair of repayment, there would be no *yeush* and the debt to such a creditor would not be discharged.

---

[106] SHULHAN ARUKH, *Hoshen Mishpat* 98:1.

[107] BLAU, *supra* note 17, ch. 2, *halakha* 29, n.73. *See also* ZVI HIRSCH BEN YAAKOV ASHKENAZI (1660–1718), SHUT HAKHAM TZVI no. 144 (Heb.).

[108] BLAU, *supra* note 17, *Hilkhot Halva'ah*, ch. 2, *halakhah* 29, n.73. *See also* MOSHE STERNBUCH, 2 TESHUVOT VEHANHAGOT no. 701 (Heb.) (relying partly on this view).

[109] ARYEH LEIB HAKOHEN HELLER (1745–1813), KITZOT HAHOSHEN, *Hoshen Mishpat* 163:3 (Heb.).

[110] MEIR AUERBACH (nineteenth century), 2 IMREI BINAH, *Hilkhot Giviyat Hov*, no. 4 (Heb.).

§ 14.05   SUMMARY AND CONCLUSION

Although Jewish law does not itself include a bankruptcy law, it is possible that the Jewish law doctrines of *minhag hasoharim* (commercial custom) and *dina demalkhuta dina* (the law of the kingdom is religiously valid law) may incorporate secular bankruptcy law into Jewish law. Nevertheless, there is considerable dispute about the applicability of these principles. The views that seem to reject the validity of bankruptcy's discharge law typically fail to examine the various ways in which the discharge law arguably promotes the public's best interests. A number of these views also emanate from rabbinic authorities in Israel, where, according to some authorities, *dina demalkhuta dina* does not apply. A leading rabbinic authority, R. Moses Feinstein, however, has ruled that a Swiss law regarding the distribution of a debtor's assets is binding under Jewish law. The logic of that responsum seems applicable to the automatic stay law as well. In conclusion, the interrelationship between Jewish law and secular bankruptcy law is an important one that warrants continued inquiry.

Chapter 15

PROFESSIONAL ETHICS AND JEWISH LAW: LAWYERING

§ 15.01 INTRODUCTION

This chapter examines how Jewish law affects one's professional life. For simplicity, we will primarily discuss only one profession, the practice of law, although many of the issues apply to other professions as well.

There are multiple dimensions to one's work as an attorney. An attorney may serve as an employee of another lawyer or of a law firm. If so, the attorney bears obligations to this employer. If the attorney is a partner in a firm, the attorney owes duties to the other partners. Whether the attorney is a partner of a firm or a sole practitioner, the attorney undoubtedly has one or more employees and has responsibilities towards them[1] — as well as to the persons from whom the attorney purchases or rents supplies, equipment or premises. Jewish law interacts with secular law with respect to all of these interrelationships and examining them would certainly be valuable.

---

[1] *See generally* Steven H. Resnicoff, *Jewish Law and Socially Responsible Corporate Conduct*, 11 FORDHAM J. CORP. & FIN. L. 681 (2006).

However, this chapter explores only the ways in which Jewish law affects how an attorney practices law and the nature of the attorney's fiduciary responsibilities to a client.

Specifically, it focuses on how Jewish law may affect the ends that an attorney can help a client pursue, the means that an attorney may employ, and the responsibilities the attorney may bear for maintaining a client's secrets or confidences. Before exploring these specific rules, however, a few overarching comments are in order.

§ 15.02 JEWISH LAW'S REJECTION OF ROLE DIFFERENTIATED MORALITY

Secular law rarely imposes specific ethical duties on a person who is not a professional. Instead, a person is generally expected to exercise independent ethical judgment. Accordingly, a person may conclude that he or she bears certain ethical duties to others in the community. A person who is a professional, however, is often charged with a long list of supposedly "ethical" duties pertaining to the person's specific profession. These professional ethics rules are typically crafted by a governmental or quasi-governmental body that regulates the particular profession.

Sometimes professionally prescribed ethics rules contradict what a given person thinks, and, indeed, what a majority of people may think, is proper conduct for a "normal" person who is not a member of the profession. The secular response is to resolve such conflicts by "role-differentiated morality," i.e., as to issues that arise in connection with the person's role as an attorney, the attorney ethics rules apply, and as to issues unrelated to the person's role as an attorney, the general ethics rules apply.[2]

Significant problems plague this secular model. First, in many professions, such as that of an attorney, there are often few clear lines distinguishing between an attorney's private and professional lives. Second, even where lines may be discernable, it seems unreasonable to expect an individual to consistently adhere to separate moral standards. In America, at least, legal professionals spend an increasingly large number of their wakeful hours practicing law. Moreover, even during their supposedly spare time, lawyers receive countless communications from clients, employees, partners and others involved in their professional careers. They spend still more time thinking about their work. It is extremely difficult for a person who is trained and habituated to follow professional ethics rules almost all of his or her wakeful hours to exercise independent moral judgment at other times. The more likely result will be that persons will simply follow the professional ethics guidelines even during the non-professional parts of their lives. This is troublesome

---

[2] Some legal ethics rules, such as the rule not to engage in misrepresentations or lies, actually purport to apply to all parts of an attorney's life and not just to interactions pertinent to the practice of law. Yet according to Jewish law, there are a number of situations in which lying is not only permitted but actually required in order to accomplish beneficial ends. *See, e.g.,* Steven H. Resnicoff, *Lying and Lawyering: Contrasting American and Jewish Law,* 77 Notre Dame L. Rev. 937 (2002); Steven H. Resnicoff, *Ends and Means in Jewish Law: Lying to Achieve Economic Justice,* Jewish Law Annual XV (Bernard S. Jackson ed., 2004).

because professional ethics rules are often inappropriate as to non-professional scenarios. Indeed, as we shall see, some professional ethics rules may not even be morally appropriate in some professional contexts.

Jewish law generally rejects secular law's schizophrenic approach to ethics. Instead, Jewish law identifies ethical rules that apply to a person, whether that person is a professional or not, and these rules apply in every aspect of a person's life. Jewish law does not generally permit a person to voluntarily undertake "fiduciary" obligations to a client that would alter preexisting duties of compliance with Jewish law.

Of course, as explained in Chapter 4, Jewish law does not require someone to give up his or her life, or even all of his or her assets, to fulfill every commandment. Instead, usually limits apply. To the extent that secular law imposes a financial penalty, or even possible imprisonment, on a person for acting in a particular way, the extent and nature of the penalty is relevant in determining what Jewish law requires of the person. But this is equally true of professionals and non-professionals.

§ 15.03 JEWISH LAW PRINCIPLES APPLYING TO THE PRACTICE OF LAW

There are various ways to approach this complex subject. We will start by briefly enumerating some of the primary Jewish law principles arising in the practice of law, as well as in many other professions.

1. The biblical obligation to avoid profaning God's name (*hillul HaShem*)[3] through one's identification with evildoers;

2. The biblical obligation to be "holy" (*kiddoshim tihiyu*)[4] and to separate oneself from technically permissible, but spiritually repulsive, conduct (*lo lihiyot novel birishut HaTorah*)[5] and to be guiltless in the eyes of man and

---

[3] *Leviticus* 22:32. R. Hayam Donin explains the seriousness of this obligation:

> According to the Talmud, the very Sanctification of God's name and the credibility of the religious life hinges, in fact, on the quality of the ethical-moral life. If someone studies Scripture and Mishna, and attends on the scholars, is honest in business and speaks pleasantly to persons, what do people then say concerning him? "Happy is the father (and teacher) who taught him Torah, . . . for this man has studied the Torah — look how fine his ways are, how righteous are his deeds!" But if someone studies Scripture and Mishna, attends on the scholars, but is dishonest in business and discourteous in his relations with people, what do people say about him? "Woe unto him who studied the Torah, woe unto his father (and teacher) who taught him Torah! This man studied the Torah; Look how corrupt are his deeds, how ugly his ways. (Yoma 86a).

HAYAM HALEVY DONIN, TO BE A JEW 29 (1972). Later Donin adds, "For a religiously learned or ritually observant person to act in a way that would invite such remarks was regarded as a Desecration of the Divine Name (hillul HaShem), a transgression of the severest spiritual magnitude." *Id.* at 43.

[4] *Leviticus* 19:2.

[5] MOSHE BEN NAHMAN (*Nahmanides*), MIKROT GEDOLOT, *Leviticus* 19:2. Nahmanides makes similar comments with respect to the biblical verse directing Jews to do that which is "good and right." *Id. at Deuteronomy* 6:18. Related principles might include the duty to do the right and the good. *See also Deuteronomy* 12:28.

God;[6]

3. The importance of protecting oneself from spiritual and non-spiritual harm as a result of close associations with wrongdoers (*oy lirosho oy lishekheno*);[7]

4. The rabbinic duty to take affirmative steps to prevent another Jew from violating Jewish law (*lihafrish meissura*)[8] and to rebuke him or her for having done so (*lihokhiah*);[9]

5. The rabbinic duty not to strengthen the hands of wrongdoers;[10]

6. The commandment not to sue another Jew in secular court;[11]

7. The biblical commandment to distance oneself from falsehood (*medevvar shekker tirkakh*);[12]

8. The biblical prohibition against enabling someone to violate Jewish law (*lifnei iver*), which we will call the "Enabling Prohibition";[13]

9. The rabbinic prohibition against assisting someone to violate Jewish law (*mesayeah bidei ovrei aveirah*), which we will call the "Facilitating Prohibition";[14]

10. The biblical injunction against passively allowing another Jew to be wrongfully harmed (*lo ta'amod al dam reyekhah*);[15]

---

[6] *Numbers* 32:22.

[7] *See, e.g.*, MOSHE STERNBUCH, 1 TESHUVOT VEHANHAGOT, *Orah Hayyim* 283 (citing *oy lirosho oy lishekheno*). *See generally* MISHNAH, *Pirkei Avot* 1:7; SHLOMO YITZHAKI (*Rashi*), BABYLONIAN TALMUD, *Berakhot* 48a; AVRAHAM YITZHAK KOOK, DA'AT KOHEN, *Inyanei Yoreh De'ah* 193. One of the meanings of *oy lirosho oy lishekheno* is that, by associating with those who are spiritually corrupt, a person's own spiritual sensitivity can be corrupted. *See also* MENASHE KLEIN, 7 MISNHE HALAKHOT no. 255. This rule certainly does not preclude efforts to persuade wrongdoers to repent, especially if the person making such efforts is especially gifted or trained for this purpose. It does, however, generally apply to other types of close interaction and should certainly apply to associations designed to assist a wrongdoer to violate Jewish law.

[8] *See, e.g.*, YITZHAK WEISS, 5 MINHAT YITZHAK no. 14; ELIEZER WALDENBURG, 15 TZITZ ELIEZER no. 15; MOSHE FEINSTEIN, IGGEROT MOSHE, *Yoreh De'ah* I:72.

[9] *See, e.g.*, MAIMONIDES, MISHNEH TORAH, *Hilkhot De'ot* 6:7. If a Jew wrongfully refrains from rebuking his fellow when the rebuke would have been successful, the Jew is considered as blameworthy as if he himself had committed the violation. *See also* SHULHAN ARUKH, *Yoreh De'ah* 157:1.

[10] AVRAHAM GOMBINER, MAGEN AVRAHAM, *Orah Hayyim* 347, *s.k.* 4; YISROEL MEIR KAGAN, MISHNAH BERURAH 347, *s.k.* 7.

[11] SHULHAN ARUKH, *Hoshen Mishpat* 26:1. This is discussed in more detail in Chapter 16, *infra*.

[12] *Exodus* 23:7.

[13] This is based on Talmudic interpretation of the verse, "Thou shalt not curse the deaf, nor put a stumbling block before the blind." *Leviticus* 19:14. *See, e.g.*, BABYLONIAN TALMUD, *Kiddushin* 32a; *see also* MEIR TAMARI, THE CHALLENGE OF WEALTH 39–44 (1995). *See generally* Steven H. Resnicoff, *Helping a Client Violate Jewish Law: A Jewish Lawyer's Dilemma*, in 10 JEWISH LAW ASSOCIATION STUDIES 191–227 (H.G. Sprecher ed., 2000); YAIR HOFFMAN, MISGUIDING THE PERPLEXED: THE LAWS OF LIFNEI IVER (2004). This rule is discussed in more detail in Chapter 3, *supra*.

[14] YISROEL MEIR KAGAN, MISHNAH BERURAH 347:7. *See generally* Chapter 3, *supra*; HOFFMAN, *supra* note 13, at 89–91.

[15] *Deuteronomy* 22:2. *See generally* Aaron Kirschenbaum, *The Good Samaritan: Monetary Aspects*,

11.   The general biblical prohibition against causing injury (*lo ligrom hezek*)[16] to another person as well as more specific rules against embarrassing (*hamalbeen pnei havero birabeem*) others,[17] verbally abusing (*ona'at devarim*) others,[18] cheating others,[19] and stealing[20] from others.

12.   The biblical commandment not to disclose someone's private information (*bal tomar* or *lo sihiyeh rokhel*);[21]

13.   The biblical commandment against saying or believing unflattering comments about another person (*loshon harah*),[22] even if the comments are true.

14.   The biblical prohibition against saying or believing false, unflattering comments about another person (*motzei shem rah*).[23]

§ 15.04   HELPING A CLIENT ACCOMPLISH AN OBJECTIVE THAT IS IMPROPER UNDER JEWISH LAW

Often a client's objectives are consistent with Jewish law. In part, this is because of doctrines such as *minhag hasoharim*[24] (that incorporates into Jewish law many commercial customs) and *dina demalkhuta dina*[25] (that makes many secular commercial laws enforceable under Jewish law). Nevertheless, there are situations in which these doctrines do not apply, and a client attempts to accomplish a goal that conflicts with Jewish law. Here are a few examples:

1.   A client, pursuant to a secularly legitimate claim, sues someone to collect money to which the client is not entitled under Jewish law.[26]

---

17 J. HALACHA & CONTEMP. SOC'Y 83, 86–87, 89–92 (1989). Note that this journal incorrectly spells the author's first name as "Aron." This principle is discussed in Chapter 3, *supra*.

16 Some authorities identify the verse, "Love your neighbor as (you love) yourself," as the biblical source of the prohibition against injuring another person's body or property. Others cite the biblical verse against theft.

17 BABYLONIAN TALMUD, *Bava Metzia* 58b (comparing a person who embarrasses someone in public to a murderer).

18 *Leviticus* 25:17. *See also Leviticus* 19:33–34; *Exodus* 22:20–23. *See generally* BABYLONIAN TALMUD, *Bava Metzia* 58b.

19 *See* SHULHAN ARUKH, *Hoshen Mishpat* 228:6–20, 231; SOLOMON GANZFRIED, CODE OF JEWISH LAW 72 (Hyman E. Goldin trans., rev. ed. 1998).

20 *Leviticus* 19:11.

21 *See, e.g.*, J. DAVID BLEICH, 2 CONTEMPORARY HALAKHIC PROBLEMS 75 n.13 (1983) (citing various sources); BARUKH HALEVI EPSTEIN, TORAH TEMIMAH, *Leviticus* 1:1 (as to *bal tomar*).

22 *See generally Lashon ha-Ra*, *in* 10 ENCYCLOPAEDIA JUDAICA 1431 (Michael Berenbaum & Fred Skolnik eds., 2d ed. 2007); *Slander*, *in* 14 *id.*, at 1651.

23 *See* ZELIG PLISKIN, GUARD YOUR TONGUE: A PRACTICAL GUIDE TO THE LAWS OF LOSHON HORA 29 (1975).

24 *See* Chapter 7, *supra*.

25 *Id.*

26 *See, e.g.*, R. OVADIAH YOSEF, YABIA OMER, *Hoshen Mishpat* II:1; R. AKIVA EGER (1761–1837), HIDDUSHEI R. AKIVA EGER, *Shulhan Arukh, Hoshen Mishpat* 26:1; R. YAAKOV BLAU, PITHEI HOSHEN, *Dinei Halva'ah*, Chapter 6, *halakha* 6 ("[W]hen one uses secular courts to take money to which he is not entitled according to the law of the Torah the money so taken is stolen property."); R. MOSHE STERNBUCH, 1

2. A client seeks to avoid liability to pay money or to perform an act even though Jewish law requires the client to pay or perform.

3. A client applies to secular court to terminate the provision of life-preserving medical treatment to a patient when such termination is forbidden by Jewish law or to authorize the taking of organs from the patient when doing so is prohibited by Jewish law.[27]

4. A Jewish client, who has converted to some other faith, tries to obtain custody rights regarding his or her children in order to turn them away from Judaism and toward another faith.

5. A Jewish client desires to completely disinherit an heir in violation of Jewish law.[28]

6. A Jewish client seeks to enter into a transaction that violates the Jewish law against the payment or taking of interest.[29]

[A]   Profanation of God's Name (*hillul HaShem*)

In cases in which a client seeks to violate Jewish law, what should an attorney do? Under secular law, so long as the client's objective is legal, the lawyer is not encouraged to refuse the representation. On the contrary, an attorney is secularly encouraged not to refuse a case because the client or the cause is unpopular. Apparently to protect attorneys who take unpopular matters, the American Bar Association's Code of Ethics actually includes a provision declaring that the fact an attorney takes a matter does not mean that the attorney personally agrees with client's agenda.[30]

TESHUVOT VEHANHAGOT no. 795 (one of the reasons why suing a Jew in secular court is impermissible is that "one collects money from his fellow even though according to Torah law this is plain theft"); R. YEHIEL MIKHAL EPSTEIN (1829–1908), ARUKH HASHULHAN, *Hoshen Mishpat* 26:2; MICHAEL BROYDE, THE PURSUIT OF JUSTICE 45 n.18 (1996) (quoting a letter from R. J. David Bleich who says that "[a]ny recovery accepted on the basis of a decision of a secular court in excess of that which would have been ordered by a [rabbinical court] . . . constitutes extortion in the eyes of Jewish law"); R. MENASHE KLEIN, 12 MISHNE HALACHOTH 387 (using a secular court to take money from someone not in accord with *Halakha* constitutes stealing); R. EZRA BASRI (contemporary), 1 DINEI MAMANOT 346 ("Someone who takes money pursuant to secular law . . . to which he is not entitled according to the Torah is a robber and is obligated to return the money he took.").

[27] Even though secular law may treat a person as "dead," Jewish law may regard the person as alive. In such a case, Jewish law proscribes the taking of the person's vital organs. *See, e.g.*, Steven H. Resnicoff, *The Legal and Halachic Ramifications of Brain Death, in* MEDICINE AND JEWISH LAW III (Fred Rosner and Robert Schulman, eds., 2005).

[28] *See generally* SHIMON DURAN, TASHBETZ no. 147; MAIMONIDES, MISHNEH TORAH, *Hilkhot Nahalot* 6:11; YITZHAK WEISS, 1 MINHAT YITZHAK no. 233; MOSHE FEINSTEIN, IGGEROT MOSHE, *Hoshen Mishpat* 2:49, 50.

[29] *See generally* Steven H. Resnicoff, *A Commercial Conundrum: Does Prudence Permit the Jewish "Permissible Venture"?*, 20 SETON HALL L. REV. 77 (1990).

[30] ABA MODEL RULES OF PROFESSIONAL CONDUCT, Rule 1.2(b) states: "A lawyer's representation of a client, including representation by appointment, does not constitute an endorsement of the client's political, economic, social, or moral views or activities." RONALD D. ROTUNDA & JOHN S. DZIENKOWSKI, PROFESSIONAL RESPONSIBILITY: A STUDENT'S GUIDE 95 (2011). This ethics "rule" is peculiar in that it really is not a "rule" at all. It provides no regulation of the practice of law, but, instead, merely makes a statement about it.

Jewish law's approach is a bit different. Assume, for a moment, that neither the Enabling Prohibition nor the Facilitating Prohibition proscribes the representation of a particular client even though the client seeks to accomplish an objective that is both morally reprehensible and that violates Jewish law. Nevertheless, often an attorney becomes identified with the client — in the eyes of the attorney's adversary, the judge, the jurors and, in notorious cases, the general public. If the client is viewed as an evildoer, the attorney may be similarly perceived. If so, by representing such a client, an attorney could violate the directive to be "guiltless before God and Israel,"[31] which is construed not only as a commandment for a person to act correctly but also to be seen as acting correctly.[32] If by representing a wrongdoer, the attorney is perceived as acting wrongfully, the attorney could violate the extremely serious rule against causing Judaism to be ridiculed or God's name to be desecrated, *hillul HaShem*.[33]

[B] Harming Another Person

Representing such a client could involve additional problems as well. For example, not only is a Jew prohibited from injuring someone else, whether physically or financially, a Jew is also forbidden *to cause* such injury, even indirectly.[34] Yet injuring an adversary, at least financially, is often what a client wants — e.g., by obtaining a money judgment to which he is not entitled under Jewish law, by gaining an award for specific performance ordering the adversary to transfer title to specific property, or by being legally relieved of a valid Jewish law monetary obligation. As a result, Jewish law may regard an attorney who successfully assists such a client as someone who has improperly caused injury to the client's adversary.

[C] Associating with a Wrongdoer

In addition, Jewish law may regard a client who seeks to violate Jewish law as a "wrongdoer," and Jewish law enjoins one from associating with a wrongdoer.[35] Yet representing such a person may involve repeated, sustained interactions with him or her. Such contact may affect the attorney deleteriously. By becoming accustomed to trying to help clients violate Jewish law, an attorney may become insensitive to the importance of upholding Jewish law and may fail to rebuke other clients whom the attorney, with little effort, could actually persuade to abide by Jewish law. Indeed, constant and intense interaction with wrongdoers — many of whom may appear to possess good qualities and may be "good clients" — could

---

[31] *Numbers* 32:22.

[32] *See* BASIL F. HERRING, JEWISH ETHICS AND HALAKHAH FOR OUR TIME: SOURCES AND COMMENTARY II 250-251 (1989).

[33] *Leviticus* 22:32.

[34] EZRA BASRI, 4 DINEI MAMANOT 12, n.1 (arguing that although Jewish law authorities disagree as to whether it is rabbinically prohibited to assist non-Jews to violate Jewish law where they could have committed the violations without the help, all authorities agree that it is forbidden to assist even a non-Jew to unlawfully harm Jews).

[35] *See, e.g.,* MOSHE STERNBUCH, 1 TESHUVOT VEHANHAGOT, *Orah Hayyim* 283; MENASHE KLEIN, 4 MISNHE HALAKHOT 255.

even tragically influence an attorney to be less diligent in his or her own religious observance.[36]

[D] Encouraging Wrongdoers

Another problem is that Jewish law forbids a person to encourage wrongdoers in their activities. Yet attorneys often are in the position of encouraging their clients. Sometimes an attorney notices that a client is depressed or anxiety-ridden and needs a "boost." On other occasions, a client, before taking the stand to testify, may ask the attorney to, "Wish me luck." Indeed, offering emotional support for a client is part of an attorney's job. If, however, the client's goal violates Jewish law, providing such support is itself impermissible.

One source for this rule is the Mishnah regarding the Sabbatical year, in which Jews are forbidden from working the land. The Mishnah states that, "one may assist Gentiles [who are tilling the field] during the Sabbatical year, but one may not assist Jews [who are tilling the field during the Sabbatical year]."[37] The Talmud explains that the Mishnah does not mean that one can actually work the field with a Gentile during the Sabbatical year, because this is clearly forbidden. Instead, the Mishnah merely means that one may utter words of encouragement, such as "May your hands be strengthened," to such Gentiles.[38] Maimonides writes:

> One may only assist [Gentiles] . . . on the Sabbatical Year with words alone. If you see him [i.e., a Gentile] plow or seed, you may say to him "May you be strengthened" or "Succeed" or some similar expression, because they are not commanded [not to till the land on the Sabbatical Year].[39]

This statement implies that if Jewish law forbade Gentiles from performing such work, it would be prohibited to provide verbal encouragement. Indeed, R. Avraham Gombiner makes this inference and writes that: "It is good manners [*derekh eretz*] to say to someone who is working, 'May your job succeed.' But if someone is doing forbidden work, it is prohibited to say such a thing to him."[40] This rule is stated by other authorities as well.[41]

[E] The Enabling Prohibition (*Lifnei Iver*)

Up to now, the discussion has ignored the efficacy of the actual legal services the attorney provides. But this issue is critical in examining the Enabling Prohibition (*lifnei iver*). In fact, according to the majority of Jewish law authorities, that prohibition only applies if the particular attorney's assistance, or at least the

---

[36] KLEIN, *supra* note 35.

[37] MISHNAH, *Gittin* 5:9.

[38] BABYLONIAN TALMUD, *Gittin* 62a.

[39] MAIMONIDES, MISHNEH TORAH, *Hilkhot Shemittah VeYovel* 8:8.

[40] AVRAHAM GOMBINER, MAGEN AVRAHAM, *Orah Hayyim* 347, *s.k.* 4.

[41] *See* YISROEL MEIR KAGAN, MISHNAH BERURAH 347, s.k. 7. *See also* YITZHAK WEISS, 4 MINHAT YITZHAK no.79; MOSHE SHICK, MAHARAM SHICK, *Orah Hayyim* 303; R. MOSHE STERNBUCH, 3 TESHUVOT VEHANHAGOT no. 491.

assistance of some Jewish attorney, is *necessary* for the client to succeed.[42] The fundamental purpose of this aspect of the Enabling Prohibition is to prevent one from causing God's Will from being frustrated. Consequently, it applies to a Jewish attorney[43] whether or not the client is Jewish.[44]

Some might argue that a Jewish attorney's assistance is not a sine qua non to a client's success. In discussing a case in which a Jewish auditor for the Internal Revenue Service discovered taxpayer fraud, R. Moses Feinstein implicitly assumed that any IRS auditor would have uncovered the fraud.[45] An Orthodox Jewish auditor told me auditors apply standardized procedures and any competent auditor should have arrived at the same findings. Nevertheless, I doubt that many attorneys would be equally willing to deny the possible uniqueness of their services.

Attorneys perform numerous tasks. They inform clients as to the likely consequences of particular tactics and advise them as to which procedures to employ. They participate personally in the processes that are pursued, whether negotiative, litigative or both. They recommend what offers to make or accept, what interests to assert and what arguments to advance. They carefully craft written documents — whether contracts, pleadings or briefs — and artfully engage in oral advocacy — inside and outside of court. With respect to litigation, attorneys design strategies, select and prepare witnesses (experts and non-experts),[46] choose the order and manner in which to present their cases and formulate questions to pose to an adversary's witnesses. Attorneys utilize their intellectual power, their eloquence, their physical energy and whatever other personal resources they can bring to bear.

---

[42] As discussed in Chapter 3, *supra*, the majority view is that if the transgression could not be accomplished without the help of *some* Jew, then any Jew who provides the help violates the biblical *lifnei iver* rule. *See, e.g.*, YEHUDA ROSANES (d. 1727), MISHNEH LAMELEKH, *Hilkhot Malveh U'Loveh* 4:2 (Heb.).

[43] This same rule would apply to other Jewish professionals or specialists as well. In the context of litigation, for instance, it could apply to a uniquely qualified Jewish expert witness or to a small group of such Jewish witnesses without whose testimony, the wrongdoer could not prevail. Similarly, it could apply to the practice of medicine if only a small number of uniquely qualified Jewish practitioners were available to perform a procedure proscribed by Jewish law and, without their participation, the procedure would not be undertaken.

[44] As discussed in Chapter 4, *supra*, Jewish law imposes certain rules upon non-Jews. The attorney discussed in the text would not be limited by the *lifnei iver* doctrine if a non-Jewish client's objective were not forbidden to the non-Jew. It would only apply if Jewish law forbade the objective to non-Jews.

[45] MOSES FEINSTEIN, IGGEROT MOSHE, *Hoshen Mishpat* 92 (implicitly assuming that any qualitative differences among auditors — at least among those who would be hired by the government — are insignificant, by arguing that if a particular Jewish auditor would not work for the government, the government would use another auditor who would find the citizen's wrongdoing).

[46] An attorney often has to gauge the psychological or emotional strengths of potential witnesses, as well as the impact such witnesses will likely have on the judge or jury.

Some lawyers are more diligent, creative, persuasive or just more fortunate[47] than others.[48] Consequently, if a particular Jewish lawyer were to refuse a case, it may be unclear in certain cases as to whether any replacement would be able to represent the client successfully. Even if we assume there are some attorneys who might do just as good a job as the particular lawyer in question, the client may not be able to determine who these attorneys are. In many instances, even lawyers are unable to accurately assess the effectiveness of other attorneys with whom they have not had substantial, direct professional interaction. Assuming both that some other attorneys could do as good a job and that the client could recognize who these attorneys are, the client, for various reasons, still might be unable to engage them without substantial inconvenience. For example, in many cases, the representation may be proscribed by some secular conflict of interest rule[49] or the attorneys may simply be unavailable. Even when assistance involves the provision of a fungible good, some *poskim* argue that if an alternative can only be obtained through some inconvenience, the biblical *lifnei iver* rule applies.[50]

In addition, assuming that the client were theoretically able to engage an equally effective alternative attorney, that attorney might be unwilling to provide services on terms as favorable as those of the particular Jewish attorney in question. As to the sale of goods, some authorities contend that if a Gentile seller does not offer wine to a Nazir (a person who has sworn, among other things, not to partake of wine) on the same attractive terms as a Jewish seller, the Jewish seller would, by selling the wine, violate *lifnei iver*.[51] Unable to find an appropriate attorney[52] willing to take his case on acceptable terms[53], a client might even decide not to file suit altogether.[54] Thus, a particular lawyer's assistance may well be

---

[47] *Rashi* explains that even the Talmudic view that says "there is no 'preordained fate' (*mazel*) as to Jews," only means that Jews, through prayer, can alter their fate. *See* RASHI, BABYLONIAN TALMUD, *Sabbath* 156b, *s.v. ayn mazel.*

[48] Of course, the practical significance of such diversity may depend on the complexity and the specialized nature of a client's case.

[49] There are many statutes and judicially promulgated ethics rules that disqualify attorneys from accepting particular clients. In many instances, an entire firm may be vicariously disqualified based on an actual or apparent conflict with respect to a single member of the firm.

[50] The relevant Talmudic text, discussed in § 3.02, *supra*, describes *lifnei iver* in a case in which the two people, the enabler and the person committing the specific transgression stand on "two sides of the river." To commit the transgression, the transgressor needs something from the side of the river where the enabler is standing. By transferring the item to the transgressor, the enabler violates *lifnei iver*. *See, e.g.*, MENAHEM HAMEIRI (1249–1315), BEIT HABEKHIRAH, *Avodah Zarah* 6a (Heb.); YAIR BACHARACH (1638–1702), HAVVOT YAIR no.185; MORDECHAI YAAKOV BREISH, 2 HELKAT YAAKOV, *Yoreh De'ah* no. 23 (where stores are scarce and locating an alternative would require effort, the renting of a store to a Jew who will work in the store on the Sabbath is a case involving two sides of the river); YITZHAK ADLER, LIFNEI IVER 332 (1988–89).

[51] BACHARACH, *supra* note 50; BREISH, *supra* note 50; ADLER, *supra* note 50.

[52] In some types of practices there is substantial personal interaction between attorneys and clients and, for the relationship to succeed, each must be comfortable with the other. As a practical matter, the number of alternative attorneys available to a particular client will depend on the client's ability to establish an effective relationship with an appropriate attorney.

[53] *See* BACHARACH, *supra* note 50 (where a Jew sells merchandise at a lower price than others or sells on credit while others do not, we do not say that the purchaser can acquire the goods elsewhere).

[54] Filing a suit typically requires a client to invest considerable time, energy and money. Even in a

necessary if the client is to be able to violate Jewish law by collecting money to which he is not entitled. This is all the more likely if the client's matter requires specialized knowledge or training, limiting the number of appropriate alternative attorneys, or if the client must be personally represented in Israel, restricting the number of available non-Jewish alternatives.

Even if, despite the foregoing arguments, the providing of legal services would be considered a "one side of the river" case, there is an additional reason for treating such assistance as a violation of *lifnei iver*. Some *poskim*, although a minority, argue that even in a "one side of the river" scenario, an assister who is directly involved in the halakhic prohibition is guilty of *lifnei iver*.[55] The lawyer's involvement in the decision to file suit in secular court, his participation in the calendaring of secular court proceedings and his vigorous appearance on behalf of the client in such proceedings — examining witnesses, cross-examining an adversary's witnesses, raising and responding to evidentiary objections, presenting opening and closing arguments — may well constitute such direct involvement in the halakhic prohibition.[56]

As discussed earlier, under Jewish law, one must act strictly with respect to a possible violation of biblical law. Consequently, so long as there is more than a de minimus possibility that a particular lawyer's services were necessary to enable the client to accomplish its impermissible purpose, Jewish law would forbid the assistance.

Assuming that a lawyer's representation of a client might violate *lifnei iver*, are there any circumstances under which Jewish law would nonetheless allow the lawyer to help the client? For all practical purposes, the answer is "no," even if the refusal to represent clients wrongfully trying to collect money would cause an attorney to suffer some financial loss.[57] The majority view is that *halakhah*

---

contingent fee arrangement, a client may have to expend sums to cover out-of-pocket expenses such as filing fees, depositions and expert witnesses.

[55] *See generally* ADLER, *supra* note 50, at 32–34; SHALOM YITZHAK TAWIL, SHA'AREI SHALOM, *sha'ar* 3, *halakhah* 3 (Heb.).

[56] If the situation is one in which the attorney's client, a Jew, is violating the biblical prohibition (*issur arkhaot*) against suing another Jewish defendant in secular court, the attorney seems clearly involved with the client's violation at the time it is committed. If the client is using the secular court to take money the client is not entitled to under Jewish law, this would violate the law against stealing (*issur gezel*). If the attorney is present and involved with the client's efforts in this regard, the attorney could also be characterized as directly involved in the *issur gezel*. Even if the attorney's involvement were in most cases deemed to be too indirect or attenuated, there seem to be situations in which an attorney may be intimately involved with the *issur gezel*. Assume, for instance, that, although a particular plaintiff was not *halakhically* entitled to any money from a defendant, the plaintiff obtained a judgment for $2,000. If, pursuant to this judgment, the defendant pays the $2,000 to the plaintiff's attorney in cash — taking a receipt in exchange — and the attorney gives the cash to the plaintiff, the attorney may be considered to have "fed" the plaintiff the "forbidden money." See also the various issues listed *supra*, note 5. Although a full discussion of this issue falls outside the purview of this paper, the specific acts taken by a lawyer could also, in particular instances, constitute his own personal and direct violations of specific biblical or rabbinic rules. *Compare, e.g.*, R. MENASHE KLEIN, MISHNE HALACHOTH vol. 7, no. 255 and vol. 3, no. 214 (suggesting that lawyers may directly violate the *issur arkhaot*) *to* BROYDE, *supra* note 26, at 49–52 (disagreeing with R. Klein and citing other views).

[57] Theoretically, a decision not to represent a particular client might lead to a loss of prospective

requires that a person comply with a biblical prohibition that proscribes action,[58] such as *lifnei iver*, even if compliance causes him to lose all of his wealth.[59]

[F] Miscellaneous Prohibitions

Assume, however, that the *lifnei iver* doctrine does not apply because the client could accomplish the forbidden goal with a non-Jewish attorney. Nevertheless, just by assisting a Jewish client's violation of Jewish law, a Jewish lawyer transgresses the rabbinic prohibition (*mesayeah bidei ovrei avierah*).[60] If the attorney could have stopped the client from having successfully pursued its wrongful objective, then the attorney has failed to fulfill the rabbinic obligation to prevent another Jew from violating Jewish law. Similarly, if the client wrongfully harmed the other party, and the lawyer could have prevented this, the lawyer violated the

---

revenue, whether from the client refused or because of professional sanctions, including possible disbarment. The loss of prospective revenue, as a practical matter, may in many instances be small. Lawyers often have more work than they have time for. The threat of professional sanction seems to be negligible. In most instances, secular law does not require a lawyer to accept a particular case. Even if a judge would otherwise want to impose a particular *pro bono* case on an attorney, the judge may well be sympathetic to switching assignments based on an attorney's religious convictions. Indeed, an attorney may have a religious freedom right — whether constitutional or statutory — that would immunize him from any such sanction. *But see* FORMAL ETHICS OPINION No. 96-F-140, 1996 WL 340719 (Tenn. Bd. Prof. Resp.), *available at* http://tbpr.org/Attorneys/EthicsOpinions/Pdfs/96-F-140.pdf (religious objection to abortion held an insufficient basis for release from court appointment as attorney for a party attacking statutory restrictions on abortions). A junior attorney at a firm who refuses to represent a specific client may face the loss of future income because of reprisals from more senior members of the firm. As to all of these concerns, however, it is noteworthy that *Halakha* does not usually treat the loss of prospective income as seriously as the loss of currently held assets. *See* R. HAYYIM MEDINI, SDEI HEMED, *Ma'arakhat Hey, Klal* 59 (Heb.).

The most probable scenario involving a serious risk to current assets would be where an attorney or firm began representation of a client and only later discovered that the client's objective violated Jewish law. Secular rules regarding withdrawal from a matter already undertaken are considerably more restrictive than the rules regarding the initial decision not to take a case. *See, e.g.*, ABA MODEL RULES OF PROFESSIONAL CONDUCT, Rule 1.16. If the client must pay the replacement lawyer to redo legal work (e.g., reviewing witness statements, deposition testimony, research, etc.), the withdrawing attorney may have to refund part or all of any fees he received when he did that work initially. Furthermore, an abrupt withdrawal, in certain circumstances, could cause the client to lose, triggering a malpractice judgment against the withdrawing attorney.

[58] AVRAHAM S. AVRAHAM, 4 NISHMAT AVRAHAM 86 (Heb.) (citing authorities).

[59] MOSHE ISSERLES, SHULHAN ARUKH, *Yoreh De'ah* 157:1; HAYYIM MEDINI, SDEI HEMED, *Ma'arakhat Halamed, Klal* 107 (Heb.) (citing views); AVRAHAM, *supra* note 58. Of course, in the improbable event that someone threatened to kill an attorney unless the attorney helped him wrongfully collect money, *Halakhah* would permit the attorney to take the case. *Id.* The issue becomes somewhat murkier where a lesser degree of physical harm is threatened.

[60] *See, e.g.*, SHABBETAI HAKOHEN (a/k/a *Shakh*, d. 1663), *Shulhan Arukh, Yoreh De'ah* 151:1, *s.k.* 7; DAVID HALEVI, *TAZ, Orah Hayyim* 347; AVRAHAM GOMBINER (1637–1683), MAGEN AVRAHAM, *Orah Hayyim* 347; SHMUEL KOLIN (1720–1806), MAHATZIT HASHEKEL *Orah Hayyim* 347:1; SHLOMO KLUGER, 2 RESPONSA TOV TA'AM VADA'AT, TELISA'AH no. 31; YITZHAK YEHUDA SHMELKES (d. 1906), SHUT, *Orah Hayyim* no. 25; SHALOM M. SHWADRON (1835–1911), 2 MAHARSHAM no. 93; SHLOMO YEHUDA BEN PESAH TZVI, EREKH SHAI, *Hoshen Mishpat* no. 26; YOSEF ISSER, SHA'AR MISHPAT, *Hoshen Mishpat* 26:1; YISROEL MEIR KAGAN, MISHNAH BERURAH 347:9; YITZHAK WEISS, 2 MINHAT YITZHAK no. 106; HAYYIM HAKOHEN (nineteenth century), LEV SHOMEA, *Ma'arekhet* 30, *oht* 39; ABDALLAH SOMEAH (1813–1889), ZIVHEI TZEDEK, *Hoshen Mishpat* 2 (citing authorities); OVADIAH YOSEF, YABIA OMER II, *Orah Hayyim* 15 and *Yehave Da'at* III:67; HAYYIM OZER GRODZINSKY (d. 1940), 3 AHIEZER no. 81(7); ADLER, *supra* note 50.

commandment not to stand idly by while his friend is harmed (*lo ta'amod al dam re'ekhah*).

The practical application of these doctrines, however, are complex. Jewish law does not impose these rules on non-Jews. They are obligations that arise out of the interrelationship between and among Jews. Consequently, the lawyer's obligations may depend on whether the client or the client's adversary is Jewish and whether they comport themselves as part of the Jewish community.[61] This is not the place to investigate these matters more thoroughly.[62]

§ 15.05   JEWISH LAW LIMITS ON PERMISSIBLE MEANS

Whether a client hopes to achieve an appropriate or an inappropriate result, Jewish law may importantly restrict the means that an attorney may employ. For example, even if a Jewish attorney could represent a client in non-litigative matters, in some instances he or she may not be permitted to file suit on behalf of one Jewish client against a Jewish defendant.[63]

Furthermore, even if it is permissible for the attorney to represent a client at trial, certain Jewish law rules may restrict the means the attorney may employ. For example, assume that a witness has truthfully testified about certain facts that are harmful to your client's position. Indeed, your client has privately confirmed to you this witness's testimony. Assume, further, that, notwithstanding these facts, you are certain that your client's position is meritorious. However, you realize that, for various technical reasons, you may not be able to adduce adequate evidence to convince others, especially if the trier of fact believes the circumstances to which your adversary's witness has testified. You believe that, in order for your client to prevail, you must persuade the judge or jury not to rely on the witness's truthful testimony.

In certain cases, a secular attorney might want to impeach a witness based on some past wrongdoings, especially wrongdoings involving dishonesty. Jewish law, however, forbids one to repeat unflattering facts about someone, even if those facts are true.[64] There are exceptions that occasionally apply to the uttering of unflattering information,[65] but usually they permit private disclosure to a particular

---

[61] A number of Jewish law authorities contend that it is nevertheless praiseworthy to refrain from assisting a non-Jew's violation of Jewish law, even if the assistance was not essential. Similarly, they contend that it is appropriate to attempt to dissuade non-Jews from violating Jewish law. *See, e.g.,* MICHAEL J. BROYDE, THE PURSUIT OF JUSTICE AND JEWISH LAW 61 (1996). One prominent twelfth century authority, Rabbi Yehuda Hehasid, writes: "If you see a non-Jew committing a transgression and you can stop him, stop him. [After all,] God sent [the prophet] Jonah to Nineveh to cause them [i.e., the non-Jews there] to repent." *See* YEHUDA HEHASID, SEFER HASIDIM 1124.

[62] Those desiring to delve into this topic in greater detail should see Steven H. Resnicoff, *Helping a Client Violate Jewish Law: A Jewish Lawyer's Dilemma,* in JEWISH LAW ASSOCIATION STUDIES X (H.G. Sprecher ed., 2000).

[63] SHULHAN ARUKH, *Hoshen Mishpat* 26:1. *See also* Chapter 16, *infra.*

[64] PLISKIN, *supra* note 23, at 29.

[65] For example, it is usually permitted to disclose to a person unflattering information about another in order to alert the person to possible harm from the other or, at least, harm arising from traits or conditions connected to the information disclosed. The case discussed in the text is a bit different because

person or persons. Disclosures in open court, in front of a judge, members of the jury, the parties and their counsel, as well as members of the public or press, would be more difficult to permit. In addition, depending on the particular past deeds of the witness, disclosure might violate the law against embarrassing someone in public, which is a quite serious offense.

Of course, it may be that the witness is guiltless of any of the type of "bad acts" that even secular law would allow to be mentioned in court. A skilled litigator might nevertheless endeavor to undermine the witness's credibility by careful cross-examination, including the use of a tough series of leading questions,[66] designed to confuse the witness (or the trier of fact) and to cast doubt either on the witness's sensory or intellectual capacities or on the witness's veracity. This type of examination might violate the Jewish law prohibition against verbal abuse.

In addition, Jewish law not only prohibits actual fraud, but it also orders one to "distance oneself from fraud" (*medevvar shekker tirkakh*). Consequently, within a Jewish court proceeding, one may not even utilize misleading tactics. For example, under the strict rabbinical court rules, a plaintiff often requires two eye-witnesses to prevail. Suppose the plaintiff is someone whom you know and completely trust. He has one eye-witness, but not two. He asks you to come to court with him and his witness. He does not ask you to offer false testimony. Instead, he simply wants the defendant to think that you will be a second witness so that the defendant will confess to the truth. Nevertheless, the Talmud and subsequent Jewish legal authorities rule that it is forbidden for you to comply with this request because of the principle that one must distance oneself from falsehood.[67]

§ 15.06   IMPACT OF JEWISH LAW ON CLIENT CONFIDENTIALITY

The Model Rules of Professional Conduct promulgated by the American Bar Association ("ABA") do not *require* an attorney to disclose a client's confidential information even if necessary to prevent an innocent person from being murdered — or, presumably, even to prevent a mass murder.[68] By contrast, Jewish law would require such a disclosure.[69] Nevertheless, as long as secular law allows an attorney to disclose, there is no direct conflict between these two bodies of law.[70]

---

no prospective harm arises from the truthful witness's past indiscretions.

[66] Consider, for example, litigator Seymour Wishman's description of his own cross-examination of an alleged rape victim and of his subsequent encounter with that party. *See* Steven H. Resnicoff, *Lying and Lawyering: Contrasting American and Jewish Law*, 77 NOTRE DAME L. REV. 937, 951–54 (2002).

[67] MOSHE ISSERLES, SHULHAN ARUKH, *Hoshen Mishpat* 28:1.

[68] *See, e.g.*, ABA MODEL RULES OF PROFESSIONAL CONDUCT, Rule 1.6 (as amended in 2003) [hereinafter, "ABA Rule 1.6"].

[69] This arises from the Jewish law doctrine, discussed in Chapter 3, *supra*, not to stand idly by when another bleeds to death.

[70] Of course, serious practical problems could arise if a supervising attorney at a firm orders an associate not to disclose. If the associate complies with his or her religious convictions by disclosing the information, query whether the firm could legitimately fire the attorney. If, however, the secular rules required such a disclosure, and an attorney's disclosure constituted a necessary compliance with the rule, it would seem that the attorney, at least in some jurisdictions, might well be insulated from termination

Over the past twenty years or so, the secular ethics rules have importantly expanded the instances in which an attorney is allowed to disclose information relating to the representation of a client. The cases in which the ABA now permits disclosure include (1) to prevent death or serious bodily harm; (2) to prevent the client's commission of a crime or fraud reasonably certain to result in substantial financial or property injury if to further the crime the client has used or is using the lawyer's services; and (3) to prevent, mitigate or rectify substantial financial or property damage that will or has resulted from the client's past commission of a crime or fraud in which the client used the lawyer's services.[71]

Nevertheless, there seem to be many situations in which ABA Rule 1.6 would at least arguably disallow a disclosure even though it would be necessary to protect an innocent third party from victimization. Suppose, for example, that the client has committed a crime or fraud that will result in substantial injury to a third party, but the attorney's services were not used in connection with that crime, fraud or tort. Although ABA Rule 1.6 would not permit disclosure, Jewish law would appear to require it. The same problem arises if we consider the attorney has information that the client will commit a crime or fraud that will inflict substantial injury to another's financial interests or property, but the client is not using the attorney's services in connection therewith. Under ABA Rule 1.6, the attorney may not disclose the information. Under Jewish law, disclosure would seem to be required.

At least one Jewish law commentator, Alfred Cohen, has argued that Jewish law might not require disclosures on a case-by-case basis if the aggregate effect of such disclosures might not serve the public interest.[72] Cohen has contended, for example, that Jewish law might not require psychiatrists to report to authorities certain cases of physical abuse if the result would be to diminish the victims' access to doctors and therapy.[73] Citing the rabbinic decree limiting one's ability to ransom a captive for more than his worth, Cohen argues that there are times that the interests of the general public outweigh those of individuals. However, one might point out that the rule regarding ransoming arose from a specific rabbinic decree. In the absence of such a decree, and no such decrees have been issued regarding professional confidences, the underlying requirement to help each individual should apply.

Cohen, however, correctly points out that Jewish law, as discussed in Chapter 4, normally limits the burden one must incur to fulfill a particular commandment and that a particular limit depends on the nature of the commandment in question. There is, of course, a lively debate as to the limits that apply with respect to disclosure of confidential information, depending upon the harm to be avoided through disclosure.[74]

---

by his firm. *See, e.g.*, Wieder v. Skala, 80 N.Y.2d 628, 609 N.E.2d 105 (1992).

[71] ABA Rule 1.6.

[72] Alfred S. Cohen, *On Maintaining a Professional Confidence*, 7 JOURNAL OF HALACHA & CONTEMP. SOC'Y 73 (1984).

[73] A disclosure requirement might deter victims from seeking treatment. *Id.* at 82–84. In the case of persons victimized by family members, a policy of disclosure could also conceivably lead adult abusers to block the victims' access to treatment.

[74] *See, e.g.*, MOSHE HALEVI SPERO, HANDBOOK OF PSYCHOTHERAPY & JEWISH ETHICS 117–148 (1986)

(carefully examining the topic of professional confidentiality and disagreeing with Cohen as to the extent of one's duty to disclose).

Chapter 16

ALTERNATIVE DISPUTE RESOLUTION AND JEWISH LAW

§ 16.01   INTRODUCTION

Jewish law offers three basic ways of resolving disputes: (1) by adjudication "according to *din*" (i.e., according to the strict law); (2) by compromise (*p'sharah*); or (3) by compromise close to the strict law (*p'sharah kerovah ledin*). Alternatively, there is the possibility of parties reaching a voluntary settlement of their disputes by participating in a mediation process without going to a rabbinic court. Studying these procedures is not only important as a matter of comparative law, but in many instances, Jewish law forbids, or restricts, resort to a non-Jewish court.[1] This chapter begins with a discussion of these restrictions.

---

[1] Nevertheless, it seems that the prohibition against going to secular courts is frequently violated. Kasdan, for example, comments: "Despite . . . [the] Torah-based prohibition [against suing someone in a non-rabbinic court], religious Jews, like others in today's litigious society, unfortunately turn to the courts of this land [i.e., the United States] to resolve disputes in which they become embroiled." Yitzchak Kasdan, *A Proposal for P'sharah: A Jewish Mediation/Arbitration Service, in* THE ETHICAL IMPERATIVE 300, 301 (Nisson Wolpin ed., 2000). *See also* Chaim Dovid Zwiebel, *Batei Din vs. Secular Courts: Where Do We Pursue Justice?, in* THE ETHICAL IMPERATIVE 266–65 (Nisson Wolpin ed., 2000).

§ 16.02 RESTRICTIONS ON RESORT TO NON-JEWISH COURTS

The Pentateuch states, "And these are the laws that you must set before them"[2] and then enumerates many laws. A question arises as to what the words "before them" mean. If it means "Jews," generally, then the verse might simply be directing Moses to teach these laws to the Jewish people. However, the Talmud states:

> R. Tarfon used to say: In any place where you find heathen law courts, even though their law is the same as the Israelite law, you must not resort to them since it says, "These are the judgments [i.e., laws] which thou shalt set before them,"[3] that is to say, "before them" [i.e., Jewish courts] and not before heathens.[4]

Based on this Talmudic source, R. Yosef Karo's still authoritative sixteenth century Code of Jewish Law (the *Shulhan Arukh*) states:

> It is forbidden to litigate before . . . [non-Jewish] judges and courts. . . . Even in a matter as to which they apply Jewish law and even if both parties agree to litigate before them, it is forbidden. [If] anyone goes to litigate before them, he is an evildoer, and it is considered as if he blasphemed, cursed and committed violence against the Torah.[5]

To be more precise, the Talmud and Shulhan Arukh both use the word "*akum*," a contraction of "*ovdei kokhavim*," which literally means "star-worshipers" and, less literally, refers to all idolaters. Nevertheless, the cited translators have respectively rendered this word as "heathen" or "non-Jewish." The word *akum* is frequently used in the Talmud to refer to all non-Jews, and virtually all Jewish law authorities explain that in this context the term is intended to apply to all non-rabbinic courts.[6] In fact, according to most authorities the prohibition applies to any courts other than rabbinic courts. According to many rabbinic authorities, including a former Chief Sephardi Rabbi of the State of Israel, the prohibition even applies to Israel's secular courts and even if all of the judges are Jewish.[7]

---

[2] *Exodus* 21:1.

[3] *Id.*

[4] BABYLONIAN TALMUD, *Gittin* 88b.

[5] SHULHAN ARUKH, *Hoshen Mishpat* 26:1. Similarly, the *Midrash Tanhuma*, *Mishpatim* 3 (Heb.) states: "For whoever abjures Jewish judges and goes before gentile [judges] has first denied the Holy One, blessed be He, and thereafter denied the Torah." *See* J. DAVID BLEICH, 4 CONTEMPORARY HALAKHIC PROBLEMS 3 (1995) (providing this translation).

[6] *See, e.g.*, SHIMON DURAN (1361–1444), 4 TASHBATS no. 6 (Heb.) (term applies to Muslim courts even though they are not star worshipers); R. Simcha Krauss, *Litigation in Secular Courts*, 3 J. HALACHA & CONTEMP. SOC'Y 35, 37–38, n.6 (1982); Mordecai Biser, *Can an Observant Jew Practice Law? A Look at Some Halakhic Problems*, 11 THE JEWISH LAW ANNUAL 101, 103 n.5 (Bernard S. Jackson ed., 1994); MICHAEL BROYDE, THE PURSUIT OF JUSTICE 42, note 5 (1996) (citing authorities).

[7] *See, e.g.*, OVADIA YOSEF, 4 YEHAVE DA'AT no. 64 (Heb.) (arguing, in fact, that the prohibition applies *a fortiori* to the submission of disputes to Jewish judges, who, although personally commanded to apply Jewish law, rule according to secular Israeli law); MOSHE STERNBUCH, 3 TESHUVOT VEHANHAGOT no. 441 (Heb.); Krauss, *supra* note 6, at 49–52.

It is worthwhile to mention the most common exceptions to this rule. First, according to most authorities, a Jewish plaintiff may go to a secular court to assert a claim against a Gentile.[8] Second, if a defendant, including a Jewish defendant, refuses to go to a rabbinic court, a Jewish plaintiff may seek rabbinic permission to proceed to secular court.[9] Without such permission, however, the normative view is that a Jewish client generally cannot file suit in a secular court against a religiously observant Jewish defendant. Even if the Jewish defendant is not religiously observant, many authorities — probably most — still specifically require a Jewish plaintiff to obtain rabbinic permission prior to commencing secular litigation.[10] Third, sometimes a lawsuit may, in name, be filed against a particular person but, in fact, any recovery may come from a third party, such as the named defendant's insurer, who is not Jewish and who is presumably unwilling to submit to a rabbinical court. In such cases, too, it is possible to obtain rabbinic approval to proceed with a suit in secular court. Fourth, a Jew who is sued in a secular court is permitted to defend himself or herself in that court.

Should someone violate this rule, sue in secular court and obtain a judgment in an amount greater than what he or she would have been entitled under Jewish law, then collecting that judgment violates the biblical law against stealing (*issur gezel*). As R. Yaakov Blau states: "[W]hen one uses secular courts to take money to which he is not entitled according to the law of the Torah, the money so taken is stolen money."[11]

In most monetary disputes between Jews and non-Jews, disputes among Gentiles, there will probably be little, if any, conflict between secular law and

---

[8] *See* BROYDE, *supra* note 6, at 43 (citing *Kovetz HaPoskim*, at 178–80). *But see* DURAN, *supra* note 6, *at* vol. 2, no. 290 (Heb.) (if a Gentile wants to litigate in rabbinic court, the Jewish litigant cannot resort to a secular court). *See also* Judah Dick, *Can Modern Legal Disputes Be Settled by Din Torah?, in* THE ETHICAL IMPERATIVE 254 (Nisson Wolpin ed., 2000).

[9] SHULHAN ARUKH, *Hoshen Mishpat* 26:2. According to Rabbi Yehiel M. Epstein, the permission should be restricted to recovery of the amount of money to which the plaintiff would be entitled under Jewish law. *See* YEHIEL MIKHAL HALEVI EPSTEIN (1829–1908), ARUKH HASHULHAN, *Hoshen Mishpat* 26:2 (Heb.).

[10] In the case of someone who has entirely rejected Judaism, R. Sternbuch suggests that the reason for this requirement may be because of the honor of the rabbinic court rather than the underlying prohibition against resorting to a secular court. *See* STERNBUCH, *supra* note 7, vol. 1, no. 795; vol. 2, no. 441. J. David Bleich (contemporary), offers a "possible justification" (a *Limud Zekhut*) for those who sue irreligious Jews in secular courts without first securing rabbinic permission, but he explicitly states that he is not ruling that such conduct is permissible. *See* BROYDE, *supra* note 6, at 44–45 (citing a letter containing Bleich's comments). *Cf.* MOSHE FEINSTEIN (1895–1986), IGGEROT MOSHE, *Hoshen Mishpat* I:8.

[11] *See* YAAKOV BLAU (contemporary), PITHEI HOSHEN, *Dinei Halva'ah*, Chapter 6, *halakha* 6 (Heb.). *See also* OVADIA YOSEF, YABIA OMER, *Hoshen Mishpat* II:1; AKIVA EGER (1761–1837), HIDDUSHEI R. AKIVA EGER, *Hoshen Mishpat* 26:1; STERNBUCH, *supra* note 7 (one of the reasons why suing a Jew in secular court is impermissible is that "one collects money from his fellow even though according to Torah law this is plain theft"); EPSTEIN (1829–1908), *supra* note 9, at *Hoshen Mishpat* 26:2; BROYDE, *supra* note 6, at 45 (quotes a letter from J. David Bleich who says that "[a]ny recovery accepted on the basis of a decision of a secular court in excess of that which would have been ordered by a [rabbinical court] . . . constitutes extortion in the eyes of Jewish law"); MENASHE KLEIN, 12 MISHNE HALACHOTH no. 387 (using a secular court to take money from someone not in accord with *halakha* constitutes stealing); EZRA BASRI, 1 DINEI MAMANOT 346 ("Someone who takes money pursuant to secular law . . . to which he is not entitled according to the Torah is a robber and is obligated to return the money he took.").

halakhah.[12] Where one or both parties are Jewish, however, the parties' rights under secular and Jewish law may in many instances differ importantly. For example, although some Jewish law doctrines, such as *dina demalkhuta dina* (the law of the kingdom is [religiously] binding) and *minhag hasoharim* (the custom of merchants), integrate some secular laws and practices into the Jewish law system, each of these doctrines is subject to possible limitations.[13] Sometimes, even if the two systems' substantive rules are the same, procedural and evidentiary rule differences may enable a Jewish plaintiff to prevail in secular court even if the case would have failed in a rabbinic court. In such cases, rabbinic authorities disagree as to whether the plaintiff is entitled to collect such a judgment.[14]

§ 16.03   SECULAR LAW'S ALTERNATIVE DISPUTE OPTIONS

Secular law, however, provides two principal mechanisms for people to resolve their disputes without first going to court: arbitration and mediation. Arbitration involves a hearing, which is generally governed by rules and procedures to which the parties agree at the outset. However, according to some statutes, certain procedural rights, such as the right to be represented by an attorney, cannot be irrevocably waived. The hearing results in an arbitral award which is similar to a judicial judgment. If the arbitration is conducted according to the relevant statute, the prevailing party is permitted to enforce the arbitral award by having it confirmed in court. Assuming compliance with the relevant arbitration statute,[15] there are very few grounds for successfully appealing an aribtral award. Indeed,

---

[12] Some authorities, however, believe that the substantive and procedural rules of Jewish law must be followed by Gentiles when they resolve disputes among themselves. According to this view, there may well be substantial conflicts between contemporary secular law and *halakha* even when all of the litigants are Gentile. Nevertheless, the majority position is that Jewish law allows Gentiles flexibility in crafting rules to apply to each other. *See generally* Michael J. Broyde & Steven H. Resnicoff, *Jewish law and Modern Business Structures: The Corporate Paradigm*, 43 Wayne L. Rev. 1685 (1997).

[13] *See generally id.*, at 1765–1773; Steven H. Resnicoff, *Bankruptcy — A Viable Halachic Option?*, 34 J. Halacha & Contemp. Soc'y 5 (1992); Moshe Feinstein, Iggerot Moshe, *Hoshen Mishpat* I:62 (while applying *dina demalkhuta dina* to at least some aspects of secular bankruptcy law, stating that the doctrine is inapplicable to certain specific areas of law); Tzvi Sendler (contemporary), *Liability for Motor Vehicle Damages*, 36 J. Halacha & Contemp. Soc'y 58, 73 (1998) (arguing that neither doctrine alters the basic Jewish laws as to tort liability). *But see* Dick, *supra* note 8, at 254 (citing an article by Rabbi Eliyahu Henkin ruling that secular rent-control laws are binding on Jews based on the *dina demalkhuta dina* doctrine).

[14] Sternbuch considers a case in which a Jewish plaintiff would be entitled to collect under substantive Jewish law, but that he would not win in a rabbinic court because of an evidentiary rule of Jewish law. If the Jewish defendant is totally irreligious and refuses to appear in a rabbinic court, R. Sternbuch concludes that the plaintiff should be able to litigate in the secular court and recover the amount of money to which substantive (albeit not evidentiary) Jewish law would entitle him. *See* Sternbuch, *supra* note 7. *But cf.* Yaakov Blau, Pithei Hoshen, *Hilkhot Nezikin, perek* 4, *halakha* 29, note 74 (citing the view of Aryeh Leib Heller (*Kitzot HaHoshen*, 1745–1813) that even if the secular law applies the same substantive law as Jewish law, if it was obtained through testimony of a witness who would have been disqualified under Jewish law, the defendant is considered to have been wrongfully injured — and is entitled to recover from the witness).

[15] For a few of the typical compliance issues, see, for example, Shlomo Chaim Resnicoff, *The Secular Enforceability of a Beis Din Judgment, in* The Ethical Imperative 292–98 (Nisson Wolpin ed., 2000);

one New York Law Journal article compared the chances of overturning a properly obtained arbitration award to a snowball's chances of surviving *Gehinnom* (i.e., Hades).[16] There are a few areas in which arbitration awards are not so readily confirmed. Principally these are awards regarding child custody and child support.[17]

A second alternative mechanism for dispute resolution is mediation. A mediator does not issue a judgment. Instead, a mediator helps the parties negotiate a settlement. Consequently, a successful mediation results in a settlement agreement that the parties execute. This agreement becomes a contract enforceable in court. Fewer rules restrict the procedures that may be employed in mediation. The same mediator might utilize different procedures in different mediations. Similarly, mediations can result in settlements that are far more creative than arbitral awards or court judgments.[18]

§ 16.04   JEWISH LAW AND SECULAR ALTERNATIVE DISPUTE OPTIONS

Assuming that a rabbinic court would adhere to an applicable arbitration statute, state law would treat the rabbinic court's judgment just as it would treat any other arbitral award. Thus, if two Jews agreed to submit a particular dispute, or any prospective dispute arising out of a contract with each other, to arbitration by a rabbinic court, and one party subsequently tried to renege, a secular court could order him or her to submit to arbitration. Challenges to such enforcement based on the constitutional doctrine regarding the separation of church and state have failed. Indeed, a court's refusal to enforce a rabbinic arbitration agreement might constitute an unconstitutional deprivation of a Jew's right to contract.[19] In addition, if the rabbinic court issues a judgment, secular courts will confirm and enforce that judgment just as they would an arbitral award from any other panel of arbitrators. Similarly, secular courts would enforce agreements produced by rabbinic mediation just as they would enforce agreements produced by any other mediators.

§ 16.05   RABBINIC COURT PROCEEDING

If a party, the plaintiff, has a claim against another, he or she may bring that claim to a rabbinic court [beis din or bet din].

Steven H. Resnicoff, *Outline Re: The Secular Enforceability of Beis Din Judgments* (2000), http://jlaw.com/Articles/resni1.html.

[16] David E. Robbins, *Vacating Arbitration Awards*, N.Y. L.J., Sept. 9, 1994, at 1.

[17] *See, e.g.*, Agur v. Agur, 298 N.Y.S.2d 772 (1969). *See also* Jeffrey Haberman, Note, *Child Custody: Don't Worry, a Bet Din Can Get It Right*, 11 Cardozo J. Conflict Resol. 613 (2010) (arguing against New York State's policy of treating rabbinic court awards of child custody differently from other types of awards).

[18] Secular courts prefer monetary judgments to awards of equitable relief. Parties to mediation, however, may voluntarily agree on continued contractual relations between them. If possible, they may even agree to a mutually beneficial restructuring of their arrangement, which is something that could not generally be accomplished in a secular court judgment.

[19] *See, e.g.*, Elmora Hebrew Center, Inc. v. Fishman, 125 N.J. 404, 413–414 (1991).

[A] Initiation of a Rabbinic Proceeding

The rabbinic court will issue a summons to the defendant calling for the defendant to respond. Typically, if a defendant ignores an initial summons, the rabbinic court will issue a second. At some point, however, if the defendant fails to respond, the court may issue a decree declaring the defendant to be someone who wrongfully refuses to appear, a *sarvan ledin,* and may issue a decree putting the defendant in *herem,* i.e., requiring others in the community to ostracize the defendant and his or her business. In addition, the rabbinic court may give the plaintiff permission to sue in secular court.[20]

However, there are some exceptions. For example, if the parties reside in different locations, a rabbinic court in the plaintiff's city may not have jurisdiction over the defendant from a different city.[21] If the court lacks jurisdiction, it may also lack the authority to issue a decree putting the defendant in *herem.* Similarly, because most rabbinical courts are not "official" courts established by the local communities, a defendant typically has the right to declare that he or she prefers a process of arbitration involving three arbitrators picked by the parties. Specifically, each party picks one arbitrator and the two arbitrators so picked choose a third.[22] Three arbitrators so assembled constitute a Jewish court for purposes of the matter submitted to it.

Once the parties are before a Jewish court, most authorities rule that they are obligated to sign an agreement stating that they will be bound by the judgment that is issued and that they agree that any such judgment may be confirmed in, and enforced by, a secular court. A failure to sign such an agreement may be regarded as the equivalent of a refusal to appear before the court and could constitute grounds for granting the plaintiff permission to proceed to secular court.[23]

[B] Enforcing a Rabbinic Court Judgment

If a defendant has been found liable in a Jewish court, but refuses to abide by the judgment despite possessing the ability to comply, the rabbinic court may issue a decree of ostracism (*herem*). Rabbi Moses Isserles writes:

> One who has been found liable to his colleague in beis din, and he transgresses the ruling of the beis din, [the beis din] writes to the communities of Israel that "we have issued a judgment against So-and-so, and he has declined to follow and paid no heed [to our judgment], and we ostracized him that people should not daven [pray] with him, and they

---

[20] Shulhan Arukh, *Hoshen Mishpat* 26:2.

[21] Of course, just as with secular law, there are sometimes exceptions to the exceptions. For example, if the dispute concerns the ownership of personal property, and the plaintiff has physical possession of the property, the court in the plaintiff's city may have jurisdiction. The same may be true if the dispute concerns real property and the real property is located in the plaintiff's city.

[22] This process is referred to as *Zablo,* an acronym from the Hebrew words *zeh borer lo ehad vezeh borer lo ehad* (*i.e.,* this party picks one and that party picks one). *See* Bleich, *supra* note 5, at 5.

[23] Dick, *supra* note 8, at 256 (citing *Divrei Gaonim,* section 52(8) (Heb.)); Yitzhak Isaac Liebes, Shut Bet Avi 156 (ruling that if a party refuses to sign such an agreement, the party is treated as if it refused to participate in the rabbinic court proceeding).

should not circumcise his son, and they should not bury his dead, and they [should] remove his children from school and his wife from shul [synagogue], until he accepts upon himself the judgment.[24]

Nevertheless, it should be noted that at the time of R. Isserles, Jewish communities were much more structured than in modern times and typically had formally established, fixed rabbinic courts. R. J. David Bleich explains:

In many communities it was customary for all householders to affix their signatures to the formal ketav rabbanut, or rabbinic contract, presented to a newly appointed rabbi specifically designating him as the presiding judge of the local Bet Din. That practice was instituted in order to assure that no person might refuse to obey a summons issued by the communal rabbi on the plea that he did not recognize the rabbi's judicial authority."[25]

As discussed in Chapter 10, the situation is much different now, and the authority, and certainly the power, of rabbinic courts to coerce compliance with their judgments is much more attenuated. However, in the case of a party's willful non-compliance, today's rabbinic courts can authorize the other party to pursue its rights in secular court.

[C]   Types of Rabbinic Court Judgments

Theoretically, a rabbinic court proceeding may take one of three forms. The first approach would be to follow "*din*," referring in this case to denote the strict law. Accordingly, the formal procedures of a rabbinic court would be applied, and the court would ultimately issue a verdict for the plaintiff for the entire amount of the claim or a verdict completely exonerating the defendant.

The second alternative is for the court to follow a less strict approach referred to as *p'sharah* (i.e., compromise). In such a case, the court does not need to comply with the strict evidentiary or procedural requirements applicable to a rabbinic court. In addition, the court may issue a judgment that reflects its view of the equities raised by all of the attendant circumstances. Consequently, the defendant may be obligated to pay less, or more, than what the strict law would require. Rabbi Zvi Spitz explains that a judgment based on compromise customarily splits the amount in dispute, but the court has the authority to reach a different result based on the equities.[26]

The third approach, *p'sharah kerovah ledin* (a compromise close to the strict *din*) can vary from the strict din by one-third.[27] Thus, under this approach, even if the plaintiff would prevail under strict law, the court could award the plaintiff up to one-third less. Similarly, even if the strict law would completely exonerate the defendant, the court could still find the defendant liable for up to one-third.

---

[24] Zwiebel, *supra* note 1, at 271 (citing and translating from Moses Isserles, *Darkhei Moshe, Hoshen Mishpat* 19). The bracketed words are Zwiebel's; the words in the curlycues are mine.

[25] Bleich, *supra* note 5, at 5.

[26] *See* R. Tzvi Spitz, 3 Mishpetei HaTorah 113 (1998) (Heb.).

[27] *Id.*

Although parties can *theoretically* choose any of these three approaches, rabbinic courts typically will not hear a case based on strict *din*. In part, this is because the Talmud, after hearing opposing views, concludes that it is a *mitzvah* to compromise.[28] In this context, it seems that the word *mitzvah* is not used to mean a "commandment," but, instead, to connote good and meritorious conduct, at least as applied to the litigants. When R. Yehiel Mikhal Epstein rules that it is a *mitzvah* for the rabbinic court to encourage the parties to agree to *p'sharah*, he may actually mean that it is a duty.[29] One of the reasons why the Talmud favors *p'sharah* is that in compromise, each person is, in some sense, a "winner;" no one loses completely. Another, however, is to protect the members of the rabbinical court from the consequences of erring as to the strict law.[30]

Nevertheless, when a rabbinic court proceeds pursuant to *p'sharah*, the parties first sign an "arbitration" agreement with the rabbinical court agreeing from the outset that they will be bound by the *p'sharah* announced by the court.[31] If the parties want, and the rabbinic court is willing, the initial agreement may limit the court to issuing a *p'sharah kerovah ledin*. Otherwise, the agreement will authorize a general *p'sharah*. In any event, the parties will be bound by the *p'sharah* announced by the court even if they do not like it, do not want it, and in fact vocally object to it. By executing the original arbitration agreement, the parties relinquish their control over their dispute to the rabbinic court.

This is, of course, very different from the secular notion of mediation. As mentioned before, in mediation, the mediator does not issue a judgment but, instead, merely helps the parties reach a voluntary agreement. In mediation, the parties retain the ultimate power to reach, or not to reach, a settlement.

§ 16.06 INTERNET RESOURCES REGARDING RABBINIC COURTS

There are many web sites of individual rabbinic courts. You can find many of them by using a search engine and the terms "Beis Din," or "Bais Din," "Beth Din," or "rabbinical court," and perhaps "United States" or the name of some specific state. Here is information about three sites that provide valuable information:

1. The web site of the Beth Din of America, at http://www.bethdin.org/index.asp.

    Its publications site, http://www.bethdin.org/forms-publications.asp, contains a number of helpful documents, including:

    a. The Rules and Procedures of the Beth Din of America;

    b. An Application to Open a Din Torah Proceeding; and

---

[28] BABYLONIAN TALMUD, *Sanhedrin* 6b. *See also* SHULHAN ARUKH, *Hoshen Mishpat* 12:2.

[29] EPSTEIN, *supra* note 9, at *Hoshen Mishpat* 12:2.

[30] *See, e.g.*, R. Dov Bressler, *Arbitration and the Courts in Jewish Law*, 9 J. HALACHA & CONTEMP. SOC'Y 105, 107 (1985) (citing various authorities).

[31] BABYLONIAN TALMUD, *Sanhedrin* 6a; SHULHAN ARUKH, *supra* note 20, at 12:7.

c.   An eight-page Layman's Guide to Dinei Torah (Beth Din Arbitration Agreements).

2.   The web site of the Chicago Rabbinical Council, at http://www.crcweb.org/bethdin.php. It contains information about the process, as well as an application to open a case and an agreement to arbitrate.

3.   The web site of the Bais Din of the Rabbinical Council of California, http://rccvaad.org/bethdin/financial-arbitration-din-torah.

Appendix 1

GLOSSARY[1]

This Appendix provides a glossary of many of the most commonly used abbreviations, words and expressions that appear in Jewish law materials written in English. Some of the descriptions refer to other terms described in this Glossary. For additional details or for terms not included here, you may want to refer to more extensive resources, such as:

1. PHILIP BIRNBAUM, A BOOK OF JEWISH CONCEPTS (New York: Hebrew Publishing Co. 1964).

2. ENCYCLOPAEDIA JUDAICA (Fred Skolnick & Michael Berenbaum eds., Detroit: MacMillan Reference USA in connection with Keter Publishing Co., 2d ed. 2007).

3. MENACHEM ELON, JEWISH LAW: HISTORY, SOURCES, PRINCIPLES (4 volumes) (Bernard Auerbach & Melvin J. Sykes trans., Philadelphia: The Jewish Publication Society 1994).

1. Agunah:

A Jewish woman who has the legal status of being married yet lacks many of the benefits of marriage usually because: (a) her husband is dead, but there is inadequate proof of his death as a matter of Jewish law; or (b) her husband has abandoned her, but will not provide her a Jewish bill of divorce (a Get).

2. Aharon (Acharon), *plural* Aharonim (Acharonim):

The singular form of this term means "the later one." The term refers to a "later" Jewish law authority, usually to one who lived after the sixteenth century. *See generally* THE EARLY ACHARONIM (Hersh Goldwurm ed., Mesorah Publications, Ltd. 1989).

3. Akum:

This is a contraction of the Hebrew words Ovdei Kokhavim, literally meaning "star-worshippers," but commonly used to mean any idolaters or even any non-Jews.

4. Amidah:

Synonymous with "Shemonah Esrei," this refers to a silent devotion which is the central component of each of Judaism's three daily prayer services.

---

[1] Some common variant transliterations appear in parentheses.

5. Amora, *plural* Amoraim:

Rabbis during the Talmudic period (from approximately 220 C.E. through the end of the fifth century). For biographical information about Amoraim, *see generally* GERSHOM BADER, THE JEWISH SPIRITUAL HEROES (New York: Pardes Publishing House, Inc. 1940).

6. Arevut:

An "Arev" or "Orev" is a guarantor for someone else. Arevut refers to the mutual responsibility that each Jew has for another.

7. Arukh HaShulhan:

Written by Rabbi Yehiel Mekhal Epstein, this is a Code of Jewish law that follows the structure of the Shulhan Arukh but does not quote the language of the Shulhan Arukh. Instead, it provides a deep analysis of each of the laws, often discussing Talmudic passages and the writings of Rishonim.

8. Ashkenazi:

A Jew from the cultural group of Jews whose medieval "hub" was in Italy and Germany and whose hub later became Eastern Europe.

9. Ashmakhtah (Asmachtah, Asmakhta, Asmachta):

A device whereby a Jewish law authority uses a Scriptural text as the supposed basis for a non-biblical ruling.

10. Bamidbar:

The Hebrew title for the fourth book of the Pentateuch, the book of Numbers.

11. Bat Kol (Bas Kol):

This term is used in rabbinic literature to refer to a heavenly voice or revelation from God as written about in the Bible.

12. Bavli:

Literally, this term means "Babylonian." It usually refers to the Babylonian Talmud, *i.e.*, the Talmud Bavli. It is this latter term that accounts for the fact that standard citations to the Babylonian Talmud are "T.B.," "TB," or "tb."

13. B.C.E.:

An abbreviation for "before the common era;" it is equivalent to "B.C."

14. Bedi'eved:

"Post facto" or "after the fact." In Jewish law, some prohibitions apply only on an a priori basis. Certain acts that are forbidden on an a priori basis are not considered violations of law when regarded post facto.

15. Bein Adam Lihavero:

Literally, "between a man and his fellow." This refers to a duty that a person owes to another person. Such a duty typically requires a particular type of active or passive conduct vis-à-vis another person. (Under Jewish law, God is the ultimate source of all duties. Nevertheless, this term is used in contrast to the phrase Bein Adam LaMakom, "between a man and God." Literally, the phrase means, between a man and "the Place." God is referred to as "the Place" because God is everywhere.)

16. Bein Adam LaMakom:

This refers to a duty that a person owes directly to God, as opposed to one owed to another person. Included among such duties, for instance, is the obligation not to commit idolatry. LaMakom means "the Place" and is a pseudonym for God.

17. Bereshit (Bereshis):

This is the Hebrew title for the first book of the Pentateuch, the book of Genesis.

18. Bet Din (Bes Din, Beis Din, Beit Din, Beth Din):

This term refers to a rabbinic court.

19. Baraitha (Braitha, Baraisa, Braisa):

A Tannaitic statement that was not included in the Mishnah. *See* Mishnah and Tanna, *infra.*

20. C.E.:

This refers to "the common era" and is equivalent to "A.D."

21. Chumash (Humash):

The Hebrew word for the Five Books of Moses, based on the Hebrew word for the number five, Chamesh (Hamesh). It is equivalent to the English word Pentateuch.

22. Chumrah (Chumra, Humrah, Humra):

A stringency that may or may not be required by Jewish law.

23. Da'at Torah (Da'as Torah):

Literally, "the Torah view," meaning, however, "what God wants." In modern times, the phrase is primarily invoked by those who urge others to conduct themselves in accordance with the directions of certain well-known rabbinic leaders even as to matters that are not strictly governed by Jewish law. Thus, if rabbis ban a book or prohibit the use of the internet, it may be asserted that the rabbis' view should be followed because it reflects "Da'at Torah."

24. Daf Yomi:

Literally, "a page a day." This term refers to a program of study in which Jews worldwide study the same two-sided *daf*, or page, of Talmud on the same day. The program was proposed by Rabbi Meir Shapiro at the First World Congress of the World Agudath Israel, held in Vienna in 1923. Participants in the program learn the entire Babylonian Talmud page by page, a process that takes seven years and five months to complete.

25. DeRabbanon (Derabbanon) or MedeRabbanon (Mederabbanon):

Rabbinic, rather than, for instance, biblical. This typically refers to a law legislated by the rabbis, rather than a law that was divinely transmitted.

26. Deoraita (Deoraitha) or Mideoraita (Mideoraitha):

Biblical, rather than, for example, rabbinic. As opposed to DeRabbanon, this term refers to a law that was part of the Written Torah or the Oral Torah.

27. Devarim:

This is the Hebrew title of the fifth book of the Pentateuch, the book of Deuteronomy.

28. Din:

This refers either to a legal rule or to a legal decision in a particular case.

29. Dina DeMalkhuta Dina (Dina Demalchuta Dina):

Literally, "the law of the kingdom is [valid as a matter of Jewish] law." When applicable, this doctrine makes violation of a particular secular law a violation of Jewish law.

30. Din Torah:

A legal dispute heard by a Jewish rabbinic court.

31. Dinei Mamonos (Dinei Mamonot, Dinei Mamonoth):

Jewish laws pertaining to monetary matters. This is often used as a synonym for "civil law."

32. Dinei Nefashos (Dinei Nefashot):

Jewish laws pertaining to life and death, including, for example, laws regarding rescuing people from harm and laws regarding the judicial execution of criminals.

33. Emunah:

Emunah means religious belief or faith.

34. Even HaEzer:

This is one of the four divisions of law in the Arba'ah Turim and in the Shulhan Arukh. It deals primarily with family law matters, such as marriage, divorce and support.

35. Five Books of Moses:

A synonym for the Chumash, the Pentateuch, the Written Law and the Written Torah.

36. Gaon, *plural* Geonim:

The heads of Talmudic Academies from approximately the end of the sixth century to the middle of the eleventh century in Ashkenazi lands and to the thirteenth century in Sephardi lands.

37. Gehinnom:

Hades.

38. Gemara:

The portion of the Talmud that contains (rabbinic, academic, or explanatory) discussions concerning the Mishnah. It excludes the part of the Talmud that quotes the Mishnah.

39. Get:

A "get" is a religious bill of divorce.

40. Get Me'usseh:

A religious bill of divorce that was given as a result of unlawful coercion. Therefore, it does not effectuate a valid divorce.

41. Gezerah (Gezera), *plural* Gezerot:

A rabbinic legal decree or takkanah.

42. Gilui Arayot (Gilui Arayos):

Certain prohibited acts involving sexual immorality.

43. Godol, *plural* Gedolim:

This word can refer to (a) an adult, generally; or (b) specifically, to a leading Jewish law authority.

44. Halakhah (halakha, halachah, halacha, halacho):

This term can refer (a) specifically, to the particular Jewish law that pertains to a given case or issue; or (b) generally, to the entire body of Jewish law.

45. Hallowing God's Name (Kiddush HaShem or Kiddush Hashem):

A religious commandment to act in such a way that will lead Jews and non-Jews to have greater respect for God.

46. HaShem (Hashem):

Literally, "the Name." Judaism recognizes various names for God, each with slightly different meanings. Under Jewish law, it is forbidden to pronounce some of these names other than in prayer or as part of some religious ritual. Consequently, people often refer to God without saying any of God's names by using the general term, "HaShem."

47. Hefker Bet Din Hefker:

A doctrine that gives a rabbinic court the power to expropriate property, at least under certain circumstances. This doctrine is often cited as a predicate for the binding Jewish law authority of various rabbinic decrees regarding financial matters.

48. Herem:

A decree ostracizing or excommunicating someone or the state of being ostracized or excommunicated.

49. Hora'at Sha'ah (Hora'as Sha'ah):

This term refers to an exceptional and temporary Jewish law ruling that is necessary in light of exigent circumstances.

50. Hoshen Mishpat (Choshen Mishpat):

This is one of the four divisions of law in the Arba'ah Turim and in the Shulhan Arukh. It principally includes laws regarding financial matters and crimes.

51. Ikkar, *plural* Ikkarim:

An Ikkar is an essential principle.

52. Imitatio Dei (Emulating HaShem):

An expression often used to refer to the concept in Jewish law that instructs Jews to emulate God by following in His ways.

53. Israeli Chief Rabbinate:

An institute of the government of Israel that includes the two Chief Rabbis of Israel, one of whom is Ashkenazi and one of whom is Sephardi.

54. Kiddush HaShem (Kiddush Hashem, Hallowing God's Name):

See Hallowing God's Name, *supra*.

55. King (Melekh, Melech):

Jewish law recognizes Jewish and non-Jewish kings.

56. King's Law (Mishpat Hamelekh, Mishpat HaMelekh):

Special powers and responsibilities of a Jewish (and, according to some authorities, a non-Jewish) king.

57. Koach D'Heter Adif:

Literally, "the power of leniency is preferred." This Talmudic expression indicates that it takes greater wisdom to find an analytic path justifying a lenient ruling than merely to rule strictly from doubt.

58. Jubilee Year:

When certain conditions are satisfied, there is a biblical counting of years. The fiftieth such year is the Jubilee Year ("Yovel") at which time certain real property returns to its previous holders, slaves are freed, etc.

59. Latzeit Yedei Shamayim:

This refers to an obligation on a Jew that cannot be enforced by a rabbinical court, but which the Jew must do to "clear his account" in Heaven.

60. Lechat'hilah (Lekhat'hilah, Lekhathilah, Lekhathila):

"A priori" or "before the fact." Some Jewish law prescriptions only apply before the fact. If someone acts without knowing of an a priori proscription, the act, retrospectively, may not constitute a violation of Jewish law.

61. LeMigdar Milta:

Literally meaning, "to safeguard the matter," this phrase refers to the basis for rabbinic authority to issue "protective" edicts prohibiting acts that might lead to violations of Torah laws. The Torah law in question is the "matter" that is protected.

62. Lex Talionis:

This is the Latin term for the rule in the Scripture, "[a]n eye for an eye." The Talmud as well as most Jewish law scholars attest to the fact that mainstream Jewish law never interpreted this verse literally but, rather, as requiring financial compensation.

63. Lifnei Iver:

This refers to the biblical commandment: (1) not to enable another person, Jewish or non-Jewish, to violate Jewish law; and (2) not to purposefully provide bad advice to another Jew. Compare Lifnei Iver to the doctrine Mesayeah Bidei Ovrei Aveirah, *infra*.

64. Lifnim MeShurat HaDin:

This doctrine calls for people to act more generously than the minimum otherwise required under Jewish law. In some ways, it is similar to the secular doctrine, "beyond the letter of the law," but different in others. For example, in some instances, Jewish law actually *requires* a person to act Lifnim MeShurat HaDin.

65. Loshon HaRah:

Literally, the "Evil Tongue," Loshon HaRah refers to derogatory communications. Jewish law contains numerous prohibitions against making, against listening to, and against believing such communications. The Chafetz Chaim is the foremost authority regarding these rules.

66. Mappah:

Rabbi Moses Isserles' gloss on the Shulhan Arukh.

67. Mederabbanon:

See entry for Derabbanon, *supra*.

68. Mideoraita (Mideoraitha):

See entry for Deoraita, *supra*.

69. Midivrei Sofrim:

Usually this term refers to a law that is rabbinic rather that biblical.

70. Mesayeah Bidei Ovrei Aveirah (Mesayeah Lidei Ovrei Aveirah):

Also referred to as Mahzik BiDei Ovrei Aveirah, this phrase refers to a rabbinic prohibition against assisting another Jew to violate Jewish law even if the other Jew could have committed the violation without such assistance. Compare this to the biblical doctrine of Lifnei Iver, *supra*.

71. Mesorah:

Mesorah means that which is handed over. It is commonly used to refer either to the entire body of Jewish law and traditions that are handed down generation to generation. It is also used to refer to the traditions as to a particular topic, as in "What is the Mesorah about X?"

72. Middah, *plural* Middot (Middos):

A Middah is a character trait. Middot is a plural term that refers to character traits generally.

73. Midrash, *plural* Midrashim:

A Midrash is an interpretation of a Scriptural text. There are legal, or halakhic, Midrashim, which derive legal rules from a text, and Aggadic Midrashim, which provide non-legal, homiletical lessons.

74. Minhag (Minhog):

Custom. In Jewish law, customs can attain the status of law. This is especially true with respect to business custom, or Minhag HaSoharim (Minhag HaSocharim).

75. Mishnah (Mishna):

The first publicly published compilation of Tannaitic teachings, including both the Oral Torah communicated to Moses and non-biblical law.

76. Mishneh Torah:

The first comprehensive codification of Jewish law according to subject matter. It is the eleventh century magnum opus of Maimonides.

77. Mishpat Ivri:

This term usually refers either to Jewish civil law or to the effort to convince the government of Israel to implement Jewish civil law into Israeli law.

78. Mitzvat Aseh (Mitzvas Aseh), *plural* Mitzvot Aseh (Mizvos Aseh):

An affirmative (or active) commandment that requires a person to do something.

79. Mitzvat Lo Ta'aseh (Mitzvas Lo Sa'aseh), *plural* Mitzvot Lo Ta'aseh (Mitzvos Lo Sa'aseh):

A negative (or passive) commandment that prohibits a person from doing something. There is a debate among Jewish law authorities whether characterization of a commandment as affirmative or negative depends on either the form of the Written Torah's wording or the practical effect of its wording. For example, the Written Torah directs a person, "Do not stand idly by while your fellow bleeds." Thus, the commandment is worded negatively, as a "do not." On the other hand, the effect of the commandment to not stand idly by is that one is obligated to act. If characterization of the commandment depends on the form of the wording, the commandment would be a Mitzvat Lo Ta'aseh. If it depends on the effect of the wording, the commandment would be a Mitzvat Aseh.

80. Mosaic Ordination (Semikhah, Semichah):

The Written Torah states that Moses invested authority in Joshua as his successor by resting his hands upon Joshua. The Hebrew word for resting one's hand on another is Semikhah. Jewish law assumes that this, in fact, became the standard mechanism for authorizing subsequent rabbinic leaders. Only those who could directly trace their authority back to Moses through a human chain of similarly ordained authorities enjoyed this authentic Semikhah. Only people with this Mosaic ordination were eligible to serve in certain roles, such as becoming members of Israel's Supreme Court (the Sanhedrin HaGadol). This chain of ordination was snapped during periods in which Jews were oppressed and the teaching of Jewish law was outlawed on pain of execution. Efforts to reinstitute the institution of Mosaic Ordination did not succeed. *See* THE EARLY ACHARONIM 22–24 (Hersh Goldwurm ed., Mesorah Publications, Ltd. 1989).

81. Naval BiRishut HaTorah (Naval BiRishus HaTorah, Naval Birishut HaTorah, Naval Birishus HaTorah):

The word "Naval" means disgusting, loathsome, or repulsive. Naval BiRishut HaTorah refers to the notion that a person could observe all of the explicit Biblical commandments (and possibly also all of the specific non-Biblical laws), yet still engage in disgusting, loathsome, or repulsive conduct. The Nahmanides makes this point in at least two places in his commentary on the Written Torah. He explains that it is impossible for a written work to cover every case and contingency and argues that the general Biblical commandments, such as "to be holy" and "to walk in God's ways," require more than mere compliance with the Written Torah's explicit rules.

82. Neder, *plural* Nedarim:

A Neder is a vow. By making a Neder, a person can make an otherwise permitted thing or action biblically prohibited.

83. Neshamah, *plural* Neshamot (Neshamos):

A Neshamah is a person's soul.

84. Noahide Laws:

God gave seven laws, or categories, of laws to all of mankind. One was given to the first man, Adam. This one and six more were given to Noah when he exited the Ark after the waters of the Great Flood receded. They are referred to as Noahide laws (or Noachide laws or the Laws of Noah) because they apply to all of mankind, who are all descendants of Noah. There is some debate as to how these laws apply to Jews, who received an additional body of laws.

85. Olam HaBah:

See World to Come, *infra.*

86. Orah Hayyim:

This is one of the four divisions of law in the Arba'ah Turim and in the Shulhan Arukh. It deals primarily with daily and holiday prayer and practices.

87. Oral Torah or Oral Law:

Generally, the biblical laws that God communicated to Moses not intended to be included in the Written Torah. The term "Oral Law" is sometimes used synonymously with the "Oral Torah." However, the "Oral Law" is also sometimes used to refer to all Jewish law, biblical and non-biblical, that is not contained in the Written Torah.

88. Ordination (Semikhah, Semichah):

The transmission of the authority to rule on Jewish law matters from recognized authorities to younger accomplished scholars. Ordination is a general term and includes Mosaic ordination and non-Mosaic ordination. *See* Mosaic Ordination, *supra.* After the chain of Mosaic ordination was broken, there remained a need to identify those who were worthy of serving as Jewish law authorities. Already recognized authorities would specifically authorize younger accomplished scholars by declaring that they have permission to rule on Jewish law matters. The conferring of this type of permission is what is now known as ordination or Semikhah.

89. Ovdei Kokhavim (Ovdei Kochavim):

Literally, this means Star-worshippers, but the term is commonly used to refer not only to all idolaters but also to all non-Jews.

90. Pentateuch:

See Synonym for Chumash, Five Books of Moses, Written Law and Written Torah.

91. Pesak (P'sak):

A Jewish law ruling in a particular case or as to a particular issue.

92. Posek, *plural* Poskim or Posekim:

This refers to a person who is qualified to render rulings regarding Jewish law.

93. Profaning God's Name (Hillul HaShem, Chillul HaShem):

Jewish law proscribes the profaning of God's name, which involves conduct that would lead Jews or non-Jews to think ill of God. There are severe stringencies regarding this law. Nevertheless, determining precisely what constitutes profaning God's Name for purposes of these rules can be rather complex.

94. P'sharah (Pesharah):

Settlement or compromise.

95. P'sharah Kerovah LeDin (Pesharah Kerovah Ledin):

A settlement or compromise that is no more than one-third off, more or less, than the strict law.

96. Rabbanon Savorai, Rabbanim Savoranim, or Savoranim:

Jewish leaders in the period immediately after the "closing" of the Babylonian Talmud (during the fifth and sixth centuries).

97. Responsa (She'elot U'Teshuvot, Shut):

Throughout much of Jewish history, questions concerning all aspects of Jewish law, including those involving disputes among individual litigants, were often submitted to Jewish law authorities, who frequently lived elsewhere. The questions were sent in writing, and the answers, which restated the questions and replied to them, were in writing. These answers are referred to as "responsa." The Hebrew word "She'elot" means "questions," and "U'Teshuvot," means "and answers." Consequently, the expression "She'elot U'Teshuvot" also refers to these questions and answers. The word "Shut" is a contraction of "She'elot U'Teshuvot."

98. Reward and Punishment (Skhar VeOnesh):

The Jewish belief in the concept of reward and punishment based on the correctness of one's deeds.

99. Rishon, *plural* Rishonim:

Jewish leaders immediately after the Gaonic period (from the eleventh through the fifteenth centuries). *See generally* HERSH GOLDWURM, THE RISHONIM 79 (Brooklyn: Mesorah Publications, Ltd., 2d ed. 2001).

100. Safek DeOraitha LiHumrah:

This principle means that if there is a more than a de minimum chance that a particular act would violate biblical law, one may not perform the act. Similarly, if there is more than a de minimus chance that failure to perform an act would violate biblical law, one is obligated to do the act. This is in contrast to the rule, Safek DeRabbanon LiKula, that applies to uncertain questions regarding non-biblical law.

101. Safek DeRabbanon LiKulah:

This principle means that if it is uncertain whether a particular act is permitted, or prohibited, under Jewish law, one has discretion as to whether to do the act, at least so long as the likelihood of a rabbinic violation is not great. This is in contrast to the rule, Safek DeOraitha LiHumrah, which applies to uncertain violations of biblical law.

102. Sanhedrin:

A rabbinic court comprised of expert judges. Such a court might be either a Sanhedrin Kattanah (a minor court), usually of 3 or 23 judges, or it might be the Sanhedrin HaGadol (the "Great Court" or the "Supreme Court"), consisting of 71 members.

103. Sanhedrin HaGadol:

The "Great Court" or the "Supreme Court" consisting of 71 members, each of whom had to possess Mosaic ordination and satisfy a variety of other criteria.

104. Sefer Hahinnukh (Sefer HaHinnukh, Sefer HaChinnukh):

This volume was written in the thirteenth century. It examines each of the 613 Biblical commandments (as its author identifies them) in the order in which they arise in the Pentateuch. Its authorship was for many years ascribed to a "Rishon" named Aharon Halevi of Barcelona. More recent scholars question this accuracy of this ascription. *See* AHARON HALEVI, SEFER HAHINNUCH, vol. 1, at vii–xiv (Charles

Wengrov trans., New York: Feldheim 2d ed. 1992).

105. Sefer HaTurim:

A legal code authored by Jacob ben (i.e., the son of) Asher (1269–1343). This was a monumental work that dealt with four major categories of Jewish law. Rav Yosef Karo adopted this same structure for his work, the Shulhan Arukh.

106. Semikhah (Semichah):

See "Ordination," *supra.*

107. Sephardi (Sefardi):

Narrowly speaking, a Jew whose ancestry traces back to the Jews of the Iberian Peninsula prior to the expulsion from Spain in 1492 and Portugal in 1497. Sephardi Jews generally resided in Arab or Oriental lands, in contrast to Ashkenzi Jews. *See* "Ashkenazi," *supra.*

108. Shavuah, *plural* Shavuot:

A Shavuah is an oath. By taking a Shavuah, a person can biblically obligate himself or herself to do, or to refrain from doing, something.

109. Shemittah:

When certain conditions are satisfied, there is a counting of years. The years are counted in cycles of seven, and the seventh year is the Shemittah year. One of the laws of the Shemittah year is that liability on certain unsecured debts is discharged.

110. Shemot (Shemos, Shemoth):

The Hebrew name of the second book of the Pentateuch, the book of Exodus.

111. Skhar VeOnesh (S'char ve-onesh):

See Reward and Punishment.

112. Shas:

This term has at least two meanings. First, and most relevant to the study of Jewish law, it is the acronym of the Hebrew for "Six Divisions" (**SH**isha Sidrei), and is used to refer to the six divisions of the Mishnah or Talmud. "Shas" is also the name of an Orthodox Jewish political party in the State of Israel. The name undoubtedly is based on the same Hebrew acrony, the message being that this party's principles are those of the six divisions of the Mishnah and Talmud.

113. Shulhan Arukh (Shulchan Arukh, Shulhan Aruch, Shulchan Aruch):

The sixteenth century Jewish legal code was authored by Rabbi Yosef Karo. Rabbi Moses Isserles, a contemporary of Rabbi Karo, wrote a gloss (the "Mappah") on Rabbi Karo's text. This gloss is so important that the two are almost invariably published together. This work, usually referred to in English as "The Code of Jewish Law," is generally regarded as the most authoritative of Jewish law codes.

114. S'tumtah:

This refers to any method, other than one that is specifically called for under Jewish law, that is customarily used by people in a community to effectuate a transfer of ownership of property. The Jewish law regarding "customs" renders S'tumtah effective as a matter of Jewish law.

115. S.V.:

"Sub verbo" or "sub voce," in Latin. It indicates the word or words to which a particular Jewish law commentary applies. The glosses of Jewish law commentators, whether printed separately or within the text of a Talmudic tractate or legal code, are typically appended to specific words in the original text.

116. Takkanah, *plural* Takkanot:

A decree issued by Jewish law authorities.

117. Talmud:

This word refers to one of the two literary works, each of which contains rabbinic discussions of Jewish law. These discussions are organized around the text of the Mishnah.

Babylonian Talmud (Talmud Bavli, Bavli, TB):

The Babylonian Talmud was the product of the rabbinic academies in Babylonia. It is the more complete and authoritative of the two Talmuds, and was redacted circa 550 C.E.

Jerusalem Talmud (Talmud Yerushalmi, Yerushalmi, TJ):

The Jerusalem Talmud was the product of the rabbinic academies in Israel.

It is less complete and less authoritative than the Babylonian Talmud and was redacted circa 352 C.E.

118. Tanakh (Tanach):

The word Tanakh is a Hebrew acronym for Torah (the Written Torah), Nevi'im (Prophets), and Ketuvim (Writings). The Tanakh represents the canon of the Jewish Bible. It is also sometimes referred to as the Masoretic text.

119. Tanna, *plural* Tannaim:

Torah scholars whose views are cited in the Mishnah, by contrast to Amoraim, later scholars, whose discussions of the Mishnah are recorded in the Talmuds.

120. Teshuvah, *plural* Teshuvot:

The word "teshuvah" has two major meanings. The first is a response by a Jewish law authority to a question that was put to the authority. When the answer is in writing it is also referred to as a "responsum." *See* Responsa, *supra*. "Teshuvah" also means "repentance," and a "Ba'al Teshvuah" is someone who has repented. Many Jews who were not raised religiously but who chose to become religiously observant later in life are referred to as "Ba'alei Teshuvah."

121. Tinokh She'Nishba:

Literally, "a kidnapped child." This term is used to refer to a Jew who was raised in a non-Jewish environment or, more generally, to one who was never properly taught about or habituated to comply with Jewish law. Because of this, if the person purposefully violates Jewish law, the violation may not be deemed to be an "intentional" violation.

122. Torah:

The word "Torah" has several alternative meanings to which it can refer: (a) all of Jewish law and teachings, whether biblical or rabbinic; (b) all biblical teachings, both in the Written Torah and the Oral Torah; and (c) only to the Written Torah.

123. Torah She'be'al Peh (Torah She-be-al Peh):

This is the Hebrew for the "Oral Torah." *See* the entry for that term, *supra*.

124. Torah She'bikhtav (Torah She-bi-Khetav):

This is the Hebrew for the "Written Torah." *See* the entry for that term, *infra*.

125. Tzelem Elokim:

Literally, "the image of God." According to the Written Torah, man was created in the image of God. Not only does this belief entail certain spiritual and philosophical consequences, it also gives rise to certain specific laws, such as respect that must be accorded to the physical remains of a deceased.

126. VaYikra:

The transliteration of the Hebrew name for the Book of Leviticus.

127. World to Come (Olam HaBa):

This expression is used in Talmudic and Midrashic literature as opposed to the present world (Olam HaZeh). The expression is usually used in the sense of the "Afterlife," the period in which people will be ultimately rewarded (or punished) for their conduct in the present world. The expression is also sometimes used to refer to Yemot HaMashiah (the Messianic days).

128. Written Torah or Written Law:

The Written Torah refers to the Pentateuch, also known as the Chumash and the Five Books of Moses.

129. Ya'avor Velo Yehareg:

A Jewish law doctrine that provides that, in most instances, if a Jew is confronted by someone who threatens to kill him unless he violates Jewish law, the Jew is obligated to commit the violation, thereby saving his life.

130. Yehareg Velo Ya'avor:

A Jewish law doctrine that provides certain limited exceptions to the doctrine of Ya'avor Velo Yehareg. In these situations, a Jew must not commit a violation of Jewish law, even if confronted by someone threatening to kill him unless he commits the violation.

131. Yoreh De'ah:

This is one of the four divisions of law in the Arba'ah Turim and in the Shulhan Arukh. It addresses a wide variety of rules not included in the other three divisions. The laws so included range from family purity laws and kosher laws to laws regarding martyrdom.

Appendix 2

SELECTED LIST OF POST-TALMUDIC JEWISH LAW SCHOLARS & SCHOLARSHIP

Jewish law scholars are not only known by their names, but also by the names of their scholarly works. In fact, the names of the works are frequently better known than the actual names of their authors. Because of this phenomenon, however, it is appropriate to provide an alphabetical list that includes both the names of selected scholars and the names of selected scholarly works. The names on this list are alphabeticalized according to the transliteration that I suspect is more commonly used for the particular person or work.

See the appendix containing the Glossary for clarification of any of the terms used below. For those who have not read the Glossary, here are three quick notes:

(1) The word "Rishon" refers to scholars who lived from the 11th through the 15th centuries.

(2) The word "Aharon" is not only used as a first name. It is also used, often transliterated as "Acharon," to refer to a rabbinic scholar since the end of the fifteenth century.

(3) An "Ashkenazi" is someone who traces his roots back to the Franco-German Jewish communities, while a "Sephardi" is someone who traces his roots to the Jewish communities that originally settled in the Iberian peninsula.

1. Abulafia, R. Meir ben Todros HaLevi of Toledo (Ramah; 1170–1244):

R. Abulafia was a Sephardi Rishon whose Talmud commentary, entitled the Yad Ramah, is especially well-known and respected.

2. Adret, R. Shlomo ben Avraham (Rashba; 1235–1310):

R. Adret, a Sephardi Rishon, was one of the foremost commentators on the Babylonian Talmud, and the author of a substantial body of responsa which has survived the travails of time.

3. Albo, Yosef (c. 1380–1444):

R. Albo, a Sephardi Rishon, was author of the Sefer HaIkkarim, an important work on Jewish philosophy.

4. Alfasi, R. Yitzhak ben Yaakov (Rif; 1013–1103):

R. Alfasi was born in a small Algerian village, but moved to the Moroccon city of Fez, which gave rise to his surname "Alfasi." A Sephardi Rishon, he is also known by the Hebrew acronym **Rif**, based on **R**abbi **Y**itzhak from **F**ez. Alfasi's greatest scholarly impact came from his work, Sefer HaHalakhot (Book of Laws). This is essentially an abridged form of the Talmud that only includes those discussions leading to practical Jewish law applications. Alfasi and his writings received extraordinary praise from numerous other Rishonim, including Maimonides. Hersh Goldwurm reports that:

> "Ravad III, who was most critical in his evaluation of other authors, states in regard to Rif, 'I would adhere to the words of the rabbi even if he were to decide that right was left.' " *See* HERSH GOLDWURM, THE RISHONIM 66 (Brooklyn: Mesorah Publications, Ltd., 2d ed. 2001).

5. Arba'ah Turim:

This work, also known as the "Sefer HaTurim" or the "Tur," was written by R. Yaakov ben Asher (1280–1340), son of Rosh, *infra*, and introduced a structure that divided practical Jewish law into four parts: Orah Hayyim, Hoshen Mishpat, Yoreh De'ah and Even HaEzer. This structure was followed by R. Yosef Karo when he wrote the Shulhan Arukh, the most widely accepted Jewish law code.

6. Arukh HaShulhan (Aruch HaShulchan):

R. Yehiel Mikhal Epstein (1829–1908), who was the Ashkenazi Rav and halakhic decisor for the city of Navahrudak for the last thirty-four years of his life, wrote the Arukh HaShulhan, which is a comprehensive code of Jewish law. It differs from many other legal codes by the way in which it carefully examines the Talmudic basis for each law as well as the pertinent views of Rishonim and earlier Aharonim. In this way, the Arukh HaShulhan is similar to R. Karo's work, Beit Yosef. Beit Yosef, however, is not itself a halakhic code but only a commentary on the Arba'ah Turim.

7. Asevelli, R. Yom Tov (Ritva; 1250–1330):

R. Asevelli, a Sephardi Rishon, spent his entire life in Spain, where he was a leading Talmudic commentator. His last name, Asevelli, is sometimes transliterated as "Ishbili."

8. Asher, Bachya (Bahya) ben (d. 1340):

R. Bachya was a Sephardi Rishon best known for his commentary on the Written Torah.

9. Ba'al HaTanya (1745–1813):

This is the Hebrew acronym for R. Shneur Zalman of Lyadi, author of the Tanya.

10. Ba'al HaTurim:

This phrase means "Master of the Turim" and refers to the author of the Sefer HaTurim, R. Yaakov ben Asher (1270–1343), son of Rosh, *infra*. When the word "Ba'al" precedes the name of a particular work, it often refers to the author of that work.

11. Ba'alei HaTosafot:

Literally, the Masters of the "Additions," this refers to the entire group of Rishonim whose greatest scholarship involved sharply analytic examination of the Talmudic texts. Many of the commentaries of the Ba'alei HaTosafot, or Tosafists, as they are also known, are printed on the outside border of each page of Talmud as "additional" material.

12. Babad, R. Yosef ben Moshe (1800–1874):

Rabbi Babad was an Ashekenazi scholar best known for his analytic commentary and supplement, entitled Minhat Hinnukh, to the Sefer HaHinnukh, which was written by a Rishon.

13. Bach (Bah):

R. Joel Sirkes (1561–1640), an early Sephardi Aharon, is known as the Bach (or Bah) based on the name of his commentary on the Arba'ah Turim, i.e., the **B**ayit **CH**adash (or **B**ayit **H**adash).

14. Beit (or Bet) Shmuel:

Written by Ashkenazi R. Shmuel Phoebus (second half of the 17th century), the Beit Shmuel is one of the foremost commentaries on the division of the Shulhan Arukh known as Even HaEzer. This commentary is routinely published on the same page as the Shulhan Arukh passage to which it refers.

15. Beit Yosef (or Bet Yosef):

This is the name of R. Yosef Karo's (1488–1575) commentary on the Sefer HaTurim. In this commentary, R. Karo identifies the Talmudic source law as well as the views of Rishonim. In this way, the Beit Yosef is similar to the much later work, the Arukh HaShulhan. R. Karo is also extremely well-known as, among other things, the author of the Shulhan Arukh (known as the Code of Jewish Law) and of the Kessef Mishneh, a commentary on Maimonides' Mishneh Torah.

16. Ben Ish Hai (Ben Ish Chai):

This is the appellation by which Sephardi Rabbi Yosef Hayim (Yosef Chaim) (1832–1909) is known. Sephardi Jews sometimes use the title "Hakham" ("Chacham") instead of Rabbi. Thus, the Ben Ish Hai is sometimes referred to as Hakham (Chacham) Yosef.

17. Caro, Rav Yosef (1488–1575):

See **Karo, Rav Yosef.**

18. Chafetz Chaim (Hafetz Hayyim):

R. Yisroel Meir Kagan (1838–1933), an Ashkenazi rabbinic authority, is known as the Chafetz Chaim (literally, "He who wants life"), which is the name of one of his scholarly works regarding the serious transgressions involved in derogatory communications. He campaigned strongly against such conduct. He is also the writer of the Mishnah Berurah, an extremely well-accepted commentary on the Orah Hayyim portion of Shulhan Arukh.

19. Chasam Sofer (or Hatam Sofer):

This is the name of the works of Ashkenazi R. Moshe Schreiber (a/k/a Moshe Sofer; 1763–1839).

20. Coucy, R. Moses — of (d. 1260):

Ashkenazi R. Moses of Coucy was a French Tosafist. In 1240, he was one of four rabbis forced to defend Judaism in a public debate in Paris. R. Moses authored the Sefer Mitzvot Gadol (the Large Book of Commandments), known by the Hebrew Acronym, SeMaG, which identifies and examines the 248 affirmative biblical commandments and the 365 negative biblical commandments which, together, add up to the traditional number of 613 biblical commandments. The SeMaG differs from many other books of commandments by providing extensive discussions of the opinions of other scholars and of their various practical Jewish law ramifications.

21. Ein Mishpat:

Written by Sephardi R. Yehoshua Boaz MiBarukh (d. mid-16th century), this gloss on the Babylonian Talmud points out where the Jewish law under discussion is cited in the major Jewish law codes, such as the Mishneh Torah, Sefer HaTurim, and the Shulhan Arukh. R. Yehoshua was the author of several other important works, including the Shiltei HaGiborim, which is a gloss on the Talmudic work of Rav Alfasi and of the Mordekhai.

22. Feinstein, Moses (1895–1986):

Ashkenazi R. Moses Feinstein succeeded R. Eliyahu Henkin as the foremost halakhic decisor in the United States. His two major works were his responsa, Iggerot Moshe, and his extensive Talmudic commentary, Dibrot Moshe. R. Feinstein was the halakhic authority whose opinion was followed in a noted case involving the treatment of conjoined twins. If nothing were done, both would die. If they were separated, one would die, but the other was expected to live. It is not possible to review the relevant halakhic analysis here, but R. Feinstein allowed the surgery.

23. Ganzfried, Shlomo (1804–1886):

R. Ganzfried was an Ashkenazi authority who authored a well-known Jewish law code. *See* Kitzur Shulhan Arukh, *infra*.

24. Gaon, R. Hai (939–1038):

R. Hai Gaon was the son of R. Sherira Gaon. He is especially known for his many responsa.

25. Gaon, R. Sherira (906–1006):

R. Sherira Gaon was the head of the rabbinical academy in the Babylonian city of Pumpeditha. He is especially well-known for his work, known as the Iggeret (Epistle) of R. Sherira Gaon, on the composition of the Mishnah and the Talmud.

26. Gerondi, R. Yonah ben Avraham HeHassid (1200–1263):

Sephardi R. Yonah was best known for his ethical work, Sha'arei Teshuvah ("The Gates of Repentence").

27. Gombiner, R. Avraham Abeli (1637–1683):

An Ashkenazi Aharon, R. Gombiner authored a major commmentary on the Orah Haim section of Shulhan Arukh known as the Magen Avraham. This commentary is routinely printed on the same page as the pertinent part of the Shulhan Arukh.

28. HaLevi, R. Yehudah (c. 1080–1145):

R. Yehuda Halevi was a Sephardi Rishon, born in Spain, who was also an expert in literary style, a poet, and a practicing physician. His best known contribution to Torah literature was the Kuzari. This was a philosophical work in which the king of the Khazar tribe seeks to find true faith by conversations with scholars of Christianity, Islam and Judaism. This book is a platform on which R. Halevi explores Judaism's fundamental beliefs and defends Jewish belief from a variety of attacks. English translations of this work are readily available.

29. Hayei (Chayei) Adam:

Ashkenazi authority R. Avraham ben Yehiel Michel Danzig (1748–1820) authored the Hayei Adam, a well-known one-volume legal code on issues usually addressed in Shulhan Arukh Orah Hayyim. He also wrote the Nishmat Adam, dealing with issues in Shulhan Arukh Yoreh De'ah.

30. Heller, R. Yom Tov Lipmann (1579–1654):

Ashkenazi R. Heller best known for his commentary, Tosafot Yom Tov, on the Mishnah. Despite the title of his work, R. Heller was not one of the Ba'alei Tosafot, who were Rishonim. In standard Hebrew editions of the Mishnah, the Tosafot Yom

Tov is routinely printed on the same page as the relevant portion of the Mishnah.

31. Henkin, R. Yosef Eliyahu (1880–1974):

R. Henkin, an Ashkenazi, was born in Belarus, which was then within the Russian empire. He immigrated to the United States in 1922, where he was one of its most recognized Jewish law authorities. In 1925, R. Henkin became director of Ezras Torah, a charitable organization that supported needy Jewish scholars, and served in that capacity until his death. Under his direction, Ezras Torah published (and still publishes) an influential calendar that details how Jewish law requires various adjustments to ritual practices on different days in the Jewish calendar. His best known Jewish law publication is his book, Edut LeYisrael.

32. Isserles, Moses (Rema; 1530–1572):

Ashkenazi R. Isserles authored a vitally important commentary to R. Karo's Shulhan Arukh. This commentary is invariably published together with the Shulhan Arukh, with his comments interspersed with those of R. Karo. He also wrote many important responsa.

33. Kaf HaHayyim:

There were two major Jewish law works named Kaf HaHayyim, meaning "Palm of Life." One is a multi-volume work on Shulhan Arukh, comprehensively addressing the division of Shulhan Arukh known as Orah Hayyim in eight volumes and with two additional volumes on parts of Yoreh De'ah. This publication, authored by Sephardi R. Yaakov Hayyim Sofer (1870–1939), is highly respected by Ashkenazi as well as Sephardi scholars. The other Kaf HaHayyim was written by an earlier Sephardi authority, R. Hayyim Pilaggi (1788–1869), who was a prolific author of important rabbinic scholarship.

34. Kanievsky, R. Ya'akov Yisroel (Steipler Rav; 1899–1985):

Ashkenazi R. Kanievsky was the head of a rabbinic school in Pinsk when, in 1934, he immigrated to Israel, where his brother-in-law, R. Karelitz, already lived. He is most known for his multi-volume work, Kehillat Ya'akov, which includes a series of Talmudic essays organized according to the tractates of the Talmud.

35. Karelitz, R. Avraham Yeshayah (Hazon Ish or Chazon Ish; 1878–1953):

R. Karelitz, an Ashkenazi authority, was undoubtedly one of the foremost Jewish law personalities of his time. He is called the Hazon Ish, which was the name of his most influential Torah scholarship.

36. Karo, R. Yosef (the Mechaber or the Mehaber; 1488–1575):

Sephardi scholar R. Yosef Karo is best known for three of his works: the Bet Yosef, the Shulhan Arukh and the Kessef Mishneh. The Bet Yosef is a prodigious commentary on the Arba'ah Turim. The Shulhan Arukh is perhaps the most highly regarded code of Jewish law. The Kessef Mishneh is a commentary on Maimonides' Mishneh Torah.

37. Kitzur Shulhan Arukh:

Written by Ashkenazi R. Shlomo Ganzfried (1804–1886), this is a comprehensive legal code. Despite the name, it is not an "abbreviated" version of R. Karo's Shulhan Arukh. Interestingly, each of these two works is also commonly referred to in English as the "Code of Jewish Law."

38. Kook, R. Avraham Yitzhak (Re'ayah; 1865–1935):

Ashkenazi R. Kook was a former Chief Rabbi of the Land of Israel in the years before the United Nations recognized the country of Israel in 1948. He was the leader of the religious Mizrachi movement. A number of Israeli organizations are named after him, and prominent among them is the Mosad HaRav Kook, which is involved in the publication of a considerable body of Jewish law literature.

39. Kotler, R. Aharon (1891–1962):

R. Kotler was an important Ashkenazi rabbinic figure in Lithuania and later one of the most influential and active rabbis in the United States. He helped create Chinuch Atzmai, the independent Jewish religious school system in Israel, and served as chairman of Moetzes Gedolei HaTorah (the Executive Committee) of Agudath Israel of America, chair of the Rabbinic Board of Torah Umesorah, an organization of rabbinic schools in the United States, and served on the presidium of Agudath HaRabbonim of the United States and Canada. In 1943, R. Kotler founded the Lakewood Yeshivah (now also known as the Rabbi Aaron Kotler Institute for Advanced Learning) in Lakewood, New Jersey, with just a few students. The Yeshivah, which promotes dedicating one's lifetime to full-time learning, developed into the largest Yeshivah in the United States, and one of the largest, if not the largest, in the world.

40. Liadi, Shneur Zalman — of (Alter Rebbe and Ba'al HaTanya; 1745–1812):

Ashkenazi R. Shneur Zalman Liadi was the first Chabad Rebbe. Among his works are the Shulhan Arukh HaRav, a legal code addressing the same topics as R. Karo's Shulhan Arukh, and the Tanya, a philosophical work.

41. Lorbeerbaum, R. Yaakov of Lisa (c. 1760–1832):

R. Lorbeerbaum, an Ashkenazi authority, is best known for publications on two of the four divisions of Shulhan Arukh. One, Havvot Da'at (Chavos Da'as), examines issues pertaining to Yoreh De'ah. The other, Netivot HaMishpat (Nesivos HaMishpat), addresses issues in Hoshen Mishpat.

42. Luzzatto, R. Moshe Chaim (R. Moshe Hayyim) (1707–1746):

R. Luzzatto, an Ashkenazi authority, wrote a number of major works on Jewish philosophy and ethics. Perhaps the best known is his book, Mesillat (Mesillas)

Yesharim, the Path of the Just.

43. Maggid Mishneh:

This is the name of Sephardi R. Vidal Yom Tov of Tolosa's (fourteenth century) commentary on Maimonides' Mishneh Torah.

44. Maimonides (1135–1204):

This is the Greek version of the name of Sephardi R. Moses ben Maimon, author of the Mishneh Torah, the Sefer HaMitzvot (Book of Commandments), Pirush LiMishnayot (Commentary to the Mishnah), Moreh Nevukhim (Guide to the Perplexed) and other works. He is also known by the acronym, Rambam, based on **R**abbi **M**oses **b**en **M**aimon.

45. Meiri, R. Menachem ben Shlomo:

Meiri (1249–1315) is perhaps best known for his extensive commentary on the Babylonian Talmud entitled Bet HaBehirah (or Beit HaBechirah). Meiri who lived in Spain, was primarily taught by a French Rishon. His work, Magen Aboth, addresses the different practices of Jews in France and Spain.

46. Mishnah Berurah:

This is the name of R. Yisroel Meir Kagan's (Chafetz Chayim or Hafetz Hayyim; 1838–1933) commentary on Shulhan Arukh, Orah Hayyim. R. Kagan is also especially known for his scholarship and personal efforts against derogatory speech (Loshon HaRa).

47. Nahmanides (1194–1270):

This is the Greek version of the name of Moses ben Nahman. He is also known by the acronym, Ramban, based on **R**abbi **M**oses **b**en **N**ahman. His many writings include commentaries on the Written Torah, the Babylonian Talmud and the Rambam's Sefer HaMitzvot (The Book of Mitzvot).

48. Or Some'ach (Ohr Somayach or Ohr Someah):

This is the name of Ashkenazi R. Meir Simha of Divinsk's (1843–1926) commentary on the Mishneh Torah. He is also the author of a profound commentary on the Torah, entitled the Meshekh Hohmah.

49. Paquda, Bachya (Bahya) ibn (c. 1080):

R. Bachya ibn Paquda, a Sephardi Rishon, authored the famous ethical (Musar) work entitled Hovot HaLevvavot (Duties of the Heart).

50. Posquieres, R. Avraham ben David — of (1120–1197):

See Ravad III, *infra*.

51. Rabbenu Hananel ben Hushiel (Chananel ben Chushiel; d. circa 1055):

A very early Sephardi Rishon, Rabbenu Hananel is also known by the Hebrew acronym Rah (Rach). He wrote a thorough commentary on the Babylonian Talmud which was studied by almost all later commentators, especially Rif.

52. Rambam:

This is a Hebrew acronym for Sephardi R. Moses ben Maimon, who is also known as Maimonides. This acronym sounds very similar to the acronym, Ramban, used for Sephardi R. Moshe ben Nahman. The convention in yeshivas is to differentiate the two by acccentuating the first syllable of Rambam and the second syllable of Ramban.

53. Ramban:

This is a Hebrew acronym for R. Moses ben Nahman, who is also known by his Greek name, Nahmanides. *See* Nahmanides, *supra*.

54. Rashba (1235–1310):

See Adret, *supra*.

55. Rashi (1040–1105):

Rashi is the Hebrew acronym for Ashkenazi **R. Shlomo Yitzhaki**, perhaps the premier commentator on the Pentateuch and on the Babylonian Talmud.

56. Ravad III (1120–1197):

Rishon R. Avraham ben David of Posquieres, whose Hebrew acronym is Ravad, is known as Ravad and as Ravad III, because two other major rabbinic figures with the same Hebrew acronym preceded him. (Ravad II actually became his father-in-law.) Ravad III was especially known for his critiques of works by others and, especially, by his critiques on Maimonides' Mishneh Torah. Similarly, Ravad III sharply responded to R. Zerahyah (Zerachya) Halevi's (Razah; 1125–1186) purported refutations of Alfasi's halakhic rulings. A collection of correspondence between Ravad III and Razah on this subject was published as Divrei Rivot.

57. Rif (1013–1103):

See Alfasi, *supra*.

58. Ritva (1250–1330):

This is the acronym by which Sephardi R. Yom Tov ben Avraham Asevelli, who spent his entire life in Spain, is known. *See* Asevelli, *supra*.

59. Rivash (1326–1407):

R. Yitzhak ben Sheshet Perfet was a prominent Sephardi Talmudist and a student of the Rabbi Nissim ben Reuven (Ran).

60. Rosh (1250–1327):

R. Asher ben Yehiel was born in Germany, but spent most of his life in Spain. Nevertheless, he maintained his Ashekenazi customs. A student of R. Meir of Rothenberg, R. Asher became a leading Talmudist. He wrote an authoritative commentary on individual Babylonian Talmud tractates that is included in all full editions of the Talmud. His book of responsa, Teshuvot HaRosh, is highly authoritative. One of his eight sons, R. Jacob, wrote the halakhic work, the Arba'ah Turim.

61. Schneerson, Menachem Mendel ("the Rebbe" or "the Lubavitcher Rebbe") (1902–1994):

Ashkenazi R. Schneerson succeeded his father-in-law as Rebbe of the Lubavitch Hasidim in 1951. Under his guidance, the movement continuously expanded its worldwide activities to spread Orthodox Judaism. Through its network of institutions and representatives, the movement has also provided significant assistance to Jews throughout the world. R. Schneerson authored a great wealth of Torah scholarship. The movement's emphasis on Messianism became controversial, especially after he suffered a significant stroke in 1992 that left him unable to speak and paralyzed on one side. The controversy continues as a number of Lubavitch Hasidim (how large a number cannot be precisely determined) await his return as the Messiah.

62. Sefer HaHinnukh:

The Sefer HaHinnukh, written in the thirteenth century, systematically clarifies the 613 biblical commandments, addressing them in the order in which they appear in the Pentateuch. Its authorship was for many years ascribed to a "Rishon" named Aharon Halevi of Barcelona. More recent scholars question this accuracy of this ascription. *See* AHARON HALEVI, SEFER HAHINNUCH vol. 1, at vii–xiv (Charles Wengrov trans., New York: Fedlheim, 2d ed. 1992).

63. Sefer Hasidim (1140–1217):

Written by Sephardi Rishon Yehudah HeHasid (1140–1217), this is a highly regarded work of law and ethics.

64. Semag (Sefer Mitzvot Gadol):

See R. Moses of Coucy, *supra.*

65. Shakh:

R. Shabbetai (or Shabtai) HaKohen (1622–1663), an Ashkenazi Aharon, is best known for his commentaries on Shulhan Arukh.

66. Shapiro, R. Avraham Duber Kahana (Devar Avraham; 1871–1943):

R. Shapiro, an Ashkenazi authority, is the author of a collection of responsa and halakhic essays entitled Devar Avraham. R. Shapiro is often referred to by the name of that publication.

67. Shulhan Arukh:

This is a sixteenth century code of Jewish law, known in English as the Code of Jewish Law, and authored by Sephardi scholar R. Yosef Karo. Ashkenazi scholar R. Moses Isserles added a gloss, known as the Mappah, to reflect Ashkenazi customs and rulings. The words of the Mappah were soon interspersed, in a different type print, into R. Karo's text, and every standard printing of the Shulhan Arukh contains this combined text. The Shulhan Arukh attracted the attention of many subsequent scholars who wrote numerous commentaries upon it, many of which are printed in virtually all editions of the Shulhan Arukh.

68. Shulhan Arukh HaRav:

One should be careful not to confuse the Shulhan Arukh HaRav with the Shulhan Arukh. The Shulhan Arukh HaRav is a much later work, written by Ashkenazi Rav Shneur Zalman of Liadi, known in Chabad circles since his death as the "Alter Rebbe" and the "Ba'al HaTanya." Kehot Publication Society, which publishes most Chabad Hasidic works, published a Hebrew-English version of the Shulhan Arukh HaRav which indicates where the conclusions of the Shulhan Arukh HaRav differ from those of the Shulhan Arukh.

69. Soloveichik, Yosef Ber/Dov (1903–1993):

R. Soloveichik, an Ashenazic rabbinic leader who spent most of his life in the United States, was Rosh HaYeshivah of the Rabbi Isaac Elchanan Theological Seminary at Yeshiva University for many years. He is widely recognized as a critical and early leader in the Modern (or Centrist) Orthodox movement in the United States. Known as simply "the Rav" both by his former students and by many Modern Orthodox Jews, R. Soloveitchik is known for strongly promoting a synthesis of Torah and secular studies known as Torah Im Derekh Eretz. His many writings include *The Lonely Man of Faith, Halakhic Man* and *Halakhic Mind*.

70. Tanya:

The Tanya is a book of Jewish philosophy written by Ashkenazi R. Shneur Zalman of Liadi, known in Chabad circules as the "Alter Rebbe" and the "Ba'al HaTanya," and first published in 1797. The work's formal title is "Likutei Amarim" ("Collection of Statements"), but it is known by the first word of its text, "Tanya," meaning "it was taught in a Baraitha."

71. Taz:

Ashkenazi R. David ben Shmuel Halevi Segal (1586–1667) is often referred to as the Taz. Taz is the Hebrew acronym for R. Halevi's very important commentary on the Yoreh De'ah portion of Shulhan Arukh. R. Segal also wrote an important commentary, Magen David, on Hoshen Mishpat. He also authored Divrei David, a supercommentary on Rashi's commentary on the Written Torah.

72. Terumat HaDeshen:

The Terumat HaDehen is a collection of responsa from R. Yisroel Isserlein (1390–1460), an Ashkenazi Rishon.

73. Tolosa, Vidal Yom Tov — of (d. 1357):

Sephardi R. Vidal Yom Tov of Tolosa is best known for his commentary, entitled Maggid Mishneh, to Maimonides' Mishneh Torah.

74. Vilna Gaon (the Gaon of Vilna):

Ashkenazi R. Eliyahu of Vilna (1720–1797) is known as the Vilna Gaon. The formal title "Gaon" referred to the heads of rabbinical academies from the sixth through the early part of the eleventh centuries. Many later Torah leaders were sometimes addressed or refered to by the honorific Gaon. R. Eliyahu, however, is singular in that, even though he lived at a time when there were numerous Torah luminaries in Vilna, he became universally known as the Vilna Gaon. His erudition is legendary, and he left a comprehensive and diverse body of Torah scholarship.

Appendix 3

TRANSLITERATIONS

Most primary Jewish law sources are written in Hebrew or Babylonian Aramaic. Some of the terms cannot be easily translated into English. Other terms, which perhaps could be translated, often are not. Instead, such terms are transliterated into English. Unfortunately, various people utilize transliteration systems that differ as to, for example, the letters, symbols or diacritical marks used or the capitalization practices employed.

This appendix *does not* provide details regarding all of the different ways in which Hebrew and Aramaic are transliterated. Such an undertaking would be overly ambitious — and far beyond the interest of most beginning (and some advanced) students of Jewish law. Instead, this appendix provides a *relatively* short outline designed to help prepare students to cope with the disparate transliterations they will encounter by explaining the reasons for the inconsistencies and by identifying some of the most common alternative transliterations.

1. Reasons different publications may employ inconsistent transliterations:

    a. Transliterations are based on how words are pronounced. One reason for inconsistent transliterations is that particular Hebrew or Aramaic words may be pronounced in more than one way.

        i. There are, for instance, some basic differences between the ways Ashkenazi Jews and Sephardi Jews pronounce Hebrew words. There are two especially common differences between traditional Ashkenazi and Sephardi pronunciations.

            (1) One difference concerns the Hebrew letter, "ת." In Hebrew, this letter is sometimes emphasized, this emphasis being shown in Hebrew by the placement of a dot within the letter. The Ashkenazi tradition pronounces the unemphasized letter as an "s" and the emphasized letter as a "t" or "th."

                 The Sephardi tradition, which is the official pronunciation used by the Israeli government, does not differentiate between the unemphasized and emphasized versions of the letter, pronouncing each version as a "t" or "th."

                 The Hebrew words for "rabbinical court" are בית דין in which the letter, ת, is not emphasized. According to the Ashkenazi tradition, these words might be transliterated as "bes din."[1] According to the Sephardi tradition, the words would be transliterated as "bet din" or "beth din."

(2) The second difference involves the pronunciation of a particular vowel, known as a kometz. This vowel is not represented by any Hebrew letter, but, like other Hebrew vowels, may be indicated through the use of diacritical marks.[2] According to Ashkenazi tradition, this vowel is pronounced as "aw" as in the word "caw." According to Sephardi tradition, this vowel is pronounced as "ah."

ii. Similarly, there are differences in pronunciation even within subgroups of Ashkenazic Jewry. Consequently, these differences can affect transliterations, particularly those appearing in less formal writings.

b. Writers sometimes use different transliteration systems based on the degree to which they are interested in the precise sounds in a particular passage or in the passage's substantive meaning. Thus, phonetics scholars may use a much more precise transliteration system than Jewish law scholars.

c. A few publications and individual writers may use idiosyncratic transliteration "systems." Some Hebrew letters are often represented by the use of an "underdot," such as beneath an "h" or a "z." But some people avoid underdots because using them can be inconvenient and because a casual reader may be put off by them. Because I believe that such marks would be confusing for most law students, I avoid them in this book.

d. For information on various specific transliteration systems, see, for example:

i. Wikipedia, entry "Romanization of Hebrew," available at http://en.wikipedia.org/wiki/Transliteration_of_Hebrew.

ii. Heshey Zelcer, "The Hakirah Guide to Writing a Scholarly Article," Hakira, available at http://www.hakirah.org/HakirahGuideToWriting.pdf (includes chart comparing systems by the Encyclopedia Judaica with the system used by Artscroll Publication).

2. Reasons for the use of inconsistent transliteration systems within a single publication:

a. Although a particular author or journal may utilize one transliteration

---

[1] Alternatively, "beis" might be used instead of "bes."

[2] In fact, however, most traditional Jewish law writings — and most modern Hebrew newspapers, magazines and books — are written without the relevant diacritical marks. Those who are familiar with the structure of Hebrew can identify the words and their correct pronunciation without the use of such marks.

system, it may quote material from a publication that used a different transliteration system. The transliteration style in the quoted material is preserved. You will find this type of "inconsistency" (at least) within this book.

b.   Although a particular author or journal may utilize one transliteration system, it may refer to a person who transliterates his or her own Hebrew name according to a different system. When the person's own transliteration of his or her name is known, it is typically honored.

c.   Note also that many names have generally accepted English equivalents. Some publications will utilize those equivalents rather than a transliteration of the Hebrew (*e.g.*, "Jeremiah," instead of "Yirmeyahu"). This practice does not represent the inconsistent use of transliteration systems but, instead, the arguably inconsistent practice of only sometimes transliterating.

3.   Examples of common alternative transliterations:

a.   The Hebrew suffix, "עָה," is sometimes transliterated as "ah," with an "h," and sometimes simply as "a," without an h.

Example: The word, מִשְׁנָה, is transliterated as "Mishnah" or "Mishna." This term refers to the pre-Talmudic teachings compiled and redacted by Rabbi Yehuda Ha-Nasi (*i.e.*, "Rabbi Yehuda the Prince").

b.   The Hebrew letter, "כ," is sometimes transliterated as "kh" and sometimes as "ch."

Examples:

* Hoshen Mishpat or Choshen Mishpat: These transliterations refer to one of the four categories of law included in the sixteenth century legal code known as "the Code of Jewish Law," but whose Hebrew title is literally translated as "the Set Table." This particular legal category deals principally with rules regarding commercial and criminal law.

c.   Sometimes terms may be transliterated in numerous ways because they involve a number of possible variants.

Here are a few examples involving both of the possible variants mentioned in "a" and "b," *supra*:

* Dina Demalkhuta Dina, Dina Demalchuta Dina, Dina De-Malchuta Dina, Dina De-Malkhuta Dina: These are some of the variant transliterations for the Jewish law doctrine, "the law of the kingdom is valid [as a matter of Jewish] law."[3] When this doctrine applies, a violation of the applicable secular law consti-

---

[3] Of course, there are also alternative translations for various Hebrew terms. For example, alternative translations of dina demalkhuta dina include "the law of the land is the law" and "the law of the kingdom is the law."

tutes a violation of Jewish law as well.

- Halakhah, Halachah, Halakha, Halacha: These transliterations are typically translated "Jewish law" and can refer either to the entire body of Jewish law or to a specific Jewish law rule applicable in a specific context or to a particular question.

d. Sometimes the Hebrew letter, "ח" is transliterated as either "h" (with or without an underdot)" or as "ch."

Here is an example that involves both this variant and the variant mentioned in "b," *supra*:

- Shulhan Arukh, Shulchan Arukh, Shulhan Aruch, Shulchan Aruch

Appendix 4

INTERNET RESOURCES ON JEWISH LAW

PLEASE NOTE: This appendix is designed to provide important information regarding resources for the study of Jewish law that are available, with or without payment, on the Internet. However, a few caveats must be clearly stated at the outset:

1. What is available on a particular internet site today may not be there tomorrow. Consequently, the particular links provided in this appendix may not necessarily work when you try them. If, however, the material is still available somewhere on the Internet, the information in this appendix may help you find it.

2. I have tried to provide links to sites that represent various perspectives on Jewish law, including perspectives with which I do not personally agree. Inclusion of a particular site in this appendix is in no way an endorsement of that site or of what is said on that site.

3. Visiting some sites or downloading materials from some sites may be harmful to your computer. Reference to a particular site in this appendix is not, and should not be interpreted as, a statement that visiting the site or downloading material from the site is safe.

4. Some of the sites that provide materials, whether for free or for a charge, may not be legally, or halakhically, authorized to provide those materials. Similarly, it may or may not be legally, or halakhically, permitted for you to view or download such materials. Reference to a particular site in this appendix is not, and should not be interpreted as, a statement that using or downloading such materials is legal. In each instance, you must make these determinations.

Free Access to Classical Jewish Law Texts

- **English Translations**

    - Jewish Scripture (Tanakh) is available at http://www.shamash.org/tanach/text.shtml

    - Mishnah, as originally translated by Philip Blackman, is available at http://www.oldinthenew.org/?p=210

    - Mishneh Torah (the eleventh century Jewish code authored by Maimonides) is available at http://www.chabad.org/library/article_cdo/aid/682956/jewish/Mishneh-Torah.htm

    - Shulhan Arukh (the sixteenth century Code of Jewish Law) is available at http://www.shulchanarach.com/

(As of the date of the publication of this book, this web site was a work in progress and provided a translation of only parts of the Shulhan Arukh.)

- Babylonian Talmud:

- The classical Soncino translation of the Babylonian Talmud, completed under the editorship of Rabbi Dr. I. Epstein, is available for free at http://halakhah.com/. (This same address provides links to other resources, including Michael L. Rodkinson's 1918 translation of portions of the Babylonian Talmud.) This Soncino translation contains a number of helpful explanatory notes, but provides relatively little context to the Talmudic discussions. This translation of the Babylonian Talmud is also available for purchase in CD and hard copy formats. A newly reformatted version is available for free at http://halakhah.com/indexrst.html.

- English lectures that include translations

  - Mishnah: Lectures are available at various sites, including

    - http://www.ou.org/torah/index#/mishna_yomit

    - http://www.shemayisrael.com/mishna/

  - Babylonian Talmud: Links to lectures (in various languages, including English) on the Babylonian Talmud are available at http://www.dafyomi.co.il/central.htm#videoaudio. One is able to hear a lecture on any page of the Talmud that one selects.

  - Jerusalem Talmud: Links to lectures in English on specific pages of the Jerusalem Talmud are available at http://www.yerushalmionline.org/audio.html

- **Sites offering Free Access to the Original Versions of the Texts**

  - Jewish Scripture, Mishnah, Babylonian Talmud, Jerusalem Talmud and other texts are available through a University of Pennsylvania site, http://www.library.upenn.edu/cajs/etexts.html

  - Jewish Scripture, Mishnah, Babylonian Talmud, Jerusalem Talmud, Mishneh Torah and other texts are available at http://www.mechon-mamre.org/mtrpromo.htm

- **Some sites contain a mixture of links providing translations and/or the original versions of primary texts of Jewish law as well as primary texts of other religions**

- Jay C. Treat, *Internet Resources for the Study of Judaism and Christianity*, available at http://ccat.sas.upenn.edu/~jtreat/rs/resources.html

Free Access to English Study Aids

- *A Page from the Babylonian Talmud*, available at http://people.ucalgary.ca/~elsegal/TalmudPage.html, is an **excellent** resource. The site presents the original of a page of the Babylonian Talmud, which, of course, contains various commentaries. Clicking on each of these separate commentaries brings the user to a site that provides clear and fairly complete information about the title of the relevant commentary, its author(s), its historical period, its purpose.

- Partial Index to the Babylonian Talmud: available at Mordechai Torczyner's site, Webshas, available at http://www.webshas.org/

- Various study aids to the Mishneh Torah and other works by Maimonides are available at http://www.panix.com/~jjbaker/rambam.html

Free Access to English (and other language) Bibliographies on Jewish Law

- An on-line version of Professor Nahum Rakover's Multi-Language Bibliography of Articles on Jewish law is available at http://www.mishpativri.org.il/english/multbibtochen.htm

- RAMBI — The Index of Articles on Jewish Studies (maintained by the Hebrew University) is available at http://jnul.huji.ac.il/rambi/about_~1.htm

- Library of the Faculty of Law at Bar-Ilan University: Index to Articles (written in Hebrew or English that address matters of Jewish law) is available by going to http://www.law.biu.ac.il/library/, choosing the top left link for "English" and then choosing "Index to Articles".

- Columbia University's Bibliographies on Jewish Studies is available at http://www.columbia.edu/cu/lweb/indiv/mideast/cuvlj/BibInfo.html

- Links to a variety of useful bibliographies can be found at the University of Toronto's Academic Guide to Jewish History, available at http://link.library.utoronto.ca/jewishhistory/getItems.cfm/majorCatID=10

- Hebrew Union College's Midrash Bibliography is available at http://www.huc.edu/midrash/

Free Access to encyclopedic work

- The Jewish Encyclopedia is available at http://www.jewishencyclopedia.com/view.jsp?artid=246&letter=M

Free Access to contemporary Jewish Law Scholarship (primarily or exclusively in English)

- Jlaw, at http://www.jlaw.com, provides links to articles, commentaries and other materials on Jewish law.

- Yeshiva University's web site, at http://www.yutorah.org/search/#, allows users to browse, and download, articles in various of its publications, including its series, *The Orthodox Forum*.

- Edah was a Modern Orthodox Organization. Although its web site, http://www.edah.org/backend/coldfusion/search/bycat.cfm?id=20, is not updated, it still contains links to archives of its journal, Meorot, and to what it calls

"The Modern Orthodox Library," a collection of articles/presentations on a wide variety of contemporary topics.

- The Rabbinic Assembly, the rabbinical organization of the Conservative/ Masorati movement, maintains a web site with links to many resources, including to decisions by its Committee on Jewish Law and Standards, at http://www.rabbinicalassembly.org/.

- The Schechter Institutes, affiliated with Conservative Judaism, maintains a web site with various resources. One page, http://responsafortoday.com/ eng_index.html, for instance, contains a variety of responsa on contemporary issues, authored by persons affiliated with their organization. In addition, it has information about its various research institutes, including the Institute for Applied Halacha and the Center for Women in Jewish Law.

- The Central Conference of American Rabbis, an organization of Reform Judaism, makes responsa by Reform Rabbis available at http://ccarnet.org/ documentsandpositions/responsa/.

- *Israel Studies*, sponsored by the Ben-Gurion Research Institute for the Study of Zionism and Israel, Ben-Gurion University of the Negev (Sede-Boker, Israel) and the Schusterman Center for Israel Studies Brandeis University (Waltham, Massachusetts, USA), provides an index to its publications through its web site, at http://cmsprod.bgu.ac.il/Eng/Centers/bgi/ Journals/israel_studies.htm

- The *Journal of Torah and Scholarship* provides tables of contents and abstracts for some of its volumes at http://www.biu.ac.il/JH/BDD/ ind_eng.shtml

- The publication, *Torah Mitzion: Religious Zionist Kollelim*, provides access to many of its articles at http://www.torahmitzion.org/eng/resources/ JewishLaw.asp

- Business Halacha: This site, http://www.businesshalacha.com/, provides newsletters and other publications addressing questions of Jewish business law.

- Torah.org: This site provides various materials on Jewish law. At http:// www.torah.org/advanced/business-halacha/5757/, the site provides links to a long list of discussions of specific questions regarding monetary transactions.

- *The Jewish Observer*: The archives of this publication are available online at http://www.shemayisrael.com/jewishobserver/archives.htm.

Fee-Based Access to Jewish Law Scholarship in English

- *Tradition* online: *Tradition* is a modern Orthodox journal with articles on a vast variety of topics. For a relatively modest fee, individuals can purchase a year's subscription to it online that provides them access to the publication's entire archive. Although some of the articles may be too advanced for beginners, others — especially in conjunction with guidance from a professor — are just right. Its web site is http://www.traditiononline.org/.

Free Access to Jewish Law Scholarship (primarily or exclusively in Hebrew)

- HebrewBooks: This web site, http://www.hebrewbooks.org/home.aspx, provides free access to, and downloads of, thousands of Hebrew books and periodicals. It also provides access to a few rare diamonds in English.

- Seforim Online: This web site, http://www.seforimonline.org/about.html, provides free access to, and downloads of, many Hebrew books.

- The Jewish National and University library, at http://www.jnul.huji.ac.il/eng/digibook.html, makes many rare Hebrew books available online.

- Tshuvos: This site, http://www.tshuvos.com/tshuvos.asp, provides free access to, and downloads of, many Hebrew books about Jewish law, including the series of responsa seforim from Rabbi Menashe Klein of Boro Park, New York.

- Online Treasure of Hebrew Manuscripts: This site, http://jnul.huji.ac.il/dl/talmud/intro_eng.htm, provides images of major Talmudic manuscripts from libraries throughout the world.

Fee-Based Access to Jewish Law Texts and Scholarship

- Various sites charge for access to Jewish law texts. One site, Otzar HaHochma, at http://www.otzar.org/otzaren/indexeng.asp, may be especially useful for people who need to do a few precise searches, as it contains more than 50,000 volumes of Hebrew texts in PDF format and, at least at the time of the printing of this book, offers relatively inexpensive licenses for periods as short as 24 hours. (The site also sells various editions of a portable database containing some or all of the texts available online.)

Miscellaneous Research and Writing Guides on the Internet

- University of Miami's Jewish Law Research Guide, at http://www.law.miami.edu/library/judaicguide.php

- Cleveland State University's Judaic Law Research Guide, at http://develdrupal.law.csuohio.edu/lawlibrary/resources/lawpubs/JudaicLawGuide.html

- Heshey Zelcer, *The Hakirah Guide to Writing a Scholarly Article*, Hakira, available at http://www.hakirah.org/HakirahGuideToWriting.pdf

- Marylin Johnson Raisch, *Religious Legal Systems: A Brief Guide to Research and Its Role in Comparative Law*, at http://www.nyulawglobal.org/globalex/Religious_Legal_Systems.htm

Miscellaneous Sites Providing Resources for Studying Jewish Law or Links to Sites That Do

- Internet Resources for Jewish Studies, at http://www2.lib.udel.edu/subj/jew/internet.htm

- D.A.F.'s Dafyomi Central Headquarters (this site provides an extensive array of links to free online resources as well as links to purchasable study aids regarding the Babylonian Talmud), at http://www.dafyomi.co.il/central.htm

- Codex: Resources for Biblical, Theological and Religious Studies, at http://biblical-studies.ca/

- Princeton University — Jewish Studies Resources, at http://www.princeton.edu/~pressman/jewish.html

- University of Manchester Centre for Jewish Studies, at http://www.mucjs.org/links.htm#8

- University of Washington's Jewish Law Resource Page, at http://www.washlaw.edu/subject/jewish.html

- H-Judaic Jewish Studies Network (JSN), at http://www.h-net.org/~judaic/

- Ehud's Assisting You to Learn, at http://www.ualberta.ca/~ebenzvi/Assist/Judaism/index.html

Material on Selected specific topics

- Agunah Problems

  - Papers of the University of Manchester Agunah Research Unit, at http://www.mucjs.org/publications.htm

- Bioethics

  - Schlesinger Institute for Medical Ethics, at http://www.medethics.org.il/

- Biographical information on Jewish law authorities

  - Acharonim

    - Wikipedia entry on "Acharonim," athttp://en.wikipedia.org/wiki/Acharonim

  - Rishonim

    - Wikipedia entry on "Rishonim," at http://en.wikipedia.org/wiki/Rishonim

    - http://www.tzemachdovid.org/gedolim/index._alphabetical.html

    - http://www.chabad.org/library/article_cdo/aid/115536/jewish/The-Rishonim.htm

  - Miscellaneous Authorities or Groups of Authorities

    - http://www.tzemachdovid.org/gedolim/index_by_type2.html

- Business and professional ethics

  - Business Ethics Center of Jerusalem, at http://www.besr.org/

- Center for Ethics at Yeshiva University, at http://www.yu.edu/ethics/

- Hebrew Union College Ethics Center, at http://huc.edu/ethics/

- Jewish Association for Business Ethics, (JABE), at http://www.jabe.org/

- The Jewish Ethicist, at http://www.ou.org/torah/je/archive.htm

- Jewish Media Resources — Jewish Ethics, at http://www.jewishmediaresources.com/topics/4/

- Judaism in the Workplace, at http://www.darchenoam.org/ethics/pe_home.htm

- Kampela Collection on Jewish Ethics (including bioethics), at http://bioethics.georgetown.edu/collections/kampelman/Kampelman.pdf

- Dictionaries

  - Comprehensive Aramaic Lexicon, at http://cal1.cn.huc.edu/

- Jewish Feminism

  - The web site of the Jewish Orthodox Feminist Alliance (JOFA) is available at http://www.jofa.org/

- Jewish history

  - The Jewish History Research Center's site is at http://jewishhistory.huji.ac.il/internetresources/historyresources/timelines_for_ancient_jewish_his.htm

  - Other sites with Jewish historical timelines include:

    - http://www.jewishhistory.org.il/history.php

    - http://www.beingjewish.com/mesorah/timeline.html

    - http://www.religionfacts.com/judaism/timeline.htm

Jewish Law Library Sites — Miscellaneous

- American Jewish University's Ostrow Library, at http://library.ajula.edu/

- Bar Ilan Faculty of Law's Library, at http://jnul.huji.ac.il/eng/

- Hebrew Union College's Library, at http://huc.edu/libraries/libcats_v4.htm

- Hebrew University of Jerusalem Faculty of Law Library Online Catalogs, at http://micro5.mscc.huji.ac.il/~lawlib/catalog.htm

- Hebrew Theological College's Saul Silber Memorial Library, at http://htc.edu/index.php/Saul-Silber-Memorial-Library-Root/Saul-Silber-Memorial-Library.html

- Israel Library Network Sites, at http://libnet.ac.il/~libnet/malmad-israelnet.htm

- Jewish National and University Library, at http://jnul.huji.ac.il/eng/

- Jewish Theological Seminary Library, at http://www.jtsa.edu/Library.xml
- Jewish Virtual Library, at http://www.jewishvirtuallibrary.org/
- Spertus Institute of Jewish Studies' Asher Library, at http://spertus.edu/asher_cja/asher_collections.php
- Yehiva University Gottesman Library, at http://www.yu.edu/libraries/index.aspx?id=31&AspxAutoDetectCookieSupport=1

Miscellaneous Jewish Associations and Organizations

- American Association of Jewish Lawyers and Jurists, at http://www.jewishlawyers.org/
- Association for Canadian Jewish Studies, at http://www.acjs-aejc.ca/
- Association for Jewish Studies, at http://www.ajsnet.org/
- Association of Jewish Law Librarians, at http://www.jewishlibraries.org/
- British Association for Jewish Studies, at http://britishjewishstudies.org/
- Decalogue Society of Lawyers, at http://decaloguesociety.org/default.aspx
- European Association for Jewish Studies, at http://eurojewishstudies.org/
- International Association of Jewish Lawyers and Jurists, at http://www.intjewishlawyers.org/
- Jewish Law Association (JLA), http://jewishlawassociation.org/
- Jewish Studies Network (H-Judaic), at http://www.h-net.org/~judaic/
- Midwest Jewish Studies Association, at http://www.case.edu/artsci/jdst/mjsa.html

Academic Centers, Departments and Programs on Jewish Law (or Israeli Law)

- Academic Jewish Studies Internet Directory, at http://www.jewish-studies.com/
- Bar-Ilan Faculty of Law, at http://law.biu.ac.il/en/
- Berkeley Center for Jewish Law, Israeli Law, Economy and Society, at http://www.law.berkeley.edu/10091.htm
- DePaul University College of Law's Center for Jewish Law & Judaic Studies (JLJS), at http://law.depaul.edu/centers_institutes/jljs/
- Harvard University Center for Jewish Studies, at http://www.fas.harvard.edu/~cjs/
- Hebrew University Faculty of Law, at http://law.huji.ac.il/eng/
- London School of Jewish Studies, at http://www.lsjs.ac.uk/

- Ono Academic College (law school, Israel), at http://www.ono.ac.il/contact-2/?lang=en

- Oxford Centre for Hebrew and Jewish Studies, at http://www.ochjs.ac.uk/

- New York University's Tikva Center for Law and Jewish Civilization, at http://nyutikvah.org/

- Princeton University Program in Judaic Studies, at http://www.princeton.edu/~judaic/

- University of Cambridge, College of Divinity, Jewish Studies, at http://www.divinity.cam.ac.uk/

- University of Manchester Centre for Jewish Studies, at http://www.manchesterjewishstudies.org/

- University of Pennsylvania Center for Advanced Jewish Studies, at http://www.cjs.upenn.edu/

- Sha'arei Mishpat College (law school, Israel), at http://www.mishpat.ac.il/main.asp?lngCategoryID=4270

- Spertus Institute of Jewish Studies, at http://www.spertus.edu/

- Tel-Aviv University Faculty of Law, at http://www.law.tau.ac.il/

- Touro Law Center's Jewish Law Institute, at http://www.tourolaw.edu/Academics/?pageid=185

- Yeshiva University Cardozo School of Law Center for Jewish Law and Contemporary Civilization, at http://www.cardozo.yu.edu/cjl/

- *See also* the Wikipedia entry on "Jewish Studies," at http://en.wikipedia.org/wiki/Jewish_studies

Appendix 5

JEWISH LAW RESOURCES (*NON-INTERNET*) FOR STUDY OF THE MISHNAH, TALMUDS, MISHNEH TORAH AND SHULHAN ARUKH

In addition to materials available on the Internet, many important English aids exist that can importantly facilitate the study of Jewish law in English. Of course, it is not possible to list all of the relevant resources. Instead, this appendix provides information on those that the author believes will be of most use to law students without substantial background in Jewish law:

A. Specifically to the study of the Written Torah;

B. Specifically to the study of the Mishnah;

C. Specifically to the study of the Jerusalem Talmud and the Babylonian Talmud;

D. More generally to the study of the Mishnah or the Talmuds;

E   Specifically to study of the Mishneh Torah; and

F. Specifically to study of the Shulhan Arukh.

A. English Aids for Studying the Written Torah

1. Translations

The Holy Scriptures, published by the Jewish Publication Society in 1917, served, for many years, as the standard English translation of the Pentateuch used by Jews. That work, however, followed the archaic style of the King James Version published in 1611. Recently, however, Jewish publishers have issued quite a number of new translations. Such new translations not only employ modern language, but often provide extensive commentaries and visual aids. One such translation, *The Living Torah*, was published by Aryeh Kaplan in 1981. Another, very popular translation, *The Chumash: The Stone Edition*, was published in 1993 by Mesorah Publications, Ltd.

2. Commentaries

Many of the classical Jewish commentaries on the Pentateuch have been translated into English. Additional commentaries continue to be published by contemporary scholars whose native language is English.

B. English Aids for Studying the Mishnah

1. Translations

The Mishnah was the first openly published compilation of the oral teachings, including portions of the Oral Torah and other non-biblical law. It was compiled by Rabbi Yehuda Ha-Nasi circa 188 of the Common Era.

The first thing one needs to study the Mishnah in English is an English translation. Herbert Danby authored a well-regarded English translation entitled, *The Mishnah*, that was originally published by the Oxford University Press in 1933 (SBN 0-19-815402-X). Nevertheless, for many reasons (see the discussion in Chapter 10), a literal translation of the Mishnah does little to communicate that work's conceptual or jurisprudential teachings. Numerous commentaries in Hebrew and Aramaic struggle to provide clarity to readers of the original Hebrew version of the Mishnah. The reader of an English translation needs similar assistance.

Philip Blackman authored a multi-volume translation of the Mishnah which included relatively brief explanatory notes. This translation was first published in 1957, although one or more revised editions came out later. Nevertheless, most law students are unlikely to find Blackman's notes to be adequate assistance in understanding the Mishnah.

A major breakthrough for the study of the Mishnah in English occurred in 1994 with publication of an English translation of the modern Hebrew commentary by twentieth century scholar Pinhas Kehati. Kehati's Hebrew commentary is a comprehensive, multi-volume work. Kehati painstakingly provides introductory and supplementary contextual information, citing pertinent Scriptural verses, Talmudic commentary, and, not infrequently, even substantially different interpretations of the Mishnah offered by early post-Talmudic commentators. Kehati's commentary is so helpful that seasoned Jewish law scholars occasionally use it as a shortcut. Talmudic passages or commentaries sometimes refer to relatively esoteric portions of the Mishnah. By referring to Kehati's interpretation, one can quickly familiarize oneself with the cited Mishnah and, thereby, more readily appreciate why it is being referenced.

In the early 1980s, Mesorah Publishers, Ltd. (part of Artscroll publications), began to publish a new translation and commentary to the Mishnah volume by volume, known as *The Mishnah, a new translation with commentary by Yad Avraham*. This series was completed in 2011, and consists of 71 volumes. Its commentary is considerably more extensive than that of Kehati and explores, in some depth, a number of the issues raised both by classical commentaries on the Mishnah and by the Talmud.

Note: Although there are a few other translations of the Mishnah, I would think that, for most purposes, the Kehati version would be best for most law students. If, for some reason, a student has further questions about a particular Mishnah, he or she might want to examine the Mesorah version.

2. Audio and Other Aids

See Appendix 4, which, among other things, provides information on internet sites with various resources regarding Mishnah studies.

C. English Aids for Studying the Talmuds

1. The Jerusalem Talmud

a. Translations

The Jerusalem Talmud, also known as the Palestinian Talmud or the Talmud Yerushalmi, is earlier and less authoritative than the Babylonian Talmud, and was redacted from 350 to 400 C.E. Jacob Neusner and Tzvee Zahavy completed their translation of the Jerusalem Talmud, published by the University of Chicago Press, in 1982. This translation is also available as *The Jerusalem Talmud, A Translation and Commentary* on CD from Hendrickson Publishers.

A detailed translation and commentary on various volumes of the Jerusalem Talmud has been published by Artscroll Publishers. A list of available volumes should be accessible at artscroll.com.

b. Audio and Other Aids

See Appendix 4, which, among other things, provides information on internet sites with various resources regarding Talmud studies. These resources include a site that allows users to access a free lecture in English on any selected page of the Jerusalem Talmud.

2. Babylonian Talmud

The Babylonian Talmud, the more extensive and authoritative of the Talmuds, was redacted circa 500 C.E.

a. Translations

i. The classical Soncino translation of the Babylonian Talmud, completed under the editorship of Rabbi Dr. I. Epstein, is available for purchase in CD and hard copy formats. (However, it is also available for free online at http://halakhah.com/, with a newly formatted version at http://halakhah.com/indexrst.html.)

ii. Mesorah Publications, Ltd., has published a 73 volume translation and commentary on the Babylonian Talmud. This is entitled the Schottenstein Edition of the Talmud Bavli. It provides truly extensive assistance not only in reading and interpreting a particular Talmudic text, but also in understanding the relationship of the text to other, ostensibly inconsistent, Talmudic texts or Jewish law doctrines. This translation is available, as individual volumes or as a complete set, for purchase in hard copy in various sizes.

b. **Audio and Other Aids**

See Appendix 4, which, among other things, provides information on internet sites with various resources regarding the Babylonian Talmud. These resources include sites that allow users to access free lectures in English on any selected page of the Babylonian Talmud.

D. English Aids for Studying the Mishnah or Talmuds, Generally

The following is a list of selected materials in English that can assist in the study of the Mishnah or Talmuds.

1. **Biographical Information About Persons Mentioned in the Mishnah or Talmuds:** GERSHOM BADER, THE JEWISH SPIRITUAL HEROES (New York: Pardes Publishing House, Inc., 1940). This is a three-volume set, each chapter of which is dedicated to biographical information about an ancient sage. One volume focuses on the sages (Tannaim) who are cited in the Mishnah. A second volume discusses the later sages (Amoraim) who were most active in the Talmudic deliberations in Jerusalem. Volume three is dedicated to the later sages (Amoraim) who were most active in the Talmudic deliberations in Babylon. The information provided about each personage is compiled from references to him throughout the Talmuds and elsewhere.

2. **Maimonides (Zvi Lampel trans.),** *Maimonides' Introduction to the Talmud* (Brooklyn: The Judaica Press, 1998). This volume is an English translation of Moses Maimonides' twelfth century introduction to his commentary on the *Mishnah*. Nevertheless, it provides an excellent introduction to both the Mishnah and the Talmud.

3. **Introductions to the Mishnah and/or Talmud that provide some detailed description of Talmudic sources and reasoning:**

    a. MEIR ZVI BERGMAN, GATEWAY TO THE TALMUD (Brooklyn: Mesorah Publications, Ltd., 1989)

    b. MOSES MIELZINER, INTRODUCTION TO THE TALMUD (New York: Block Publishing Company, 1968, 5th ed.)

    c. HERMANN L. STRACK, INTRODUCTION TO THE TALMUD AND MIDRASH (Massachusetts: Atheneum, 1974)

4. **Aids or Tools for studying Talmud or the Talmudic Commentary of Tosafos:**

    a. ARYEH CARMELL, AIDS TO TALMUD STUDY (Jerusalem: Feldheim Publishers, 1975, 3d ed.)

    b. HAIM PERLMUTTER, TOOLS FOR TOSAFOS (Michigan: Targum Press Inc., 1996)

5. **General Introduction to the Talmud:** ADIN STEINSALTZ, THE ESSENTIAL TALMUD (Chaya Galai trans.) (USA: Basic Books, 1976)

E. English Aids for Studying the Mishneh Torah

The Mishneh Torah is the magnum opus of Moses Maimonides. Written in the twelfth century, the Mishneh Torah provided a novel, logically arranged code encompassing all facets of Jewish law.

The complete, or nearly complete, English translations of the Mishneh Torah include publications by:

1. The Yale University Judaica Series;

2. Moznaim Publishing Company. Twenty-nine volumes are published. The only untranslated volume is book 10 on Tohoroth (Purity).

3. Chabad.org provides an online translation at http://www.chabad.org/library/article_cdo/aid/682956/jewish/Mishneh-Torah.htm.

Other study guides for the Mishneh Torah and other works by Maimonides are available at http://www.panix.com/~jjbaker/rambam.html. Additional useful information about the Mishneh Torah, including a list of the commentaries on it may be found at http://en.wikipedia.org/wiki/List_of_commentaries_on_Mishneh_Torah.

F. English Aids for Studying the Shulhan Arukh

The Shulhan Arukh is a sixteenth century work written by Rabbi Yosef Karo. As of the time this book is being printed, the Shulhan Arukh has NOT yet been completely translated into English, although a partial translation is available at http://www.shulchanarach.com/.

A common mistake is to confuse the Shulhan Arukh, written by Rabbi Yosef Karo in the sixteenth century, with a completely different work, entitled the Kitzur Shulhan Arukh, written by Rabbi Shlomo Ganzfried in the nineteenth century, of which there are English translations. The confusion arises from the fact that the word "Kitzur" means "abbreviated." Consequently, many people mistakenly believe that the Kitzur Shulhan Arukh is an abbreviated version of Rabbi Karo's work.

One of the Shulhan Arukh's four sections, Hoshen Mishpat, is devoted primarily to commercial and criminal transactions. Emanuel Quint is the author of an eleven-volume work entitled, "A Restatement of Rabbinic Civil Law." The first eight volumes of this series were originally published by Jason Aronson Inc., and the final three volumes by Gefen Books. These volumes do not translate the Shulhan Arukh's section on Hoshen Mishpat, but they do examine many of the same issues, following the same numbering scheme.

Appendix 6

SELECTED BIBLIOGRAPHY OF BOOKS & JOURNALS IN ENGLISH

The purpose of this appendix is to provide information about selected contemporary English journals and books devoted, in whole or part, to Jewish law. The available articles on Jewish law are too numerous to include. However, this list includes several bibliographies of such articles including one bibliography that is available for free on-line. In addition, one of the journals on the list, *Tradition*, provides its subscribers with a list of the voluminous (and high quality) articles in its archives. Information on free, on-line bibliographies may be found in Appendix 4: Internet Resources.

Journals:

- *Crossroads: Halacha and the Modern World* (Alon-Shvut, Israel: Zomet Institute)

- *Dinei Yisrael*, published annually by the law faculty of Tel Aviv University (contains articles in English and Hebrew)

- *Israel Law Review*, published by the law faculty of Hebrew University

- *Hakirah, The Flatbush Journal of Jewish Law & Thought*, published by Hakirah, Inc. (Brooklyn, NY, USA). This journal's website is at http://www.hakirah.org/Editor in Chief: R. Asher Benzion Buchman

- *Jewish Medical Ethics and Halacha*, published by The Schlesinger Institute, Shaare Zedek Medical Center, P.O. Box 3235, Jerusalem, Israel 91030. Editors: Shimon Glick, Mordechai Halperin, David Fink

- *Journal of Halacha & Contemporary Society*, published by Rabbi Jacob Joseph School, 3495 Richmond Road, Staten Island, NY 10306. This journal offers a CD containing all of its editions from 1981–2007 for a fee of $36. *See* http://daniel.lrehosting.com/rjj/ Editor: Alfred Cohen

- *Tradition: A Journal of Orthodox Jewish Thought*, published by Rabbinical Council of America, 305 Seventh Avenue, New York, NY 10001. One may subscribe to a hard-print and/or online subscription. Online subscribers enjoy access to its entire archives. Editor: Shalom Carmy

- *Torah U-Madda Journal*. Many articles from this journal are available for free through the yutorah.org website.

Book Series

- *The Orthodox Forum* (Yeshiva University) Publisher: Michael Scharf Publication Trust of Yeshiva University Press (Jersey City, NJ, USA). Note: Several different publishers have been involved in this series.

- *Jewish Law Association Studies.* Several different publishers (including Scholars Press) have been involved with this series. The series is currently self-published by the Jewish Law Association, which is an independent international association that promotes the study of Jewish Law in English).

- *The Jewish Law Annual*, The Institute of Jewish Law at Boston University School of Law, Routledge (2009).

Teaching Materials:

- Hanina Ben-Menahem and Neil S. Hecht (eds.), *Selected Topics in Jewish Law* (Israel: The Open University of Israel Publishing House, 1988–1993), six volumes

- Menachem Elon et al., *Jewish Law (Mishpat Ivri): Cases and Materials* (New York: Matthew Bender & Co., Inc., 1999)

Treatises and Similar works

- Menachem Elon (Bernard Auerbach and Melvin J. Sykes trans.), *Jewish Law: History Sources, Principles* (Philadelphia: The Jewish Publication Society, 1994), four volumes

- Isaac Herzog, *The Main Institutions of Jewish Law* (New York: The Soncino Press, Ltd., 2d ed., 1967), two volumes

- Aryeh Kaplan, *Handbook of Jewish Thought* (Jerusalem: Moznaim Publishing Corporation, 1979)

- Aryeh Kaplan, *Handbook of Jewish Thought Vol. II* (Jerusalem: Moznaim Publishing Corporation, 1992)

- Emanual Quint, *A Restatement of Rabbinic Civil Law*, eleven volumes (the first eight volumes were published by Jason Aronson, Inc.; volumes nine to eleven published by Gefen Publishing House)

Introductions/Overviews to Jewish Law

- Arnold Cohen, *An Introduction to Jewish Civil Law* (New York: Feldheim Publishers, 1991)

- E. N. Dorff and A. Rosett, *A Living Tree* (Albany: State University of New York, 1988)

- Elliot N. Dorff, *The Unfolding Tradition: Jewish law After Sinai* (New York: Aviv Press, 2006)

- Menachem Elon (ed.), *The Principles of Jewish Law* (Jerusalem: Keter Publishing House Jerusalem, 1975)

- N. S. Hecht et al. (eds.), *An Introduction to the History and Sources of Jewish Law* (Oxford: Clarendon Press, 1996)

- George Horowitz, *The Spirit of Jewish Law* (New York: Bloch Publishing Company, 1973)

- Abraham Hirsch Rabinowitz, *The Jewish Mind in its Halachic Talmudic Expression* (Jerusalem: Hillel Press, 1978)

- H. Chaim Schimmel, *The Oral L* aw (New York: Feldheim Publishers, 1996, revised edition)

Introductions to Jewish Law Literature

- Meir Zvi Bergman, *Gateway to the Talmud* (Brooklyn: Mesorah Publications, Ltd., 1989)

- Moses Mielziner, *Introduction to the Talmud* (New York: Block Publishing Company, 1968, 5th ed.)

- Hermann L. Strack, *Introduction to the Talmud and Midrash* (Massachusetts: Atheneum, 1974)

- Adin Steinsaltz, *The Essential Talmud* (Chaya Galai trans.) (USA: Basic Books, 1976)

Bibliographies and Reference Works

- Nahum Rakover, *The Multi-language Bibliography of Jewish Law* (Jerusalem: The Jewish Legal Heritage Society 1990)

- Nahum Rakover, *A Guide to the Sources of Jewish Law* (Jerusalem: The Jewish Legal Heritage Society 1994)

- Phyllis Holman Weisbard, *Jewish law: Bibliography of Sources and Scholarship in English* (Littleton, Colo.: F.B. Rothman, 1990)

- Although not a book, see also Chad Baruch and Karsten Lokken, *Research of Jewish Law Issues: A Basic Guide and Bibliography for Students and Practitioners*, 77 U. Det. Mercy L. Rev. 303 (Winter 2000).

Books on a Variety of Contemporary Issues

- J. David Bleich, *Contemporary Halakhic Problems*

  vol. 1 (New York: Ktav Publishing House, Inc., 1977)

  vol. 2 (New York: Ktav Publishing House, Inc., 1983)

  vol. 3 (New York: Ktav Publishing House, Inc., 1989)

  vol. 4 (New York: Ktav Publishing House, Inc., 1995)

  vol. 5 (Michigan: Targum Press, Inc., 2005)

- Barry Freundel, *Contemporary Orthodox Judaism's Response to Modernity* (Jersey City: Ktav Publishing House, 2004)

- Basil Herring, *Jewish Ethics and Halakhah for Our Time: Sources and Commentary* (Hoboken: Ktav Publishing House, 1984)

- Basil Herring, *Jewish Ethics and Halakhah for Our Time: Sources and Commentary II* (Hoboken: Ktav Publishing House, 1989)

- Chaim Jachter, *Gray Matter*

  vol. 1 (Teaneck, NJ: H. Jachter, 2000)

  vol. 2 (Teaneck, NJ: H. Jachter, 2006)

  vol. 3 (New Jersey: Kol Torah Publications, 2008)

- Daniel Pollack, *Contrasts in American and Jewish Law* (New York: KTAV/Yeshiva University Press 2001)

Works Comparing Jewish and Roman Law:

- Boaz Cohen, *Jewish and Roman Law: A Comparative Study* (New York: Jewish Theological Seminary, 1966)

- K. Kahana Kagan, *Three Great Systems of Jurisprudence* (London: Stevens, 1955), comparing Jewish, Roman and English law

Selected Topics:

Bioethics

- Abraham S. Abraham, *Nishmat Avraham* multi-volume — from Mesorah Publications, Ltd.

  vol. 1 *Orach Chaim* (Brooklyn, NY: Mesorah Publications, 2000)

  vol. 2 *Yoreh Deah* (Brooklyn, NY: Mesorah Publications, 2003)

  vol. 3 *Even Haezer and Choshen Mishpat* (Brooklyn, NY: Mesorah Publications, 2004)

- J. David Bleich, *Bioethical Dilemmas: A Jewish Perspective* (Hoboken: Ktav Publishing House, Inc., 1998)

- J. David Bleich, *Bioethical Dilemmas: A Jewish Perspective* II (Hoboken: Targum Press/Feldheim, 2006)

- J. David Bleich, *Judaism and Healing: Halakhic Perspectives* (New York: Ktav Publishing House, Inc., 1981)

- J. David Bleich, *Time of Death in Jewish Law* (New York: J. Berman Publishing Co., 1991)

- Elliot N. Dorff, *Matters of Life and Death: A Jewish Approach to Modern Medical Ethics* (Philadelphia: The Jewish Publication Society, 1998)

- Gad Freudenthal (ed.), *AIDS in Jewish Thought and Law* (Hoboken: Ktav Publishing House, Inc., 1998)

- Immanuel Jakobovitz, *Jewish Medical Ethics* (New York: Block Publishing Company 1959)

- Fred Rosner & J. David Bleich (eds.), *Jewish Bioethics* (New York: Sanhedrin Press, 1979)

- Fred Rosner and Robert Schulman (eds.), *Medicine and Jewish Law*

  vol. 1 (New Jersey: J. Aronson, 1990)

  vol. 2 (New Jersey: J. Aronson, 1993)

  vol. 3 (Brooklyn: Yashar Books, Inc., 2005)

- Daniel B. Sinclair (ed.), *Jewish Biomedical Law* (New York: Global Academic Publishing, 2005)

- Avraham Steinberg, *Encyclopedia of Jewish Medical Ethics*, three volumes (New York: Feldheim, 2003)

- Moshe Dovid Tendler, *Responsa of Rav Moshe Feinstein, Translation and Commentary, Vol. 1: Care of the Critically Ill* (Hoboken: Ktav Publishing House, Inc., 1996)

- Noam J. Zohar, *Alternatives in Jewish Bioethics* (New York: State University of New York Press, 1997)

Business and Professional Ethics:

- Jerold S. Auerbach, *Rabbis and Lawyers: The Journey from Torah to Constitution* (Indiana 1990). Note: This book is not included because of its discussion of Jewish law, but because of its relevance to prospective Jewish lawyers.

- Michael J. Broyde, *The Pursuit of Justice and Jewish Law: Halakhic Perspectives on the Legal Profession* (Brooklyn: Yashar Books, 2007, revised and expanded ed.)

- Yisroel Pinchos Bodner, *Halachos of Other People's Money* (New York: Feldheim Publishers, 2003)

- Shlomo Cohen, *Pure Money, Volume One: Integrity* (Michigan: Targum Press, Inc., 2007)

- Shlomo Cohen, *Pure Money, Volume Two: Responsibility* (Michigan: Targum Press, Inc., 2007)

- Menachem Marc Kellner (ed.), *Contemporary Jewish Ethics* (New York: Hebrew Publishing Company, 1978)

- Aaron Levine, *Case Studies in Jewish Business Ethics* (Hoboken: Ktav Publishing House, Inc., 2000)

- Aaron Levine, *Economic Public Policy and Jewish Law* (Hoboken: Ktav Publishing House, Inc., 1993)

- Aaron Levine, *Free Enterprise and Jewish Law: Aspects of Jewish Business Ethics* (New York: KTAV Publishing House, Inc. 1980)

- Aaron Levine, *Moral Issues of the Marketplace in Jewish Law* (Brooklyn: Yashar Books Inc., 2005)

- Asher Meir, *The Jewish Ethicist* (Jerusalem: Ktav Publishing House, Inc., 2005)

- Moses L. Pava, *Business Ethics* (Hoboken: Ktav Publishing House, Inc., 1997)

- Nahum Rakover, *Ethics in the Market Place: A Jewish Perspective* (Jerusalem: Library of Jewish Law, 2000)

- Nahum Rakover, *Unjust Enrichment in Jewish Law* (Israel: Library of Jewish Law, 2000)

- Tzvi Spitz, *Cases in Monetary Halachah* (Brooklyn: Mesorah Publications, Ltd., 2001)

- Meir Tamari, *The Challenge of Wealth: A Jewish Perspective on Earning and Spending Money* (Northvale, New Jersey: Jason Aronson Inc., 1995)

- Meir Tamari, *"With All Your Possessions": Jewish Ethics and Economic Life* (New York: The Free Press, 1987)

Criminal Law

- Aaron Kirschenbaum, *Self-Incrimination in Jewish Law* (New York: The Burning Bush Press, 1970)

- Walter Jacob and Moshe Zehmer, *Crime and Punishment in Jewish Law: Essays and Responsa* (USA: Berghahn Books, 1999)

Ethics — Generally

- Aaron Kirschenbaum, *Equity in Jewish law: Halakhic Perspectives in Law* (Hoboken: Ktav Publishing House, Inc., 1991)

- Aaron Kirschenbaum, *Equity in Jewish law: Beyond Equity: Halakhic Aspirationism in Jewish Civil Law* (Hoboken: Ktav Publishing House, Inc., 1991)

Family Law and Marital Relations

- Kenneth Auman and Basil F. Herring (eds.), *The Prenuptial Agreement: Halakhic and Pastoral Considerations* (New York: Jason Aronson 1996)

- Irving Breitowitz, *Between Civil and Religious Law: The Plight of the Agunah in American Society* (Greenwood 1994)

- Louis Epstein, *The Jewish Marriage Contract; a Study in the Status of the Woman in Jewish Law* (New York: Arno Press 1973)

- Mendel Epstein, *A Woman's Guide to the Get Process* (s.n., 1989)

- David Feldman, *Marital Relations, Birth Control, and Abortion in Jewish Law* (New York: Schocken Books 1975)

- Irwin H. Haut, *Divorce in Jewish Law and Life* (New York: Sepher-Hermon Press, 1983)

- Shlomo Riskin, *Women and Jewish Divorce: The Rebellious Wife, the Agunah and the Right of Women to Initiate Divorce in Jewish Law; A Halakhik Solution* (Hoboken: Ktav Publishing House, Inc., 1989)

- Joel Wolowelsky, *Jewish Law and the New Reproductive Technologies* (New Jersey: Ktav Publishing House, Inc., 1997)

Halakhic Process

- Hanina Ben-Menahem, *Judicial Deviation in Talmudic Law: Governed by Men, Not by Rules* (New York: Harwood Academic Publishers, 1991)

- Hanina Ben-Menachem and Neil S. Hecht (ed.), *Authority, Process and Method: Studies in Jewish Law* (Amsterdam: Harwood Academic Publishers, 1998)

- Eliezer Berkovits, *Not in Heaven: The Nature and Function of Jewish Law* (New York: Ktav Publishing House, Inc., 1983)

- Michael J. Broyde, *Innovation in Jewish Law* (Israel: Urim Publications, 2010)

- Aryeh Hendler (editor-in chief), *HaMelucha Ve-HaMemshala: Issues of Authority and Leadership* (Israel: Rabbi Dr. Sol Roth Torah Publications, 2007)

- Aaron Schreiber, *Jewish Law and Decision-Making: A Study Through Time* (Philadelphia: Temple University Press, 1979)

- Michael Walzer et al, *The Jewish Political Tradition, Vol. one: Authority* (New Haven: Yale University Press, 2000)

Holocaust Issues

- Ephraim Oshry (Y. Leiman trans.), *Responsa from the Holocaust* (New York: Judaica Press, 1989)

- Irving J. Rosenbaum, *The Holocaust and Halakhah* (Hoboken: Ktav Publishing House, Ltd., 1976)

Inheritance Law

- Ezra Basri, *I, Hereby, Bequest* (Jerusalem: Haktav Institute 1984)

- R. Feivel Cohen, *Kuntres MiDor LiDor* (New York: Star Composition Service 1987)

- Dayan Grunfeld, *The Jewish Law of Inheritance* (Michigan: Targum Press, 1987)

Insurance Law

- S.M. Passamaneck, *Insurance in Rabbinic Law* (Edinburgh: Edinburgh University Press, 1974)

- Menachem Slae, *Insurance in the Halachah* (Tel Aviv: Israel Insurance Association, 1982)

Intellectual Property

- Nachum Menashe Weisfish (Tzvia Ehrlich-Klein ed.), *Copyright in Jewish Law* (Jerusalem: Feldheim Publishers, 2010)

Jewish History

The volumes listed below are a sampling of books that provide information in formats that are easily understood. They are not necessarily deep scholarly works for historians.

- Zechariah Fendel, *Anvil of Sinai* (Brooklyn: Hashkafa Publications, 1977)

- Zechariah Fendel, *Challenge of Sinai* (Brooklyn: Hashkafa Publications, 1978)

- Zechariah Fendel, *Legacy of Sinai* (Brooklyn: Hashkafa Publications, 1985, 2d ed.)

- Zechariah Fendel, *Charting the Mesorah: Creation through Geonim* (New York: Hashkafah Publications, 1994)

- Shlomo Rotenberg, *Am Olam* (Brooklyn: Keren Eliezer, 1988)

- Shlomo Rotenberg, *Am Olam Volume II* (Brooklyn: Keren Eliezer, 1995)

- Pinchas Winston, *The Unbroken Chain of Jewish Tradition: A Visual Overview of the History of the Jewish People* (Canada: Aish HaTorah, 1986)

Jewish Law and Secular Courts or Secular Law

- H. Cohn, Jewish Law in Israeli Jurisprudence (Cincinnati: Hebrew Union College Press, 1968)

- J.J. Rabinowitz, *Jewish Law, Its Influence on the Development of Legal Institutions* (New York: Bloch Publishing Company, 1956)

Mishnah, Talmud and Other Jewish Legal Literature (Translations and Commentaries)

- Philip Blackman, *Mishnayot* (New York: The Judaica Press, 1963-1964)

- Herbert Danby, *The Mishnah* (Oxford: Oxford University Press, 2008)

- Isadore Epstein (ed.), Soncino Press Complete Babylonian Talmud (U.S.: Bloch Publishing Co., 1990)

- Hersh Goldwurm and Yisroel Simcha Schorr (general eds.), *The Schottenstein Edition: Talmud Bavli* (Brooklyn: Mesorah Publications, Ltd., 2005)

- Zvi Horowitz, *The Mishnah a New Translation with a Commentary, Yad Avraham* (Brooklyn: Mesorah Publications, Ltd., 2010)

- Pinhas Kehati, *The Mishnah: A New Translation with a Commentary* (Jerusalem: Eliner Library, 1987)

- Zvi Lampel (translator), *Maimonides' Introduction to the Talmud* (Brooklyn: The Judaica Press, 1998).

- Nosson Dovid Rabinowich (trans.), *The Iggeres of Rav Sherira Gaon* (Jerusalem: Rabbi Jacob Joseph School Press, 1988)

Sexual Abuse

- Eishes Chayil [pseud.], *Hush!* (New York: Walker, 2010)

- Daniel Eidensohn and Baruch Shulem, *Child & Domestic Abuse* (two volumes) (Jerusalem; New York: Emunah Publishing 2010)

- David Mandel and David Pelcovitz, *Breaking the Silence: Sexual Abuse in the Jewish Community* (Jersey City: Ktav Publishing House, 2011)

- Amy Neustein (ed.), *Tempest in the Temple: Jewish Communities and Child Sex Scandals* (Hanover: University Press of New England, 2009)

Women and Jewish Law

- Rachel Adler, *Engendering Judaism: An Inclusive Theology and Ethics* (Philadelphia: Jewish Publication Society, 1998)

- Rachel Biale, *Women and Jewish law: the Essential Texts, Their History, and Their Relevance for Today* (New York: Schocken Books, 1995)

- Blu Goldberg, *On Women and Judaism: A View from Tradition* (Philadelphia: The Jewish Publication Society of America, 1994)

- Yehuda Henkin, *Responsa on Contemporary Jewish Women's Issues* (Hoboken: Ktav Publishing House, Inc., 2003)

- Moshe Meiselman, *Jewish Woman in Jewish Law* (Hoboken: Ktav Publishing House, Inc., 1978)

- Avraham Weiss, *Women at Prayer: A Halakhic Analysis of Women's Prayer Groups* (Hoboken: Ktav Publishing House, Inc., 2001, rev. ed.)

Appendix 7

BRIEF OUTLINE OF THE DEVELOPMENT OF JEWISH LAW LITERATURE

A. The Sinaitic Revelation: 2448, 1313 B.C.

Jewish authorities state that the Sinaitic Revelation took place in the year 2448, according to the Jewish calendar's counting of years. According to the secular calendar, this occurred in the year 1313 B.C.[1]

1. Part of the Sinaitic Revelation was written as the Five Books of Moses, which is also known as the Chumash, the Pentateuch, the Written Torah and the Written Law. It comprises the books known in English as Genesis (Heb., Bereishit), Exodus (Heb., Shemot), Leviticus (Heb., VaYikra), Numbers (Heb., Bamidbar) and Deuteronomy (Heb., Devarim).

2. The other part of the Sinaitic Revelation was to be transmitted orally, from teacher to student. This portion of the tradition is known as the Oral Torah or the Oral Law.[2] The Oral Torah explicates and supplements the Written Torah.

B. Other Scripture — Prophets (Nivi'im) and Writings (Ketuvim)

These writings are referred to as *Divrei Kabbalah*. The Talmud sometimes states that Jewish law is not derived from these writings, *Divrei Torah Midivrei Kabbalah Lo Yalfinan* (Jewish law is not derived from *Divrei Kabbalah*). See, e.g., *Babylonian Talmud, Bava Kamma* 2b. Nevertheless, this statement is not as unqualified as it sounds. There are a variety of ways in which Talmudic and later sages have managed to derive certain laws from close scrutiny of the prophets and writings. For example, as described in Chapter 6, Rabbi Moses Schreiber (a/k/a Moses Sofer) argued that the basis for the important doctrine of *dina demalkhuta dina* arises from a verse in Song of Songs (*Shir HaShirim*). *See also* MENACHEM ELON, JEWISH LAW: HISTORY, SOURCES, PRINCIPLES vol. 1, at 203–04 (Bernard Auerbach & Melvin J. Sykes trans.; Jewish Publication Socy., 1994).

---

[1] *See generally* Appendix 8, *infra*, as to the differences between the Jewish and Catholic counting of years.

[2] The "Oral Torah" has other meanings as well. *See* Appendix 1: Glossary, *supra*.

C. The Oral Torah Becomes Written, at Least in Part

1. Privately kept notes:

   At first, "no work of the . . . [Oral Torah] was written to be studied publicly."[3] Instead, distinguished individual authorities kept their own private notes regarding the teachings of the Oral Torah. Sometimes these notes contained the disagreeing views of earlier authorities.

2. The Mishnah: circa 190:

   Rabbi Yehudah HaNasi (also known as *Rebbe*) compiled and organized many of these teachings, and they were published as the *Mishnah*. Rav Sherira Gaon (906–1006), head of the Yeshiva in Pumbeditha, wrote that "Rebbe arranged and wrote the Mishnah. . . . Rebbe did not produce these words with his own mind; rather, they were the teachings of the early sages who preceded him."[4] Many other commentators agree.[5] However, some disagree, arguing that, while Rabbi Yehudah HaNasi may have compiled and arranged these teachings, the teachings were not published during his lifetime.[6] In any event, the Mishnah became the most authoritative collection of Tannaitic teachings and was the focus of the rabbinic debates that were later recorded in the Jerusalem and Babylonian Talmuds.

3. Another volume of Tannaitic statements is entitled the *Tosefta*, which, according to tradition was produced by Rabbi Hiya (and his student, Rabbi Oshaiah).[7] The word Tosefta is Aramaic and means "addition." The traditional view is that the Tosefta was written sometime in the third century, after publication of the Mishnah, and serves both to clarify and to supplement the teachings included in the Mishnah.[8] Unsurprisingly, a

---

[3] *See, e.g.*, MAIMONIDES, MAIMONIDES INTRODUCTION TO THE TALMUD 69 (Zvi Lampel trans., 1998). Rav Sherira Gaon (906–1006) actually writes that "none of the early sages had written anything [regarding the Oral torah]" until near the end of Rabbi Yehudah HaNasi's life. *See* SHERIRA GAON, THE IGGERES OF RAV SHERIRA GAON 14 (Nosson Dovid Rabinowich trans., 1988). But other commentators disagree, arguing that, even before Rabbi Yehudah HaNasi's compilation, there seem to have been some other collections of Tannaitic teachings. *See* NAHUM RAKOVER, A GUIDE TO THE SOURCES OF JEWISH LAW 33 (1994); ZEVI HIRSCH CHAJES, THE STUDENT'S GUIDE THROUGH THE TALMUD 254–57 (Jacob Schachter trans., 3d ed., 2005).

[4] RAKOVER, *supra* note 3, at 20.

[5] Consider, for instance, the words of Maimonides in his introduction to the Mishnah:

   He [Rabbi Yehudah HaNasi] collected all the lectures and the laws, and all the clarifications and explanations heard from Moses, which were taught by the Great Bes Din in each and every generation, on the entire Torah and compiled from it all the book of the Mishna. He reviewed the completed work with the Sages in public and it was revealed to all Israel, and they all copied it. He disseminated it everywhere so that the Oral Torah would not become forgotten by Israel.

MAIMONIDES, *supra* note 3, at 69, 76 n.15.

[6] CHAJES, *supra* note 3, at 257–61 (citing evidence for this dissenting view, with which he agrees).

[7] *See, e.g.*, SHLOMO YITZHAK, BABYLONIAN TALMUD, *Sanhedrin* 33a, *s.v.*, *ve'afilu ta'ah b'rebbi Hiyya*.

[8] Rav Sherira Gaon writes, "Concerning the Tosefta: Certainly R. Chiyya arranged it, but there is no definite indication whether he arranged it in Rebbe's lifetime or afterwards. However, it undoubtedly was arranged after the halachos of our Mishnah. It is clear that the teachings of the Tosefta are based upon

number of the baraithot that appear in the Tosefta involve teachings that predate publication of the Mishnah itself.

4. Halakhic Midrashim

The Hebrew word *Midrash* (plural, *Midrashim*) means exposition or interpretation.

There are two types of Midrashim — Haggadic Midrashim and Halakhic Midrashim. The former are non-legal teachings that convey ethical or spiritual lessons. By contrast, Halakhic Midrashim explain how biblical verses provide the basis for specific legal rules. Halakhic Midrashim were primarily taught by Tannaim, the same authorities whose views are cited in the Mishnah, and many of these teachings preceded the Mishnah. Nevertheless, the various sets of Halakhic Midrashim are believed to have been published only after publication of the Mishnah.

Of the various collections of Halakhic Midrashim, a few should be specifically mentioned. Two of these, the *Mekhilta de-Rabbi Yishmael* (attributed by several Rishonim to the Tanna Rabbi Yishmael but by recent scholars to the School of a different Rabbi Yishmael)[9] and the *Mekhilta de-Rabbi Shimon* (also known by several other names, including *Mekhilta de-Sanya*, *Mekhilta*, *Sifrei*, *Sifri-de-Vei Rav*),[10] focus on the book of Exodus. The *Sifra* (also known as *Torat Kohanim* and *Sifra debe Rab*), attributed to the third century Amora, Rav,[11] addresses the book of Leviticus. *Sifre*, also attributed to Rav,[12] interprets verses in both Numbers and Deuteronomy. Very little of another Halakhic Midrash, *Mekhilta de-Sefer Devarim* (or *Mekhilta Deuteronomy*) is extant.[13]

5. The Talmuds

None of the Tannaitic halakhic literature was as accepted as the Mishnah. As Maimonides writes, "[T]he Mishna was the basic text to which all the other works were secondary and subordinate, it being the work unanimously esteemed over all the others."[14] At the time of the Mishnah, there were two main centers for rabbinical study, the land of Israel and Babylonia. In each of these locations, the rabbinic academies centered their Jewish law inquiries around the Mishnah, and, in each location, produced a Talmud.

---

our Mishnah and teach about [its halachos]." *See* SHERIRA GAON, *supra* note 3, at 34. Maimonides writes, "Rebbi Yehuda's words, presented in the Mishna, are brief, yet they encompass many concepts . . . Rabbi Heeya, one of Rebbi's disciples, thereupon decided to compose a text tin which he would follow after his master's work, explicating that which might not be easily comprehended from his master's own words. This is the Tosefta [Addition]." MAIMONIDES, *supra* note 3, at 143.

[9] *See* Menahem I. Kahana, *Mekhilta of R. Ishmael*, in 13 ENCYCLOPAEDIA JUDAICA 794 (Michael Berenbaum & Fred Skolnick eds., 2d ed. 2007).

[10] *Id.* at 795.

[11] Maimonides is among those who so attribute the work. MAIMONIDES, *supra* note 3, at 143.

[12] *See, e.g.*, MEIR A BERGMAN, GATEWAY TO THE TALMUD 56 (1989).

[13] *See* Menahem I. Kahana, *Mekhilta Deuteronomy*, in ENCYCLOPAEDIA JUDAICA, *supra* note 9, at 792.

[14] MAIMONIDES, *supra* note 3, at 143–44.

a.   The Jerusalem Talmud (the Talmud Yerushalmi or, simply, the *Yerushalmi*): circa 350:

Rabbinical academies in the land of Israel engaged in considerable debates, over a long period of time, regarding many parts of the Mishnah. The relevant portions of the Mishnah and these debates were published, circa 350, as the Jerusalem Talmud.

b.   The Babylonian Talmud (the Talmud Bavli or, simply, the *Bavli*):

The Babylonian academies also produced a Talmud. The process within the Babylonian academies covered a larger portion of the Mishnah and lasted a longer period of time. The Babylonian Talmud was not finally redacted until circa 550.

For a variety of reasons, the Babylonian Talmud is the more authoritative of the two Talmuds. Indeed, if someone simply refers to "the Talmud," one assumes that the reference is to the Babylonian Talmud.

6.   Post-Talmudic halakhic literature

a.   In the post-Talmudic period (at least until recent times), most halakhic literature took one of two forms.

i.   First, was *responsa* literature. Individuals — or parties to disputes — would send (either directly or through a local rabbi) legal questions to distinguished Jewish law authorities who often lived elsewhere. The rabbi receiving such an inquiry would send a response that summarized the facts and rendered a decision, often providing a detailed legal explanation for the decision. There are hundreds of thousands of such responsa literature, which, to a certain extent, serve as case law that may inform contemporary authorities confronted with similar questions. Of course, in many instances, different authorities may have rendered different rulings in cases that are ostensibly similar.

ii.   Second, much halakhic literature was published as a collection of legal rules, organized in various ways.

(1)   The Gaonim were the heads of rabbinical academies roughly from the seventh century through the tenth century. Although a number of their treatises on specific legal topics are extant, only three comprehensive manuscripts have survived. Two of the broader collections, the *She'iltot*, authored by Rav Ahai Gaon (d. 760), and the *Halakhot Gedolot* written by R. Shimon Kaira (ninth century), organize the law in accordance with the order of the Written Torah. The other such collection, Rav Yehudai Gaon's (eighth century) *Halakhot Pesukot*, is arranged according to the order of the Babylonian Talmud. It provides the laws arising out of the Talmudic discussions, but excludes the discussions themselves.

(a) This approach has several benefits. The first is for the reader, who can easily ascertain the Talmudic source for a particular legal conclusion and, therefore, can evaluate whether the conclusion is sound. The second is for the writer, who is spared the challenging chore of devising a method of organizing the laws effectively.

(b) The shortcomings of following the order of the Talmud, however, can be best appreciated by those with experience in Talmudic study. The Talmud does not address all of the laws of a particular subject in a single place. Indeed, the Talmud's chain of thought is abstract. If the applicable legal reasoning is similar, it will move from one subject, such as criminal law, to another, such as a question of family purity. If one misses the conceptual connection, the transition may seem to be a complete tangent. As a result, although the various Talmudic tractates are titled, each contains halakhic rulings about completely different topics. Consequently, suppose someone wants to learn all of the laws regarding a particular subject. If the legal code follows the order of the Talmud, the only way to be sure one has seen all of the rules about any subject is to read through the entire code. This, of course, is not very practical.

(2) The Rishonim were the leading Jewish law authorities immediately after the Gaonic period (from the eleventh through the fifteenth centuries).

(a) A number of the Rishonim (including Rav Alfasi (1013–1073), who preceded Maimonides, and Rav Asher, who followed Maimonides, used Rav Yehudai Gaon's approach of following the order of the Talmud.

(b) There were, however, three important innovations during the period of the Rishonim.

(i) The first, and probably the most breathtaking, was publication of Maimonides' *Mishneh Torah*. This was the first truly comprehensive Jewish law code that was clearly, coherently and ingeniously organized according to subject matter. However, the Mishneh Torah introduced a new problem, because Maimonides chose not to identify or explain the Talmudic basis for his halakhic rulings. This made it more difficult for a reader to independently evaluate these rulings, and it led to considerable early criticism of the publication. It has also engendered an enormous body of Jewish scholarly literature regarding those conclusions.

(ii) Jewish law authorities often state that there are 613 biblical commandments, 248 affirmative commandments and 365 negative commandments, although there is considerable disagreement as to the identity of the commandments that are included in this count. A second innovation in the period of the Rishonim was the publication of a number of halakhic books organized around various lists of these commandments. One of these books, the *Sefer HaHinnuch*, has been translated and published by Feldheim Publishers as a multi-volume with each Hebrew page facing a corresponding page of English translation.

(iii) The second major innovation was introduced by Rabbi Jacob ben Asher's code, entitled the *Sefer HaTurim*, literally, the Book of Rows (Turim).[15] Rabbi Jacob's code did not address laws pertaining to the Holy Temple or the services therein, because he lived more than a thousand years after the Second Temple was destroyed. Instead, he focused on those Jewish laws that continued to have contemporary practical applications. He divided these into four major categories.[16] The first, *Orah Hayyim*, covers issues of daily life, such blessings, individual and communal prayer, laws regarding the various Jewish holidays and holy days, etc.

The second, *Yoreh De'ah*, deals with a variety of topics, including dietary restrictions, oaths, vows, mourning, etc. The third, *Even Haezer*, primarily encompasses family law, including laws of marriage and divorce. The

---

[15] The word "Turim", which is the title is an allusion to Exodus 28:17 in which the word refers to the rows of jewels — there were four such rows — that adorned the High Priest's breastplate. *See* DAVID M. FELDMAN, MARITAL RELATIONS, BIRTH CONTROL AND ABORTION IN JEWISH LAW 12 (1975).

[16] This work is therefore sometimes referred to as the *Sefer Arba'ah Turim* or the *Arba'ah Turim* (literally, the "Four Rows"). It is also known simply as the *Turim* or the *Tur*.

fourth, *Hoshen Mishpat*, focuses on commercial and criminal matters.

(3)   The Aharonim succeeded the Rishonim and produced a variety of important halakhic publications. The most important, however, was Joseph Karo's sixteenth century tome known in Hebrew as the *Shulhan Arukh* (literally, the "Set Table"), but referred to in English as the "Code of Jewish Law." Rabbi Karo, who had previously authored the foremost commentary on Rabbi Jacob ben Asher's Sefer HaTurim, followed that book's structure. Rabbi Karo was a Sephardi Jew and his rulings were heavily influenced by the rulings of the Mishneh Torah, authored by Maimonides, who was also Sephardi. In addition, Karo's rulings, particularly as to non-biblical matters, such as customs, reflected practices and takkanot in Sephardi communities. As a consequence, the Shulhan Arukh, in its original format, was of limited use to Ashkenazi Jews. An Ashkenazi contemporary of Rabbi Karo, Rabbi Moses Isserles, however, provided a gloss, referred to as the "Mappah" (i.e., Tablecloth) that reflected Ashkenazi customs and rulings. Standard editions of the Shulhan Arukh always include both R. Karo's text plus R. Isserles' Mappah. This text is centered on each page and surrounded by a number of super-commentaries.

Appendix 8

A BRIEF CHART OF JEWISH LEGAL AND NATIONAL HISTORY

Introductory Notes About the Counting of Years:

A few notes about the terminology used in counting the years in the Catholic and Jewish traditions are appropriate.

The Catholic Counting is the one with which everyone is familiar. It purports to start the count of years from the birth of Jesus of Nazareth. Years prior to that birth are referred to as "B.C.," "before Christ," and years after that birth are referred to as "A.D.," which are the initials of the Latin words for "the Years of Our Lord." Before exploring why I use the word "purports," let me just mention that the Jewish Counting purports to count continuously from a tradition date for the creation of Adam to the present time. However, to avoid confusion, it is sometimes useful to refer to the year according to the Catholic Counting that everyone else knows. Because Jews do not regard Jesus as "Our Lord," they eschew using "A.D." In its place they may use "C.E.," which stands for the "Common Era." Thus, instead of referring to 2012 A.D., Jewish literature might refer to 2012 C.E. Similarly, the year 10 B.C. stands for 10 years "before Christ." Jewish literature might refer to the same year as 10 B.C.E., i.e., 10 years "before the Common Era." The chart below shows the dates either in accordance with the continuous Jewish count or in relationship to the Common Era.

Back to Catholic Counting. It was initiated by a Catholic Priest named Dionysius Exiguus. This was not done in Jesus's lifetime. Nor was it begun within a hundred years of Jesus's death, or two hundred years or three hundred years. In fact, there are inconsistent reports as to exactly when Dionysius lived. Collier's Encyclopedia reports that he lived from 475–500 of the Common Era.[1] By contrast, the Encyclopedia Britannica, in one place, says he lived from 496–540, and in another place, says he lived from 500–560! In any event, he lived long after Jesus's death, and he retroactively put his counting into place. Yet, in the interim, the non-Jewish world lacked any continuous count. Instead, the date was customarily counted simply as the particular year of the current king's reign. Indeed, the number of days in a given non-Jewish year varied dramatically from time to time. The Roman Emperor Julian, for instance, used a year of 445 days. Consequently, it is not at all clear, in the year 2012, how long ago Jesus was born.

---

[1] This description of the Catholic Count is based on SHLOMO ROTENBERG, 1 AM OLAM: THE HISTORY OF THE ETERNAL NATION 77–81 (1988).

Another important note is that two factors interrelate to make it sometimes difficult to determine the secular year in which a particular Jewish book was published. First, unlike the secular year, the Jewish year does not begin on January 1st. For example, the Jewish year 5772 began on the evening of September 28, 2011, and ends on the evening of September 16, 2012. Consequently, a book published in the Jewish year of 5772 may have been published in 2011 or 2012. If one only knows the Jewish year of publication but not the month (and sometimes even the day) of publication, there are always two possible secular years of publication. A number of Hebrew language publications — both ancient publications and some newer ones issued in Israel — only indicate the Jewish year of publication. As a result, sometimes you will see the "English" date of publication reported by various authorities as two years, such as 2011/2012.

	Jewish Year	BCE or CE
Creation of Adam, the first person (The first of what are now referred to as the seven Noahide Laws was given to Adam.)	1 BCE	3761 BCE
The Flood	1056	2705 BCE
Noah's exit from the Ark (The first Noahide law was repeated and given, along with the other six Noahide laws, given to Noah.)	1057	2704 BCE
Jacob and his family go to Egypt	2238	1523 BCE
Sinaitic Revelation — Written & Oral Torahs	2448	1313 BCE
Moses to Ezra	3317	444 BCE
Ezra to Hillel	3377	384 BCE
Mishnah — Rabbi Yehuda HaNasi, compiler	3950	190 CE
Tosefta (Work of Tannaim)	3960	200
Baraithot (Work of Tannaim)	3960–3980	200–220
Legal Midrashim (Works of Tannaim): E.g.: • *Sifra De-Vei Rav* (*Torat Kohanim*), • *Sifrei De Vei Rav*	3960–3980	200–220
Palestinian Talmud — *Talmud Yerushalmi* (Work of Amoraim, followed by Savoraim)	4135	375 CE
Babylonian Talmud — *Talmud Bavli* (Work of Amoraim, followed by Savoraim)	4260	500
Savoranim	Until circa 4360	Until end of sixth century C.E.
Geonim — Ended with death of R. Hai Gaon — 1038	From circa 4360 until 4798	From end of sixth century until 1038
Hilkhot — author, Rav Alfasi (*Rif*) 1013–1103	c. 4848	c. 1088
R. Shlomo Yitzhaki (*Rashi*)	4800–4865	1040–1105
Rabbenu Tam, one of the first *Ba'alei HaTosafot*	d. 4931	d. 1171
Commentary on the Mishnah — author, Maimonides (Rambam; 1135–1204)	4928	1168

	Jewish Year	BCE or CE
Mishneh Torah — author, Maimonides	4940	1180
Halakhot — author, Rabbeinu Asher (*Rosh*; 1250–1327)	5060	1300
Sefer Arba'ah Turim — author, R. Yaakov b. HaRosh (1270–1343)	5090	1330
First Printed Edition of the Babylonian Talmud — by Bomberg in Venice	5280–5282	1520–1522
Shulhan Arukh — author, R. Yosef Karo (1488–1575)	5310	1550
HaMappah — commentary to Shulhan Arukh by R. Moses Isserles (1530–1572)	Printed as integrated part of Shulhan Arukh since 5338	Printed as integrated part of Shulhan Arukh since 1578
Kitzur Shulhan Arukh — author, R. Shlomo Ganzfried (1800–1886)	5624	1864
Arukh Hashulhan — author, R. Yehiel Mikhal Epstein	5644–5653	1884–1893
Mishnah Berurah — author, R. Meir Kagan	5644–5667	1884–1907

Appendix 9

JEWISH SCRIPTURE

The Jewish canon consists of three parts, namely the Written Torah ("Torah"), Prophets ("Nevi'im"), and Later Writings ("Ketuvim" or Kesuvim). The Hebrew acronym is "TaNaKh."

I. The Written Torah

(a/k/a The Chumash, the Pentateuch, and the Five Books of Moses)

	English Name	Hebrew Name
Book 1:	Genesis	Bereishit (Bereishis)
Book 2:	Exodus	Shemot (Shemos)
Book 3:	Leviticus	VaYikra (a/k/a Torat Kohanim or Toras Kohanim)
Book 4:	Numbers	BaMidbar
Book 5:	Deuteronomy	Devarim

II. The Books of the Prophets — The Nevi'im

English	Hebrew Name/Transliteration
Joshua	Yehoshua
Judges	Shoftim
Samuel I & II	Shmuel I & II
Kings I & II	Melakhim I & II
Isaiah	Yeshayahu
Jeremiah	Yirmiyahu
Ezekiel	Yehezkel
Hosea	Hoshea
Joel	Yoel
Amos	Amos
Obadiah	Ovadiah
Jonah	Yonah
Micah	Mikhah
Nahum	Nahum
Habakkuk	Habakkuk
Zephaniah	Zephaniah
Haggai	Haggai

English	Hebrew Name/Transliteration
Zechariah	Zekhariyah
Malakhi	Malakhi

III. The Writings — Kituvim

English	Hebrew Name/Transliteration
Psalms	Tehillim
Proverbs	Mishlei
Job	Eyov
The Song of Songs	Shir HaShirim
Ruth	Ruth (or Rut)
Lamentations	Eikhah
Ecclesiastes	Koheleth
Esther	Esther (or Ester)
Daniel	Dani'el
Ezra-Nehemiah	Ezra-Nehemiah
Chronicles	Divrei HaYamim

INDEX

[References are to sections.]

[References are to sections.]

[References are to sections.]

[References are to sections.]

[References are to sections.]

[References are to sections.]